THE FAMILY
IN
THEOLOGICAL PERSPECTIVE

THE FAMILY
IN
THEOLOGICAL PERSPECTIVE

Edited by

STEPHEN C. BARTON

T&T CLARK
EDINBURGH

T&T CLARK LTD
59 GEORGE STREET
EDINBURGH EH2 2LQ
SCOTLAND

www.tandtclark.co.uk

First published 1996
Latest impression 2000

ISBN 0 567 08522 8

British Library Cataloguing-in-Publication Data
A catalogue record for this book is available from the British Library

Typeset by Trinity Typesetting, Edinburgh
Printed and bound in Great Britain by Page Bros, Norwich

To Walter and John-Paul Moberly
and in memory of
Meredith

Contents

Preface

This volume is the result of collaboration between a number of academics interested in taking further Christian understanding of the family. It is my pleasure to acknowledge here the help of those who made the venture possible. The Durham Centre for Theological Research, under the directorship of Professor Jimmy Dunn, accepted my proposal for a series of research seminars in 1994–95 and gave the series its full support. Financial backing was provided by the Public Lectures Committee of the University of Durham. I am very grateful to both these bodies.

The seminar itself lasted more than two terms, meeting on a weekly basis – a test enough of anyone's endurance! But it was quite noticeable how a sense of collegiality developed and, just as important, how members' competence in thinking about the family increased. So I would like to place on record my appreciation to all those who contributed to the seminar: students, academic colleagues, and members of the public alike. A special word of thanks must go to those who presented papers and who were prepared subsequently to write them up for publication. Their efficiency has meant that there has been very little delay between presentation and publication.

A crucial stimulus for my original initiative in proposing the seminar programme was the on-going work of the Church of England Board for Social Responsibility Working Party on the Family, between 1992 and 1995, culminating in the publication of the report, *Something to Celebrate. Valuing Families in Church and Society* (London: Church House Publishing, 1995). As a member of the working party, I was stimulated and challenged in all kinds of ways to take further the historical, moral and theological dimensions of understanding family life. My enormous gratitude goes, therefore, to the members of the working party: Bishop Alan Morgan (chairman), Anne Borrowdale, Jonathan Bradshaw, Deborah Cunningham, Elisabeth Dodds, Antony Hurst, Jennifer Jenkins, Ermal Kirby, Christine McMullen, George Nairn-Briggs, Alan Storkey, Sue Walrond-Skinner and Alison Webster.

Stephen C. Barton
July, 1996

Introduction

The year 1994 was designated by the United Nations as 'International Year of the Family'. This is indicative of the fact that concern about the fate of the family is stronger today than perhaps ever before. If we confine our observations to Western society, it is possible to point to a number of factors which have contributed to this high level of concern. I draw particular attention to the following.[1]

First, there is the impact of contemporary social trends.[2] The data following is an illustrative sample only, but it makes the point. The divorce rate in Britain is second only to Denmark in the European Community and stands at about forty per cent of all marriages. The rate of re-marriage is also high (although declining), one of the consequences of which is the growing number of step-relationships in families – families, by the way, which are taking increasingly complex forms. The number of births out of wedlock continues to rise and the number of lone parent families has more than doubled between 1971 and 1991. There are now 1.3 million lone parent families containing 2.2 million children; and 90 per cent of these families are headed by a woman. Cohabitation, either prior to or as an alternative to marriage, has become widely accepted in society-at-large. The percentage of cohabitees doubled in the 1980s. In addition, demographic shifts due to changing economic circumstances and high rates of national unemployment have contributed significantly to family poverty and homelessness. Child poverty is now recognised as a major problem. These kinds of social trends are pervasive and affect the churches as well as the wider society.

---

[1] What follows is an abbreviation of points I made in an earlier essay: 'Marriage and Family Life as Christian Concerns', *Expository Times* 106/3 (1994), 69–74.

[2] I am indebted for most of the information in this section to an unpublished paper entitled, 'Family Trends and the Church' by Jonathan Bradshaw, Professor of Social Policy at the University of York. See further the Church of England report, *Something to Celebrate* (London: Church House Publishing, 1995), ch. 2.

Then there is the impact of the women's movement and feminism in its various forms. The critical analysis of marriage, child-bearing and the family from the perspective of a feminist hermeneutic of suspicion has had a major impact, especially in the latter part of the twentieth century. We are more aware than ever before of the ways in which family, church and society have been organised along patriarchal lines, the effect of which has been to marginalise women in the public domain of politics and work and to subordinate them in the private domain of the family. Taking as a starting-point women's own experience of oppression, abuse and powerlessness, and the ways in which this experience is reinforced by the distribution of power and opportunity along lines of gender difference, feminists have raised major questions about all our social institutions, including marriage and the family.[3]

A third factor has to do with questions raised by advances in science and medicine. As is well known, the advent in the second half of the twentieth century of mass-produced artificial contraceptives has raised in a more acute way than before questions about the nature and purpose of sexual intercourse and the place of children in marriage.[4] The availability of, and increasingly common recourse to, legal abortion has served to reinforce these questions. In addition, recent developments in biotechnology and scientific research have had a significant impact. There is now a wide social and moral–theological debate taking place about issues like *in vitro* fertilisation, surrogate motherhood, genetic engineering, and the use of aborted foetal tissue for experimentation.[5] At the macro-social level, the debate over

[3] See on this: Monica Furlong, ed., *Mirror to the Church, Reflections on Sexism* (London: SPCK, 1988); Janet Martin Soskice, 'Women's Problems', in A. Walker, ed., *Different Gospels* (London: SPCK, 1993), 194–203; and Elisabeth Schüssler Fiorenza and Mary Shawn Copeland, eds., *Violence Against Women* (London: SCM, 1994).

[4] Of course, the use of artificial contraception goes back to antiquity and has been a subject of moral debate throughout Christian history. See on this, J. T. Noonan, Jr., *Contraception. A History of its Treatment by the Catholic Theologians and Canonists* (Cambridge, MA: Harvard University Press, 1965), and A. S. McLaren, *A History of Contraception* (Oxford: Blackwell, 1992).

[5] See for example J. Mahoney, *Bioethics and Belief* (London: Sheed & Ward, 1984), and *The Making of Moral Theology* (Oxford: Oxford University Press, 1987); also helpful are K. Boyd et al., *Life Before Birth* (London: SPCK, 1986), and Kevin T. Kelly, *Life and Love. Towards a Christian Dialogue on Bioethical Questions* (London: Collins, 1987).

human fertility control is related also to ecological concerns about over-population and the protection of the environment.[6] In various and complex ways, all of these issues bear on marriage and the family, and raise moral and practical issues which are important for society and the churches to address.

Fourth, there is our increased awareness of problems in family life. It is probably fair to say that the institutions of marriage and the family are widely perceived to be in a state of crisis. Former Chief Rabbi Lord Jakobovits articulated this perception in a recent address when he said:

> I am not quite sure that we yet appreciate the depth of the crisis that currently besets the home, and the awesome price that we pay for the alarming breakdown of the family, on a scale that has made the family a disaster area of modern times. Marriage is under siege, and married couples in their relationship to children with a loving home are almost beginning to be an endangered species. The price we pay is a crippling price in moral terms, in social terms, in economic terms....[7]

But our perceptions are shaped also by an increased awareness of problems that hitherto have remained largely hidden from public view. One of these is child sexual abuse. This phenomenon has been a subject of press reports for some time and was given special prominence with the 'Cleveland affair' of 1987.[8] Testimony to the fact that the problem touches the lives of Christian as well as non-Christian families is the recent founding of the organisation, Christian Survivors of Sexual Abuse, whose first national conference was held in 1993. A number of underlying issues need to be addressed, not least within the churches. Above all, it needs to be asked: Do we have a theology of children profound enough to protect them from being taken advantage of? To what extent do patriarchy and the dominant modes of

---

[6] See on this Edward P. Echlin, 'Population and Catholic Theology: Discovering Fire Anew', *The Month* (January 1992), 35–8.

[7] 'The Family – A Community of Giving', in J. Bogle, ed., *Families for Tomorrow* (Leominster: Fowler Wright, 1991), 5. Jonathan Sacks, the present Chief Rabbi, has taken up his predecessor's concerns about the family, notably, in his Reith Lectures of 1990, *The Persistence of Faith. Religion, Morality & Society in a Secular Age* (London: Weidenfeld & Nicolson, 1991), 48–58.

[8] See the account by social anthropologist Jean La Fontaine, *Child Sexual Abuse* (Oxford: Polity Press, 1990), esp. 1–13.

gender construction in our society contribute to child sexual abuse? In some of these areas, adequate reflection and action have only just begun.[9]

Yet another factor is the use of 'family' rhetoric in political debate. Because claims about the family relate to the larger political and cultural context, it is not surprising to find that a certain conception of the family often becomes a political tool serving the interests of a larger agenda. For conservatives, this usually has to do with preserving or re-establishing a desired *status quo* of 'traditional family values', often linked to a free-market economic philosophy. For liberals, it has to do with social reform aimed at protecting individual rights. For fundamentalists, the family is a symbolic and practical bulwark against the moral ambiguities of secular modernity. For feminists, it is an instrument of the patriarchal oppression of women. And so on. My point here is not to evaluate these larger political interests, only to draw attention to (sometimes hidden) political dimensions of talk about the family which make it an important and legitimate focus of concern.

Mention should be made, finally, of specifically Christian or ecclesiastical concerns. Many developments in contemporary church life touch on marriage and the family in various ways, so it is worth mentioning a few here. In the Roman Catholic Church, the official ban on artificial contraception, taken further in *Humanae Vitae* and recently reiterated in *Veritatis Splendor*, represents in a very clear and uncompromising way a line of demarcation between the church as a moral community and the moral values of the modern world.[10] This line of demarcation runs right through marriage and family life. At the same time, the dramatic decline in priestly vocations has reopened the question of priestly celibacy and the eligibility of married men for the priesthood. In the Church of England and the Anglican com-

---

[9] See the excellent survey by Ann Loades in her John Coffin Memorial Lecture 1994, *Thinking about Child Sexual Abuse* (University of London, 1994), and the literature cited there. Also important are the essays in Joanne Carlson Brown and Carole R. Bohn, eds., *Christianity, Patriarchy and Abuse* (Cleveland OH: The Pilgrim Press, 1989).

[10] On the encyclicals, see Janet E. Smith, *Humanae Vitae: A Generation Later* (Washington DC: Catholic University of America, 1992); and Charles Yeats, ed., *Veritatis Splendor: A Response* (Norwich: Canterbury Press, 1994).

munion world-wide, the debate over the ordination of women to the priesthood has raised important theological and practical questions about gender construction and power relations directly relevant to marriage and the family. On another front, the increasingly common practice of cohabitation among Christian couples across the denominations has renewed the debate about the centrality of marriage in Christian sexual theology.[11] Not unrelated are concerns of a yet more general kind about how to respond to cultural and moral pluralism in contemporary society and how to respond also to what is perceived to be widespread moral breakdown in people's social relations. Here again, attitudes to marriage and the family have a pivotal role.

The essays which follow are written against this backdrop. Taken as a whole, their aim is to serve as a resource for theological reflection on the family as we approach the beginning of a new millennium. Such resources are urgently needed if the problems facing the family are to be adequately addressed. It is remarkable, and worth pointing out, that while historical, sociological, anthropological and psychological study of the family abounds, there is a relative dearth of serious theology on the family. Christian writing at a more popular level abounds and contains much positive insight, alongside wisdom of a more questionable kind.[12] But foundational issues remain to be explored more thoroughly and from across a broad range of denominational positions. The eighteen contributions to this volume mark an important beginning. It is to be hoped that they will in turn stimulate further research and reflection on the theology of the family.

As the Table of Contents indicates, the essays have been organised around two main categories: biblical and historical perspectives on the one hand, and contemporary issues on the other. This kind of division is quite conventional in that it works with a framework of a broadly chronological kind and moves

[11] See, e.g., A. E. Harvey's two-part essay, 'Marriage, Sex and the Bible', *Theology* XCVI (1993), 364–72, 461–8, and the letters it provoked by Walter Moberly and Simon Barrington-Ward in the two subsequent numbers of the journal. See also Adrian Thatcher, *Liberating Sex. A Christian Sexual Theology* (London: SPCK, 1993).

[12] For a recent evaluation of some of this literature, see Anne Borrowdale, *Reconstructing Family Values* (London: SPCK, 1994).

from the past to the present. It is not meant, however, to give the impression that the essays in Part One are of antiquarian interest only while those in Part Two are the 'relevant' ones. Nor is it meant to convey the idea that Part One is about 'foundations' while Part Two is about 'application to today'. Such dichotomies only get in the way of wise theological reflection, not least in the area of the family. Reflection on the Bible and history is as indispensable and relevant as reflection on contemporary experience in the modern world, and the one cannot be done without the other.

This very point is made in my opening essay on biblical hermeneutics which notes the prominence given to the Bible in Christian books and reports on the family, and then looks at the way the Bible is actually used in three recent books. This examination shows how easy it is misinterpret the Bible in the interests of a predetermined, modern agenda. What is needed instead, by way of corrective, are ways of reading the Bible which are grounded more firmly, both in historically-informed theology and in the worship and discipleship of communities of faith. John Rogerson shows what historically-informed theology involves, at least so far as the Old Testament is concerned. His essay draws heavily on anthropological and social–historical method to convey some sense of the actualities of family life in Old Testament times, and to show what 'structures of grace' were put in place to counteract the forces that undermined the family: all of which has important implications for people concerned about the fate of the family today. Jimmy Dunn engages likewise in a historical analysis of the rules in the New Testament governing household relationships, rules which show how important was the right ordering of household life in early Christianity. He shows *inter alia* that the contempt in which such rules are held by some moderns is misplaced if it fails to take fully into account the original context in which the rules took shape and the quality of life and responsible witness they made possible.

Christian theology and the church have not always been very good at attending to children, and much more work needs to be done in this area.[13] James Francis's essay on 'Children and Childhood in the New Testament' is one of several essays in the

---

[13] See now D. Wood, ed., *The Church and Childhood* (Oxford: Blackwell, 1994).

collection to help fill this gap. He emphasises how striking is the honour accorded children in the teaching and practice of Jesus and how important this is for the related issue of a theology of power. How little this aspect of New Testament tradition has been heard in Western culture is illustrated further on by Anthony Fletcher's description of Puritan teaching on the punishment of children, Jon Davies' sociological analysis of the neglect of children, and Ann Loades' essay on child sexual abuse.

Carol Harrison begins her essay by reminding us that virginity and asceticism, rather than the family, dominate the writings of the Church Fathers. The value of her presentation is that it sets patristic thought in the wider context of the Greco-Roman family. This helps us to understand what family life was like for most people (women and children, as well as men) and why the Fathers placed a premium on asceticism. She makes the intriguing suggestion that part of the appeal of the ascetic life was the moral and social authority it lent to its practitioners.

The teaching and practice of the English Puritans constitutes a significant and rather startling contrast to the patristic tradition. For, as Anthony Fletcher shows in his study of Puritan advice books on the regulation of marriage and family life, the Protestant Reformation represents a re-evaluation of the relation between religion and gender and a reversal of the long tradition which distrusted sex. But what he also shows is how strongly Puritanism contributed to hierarchical family relations in the form of an entrenched patriarchalism, with all that meant in terms of restrictive roles for women and a punitive approach to the upbringing of children.

From the Reformation and Puritanism, we turn in Sheridan Gilley's essay to G. K. Chesterton as a historical case-study in Roman Catholic moral theology on the family. Once again the issue of authority comes to the surface, this time in relation to the question of who decides in matters of morals. What Gilley seeks to show is how powerful were the threats to family life at the turn of the twentieth century and how Chesterton's responses represent a particularly telling instance of a traditional Catholic teaching on the family held to be universally true.

From essays held to be their theology from the Bible and the study of history, we turn with Peter Selby's contribution to essays which do their theology from other starting-points. Selby's starting-point is ecclesiology. Out of a concern that, in spite of the existence of very real threats to family life, there is the danger also of valuing the family too highly, he calls for attention to 'a larger project', participation in which is not a matter of blood ties but of *huiothesia*: adoption by God into the family of God. Michael Vasey's essay points in a not dissimilar direction from the neighbouring field of liturgy. One of his most important suggestion is that one of the roles of liturgical worship is to call into question ways of organising human desire (such as 'the modern family') which do not have God as their primary goal.

Jeff Astley engages with the family from his background in the philosophy and psychology of Christian education. His essay is a contribution to reflection on what the family is for, focusing specific attention on the crucial role of the family both in Christian nurture and faith formation and in the criticism of faith as well. Nicely complementing this study is that of Anne Borrowdale on the importance of the willingness to forgive if family life is to be a context for 'right relations'. Her essay helpfully distinguishes four levels of offence in family life and suggests that the level of offence has an important bearing on the possibility of forgiveness and the form it might take. And an important reflection on the doctrine of the atonement comes at the end.

The danger of doing a theology of the family without attention to the empirical sociological data on marital and family breakdown is the focus of Jon Davies' essay. In one of the most combative pieces in the collection, he argues that liberal theologies on the one hand and the worldview of modernity and postmodernism on the other have produced an 'adults only' society inimical to the well-being of children and to the stability of family life, especially among the poor. The best solution, argues Davies, is 'a preferential option for the family' grounded on traditional Christian values.

From empirical sociology we move, with Alan Suggate's essay, to a study of ideology in twentieth-century Britain. Two ideologies are described and evaluated in terms of their impact on the family: the ethical socialism of R. H. Tawney and the ethical capitalism of Margaret Thatcher. While Suggate finds strengths and weaknesses in both, his clear preference is for the tradition of Tawney and the social theology of William Temple; and the essay ends with a significant case-study showing how empowerment at the local community level can take place.

But it is becoming clearer to many that an adequate understanding of empowerment has to face up to the kinds of distortions of power in family, church and society which are manifested in the sexual abuse of children. Ann Loades' essay addresses this issue quite directly. Her subtle delineation of the contours of the problem and the adequacy or otherwise of attempts to solve it represents a persuasive invitation to those engaged in Christian ethics and theology to 'take children seriously'. Of course, one of the contours of the problem is that of patterns of domination which are related to gender and, in particular, patriarchy. Susan Parsons' essay on 'Feminism and the Family' is relevant here. She addresses the ethical question of the relation between theories of justice and family life and shows that feminists take a variety of approaches: some stand in the liberal tradition, others in the communitarian tradition, others yet again in a tradition of a more postmodern kind oriented around a particular notion of friendship. Parsons' own suggestion – and it is a highly significant one – is that a reconstruction of the natural law tradition is likely to be the most hopeful way forward.

This natural law tradition, according to Parsons, will enable us to discover our humanness 'as persons intended for love, love of self, and love of others, and love of the earth, and love of God'. Mention of 'love of the earth' reminds us that there is a crucial ecological dimension to thinking about the family which we too often overlook. This is the issue which Edward Echlin takes up. He points to the interdependence of human families with the wider earth community, and shows how the Christian heritage of scripture, tradition and liturgy testifies to the importance of preserving and nurturing this interdependence as part of the praise of God.

The last two essays in the collection are, appropriately enough, about the family in the light of eschatology. This is justified on the grounds that, as Gerard Loughlin says in his contribution, 'thinking about how we will be is thinking about how we are, from the perspective of our eternal destiny'. Loughlin gives a fascinating analysis of what the postmodern family looks like from the evidence of recent Hollywood cinematic images. He then proceeds to examine alternative visions of the family from within Christianity. In the process, he argues that postmodernism offers us a kind of realised eschatology, the heavenly family now, in the form of sexual promiscuity and infinite consumption. The Christian eschatological tradition, however, knows that the end has not arrived, and that what is important is to participate in the life of the heavenly family through relationships of 'mutuality, fidelity and dispossession'.

Colin Crowder also takes up eschatology, this time to see what we can learn from the widely-held belief that heaven is the place for 'the ultimate family reunion'. He shows that doctrines of heaven have tended to oscillate between those which stress discontinuity between this life and the life to come and those which stress continuity. What is of overriding importance, however, is the reality of the 'hunger' which lies behind the human desire for the reunion of the family in heaven and to let that hunger move us to acknowledge that families 'matter' and that in consequence we 'must make our relationships good – or "good enough" – while we can'.

Contributors

Rev Dr Jeff Astley is an Anglican priest and Director of the North East Institute of Christian Education, an educational research centre for Christian learning. He is also an honorary lecturer in the Departments of Theology and Education, Durham University. He is the author or editor of seven books on Christian education and faith development issues, most recently, *The Philosophy of Christian Religious Education* (SPCK, 1994).

Rev Dr Stephen C. Barton is a Lecturer in New Testament in the Theology Department, Durham University, and a non-stipendiary minister at St John's, Neville's Cross. He was a member of the Church of England Working Party on the Family and a contributor to its report, *Something to Celebrate* (Church House Publishing, 1995). His doctoral thesis was published recently as *Discipleship and Family Ties in Mark and Matthew* (SNTSMS 80; Cambridge University Press, 1994).

Dr Anne Borrowdale is a freelance writer and teacher, having served until 1994 as Oxford Diocesan Social Responsibility Officer. She is an Associate Tutor on the St Alban's and Oxford Ministry Course, and was a member of the Church of England Board for Social Responsibility Working Party on the Family. Awarded a doctorate from Durham University for a thesis on a feminist theology of work, she has written and spoken widely on gender issues. Her most recent book is *Reconstructing Family Values* (SPCK, 1994).

Dr Colin Crowder lectures in philosophy of religion, modern theology and modern atheism in the Theology Department, Durham University. He has published articles on the philosophy of religion and on theology and literature, and is the editor of *God and Reality: Essays on Christian Non-Realism* (Mowbray, 1996), and co-editor (with Jeff Astley and Leslie J. Francis) of *Theological Perspectives on Christian Education* (Gracewing, 1996).

Jon Davies is Senior Lecturer and Head of the Department of Religious Studies at the University of Newcastle upon Tyne. He has written on town and country planning, religion and war, and the family, religion and capitalism. He is currently working on two volumes: *Death in the Early Christian Centuries* (Routledge) and *Sex These Days* (Sheffield Academic Press).

Professor J. D. G. Dunn is Lightfoot Professor of Divinity in the Department of Theology, Durham University, and Director of the Durham Centre for Theological Research. He teaches New Testament theology and the history of Christian origins, and his recent publications include *The Partings of the Ways Between Christianity and Judaism and their Significance for the Character of Christianity* (SCM / TPI, 1991); *A Commentary on the Epistle to the Galatians* (A. & C. Black / Hendrickson, 1993); and *The Epistles to the Colossians and to Philemon* (Paternoster / Eerdmans, 1996).

Dr Edward P. Echlin is an Honorary Research Fellow in Theology, Trinity and All Saints College, Leeds University. He has written a number of books in the area of church and ministry, including *The Deacon in the Church* (Alba House, 1971) and *The Story of Anglican Ministry* (St Paul Publications). His strong ecological concerns are reflected in two studies: *Christian Green Heritage* (Grove Books, 1989), and *The Deacon and Creation* (Church Union, 1992).

Professor Anthony Fletcher is Professor of History at Essex University, having been Professor of Modern History at Durham University until 1995. He has researched and written extensively in the early modern period of English history. His two most recent books are: *Reform in the Provinces: The Government of Stuart England* (Yale University Press, 1986), and *Gender, Sex and Subordination 1500–1800* (Yale University Press, 1995).

Rev Dr James Francis is Senior Lecturer in the Department of Religious Studies, Sunderland University, a non-stipendiary minister and curate of St Chad's, Sunderland, and the Bishop of

Durham's Advisor for Non-Stipendiary Ministry. He has published a number of articles, the most recent being, 'Reflections on Ministry in Secular Employment', in J. Davies, ed., *God and the Marketplace* (Institute of Economic Affairs, 1993), 125–140.

Dr Sheridan Gilley is Reader in Theology in the Department of Theology, Durham University. His recent publications include *Newman and his Age* (Darton, Longman & Todd, 1990); *A History of Religion in Britain* (co-edited with W. J. Sheils, Blackwell, 1994); and various articles on Newman, Manning, Pusey, Frederick Lucas, Walter Hook, J. B. Dykes, G. K. Chesterton, and the historiography of religion in modern Britain and Ireland.

Dr Carol Harrison is Lecturer in the Theology and History of the Latin West in the Department of Theology, Durham University. She specialises in the work of St Augustine and, in addition to numerous articles, has published a study of his aesthetics, entitled *Revelation and Beauty in the Thought of St Augustine* (Oxford University Press, 1992).

Professor Ann Loades is Professor of Divinity in the Department of Theology, Durham University, where she lectures in systematic and philosophical theology and Christian ethics. She has written and edited a number of books, including *Feminist Theology, A Reader* (SPCK, 1990) and, with David Brown, *The Sense of the Sacramental* (SPCK, 1995) and *Christ the Sacramental Word* (SPCK, 1996).

Dr Gerard Loughlin is a Senior Lecturer in Religious Studies at the University of Newcastle upon Tyne, where he teaches Christian theology, ethics and philosophy of religion. He has published articles in a number of leading journals, including *Modern Theology* and *New Blackfriars,* and is the author of *Telling God's Story: Bible, Church and Narrative Theology* (Cambridge University Press, 1996).

Dr Susan Parsons is Principal of the East Midlands Ministry Training Course. She has written a number of articles in the field of Christian ethics and recently completed *Feminism and Christian*

Ethics (Cambridge University Press, 1996) for the series New
Studies in Christian Ethics.

Rev Professor John Rogerson was Head of the Department of
Biblical Studies at Sheffield University from 1979 to 1994, having
previously taught in Durham. He is retiring in 1996 in order to
concentrate on writing on ethical and theological issues connected with Biblical Studies. His recent writings include *W. M. L.
de Wette, Founder of Modern Biblical Criticism* (JSOT Press, 1992) and
The Bible and Criticism in Victorian Britain (Sheffield Academic
Press, 1995).

Rt Rev Professor Peter Selby is William Leech Professorial Fellow
in Applied Christian Theology in the University of Durham, and
an Honorary Assistant Bishop in the dioceses of Durham and
Newcastle. His most recent books are *BeLonging: Challenge to a
Tribal Church* (SPCK, 1991), and *Rescue: Jesus and Salvation Today*
(SPCK, 1995).

Dr Alan M. Suggate is a Senior Lecturer in Theology in the
Department of Theology, University of Durham. His special
field is twentieth-century Christian social ethics. As well as his
book, *William Temple and Christian Social Ethics Today* (T. & T.
Clark, 1987), he has written on the Western tradition more
widely, and also has a particular interest in East Asian theologies
(especially Japan) and dialogue between East and West.

Rev Michael Vasey lectures in Christian Liturgy at St. John's
College, University of Durham. He is a member of the Church
of England Liturgical Commission, Anglican Observer to the
Roman Catholic Pastoral Liturgical Committee, and one of the
Anglican members of the ecumenical Joint Liturgical Group.
He is a contributor to *On the Way: Towards an Integrated Approach
to Christian Initiation* (Church House Publishing, 1995). He has
also written a new study of homosexuality: *Strangers and Friends*
(Hodder & Stoughton, 1995).

PART I

Biblical and Historical Perspectives

1

Biblical Hermeneutics and the Family

Stephen C. Barton

1. *Introduction*

Christian reflection on the family has always paid considerable attention to what the Bible says. Jesus cites Genesis in
support of his prohibition of divorce (Mk 10.2–9, at vv. 6–8),
and the fifth commandment in support of his protest against
abuses of filial obligation related to the custom of Corban (Mk
7.1–13, at v. 10). The author of Ephesians quotes Gen 2.24 as
an authoritative scriptural warrant for husbands to love their
wives as Christ loved the church (Eph 5.21–33, at v. 31).[1] The
author of 1 Timothy likewise appeals to the story of Adam and
Eve as a warrant for imposing silence on women in church
and denying them a teaching ministry or authority over men
(1 Tim 2.11–14).

Such examples could be multiplied from Christian history as
a whole. Peter Brown has given us an authoritative account of
attitudes to sexuality, marriage and family ties in the patristic
period, and there too biblical interpretation is acknowledged as
playing a vital role.[2] From a much later period, we could instance
the English Puritans as a further case in point.[3] Their conception

---

[1] For full discussion, see J. Paul Sampley, *'And the Two shall Become One Flesh':
A Study of Traditions in Ephesians 5:21–33* (Cambridge: Cambridge University
Press, 1971), esp. ch. VII.

[2] Peter Brown, *The Body and Society. Men, Women and Sexual Renunciation in
Early Christianity* (London: Faber & Faber, 1990).

[3] See further, R. E. Clements, *Wisdom in Theology* (Carlisle: Paternoster Press,
1992), esp. 126–30. On the Puritans, Clements refers to Christopher Hill's *Society
and Puritanism in Pre-revolutionary England* (Harmondsworth: Penguin, 1986),
429–66.

of the home as 'the spiritualization of the household' (to use Christopher Hill's phrase) was derived, at least in part, from their reading of the Bible. Of particular importance was the Book of Proverbs with its strong focus on the individual household, rather than the temple or the palace, as the primary sphere of moral formation and social duty. In a way which is interestingly analogous to this, the Puritans made the home a centre of Christian nurture and education, and saw themselves as developing an alternative to traditional patterns of piety fostered by the churches and the (suspect) ordained priesthood.

The central role accorded the Bible is no less true of Christian reflection today. Denominational church reports on human sexuality or marriage and the family invariably include a chapter early on which attempts to lay some biblical foundations.[4] A current series in the *Expository Times* entitled 'New Occasions Teach New Duties?', has as its first two contributions essays on, respectively, 'The Use of the Old Testament in Christian Ethics' and 'The Use of the New Testament in Christian Ethics'. The recent papal encyclical *Veritatis Splendor* builds its call for a reformation of Christian morality upon an exposition of the story of Jesus' encounter with the rich young man, in Matthew 19. Recent writing of a more systematic theological kind on the family also gives considerable prominence to the biblical material. For example, Adrian Thatcher, in his recent book *Liberating Sex. A Christian Sexual Theology,* addresses as early as chapter 2 the question of 'The Place of the Bible in Christian Sexual Theology'.[5]

The prominence accorded the Bible is related to a number of factors. At a fundamental level, it has to do with the fact that Christianity is what George Lindbeck calls a 'textualized religion', where reality has an inscribed, 'it-is-written', quality about it.[6] A related factor is the history of Christian thought, in which the art of biblical interpretation has been a recurrent and

---

[4] E.g. the Church of England document, *Issues in Human Sexuality. A Statement by the House of Bishops* (London: Church House Publishing, 1991), ch. 2 of which is on 'Scripture and Human Sexuality'.

[5] Adrian Thatcher, *Liberating Sex. A Christian Sexual Theology* (London: SPCK, 1993).

[6] George Lindbeck, 'Barth and Textuality', *Theology Today* 43 (1986–87), 361–76, at 361.

dominant concern. There is a sense in which it is true to say that the history of the church *is* the history of the interpretation of the Bible. To put is another way: one of the main forms of Christian religious activity has always been scribal and exegetical. At the level of doctrine, the warrant for such activity is the Christian doctrine of revelation, where the words of Scripture have a pivotal role as the unique and inspired testimony to the Word of God incarnate. More recently, the advent of historical criticism and the hegemony of this method of Bible reading in academic theology has made finding meaning in the Bible something of a problem. Now, for many readers, the Bible presents an unavoidable obstacle which has to be circumvented: a minefield of exegetical difficulties rather than a fount and wellspring of truth for life. The Bible is still important, but now for reasons more negative than positive.

More specifically in relation to Christian reflection on human social patterns like marriage and the family, the Bible bulks large precisely because it is the story of the revelation of God in and through God's relations with men and women in their common life. In this story, composed in a wide variety of literary genres, human relatedness through blood, marriage, household ties, land and cult provides the major idiom for exploring and experiencing relatedness with God.[7] The former Chief Rabbi, Lord Jakobovits, expressed this conception of things in a recent address on the family, when he said:

> I belong to the people who first taught the human race that we were all originally descended from an identifiable father and an identifiable mother, that we all derive from a human pair, man and woman, out of whom the human race eventually evolved. I belong to a people that trace their origin to the idyllic couples of Abraham and Sarah, of Isaac and Rebecca, of Jacob and Rachel. In other words we are a people who were born at home, and therefore the entire focus of our national thinking is perhaps best expressed by the collective term by which we have been known since Biblical times: either 'the house of Israel' or 'the children of Israel'. We see ourselves as

---

[7] See further, Christopher J. H. Wright, *God's People in God's Land. Family, Land, and Property in the Old Testament* (Grand Rapids: Eerdmans, 1990).

a family that has a house, a home, that constitute the fellow-ship, the brotherhood, the family unit of children of Israel.[8]

Of course, Jakobovits is talking of the Jewish Scriptures only. But the same idiom, transformed in interesting ways, continues into the New Testament as well. Jesus speaks of his followers belonging to households one hundredfold (Mk 10.28–30); the Acts of the Apostles tells of conversion by household and the practice of hospitality among the early Christians; Paul uses familial imagery of his fellow-believers and gives instruction on matters of marriage and household order; the letter to the Ephesians, already mentioned, uses biblical marriage symbolism to describe the relation between Christ and the church (Eph 5.21–33); and so on. Taken as a whole, then, the Bible is for Christians a book which reveals the true nature of human identity under God, an identity which is explored in the predominantly social-economic-political-religious idiom of marriage and the family.

However, what the Bible 'says' and how the Bible 'speaks' are not the same thing. The literal meaning of the text is not necessarily the true meaning or the meaning 'for us'. For the Bible to speak, acts of interpretation and discrimination on the part of the reader in his or her 'reading community', under the guidance of the Holy Spirit, are required. What I want to do in the remainder of this chapter, therefore, is to take several specific and recent examples of acts of biblical interpretation which are used to underpin different kinds of Christian understanding of the family. My aim in so doing is to assess the strengths and weaknesses of these various interpretations with a view to fostering a more adequate use of the Bible in theological reflection in this area.

2.   Case studies

1. As a first case study, I have chosen Adrian Thatcher's afore-mentioned book *Liberating Sex,* published in 1993. Chapter 2 of this book is a particularly clear attempt to define how to use the Bible in constructing a Christian sexual theology. The main

---

[8] 'The Family – A Community of Giving', in Joanna Bogle, ed., *Families for Tomorrow* (Leominster: Fowler Wright, 1991), 5–7, at 5.

argument is that 'a distinction must be made between a *biblical* sexual theology and a *Christian* sexual theology'.[9] This is because the biblical text is pervasively hierarchical and patriarchal in its assumptions about relationships between men and women, and anachronistic in its understanding of male and female homosexuality. Therefore, if the Bible is to contribute to theology, it has to be set firmly within a hermeneutical framework: that of Christian faith centred on Christ. 'What is required', says Thatcher, 'is a full, Christian sexual theology, as opposed to a mere biblical one, where that Love which God is and which is spread abroad in Christ is both our norm and gift. This will give us a point of reference in making ethical judgments, and a framework for interpreting biblical material'.[10]

To make his point, Thatcher proceeds in two ways. The first is the negative one of criticising both biblical texts for their sexism and church reports for their biblicism. The second is the constructive one of proposing what we might call a hermeneutic of retrieval. Here, a christological principle and a traditional doctrinal framework are advanced as the essential basis for renouncing 'sub-Christian', literalist readings of the Bible in favour of readings which testify to the revelation of the love of God in Christ: 'Sexual theology is Christian when it derives from a sharing in the vision and experience of God as love, made known in Jesus Christ. The role of the Bible in sexual theology must be that of testifying to that vision and experience.'[11]

In my view, this approach has much to commend it. It is genuinely theological in its focus on Christ as the norm for interpreting Scripture, a theological hermeneutic rooted in early Christian interpretation of the Hebrew Bible and given classic definition by Luther at the time of the Reformation. It also avoids being reductionist in the fashion of certain kinds of historical criticism which have no hermeneutical means for interpreting the Bible as Scripture. On the contrary, Thatcher argues quite properly that the framework he is adopting for interpreting the Bible is not alien, but is itself biblical and traditional. He says, for example:

---

[9] Adrian Thatcher, *Liberating Sex*, 15. Author's emphasis.
[10] Ibid., 22.
[11] Ibid., 28.

Christian faith is a sharing in divine love. Critical scholarship is one of the tools for identifying the patriarchy that mars this vision and experience of love. The interpretative task in relation to the Scriptures is to let their testimony point to Christ (John 5.39), the revelation of divine love in human, embodied, relational being. ... This sharing in divine love is the basis for thinking about and having sex. The biblical themes of creation and re-creation, sin and redemption, brokenness and wholeness, estrangement and reconciliation, fill out the basic framework.[12]

Nevertheless, while endorsing Thatcher's basic approach, there are certain weaknesses which are worth teasing out. For instance, when it comes to treating the *text* of the Bible – as distinct from elucidating its broad *themes* – the overwhelming impression given is of the text as a source of danger, threat and damage. Take his first example of texts about husband–wife relations. Here, Thatcher's tactic is to quote texts (such as Col 3.18; 1 Pet 3.1; Eph 5.22ff.) which support the claim that New Testament teaching in this area is vitiated by unquestioned assumptions about the propriety of relations of domination, whether of husband over wife or of master over slave. He concludes: 'If the teaching on marriage in the New Testament letters is accepted, women are forever to be submissive to men and the same teaching justifies owning slaves. It is inadmissible to appeal to biblical teaching on marriage while at the same time rejecting slavery since marriage and slavery are as indissolubly linked as a man and woman are linked in marriage.'[13]

My problem with this is twofold. On the one hand, Thatcher is not critical enough – or perhaps I should say, not properly critical. When he wants to score a point, he resorts to the very proof-texting methods used by his imagined literalist opponents. What he should do is to seek first to understand these 'subordinationist' texts by setting them carefully in their respective rhetorical and historical contexts. This might help him to see, for example, that the household code in 1 Peter springs from a specific, historically-conditioned apologetic concern: to defuse criticism by outsiders that conversion to Christianity is socially

[12] Ibid., 27.
[13] Ibid., 16–17.

irresponsible because it subverts family loyalties and household duty.[14] In other words, the issue is not hierarchy and patriarchy *per se*, but the defence of the gospel and the maintenance of an effective witness to the rule of God. Furthermore, a closer look at the changing status and roles accorded women and slaves within the early 'house churches' would help Thatcher to see that a process of deconstruction of patriarchal norms had begun, and that hierarchy and patriarchy in the conventional sense were *not* taken for granted in the way he suggests.[15] But all this requires a degree of attention to the text in its historical context which Thatcher skates over.

His approach, by contrast, has the serious consequence of appearing to trivialise the text. Large sections are so dangerous as to be dispensable – as in his devastating reference to 'the miserable subordinationism of some of the New Testament letters'.[16] If this is the case, why bother with the Bible at all? Is it not completely irretrievable, as Daphne Hampson argues, for instance?[17] And if the Bible is irretrievable, are not the broader themes and the christological testimony upon which Thatcher puts heavy weight irretrievable as well? Now, it is not necessarily the case that an all-or-nothing approach is the only viable one: and this, I think, is what Thatcher himself believes. But his deep ambivalence about the Bible is in danger of being the thin end of a large wedge which eventually cuts Christian theology off from its scriptural roots altogether.

In addition to this, it is possible to suspect that, in spite of Thatcher's avowed christological hermeneutic, there is another, virtually hidden, hermeneutic at work in his treatment of these texts as well. The tip of the iceberg appears in the statement: 'What is needed is a fresh approach to marriage and human relations generally which is not based on domination at all, *but on equality*.'[18] From a Christian theological viewpoint, we are justi-

[14] See on this D. L. Balch, *Let Wives Be Submissive. The Domestic Code in I Peter* (Chico, CA: Scholars Press, 1981).

[15] On slavery, see further, Dale B. Martin, *Slavery as Salvation. The Metaphor of Slavery in Pauline Christianity* (New Haven: Yale University Press, 1990). On women, see, from a vast literature, Antoinette Clark Wire, *The Corinthian Women Prophets* (Philadelphia: Fortress Press, 1990).

[16] Adrian Thatcher, *Liberating Sex*, 21.

[17] See Daphne Hampson, *Theology and Feminism* (Oxford: Blackwell, 1990).

[18] Adrian Thatcher, *Liberating Sex*, 16–17. My emphasis.

fied in asking: Where has this norm of 'equality' come from? What is its genealogy? If it comes from post-Enlightenment, secular individualism, what justifies appeal to it as a basis for interpreting the testimony of Scripture to the will of God for human relations?

Such questions are not meant to disparage the legitimacy of the search for equality in man–woman relations today, nor to play down the human rights tradition in ethics. It is important nevertheless to observe that the goal-posts have been shifted away from the Christian field, and that the distinctive Christian way of seeing things is in danger of being subverted. Unfortunately, this danger becomes alarmingly real when Thatcher quotes Eph 5.25 ('Husbands, love your wives, as Christ loved the church and gave himself up for it'), and then goes on to remark, 'This is no basis for love.'[19] At this point, it appears that Thatcher's own christological hermeneutic has been left behind in favour of a liberal Enlightenment notion of marriage as a contract between interested parties and a notion of family life as a constant juggling of individual rights. From a Christian theological understanding of love and marriage, such a view, however fashionable today, is a long way from the truth.

2. A second case-study worthy of notice for the attention it gives to the Bible is Rodney Clapp's book *Families at the Crossroads*, also published in 1993, but coming from the other side of the Atlantic, and praised by Christian ethicist Stanley Hauerwas as 'quite simply the best book we have on the family by a Christian theologian'![20] Unlike Thatcher, Clapp does not distinguish explicitly between a 'biblical' theology and a 'Christian' theology, but some such distinction is important for him all the same. This is because one of Clapp's main concerns is to counteract a strong tendency he discerns in American evangelical Protestantism to assume that the 'traditional' nuclear family is both 'natural' and 'biblical'. The disastrous consequence of this, as he sees it, is to turn Christian values on their head. Christianity gets defined in

---

[19] Ibid., 16.
[20] Rodney Clapp, *Families at the Crossroads. Beyond Traditional and Modern Options* (Downers Grove: Inter Varsity Press, 1993). The quotation comes from the back cover.

terms of (a particular, bourgeois conception of) 'the family', rather than the family being understood in terms of Christianity. Or, in ecclesiological terms, the family usurps the place of the church as the primary locus of Christian nurture and self-understanding. Clapp epitomises his approach to biblical interpretation in this way:

> So the Bible itself is not a list of abstract, timeless formulas. It simply provides no detailed guidance or techniques, for all times and places, on disciplining children or seeking a mate or determining whether a wife should or should not work outside the home. Rather, the Bible is centrally and first of all the *story* of Israel and Jesus. Beyond that, it includes the poetry and prison letters of people who faithfully responded to that story in their own times and places. To create and live in a truly Christian family, the church in every generation and culture must read the biblical story anew.... What I offer, instead, is a reading of the biblical story with special relevance to the Western Christian family in the late twentieth and early twenty-first centuries. My aim is to discover what purposes and hopes our families should assume to remain faithful. Remaining faithful means witnessing to the living truth of the God revealed in Scripture. Witnessing means incarnating the family in peculiar shapes and rich practices *that can only be explained by resorting to the story of Israel and Jesus Christ.*[21]

Let us consider now how this works out in practice in what Clapp says theologically about the family. At one level, the Bible is used as a tool for deconstructing the widespread assumption among Clapp's evangelical readership that the 'traditional', nuclear family is the most natural and most biblical thing in the world.[22] Whereas the nuclear family is monogamous, the families of biblical times accept polygamy. Whereas the former sharply separates private and public worlds, in the latter these worlds substantially overlap. Whereas the one consists on average of 2.63 people, the average Hebrew household can range between 50 and 100 people. Whereas the modern family places a high

---

[21] Ibid., 15–16. Author's emphasis.
[22] Ibid., 27–47.

premium on romantic love and sentimental bonds, biblical family life is bound above all by concerns of economic survival, property and inheritance.

Rhetorically-speaking, Clapp is fighting his evangelical opponents on their own territory. He is using biblical data about ancient Israel to undermine the assumption that the traditional family is all that traditional, and argues to the contrary that it is a relatively modern, Victorian invention, which is quite unlike families in the Bible. This is a ground-clearing exercise on Clapp's part. What he wants to make space for is a theology of the family which involves, not an attempt to return to 'the biblical family', but an attempt to live in families in ways which flow from the biblical testimony to God-in-Christ: which means living in families in ways which are nurtured by the values of the kingdom and life together in the church. Kingdom and church first, family second: that is the order of priorities he is concerned to establish in order to dethrone the family as it is understood in the evangelical circles he is addressing.

In a chapter on 'Advanced Capitalism and the Lost Art of Christian Family',[23] Clapp goes on to argue that the modern family has been trivialised and subverted by capitalism and the economic exchange model of society. Family life has become privatised, sentimentalised and oriented towards consumption; marriage has become a matter of secular, inter-personal contract rather than a religious communally-acknowledged covenant; and having children has become problematic because of the limitations they place on the autonomy and mobility of adults. Clapp's proposed solution to this problem is not, however, to reassert the central significance of the family. That is the tendency of the religious Right, and it only exacerbates the problem by attempting to replace the late twentieth century family by the nineteenth-century bourgeois family in the guise of 'the biblical model'. Rather, Clapp seeks to go one step back by arguing that unless we start with the kingdom and the church we will have no basis upon which to decide how to live as Christians, whether in families or not.[24]

[23] Ibid., 48–66.
[24] Ibid., 67–88, on 'Church as First Family'.

At this point, the Bible becomes important again. Previously, Clapp has used the Bible as a source of *historical information* about family forms in ancient Israel to undercut the claim that getting back to the traditional family is a getting back to the biblical family. Now he uses the Bible *theologically* to argue that, seen in the light of Christ, it is not the biological family which is 'the primary vehicle of God's grace and salvation', but the family of the church. In line with his methodological aim to develop a theology out of the story of Israel and Jesus, Clapp argues, for example, that in Israel's covenantal theology, Israel's identity as the 'children of God' was above all a matter of election and obedience, even if ties of blood and kinship were important also. Turning to Jesus, Clapp emphasises those gospel traditions which firmly subordinate ties of natural kinship to the higher priority of obedience and discipleship in the light of the coming of the kingdom.[25] He then develops this strand of thought both with reference to the story of Mary the mother of Jesus, and with reference to Paul's transfer of kinship and household language to that solidarity which was of supreme importance for him – namely, the church.

So if, at an earlier point, Clapp has used historical interpretation of the Bible to dethrone the family, here he has used theological interpretation. In place of the family as the bastion against modernity and postmodernism, it is 'the church and its story' which give us a place to stand and which provide the resources for living together Christianly.[26] Among the consequences of this reordering of priorities around the kingdom and the church, Clapp has interesting things to say about the importance of the vocation to singleness, testimony to which is provided in the Bible not least by both Jesus and Paul. He also has interesting things to say about the nature of true fidelity and the importance of the ethic of hospitality to strangers, ideas of direct relevance to family life (and much else) but springing out of the biblical story of Israel and Jesus as mediated by and practised in the church.[27]

---

[25] For further exploration of these gospel texts, see Stephen C. Barton, *Discipleship and Family Ties in Mark and Matthew* (Cambridge: Cambridge University Press, 1994).

[26] *Families at the Crossroads*, 84ff.

[27] Ibid., 89–148.

When we start to evaluate Clapp's work, what strikes us immediately is the remarkable absence of the sense of deep ambivalence and of the danger posed by the biblical text which so characterises Adrian Thatcher's approach. Put in other words, where Thatcher's reading bears the marks of a hermeneutic of suspicion, Clapp's reading bears the marks of a hermeneutic of trust. Even though both authors interpret the Bible in the light of an explicit theological and christological framework, so that what is important is the words as witness to the Word, there is a sense in which Clapp is 'at home' with the Bible in a way which Thatcher is not.

The clue to this difference lies, I think, in the area of the sociology of knowledge. Thatcher writes in a way characteristic of liberal Anglicanism. His indebtedness to liberalism shows itself on the one hand in the way his agenda for a new sexual theology is heavily determined by issues of modernity such as patriarchy and homophobia. On the other hand, it comes through also in his modernist commitment to post-Enlightenment values such as equality between the sexes and individual human rights. Rodney Clapp writes from somewhere within the orbit of American evangelical Protestantism. His agenda is not a modernist one, however, but a postmodern one – something reflected in his book's subtitle, 'Beyond Traditional and Modern Options'. This allows him to capitalise upon the otherness and particularity of the biblical tradition, rather than being embarrassed or threatened by it. At the same time, his application of a christological hermeneutic and his strong ecclesiological orientation frees him to explore the spirit of the text without being irresponsible with regard to the letter.

But I would want to express a number of reservations, nonetheless. My main one concerns Clapp's hermeneutical decision to make 'story' his primary category of biblical interpretation, as when he says: 'the Bible itself is not a list of abstract, timeless formulas. ... Rather, the Bible is centrally and first of all the *story* of Israel and Jesus. Beyond that, it includes the poetry and prison letters of people who faithfully responded to that story in their own times and places'.[28] Now, the strengths of the category 'story' as a kind of organising metaphor for biblical interpretation are

----

[28] Ibid., 15.

evident: it does justice to the massive amount of narrative material in the Bible; it allows the Bible to be read as one book rather
than being broken up into disparate and conflicting parts; it fits
in with the turn to literary models in recent biblical scholarship;
and it allows a high degree of flexibility in the ways in which the
text is theologically and christologically appropriated.

The weakness, however, is that it is too general to be of any real
use. Or, to put it another way, it is so general that it says everything
and nothing at the same time. On the one hand, it represents a
refusal to engage with the detail of the text in all its complexity,
diversity and historicality. In that sense, it shares some of the
problems of its predecessor in the history of ideas, the 'salvation
history' approach to interpretation.[29] It also has the appearance of
taking seriously the Bible as literature without being at all literary-
critical. On the other hand, it represents a refusal to engage with
systematic theology, since truth is now a matter of somehow 'living
within the story' rather than of the application of critical reason to
the claims about God and reality which the biblical text conveys.

This does not necessarily mean that what he says about the
family is mistaken, only that it is not as well grounded as it might
be. In the end, a lot hangs on the communitarian dimension of
Clapp's approach; that is, a lot depends on the quality of life in
the church if the biblical story of Israel and Jesus is to function in
a life-giving way for people trying to live together in families. One
wonders if, in the end, Clapp has succeeded only in replacing one
kind of traditionalist approach with another: instead of 'back to
the Bible', he invites us to get 'back to the church' (or, even more
appealingly, 'back to the kingdom of God'!). Of course, from a
Christian point of view, none of these is a bad place to go. But
Clapp's work provides only the barest outline of what we should
do when we get there, not least in respect of marriage and the
family. Adrian Thatcher's honest grappling with issues like sexism, cohabitation, homophobia, gay and lesbian relationships,
and so on, is strangely missing. If Thatcher's broadly liberal
approach at least takes seriously the need for a new Christian

---

[29] I owe this and several other points in this paragraph to my colleague
Dr Colin Crowder in conversation.

casuistry, Clapp's narrative–communitarian approach appears to leave that crucial dimension relatively undeveloped.[30]

3. My third and final case-study again comes from 1993. It is clear how many authors and publishers were gearing up for the International Year of the Family in 1994! The book is *The Fulcrum and the Fire. Wrestling with Family Life*, written by Sue Walrond-Skinner who is a family and marital therapist and also Adviser in Pastoral Care and Counselling in the (Anglican) Diocese of Southwark. In the course of a very wide-ranging and multi-disciplinary analysis of family life, Walrond-Skinner devotes chapter 3, entitled 'Kingdom', to the question of biblical perspectives.

Her argument may be summarised thus. First, there is a polemic against what she calls 'the biblical approach to the family'. What concerns Walrond-Skinner are Christian approaches to family life which assume that the Bible tells us all we need to know about the family, and that the family is all there is. She says, for example:

> There is a kind of double difficulty about the biblical approach to the family. It is both imperialist (family life is 'Christian in its essence'; marriage is a 'Christian institution'; 'Christians should set a standard, God's standard, for everyone else to follow'); and exclusive as though there cannot and could never have been any other social institutions that fill the essential requirements of human aspiration within the will of God.[31]

Then she goes on to argue that the Bible in general and the Old Testament in particular is vitiated in what it says about the family by its pervasive patriarchalism. Nor is it safe to argue that monogamy is 'the biblical ideal', since that particular way of ordering social and sexual relations developed only gradually and in a way which brought advantage only to the male household head. Women remained subjugated and exploited.[32] Never-

---

[30] Of course, the same could not be said of Stanley Hauerwas, whose approach to theological ethics underlies much of Clapp's work. Of Hauerwas' work, see especially, *A Community of Character* (Notre Dame, IN: University of Notre Dame Press, 1981), part three of which contains essays on the family, sexual ethics, and abortion.

[31] Sue Walrond-Skinner, *The Fulcrum and the Fire* (London: Darton, Longman & Todd, 1993), 28.

[32] Ibid., 30–34.

theless, there are redeeming strands in the biblical tradition, such as the prophets' denunciation of relations of injustice and oppression. There are also pictures of loving relationships, such as Jacob's love for Rachel, the love between Naomi and Ruth, and between David and Jonathan, the love poetry of the Song of Songs, and so on. The principle and practice of hospitality to aliens are important too.

Over against this oppressive patriarchalism and transforming these faint glimmerings of light in the dark comes the 'startlingly different approach' of Jesus, with his 'revolutionary approach to personal and familiar relationships ... [by which the] family as a central social and religious unit of Israelite society is now radically redefined'.[33] She continues:

> So far as we know, Jesus neither married nor founded a family himself and much of what he says about family and marriage severely challenges the *status quo* of a lineally descended conjugal, consanguineous household. On the contrary, the new command is to become a beloved community of equals brought into being not by the blood of parenthood nor the legality of marriage but by the grace of adoption.[34]

The argument is developed by pointing to strong evidence from the gospels of the priority Jesus gave to the demands of the kingdom of God, demands which necessitated leaving families behind and which even split families apart. Jesus' teaching on divorce is interpreted as also reflecting kingdom values. What Jesus does is to prohibit a practice which allowed a man to control his wife by divorcing her on the slightest pretext, putting in its place God's original intention of the equality and unity of female and male.

Walrond-Skinner then presents two cameos of Jesus' revolutionary approach. The first is Jesus and the Samaritan woman of Jn 4. What is remarkable in this encounter is Jesus' lack of interest in 'the form of her personal relationships either past or present.... Not only is she not asked to repent or amend her living relationships, *it is the fact that they have been revealed and accepted by Jesus* that enables her to believe and to tell others about her belief. She is

---

33 Ibid., 36.
34 Ibid., 37.

accepted by Jesus just as she is and his acceptance kindles her apostolic zeal. Jesus' eye is on the kingdom, not on the outward form of things'.[35] The second cameo is Jesus' encounter with Martha in Jn 11. This is emphatically *not* the 'domestic' Martha of Lk 10.38–42 and subsequent Christian tradition. Rather, it is the woman with whom Jesus explores profound spiritual and theological truths and who confesses him to be the Messiah – all this taking precedence over her natural, family concerns to do with the deceased Lazarus. Once again, therefore, kingdom values take priority over the family.

In a final section, Walrond-Skinner addresses the problem the church has had historically in getting the balance right between 'the primary claims of the kingdom and the subordinate claims of social and familial relationships'.[36] At certain times in history, sexuality and natural relationships generally are denigrated. At other times, especially when 'traditional values' are at risk in society-at-large, kingdom values are forgotten and an idol made of the family. Interestingly, Paul is upheld as someone who worked quite hard at getting the balance right:

> Much of what he teaches is good news... the equality of marriage partners; the mutuality of marriage; the freedom of choice between marriage and celibacy; the acceptance that divorce is sometimes the right and necessary step to take; the valuing of the contributions of each person within the organic whole of the Body of Christ. And always his emphasis on the wider concerns and commitment to the community of Christ and to the primary claims made by membership of his Body and to the call of the kingdom. Moreover, Paul is always clear that the letter (or outer form) brings death and only the Spirit (or inner form) gives life.[37]

What are we to make of Walrond-Skinner's attempt to use the Bible theologically to reflect on marriage and family life? Her main goals appear to be of two kinds: on the one hand, to counter both Christianity's weighty heritage of biblical patriarchalism and its tendency to make an idol of (a particular form of) the family; on the other hand, to advance a theology

[35] Ibid., 42–3. Author's emphasis.
[36] Ibid., 46.
[37] Ibid.

of the kingdom of God which both relativises the claims of the family and provides values which make new kinds of relationship possible. In my view, these are worthy goals, shared to a high degree by the two other writers we have looked at, and Walrond-Skinner goes some way to achieving them. But I have major reservations also.

In the first instance, the overall structure of her argument seriously diminishes the effective contribution of the Old Testament to Christian moral theology. For in advancing what amounts to a kind of contamination theory, according to which the Old Testament in particular is polluted by patriarchalism, Walrond-Skinner makes the Old Testament as a whole almost unusable. Nor will it do to try to retrieve certain texts as passing the test of 'political correctness' on this issue. The fact that Jacob worked seven years more for Rachel, 'and the time seemed like only a few days to him, because he loved her' (Gen 29.20), does nothing to alter the fact that the marriage was a transaction between two men, Jacob and Laban. Nor are we told whether or not Jacob's strong feelings for Rachel were reciprocated. Again, to cite another of Walrond-Skinner's examples, the 'mutual love and self-sacrifice of Naomi and Ruth' does nothing to alter the fact that their indigence was caused by the deaths of their respective husbands, Elimelech and Mahlon, upon whom the women were completely dependent for their subsistence; and that salvation comes in the form of another significant male member of the clan, Boaz, to whom Ruth attaches herself upon the women's return to the land of Judah.

In short, what is needed here is another way of reading the Old Testament which allows it to speak as Christian Scripture. This will involve taking the text much more seriously than Walrond-Skinner does – by which I mean a willingness to read the text with historical sympathy and engage with it on its own terms, rather than prejudging it according to political and moral notions which belong to another time and place. It is worth noting that the effect of Walrond-Skinner's approach, ironically, is to deprive us of most of what the Old Testament says which might be thought relevant to family life, not least the second table of the decalogue and the biblical laws relating to marriage and household management.[38]

---

[38] For a much better way forward, see Christopher J. H. Wright, *Living as the People of God, The Relevance of Old Testament Ethics* (Leicester: Inter-Varsity Press,

This brings me to a second criticism. What is striking about Walrond-Skinner's interpretation of the Bible is the way it is skewed in an overwhelmingly 'personalist' direction. It is not coincidental that she can do little with the Old Testament, since so much of that tradition is devoted to building social, legal and religious *structures* to enable a people to live together in responsible freedom under God. Instead, theologically-speaking, a false polarisation is introduced between law and grace and between structures and values; and a kingdom of God theology is used, in effect, to draw a line between the testaments.

This polarisation is reflected further in the way she talks of Jesus' 'revolutionary approach': for without the language of revolution it is difficult to play down Christianity's damaging inheritance in the way Walrond-Skinner wants to do. And if she is forced to isolate Jesus and his kingdom preaching from their biblical roots, she is forced also to isolate them from what came after! Conscious of a Jesus tradition apparently hostile to family ties, she says, for example: 'Indeed, it is hard to understand how "the family" as a structure has ever become so inordinately preoccupying for Christians from the way in which it is treated in the Gospels themselves'.[39] In short, if the Old Testament got it wrong, so did the church; and all we are left with is the Jesus of the gospels and Paul.

But even Jesus and Paul are treated in curiously selective ways. On Paul, no explicit mention is made of the 'household codes' and their importance for Christian social ethics. Instead, 'outer form' is disparaged and 'inner meaning' is exalted. When it comes to Jesus, great emphasis is placed on the sayings of Jesus which subordinate family life to the demands of the kingdom. But there is no mention of the rhetorical, hyperbolic dimension of these 'hard sayings', nor of the fact that these sayings stand themselves in strong continuity with biblical and Jewish monotheism according to which the demands of God must always take precedence over everything and everyone else, even family.[40] There is no mention either of traditions which show Jesus' respect for the obligations of filial piety.

1983); *idem*, 'The Ethical Authority of the Old Testament: A Survey of Approaches', *Tyndale Bulletin* 43 (1992), 101–20, 203–31.

[39] *The Fulcrum and the Fire*, 36.

[40] See on this Stephen C. Barton, *Discipleship and Family Ties*, esp. ch. 2.

Interestingly, when it comes to case studies from the gospels, Walrond-Skinner leaves behind the Synoptic gospels (where the emphasis on 'the kingdom' is most pronounced) and turns to the Fourth Gospel which is so distinctive in the way it structures its story of Jesus around significant, one-to-one encounters between Jesus and one other individual. Her exploration of Jesus' conversations with, first, the Samaritan woman and then Martha allows her to portray Jesus as someone not really interested in forms and structures such as marriage and the family, but as someone who is supremely interested in 'relationships' and 'values' and the quest of the individual for personal truth.[41] The representative status of the Samaritan woman and of Martha is passed over. In the end, one is left with the suspicion that Jesus the proclaimer of the kingdom has been transformed into Jesus the therapeutic counsellor, and that Jesus' concern for the repentance of Israel and the nations has been replaced by Jesus' concern for growth in personal self-discovery.

3. *Conclusion*

By way of conclusion, it may be worthwhile to reflect on two issues in biblical hermeneutics and the family that have arisen out of the preceding three case-studies.

First, there is the issue of how to interpret the Bible in an age such as ours whose intellectual and moral horizons are strongly affected by the feminist critique of patriarchy. This is a very big question which is attracting increasing attention in biblical studies and in theological hermeneutics generally.[42] What I would say here is that a certain humility and circumspection are required if our reading is not to become 'single issue' or 'tribal' in ways which are unhelpful.

---

[41] Symptomatic is the following, from *The Fulcrum and the Fire*, 42: '... Jesus seems to be not at all interested in the form of her [the Samaritan woman's] personal relationships either past or present. Rather, he responds to this woman in her capacity to be transparently truthful herself...'.

[42] Foundational works are Elisabeth Schüssler Fiorenza, *In Memory of Her* (London SCM, 1983), and *Bread Not Stone* (Boston MA: Beacon Press, 1984) in the area of biblical interpretation; and, in systematic theology, Rosemary Radford Ruether, *Sexism and God-Talk* (London: SCM, 1983).

A lot depends on what we are trying to achieve. If we are trying to expose patriarchal domination by exploring its historical roots in western civilisation, then it is legitimate and necessary to inquire into the role of sources of traditional authority like the Bible and interpreters of the Bible. But it would be a mistake if, in so doing, we came to the conclusion that the Bible is *only* about gender relations, or that it only speaks about gender relations in one way. It would also be a mistake to argue *with* the Bible as if the Bible has a mind of its own, ideologically committed to patriarchy or, for that matter, egalitarianism.

We have to reckon very often, instead, with ways in which, for good and ill, the Bible has been interpreted in particular reading communities. And we have to ask the question, what virtues and skills does a community of readers require in order to read the Bible in ways which are wise and life-giving (for families or whoever), and how might reading the Bible itself help to inculcate such virtues?[43] On this approach, attention is directed not only at the text but also at those who are doing the reading. If, however, we begin with the assumption that the Bible is only part of the problem instead of being also part of the solution, we are likely to adopt strategies which either trivialise the text or result in major amputations, usually at the cost of the Old Testament.

Second, if it is essential to recognise the contribution of the reading community and the need for virtues and skills which make it possible to read the Bible well, it is also essential to recognise the importance of interpreting the Bible theologically and doxologically. In the context of theological reflection on the family, this means that we should read the Bible with a view to discerning more clearly how the biblical testimony to the love and justice of God *is* reflected and *ought to be* reflected in our life together in families.

If we do this, I think we will begin to see that marriage and family life are God-given ways – and, of course, not the only ways – of sharing in the life of God who is love. We will see that God's desire for the nurture and growth to mature personhood of ourselves as God's creatures is a task and calling in which marriage and family life have an important role to play. We will

---

[43] See further, Stephen E. Fowl and L. Gregory Jones, *Reading in Communion* (London: SPCK, 1991).

see that the gift of procreation is one of God's ways of entrusting the future of his world to men and women, and that raising children is for us an act of trust that the future is in God's hands. We will see, yet further, that sharing as families in the life of God is a calling that requires the practical outworking of the values of the kingdom of God revealed in both the life of the nation of Israel and the life of the person of Christ. The values I have in mind are values like love, sacrifice, forgiveness, obedience, fidelity, friendship, neighbourliness and hospitality. But values are meaningless unless they are given shape and form in relationships and structures. That is why the fidelity of God is embodied in a covenant. It is also why the institutions of marriage and the family are not to be disparaged. In the providence of God, and as the Bible testifies so amply, they are important ways of giving shape and form to the life for which God has made us.

2

The Family and Structures of Grace in the Old Testament

John Rogerson

To attempt to describe the family in the Old Testament in one essay is to attempt the impossible. We are dealing with a literature which, whenever it was put into its final form, claims to describe a society that existed for at least a thousand years – a period which saw enormous social changes and upheavals. Further, this literary evidence as well as the evidence from archaeology contains so many difficulties and obscurities that the scholarly literature is by no means agreed about its interpretation. What follows in this essay, then, is essentially a broad brush approach, and yet one that will try to show how theologically-driven attempts were made to compensate for the failures of the family structure to cope with the crises of ordinary life.

The essay will be structured as follows. I shall begin by reviewing the impression of the family in the Old Testament that is gained by a surface reading of the literature. This will be followed by a sociological and archaeological analysis which, thirdly, will lead to a social historical review of the family in ancient Israel designed to illustrate what, in the title, is called 'structures of grace'.

The family in Old Testament literature

The families that we read about in the Old Testament are almost entirely ruling or leading families, the notable exception being the family of the Bethlehemites Naomi and Elimelech. This should not surprise us. The recorded story, even the religious story, of a nation such as Israel is the story of its rulers and leaders; and if we wish to learn about the ordinary people who lived in small villages we have to interpret the mute evidence discovered by the archaeologist. And we also have to recognise that if our literature is concerned mostly with ruling families, the picture that we get from a surface reading will reflect *their* interests, and not the interests of the ordinary people. What picture do we get?

The most striking thing about the leading Israelite families is that they were polygamous. Leaving aside Abraham's servant-woman Hagar, by whom he had a son although already married to Sarah, Jacob married the two sisters Leah and Rachel (and also had children by their servants Zilpah and Bilhah), while the so-called judges must have had several wives. It is explicitly said of Gideon that he had many wives (Judg 8.30) and we can assume that the same is true of Jair the Gileadite who had thirty sons (Judg 10.4), Ibzan of Bethlehem who had thirty sons and thirty daughters (Judg 12.9) and Abdon the Pirathonite who had forty sons (Judg 12.14). Seven wives who bore children to David are listed at 1 Chron 3.1–9, to whom we must add the childless Michal, daughter of Saul. The Chronicles passage also mentions that David had concubines. With regard to Solomon we are told that he had seven hundred princesses as wives in addition to three hundred concubines (1 Kings 11.3).

In the narratives following the reign of Solomon less stress is placed upon the number of wives of the kings, and we might even conclude from the study of the illness of Jeroboam's son Abijah, that Jeroboam, at least, was monogamous. The narrative refers consistently to 'his wife' or 'the wife of Jeroboam' (e.g. 1 Kings 14.2, 4). Yet the accounts of the palace revolutions in which the houses of Jeroboam and Baasha are completely wiped out suggest that this was a bigger job than simply eliminating a small family (cf. 1 Kings 15.29, 16.11), and we are told that Ahab had seventy sons whose slaughter by Jehu needed to be carefully organised to ensure that none escaped (2 Kings 10.1-11). This indicates that Ahab had wives in addition to the notorious Jezebel.

There is no more mention of polygamous leading families after the story of the destruction of the house of Ahab. But two late passages indicate the persistence of polygamy. Deut 21.15–17 explicitly legislates for the case of a man who has two wives, ensuring that his inheritance will pass mainly to the firstborn son, even if that son is born to the less favoured of the two wives. The other passage is in Lev 18.8, a text prohibiting sexual relations

with members of the family. The statement 'You shall not un-
cover the nakedness of your father's wife' following on from the
prohibition of sexual relations between a man and his mother
clearly envisages a situation where a man will have more than one
wife. On the other hand, material dated towards the end of the
Second Temple period points strongly towards monogamy. Thus,
in the book of Tobit, Tobit's father and son and Tobit himself are
monogamous; and the same can be concluded about Mattathias
in 1 Maccabees.

The fact that ruling families were polygamous should not
surprise us. The kings needed to ensure that they had male heirs,
and polygamy assisted that, as well as enabling treaties with
neighbouring small states to be cemented by marriage. The
'judges', with their many sons, no doubt exerted political control
through having these sons as rulers of small towns in an area
presided over by the 'judge' as a sort of chief. But the 'judges' also
had responsibilities to the people as a whole, and especially the
obligation to defend the people from attacks from their enemies.
This, indeed, is a principal function of the 'judges' in the book
of that name; and in return for these and other civic responsibilities they could claim the right to several wives.[1] How far ordinary
families were monogamous is difficult to say. The story of Ruth
implies monogamy, while the story of Samuel, reminiscent of the
law in Deuteronomy about a man with two wives, recounts how
Samuel was born to Hannah, the favourite of the two wives of the
Ephraimite Elkanah (1 Sam 1.1–2).

If the literature of the Old Testament presents families whose
structure is mostly polygamous, its glimpse of how families
worked in practice is not always reassuring. The story of Cain and
Abel is one of fratricide, with Cain acting totally against the claims
of kin support that his brother might reasonably expect from
him (Gen 4.1–15). Jacob and Esau are similarly brothers in
conflict, albeit with less drastic consequences, while the relationship between Jacob and his maternal uncle Laban has strong
undercurrents of suspicion and trickery (Gen chs. 27, 29). Nor is

---

[1] Cf. the article by C. Lévi-Strauss, 'The Social and Psychological Aspects of
Chieftainship in a Primitive Tribe: the Nambikuara of Northwestern Mato
Grosso', *Transactions of the New York Academy of Sciences* 7 (1944), 16–32, reprinted
in R. Cohen and J. Middleton, eds., *Comparative Political Systems* (New York: The
Natural History Press, 1967), 45–62.

conflict within the family confined to males. The two sister wives of Jacob envy each other, so do the two wives of Elkanah in the story of Samuel. The story of David's family is even more alarming, as his firstborn son Amnon rapes his half-sister Tamar. In turn, Amnon is later killed by the servants of Tamar's brother Absalom, on Absalom's instructions (2 Sam 13). David appears to be powerless to prevent or punish these actions. Again, where the head of a family suffered misfortune either by illness or by destruction of property at the hands of an invader, the rest of the family could turn against him. In Chapter 19 Job complains that

> He (God) has put my family far from me,
> and my acquaintances are wholly estranged from me.
> My relatives and my close friends have failed me;
> the guests in my house have forgotten me;
> my serving girls count me as a stranger;
> I have become an alien in their eyes.
> I call to my servant but he gives no answer;
> I must myself plead with him.
> My breath is repulsive to my wife;
> All my intimate friends abhor me,
> and those whom I loved have turned against me.

These words of Job precede, of course, the famous passage in which Job declares that in spite of his alienation from his family he has an advocate or *goel*, namely God, who will vindicate him. This reminds us of the other side of the family in the Old Testament, to set against the negative stories that I have mentioned so far. It was the family that was meant to protect the individual within it. Through the institution of blood revenge, a kinsman of anyone who was murdered had the right to pursue the murderer and exact vengeance by killing him (Num 35.9–34). This kinsman was called the *goel*. Families also had the duty to ensure that a childless widow bore a child by having sexual relations with a brother-in-law (Deut 25.5–10). Also, smaller units within the larger family that fell on hard times were to be supported materially by the larger family. These aspects will be discussed later; but they need to be mentioned here in order to prevent us from getting a one-sidedly negative view of the family from this surface reading.

When we look at the picture as a whole it appears as follows. The family is a natural unit which, ideally, supports and protects the individuals and smaller groups within it. But its members are human; which means that the ideal is subverted by rivalry, ambition and inadequacy. To what extent all families were like the ones whose failings are recounted in the Old Testament we cannot say. How do families in our society compare with the families whose failings are described daily in our newspapers and on radio and television? Was David's family as typical of Israelite families as 'Brookside' families are typical of British families? The answer probably is that neither was or is entirely typical, but that stories of family breakdowns have an appeal and entertainment value that unites cultures separated by time and space. One thing at least should be clear from the survey so far. If anyone wishes to appeal to the Old Testament family in support of a view about how society should be organised in the West today, the appeal cannot operate at the level of a surface reading of the literature. That reading simply gives us a picture of ruling, polygamous, families that were more often than not the setting for rivalry and inadequacy, for all that there are also positive aspects in the ideals of support and protection.

The sociology of the Israelite family

This leads to the main section of the essay, that dealing with the sociology of the family in ancient Israel. At the outset, a question has to be addressed that has so far been deliberately ignored, namely, what are we talking about when we use the word 'family' in connection with the Old Testament? That question can be partly answered by posing another question: What are *we* talking about when we use the word family in connection with modern British society? Do we mean the nuclear family contained in a single household, or do we mean an extended family with the very strong ties that certainly existed in Durham and surrounding villages in the not-too-distant past when I worked there, and which most likely still exists? Do we mean leading families such as may exist in shire counties with social activities and networks that are very powerful? If reflection upon possible answers to these questions helps us to see that, even without sociological rigour, the matter is far from straighforward, we shall be well on the way to understanding something about the family in the Old Testament.

There is no clear equivalent in biblical Hebrew for the English 'family'; there are three main designations in Hebrew for social units, of which one, *shevet*, usually translated as 'tribe', can be disregarded if we are considering the Hebrew family. The other two terms, *bet av*, father's house, and *mishpachah*, often (misleadingly in my view) translated as 'clan', can be translated by 'family', depending on the context.

Bet av, or simply *bait* (house), has several senses. First, it can refer to a nuclear family living in one household. This appears to be its sense in Gen 50.7–8. These verses record the burial of Jacob whose interment is witnessed, among the Israelites, by Joseph's *bait* (house), by his brothers and by his late father's house (*bet aviv*). According to the story, Joseph had a wife and two children (Gen 41.50–52), so that his *bait* would consist of four people including himself. His brothers, who are mentioned separately, each presumably had his own *bait*, while Jacob's *bait* or household presumably consisted of his one surviving wife Leah, his two servant wives Bilhah and Zilpah, and any daughters that they might have had. Gen 50.22 implies that these women henceforth lived under Joseph's protection in the words: 'So Joseph remained in Egypt, he and his father's household' (*bet aviv*).

Against the use of *bet av* to designate a nuclear family living in a single household, there is the instance of Gen 7.1 where Noah is instructed by God to enter the ark together with his *bait* (house). However, in this story Noah has three married sons who are included in the term *bait*, which therefore designates in this context an extended family. So far *bet av* has had a primarily territorial meaning, covering people living together or in close proximity. In Gen 24.38, however, *bet av* has the meaning of a descent group. Abraham instructs his servant to travel to Mesopotamia to his father's house (*bet avi*) to seek out a bride for Isaac. He cannot be thinking of the house in a territorial sense, but as a descent group or lineage from which he has separated, setting up in the process his own *bet av*.

In this same passage, the Hebrew *bet avi* is followed immediately by *ve'el mishpachti*, translated by NEB as 'my family' and NRSV as 'my kindred'. Both renderings get the general sense. The reference is to relatives generally, as we might talk about our own families, meaning to include aunts, uncles and cousins, some of whom we may not have seen for years, or even ever. Certainly, in the story, Abraham will never have met his nephew Bethuel, whose daughter Rebekkah becomes Isaac's wife.

A *mishpachah*, then, is best thought of as a family in the sense of a descent group whose members are linked by descent from a common ancestor who may no longer be living, such as a great-grandparent. Sometimes the ancestor can be too remote to be designated genealogically, but can nevertheless be a real factor in helping people to establish their identity. At Amos 3.1 the prophet addresses 'the whole family (*kol hamishpachah*) that I brought up out of the land of Egypt'. Here, the whole people is described as a *mishpachah* that is conceived as descended from the ancestor Jacob.

A much discussed question is whether a *mishpachah* owned land, given that a *mishpachah* could be a territorial unit as well as a widely scattered descent group. The answer probably is that while a *mishpachah* did not itself own land, it had a responsibility to ensure that land remained the property of the smaller units, the father's houses, that were part of the *mishpachah*. This is illustrated by the case of the daughters of Zelophehad in Num 27.1–11, 36.1–9. Zelophehad had died in the wilderness leaving five unmarried daughters and no sons. They were thus members of a *bet av* without a male head. Although in the story the Israelites had not yet possessed any land, some of them were soon to gain land on the eastern side of the river Jordan, among them the group to which Zelophehad's immediate family belonged. The daughters thus appeal to Moses that when land is apportioned they should receive some on behalf of their deceased father. The ruling that is given by God to Moses is informative:

> If a man dies, and has no son, then you shall pass his inheritance to his daughter. If he has no daughter, then you shall give his inheritance to his brothers. If he has no brothers, then you shall give his inheritance to his father's brothers. And if his father has no brothers, then you shall give his inheritance to the nearest kinsman (*haqarov elav*) of his clan (*mimishpachto*) and he shall possess it. (Num 27.8–11)

Thus land, according to this passage, belongs to a *bet av* and must be inherited by a *bet av* within the *mishpachah*. However, this ruling raises a further problem, dealt with in Num 36.1–12. If a female inherits land and then marries a man from another tribe, the husband becomes entitled to the land, and it is added to his tribe and lost to the tribe to which the woman belongs. It is thus ruled that a female who inherits must marry within her *mishpachah* so that land is not lost from one tribe to another.

This leads conveniently to a consideration of the incest law of Lev 18.7–18 and its implications for the sociology of the family in the Old Testament. The person addressed (Ego) is forbidden to have sexual relations with the following people (underlined):

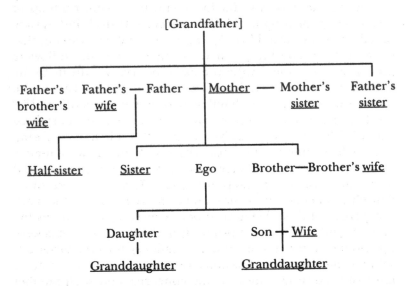

In terms of what has been discussed so far, we have an extended family (the *bet av* of the (deceased) grandfather) which is itself made up of at least five smaller *bate av*, those of Ego's father, uncle, brother and son, as well as Ego himself, while, of course, Ego's father's *bet av* considered as a descent unit will include Ego, Ego's brother and Ego's children, while Ego's *bet av* considered as a descent unit will include his own son. Territorially, as we shall see shortly, such a group would probably occupy two or three houses, assuming that Ego's sister, half-sister and daughter lived with their husbands. This extended family is a small exogamous unit, but it does allow marriage with cousins on both the father's and mother's side. To what extent people married only within their *mishpachah* or tribe we cannot say. The story of the daughters of Zelophehad envisages marriage with members of another tribe; but in practice people probably married within their own territorial areas whenever possible. We notice that the family system as described advantaged males and disadvantaged females. Only males could inherit; even females who inherited lost their inheritance to their husbands on marriage. Women, upon marriage, were expected to leave their *bet av* and become a member of their husband's *bet av*. It was also possible that they would not be the only wife of their husband.

How do the results so far fit in with the recent findings of archaeology? Bearing in mind that archaeological findings are mainly from the period Iron Age I while the literary evidence that we have been considering may be much later, the following points can be made. In the pre-exilic period two thirds of the settlements in the northern hill country of ancient Israel were hamlets or villages.[2] The hamlets had only between 20 and 50 residents and would therefore comprise two or at the most three extended families. Villages had up to 100 residents comprising four or five extended families. These settlements were mainly agricultural and self-sufficient, growing cereals, vegetables and herbs, and pasturing sheep and goats. The cities were more densely populated with a thousand or more residents, the more prosperous of them living in superior dwellings.[3] Whereas the hamlets and villages were primarily agricultural, the cites were the home of the trades and professions, including potters, soldiers, merchants and administrators. Undoubtedly some or most of these trades were family concerns, and such families would come to form a wealthy and powerful group within society in comparison with the families in the hamlets and villages that were entirely dependent upon agriculture.

The Israelite family in social-historical perspective

I now come to the social-historical account of the family. In the pre-monarchic period in Israel, we must envisage a primarily

---

[2] See I. Finkelstein, *The Archaeology of the Israelite Settlement* (Jerusalem: Israel Exploration Society, 1988), 185–204. There is a useful summary of the evidence in H. L. Bosman, et al., *Plutocrats and Paupers. Wealth and Poverty in the Old Testament,* (Pretoria: J. L. van Schaik, 1991), 144–53.

[3] See generally, V. Fritz, *Die Stadt im alten Israel* (Munich: C. H. Beck, 1990).

agricultural society ruled locally by prominent families whose leaders had a number of wives and who controlled the larger settlements, as in the case of the 'judges' Jair, Ibzan and Abdon mentioned earlier. Theirs was probably a genial style of leadership which did not tax or oppress the families that constituted most of society, but which enjoyed privileges in return for responsibility. They were probably also judges in the strict sense, adjudicating disputes where these could not be settled within the family. This situation was changed by the expansion of the Philistines eastwards towards the end of the eleventh century BCE. The Philistines began to tax the people in the form of exacting agricultural produce and setting up garrisons which had to be fed by the ordinary Israelites. A new form of leadership developed to cope with this threat, with the implication that the leader could make demands upon families to supply fighting men and food to support them. Whether or not it is appropriate to call Saul a king, his leadership ushered in a long transition period which led to Israel becoming two states, with significant implications for the family.

Historical and archaeological orthodoxy tell us that it was in the tenth century, in the reigns of David and Solomon, that what we might call loosely the Israelite state came into being, with all the demands of such a state upon its citizens, such as conscription for civil and military purposes, and taxation to support an increasing number of state officials. Further, an increase in the number of merchants and traders inevitably put pressure on the food-producing agricultural families. This orthodox picture is beginning to be challenged by excavations and by reassessment of evidence, particularly from Judah and Trans-Jordan, and it seems increasingly likely that it was not until the ninth century or, in the case of Judah, the eighth century at the earliest, that small states began to emerge in ancient Israel, Ammon, Moab and Edom, with the appropriate centralised administration.[4] There are complex issues here for experts to resolve. For our purposes, whenever these small states may have emerged, they certainly

---

[4] See D. W. Jamieson-Drake, *Scribes and Schools in Monarchic Judah. A Socio-Archeological Approach*, JSOTSSup 109 (Sheffield: Sheffield Academic Press, 1991). For Edom and Moab see the essays in P. Bienkowski, ed., *Early Edom and Moab. The Beginning of the Iron Age in Southern Jordan*, Sheffield Archaeological Monographs 7 (Sheffield: J. R. Collis Publications, 1992).

began to make demands upon agricultural communities, and we must remember that these communities were often living on a knife-edge of existence, given the agricultural conditions in the land and its unreliable rainfall. An attentive reader of the Old Testament will notice how often the word 'famine' occurs in its stories. At random, the stories of Abr(ah)am and Sara(i) (Gen 12.10–20), Joseph (Gen 41), Ruth, and Elijah (1 Kings 17) come to mind, while the stories of Gideon (Judg 6) and the Philistines (1 Sam 13) are a reminder of how an invader could disrupt and appropriate the production of food. Whether or not these stories are historical, they imply a credible and familiar world on the part of the presumed author and readers.

Famine would be a double blow for agricultural communities and the families of which they consisted. Not only would there be insufficient food to feed the families; it would be impossible to pay the taxes in kind levied by the king. In order to pay them, it would be necessary to borrow from rich landowners or merchants. If the famine continued and the debt increased, members of the family might have to be sold into slavery. Ultimately, the family could lose its land and the former landowner could be reduced to being a hired worker working his own land, or he could become a landless unemployed worker seeking casual work wherever he could find it or he could himself become a slave.

There is plenty of evidence for the existence of this state of affairs in the eighth century from the prophetic critiques that we find in Isaiah 5 or Amos 2 and 4. Isaiah criticises those who join house to house and field to field, the reference being to landowners who acquire ever larger estates by taking land from poorer families that have fallen into debt (Isa 5.8). Amos criticises those in Israel who

> sell the righteous for silver,
> and the needy for a pair of sandals
> ...who trample the head of the poor into the dust of the earth...
> [who] lay themselves down beside every altar on garments taken
> in pledge (Amos 2.8),

where the reference to the garment taken in pledge is to the practice of a man pawning his cloak, probably as a deposit against his wages for a few days' work as a casual labourer.[5]

---

[5] On this point see the Hebrew text from Mesad Hashavyahu, normally dated to the last third of the seventh century BCE, where a worker complains that his

This state of affairs is also mirrored in those parts of the so-called Book of the Covenant (Exod 21.1–23.19) that come from the pre-exilic period. Exod 21.2–11 accepts that a Hebrew might buy Hebrew men and women as slaves, and the law seeks to mitigate that situation by specifying that men must be released after six years, and that women slaves who are married by their owner or his son cease to be slaves and receive the privileges of being wives.[6] In Exod 22.25–27 (Hebrew 22.24–26) it is decreed that any loan made to a poor person must be interest free, and that a cloak taken in pawn must be restored to its owner before nightfall, 'for it may be your neighbour's only clothing to use as a cover; in what else shall that person sleep?' (Exod 22.27, Hebrew 22.26). Such a person who has to pawn what does double duty as garment and bedding is indeed in dire straits.

The framework of Exod 22.25–27 is important for the purposes of this chapter for it brings to us what I call a 'structure of grace', that is, a social arrangement designed to mitigate hardship and misfortune, and grounded in God's mercy. Exod 22.25 (Hebrew verse 24) begins 'If you lend money to _my people_, to the poor among you...', where the phrase '_my people_' indicates God's concern for and involvement with those whom this law envisages. The passage ends with the words, 'and if your neighbour cries out to me, I will listen, for I am compassionate' (Exod 22.27). In a series of articles and, most recently, in his _Theologische Ethik des Alten Testaments_, Eckard Otto has investigated the process of composition of the Book of the Covenant, and argued for a bringing together of secular laws and theological principles such that, in its pre-exilic form, the Book of the Covenant is an expression of the practical implications of the compassion of God. As Otto says in an important passage:

Im Bundesbuch wird der einzelne Mensch direkt angesprochen und mit JHWH als dem Barmherzigen konfrontiert ... Nicht

---

garment has been taken from him by a supervisor, and has not been returned. For the most recent edition, together with bibliography see J. Renz and W. Röllig, _Handbuch der Althebräischen Epigraphik_, Band I (Darmstadt: Wissenschaftliche Buchgesellschaft, 1995), 315–29.

[6] There is a famous k⁰thiv and q⁰re variant in the passage which, although affecting the interpretation slightly, does not affect the overall point.

also weil der König es gebietet, soll der Mensch solidarisch sein, sondern weil Gott solidarisch mit dem Menschen ist...[7]

The ordinances of the pre-exilic Book of the Covenant arose, according to Otto, in the family before becoming (if they did become) the responsibility of the state. They were ultimately theologically based and justified, and were designed to operate when the existing social structures broke down in the face of economic pressures.

The strictures of the prophets seem to indicate that these 'structures of grace' were often, if not largely, ignored, and in the second half of the seventh century, in the pre-exilic edition of Deuteronomy, the attempt was made to re-emphasise and indeed extend the 'structures of grace'. Whether or not there had been a complete breakdown of the social structure in terms of the family in its narrower and broader senses in the early seventh century,[8] Deuteronomy is remarkable in the way in which it assumes that duties that were hitherto the responsibility of the family are now the responsibility of each Israelite to his (sic) neighbour.

The most famous illustration of this is Deut 15 where, incidentally, readers of the Old Testament who do not know Hebrew need a translation that has not been edited for gender-free language in order to understand the point. Accordingly, I quote from the RSV:

> If there is among you a poor man, one of your brethren, in any of your towns within your land which the LORD your God gives you, you shall not harden your heart or shut your hand against your poor brother, but you shall open your hand to him, and lend him sufficient for his need, whatever it may be. Take heed lest there be a base thought in your heart, and you say, 'The seventh year, the year of the release is near', and your eye be hostile to your poor brother, and you give him nothing, and he cry to the LORD against you, and it be sin to you ... therefore I

[7] E. Otto, *Theologische Ethik des Alten Testaments* (Stuttgart: Kohlhammer Verlag, 1994), 90. The German can be translated as follows: 'In the Book of the Covenant the individual is addressed directly and confronted by YHWH as the merciful one ... Humans must thus practise solidarity not because the king commands it, but because God is in solidarity with humankind.'

[8] So Otto, *Ethik*, 192.

command you, you shall open wide your hand to your brother,
to the needy and to the poor, in the land. (Deut 15.7–9, 11b)

What is striking is the repetition of the word 'brother', which
occurs four times in the verses quoted, and is common elsewhere.
The phenomenon has been called the 'brother-ethic' in Deuteronomy; the point is that any needy Israelite, regardless of family
or genealogy, has a claim upon his more prosperous neighbour,
a claim grounded in the fact that the people as a whole are called
by God to be a holy people. The term 'brother' is even extended
to include one's enemy. Thus, if Exod 23.4–5 ('If you meet your
enemy's ox or his ass going astray, you shall bring it back to him')
is compared with Deut 22.1 ('You shall not see your brother's ox
or his sheep go astray, and withhold your help from them; you
shall take them back to your brother') it is seen that in the
deuteronomic revision of the law, enemy has become brother.
There are no enemies in Judah, only brothers.

Another feature of the late pre-exilic edition of Deuteronomy is its more positive attitude to women compared with the
Book of the Covenant. Thus female slaves are given the same
right of release as male slaves in Deut 15.12, and there is a
regulation about not taking a widow's garment as a pledge.
Further, regulations that protect a newly-married bride against
the allegation of her husband that she was not a virgin when she
was married, or that protect a betrothed or unmarried woman
against rape, have led to parts of Deuteronomy being called a
'Frauenspiegel' (women's charter) although its provisions fall
far short of what we today would understand by a women's
charter. Otto sums up the aims of this version of Deuteronomy
as follows:

> Einen Zerfall der gentilen Gemeinschaften, in denen ein
> naturwüchsiges, genealogisch geleitetes Bruderethos einen
> Ort hatte, wird das in Privilegrecht in der Herrschaft JHWHs
> über Volk und Land verankerte und also theologisch
> begründete Bruderethos entgegengesetzt. Jeder Judäer,
> einschließlich des Feindes und Prozeßgegners, nicht nur der
> Verwandte, ist der Bruder, dem solidarische Hilfe zukommt,
> wenn er ihrer bedarf. Insbesondere den Landlosen, Fremden,
> Witwen und Waisen gilt die Solidarität, die im Drittjahreszehnt,
> im Erlaßjahr, in der Sklavenfreilassung und im zinslos
> gewährten, auf Pfandsicherung weitgehend verzichteten

Notdarlehen konkret wird. Aber auch im Familienrecht gilt die Solidarität den Schwächern, insbesondere den Frauen.[9]

In my terminology, Deuteronomy is an attempt to introduce a whole series of structures of grace.

The composition of Deuteronomy in the second half of the seventh century was followed within a generation by the massive upheaval of the destruction of Jerusalem in 587, preceded ten years earlier by the transportation of the so-called cream of society to Babylon. It may well be that for those remaining in Judah, the exilic period was one in which ordinary family life was able to recover from the pressures of the two previous centuries. The nobility and the wealthy had gone, and perhaps there was little or no taxation on the part of the Babylonian authorities. For those in exile, it was necessary for new social structures to be developed, and the exilic period thus saw the rise of the *bet avot*, which is not a plural of *bet av* but a term meaning 'house of fathers'. In practice it was an extended family similar to a *mishpachah*, but named after a leader or founder. In Nehemiah 7.7–38 some of the names of these leaders or founders are given as Parosh, Shepatiah and Arach. The *bet avot* probably enabled new groupings to be formed where existing families were deliberately dispersed in exile, or had been virtually destroyed by the fighting with the Babylonians and the executions that followed the Babylonian triumph. It is also likely that on their return to Judah, these new extended families took over the leadership of the community and began once more to exert pressure on the agricultural families. The Persian government also expected heavy taxes to be paid.[10]

---

[9] Otto, *Ethik*, 192. The German can be translated as: 'An ethics of brotherhood, theologically grounded and also anchored in the laws protecting individuals stemming from YHWH's sovereignty over the people and the land, is opposed to the breakdown of the communities, in which a natural, genealogically-based ethics of brotherhood has its place. Every Judahite, including enemies and adversaries at law, and not just a relative, is a brother, to whom assistance borne of solidarity comes, when it is needed. In particular, the landless, foreigners, widows and orphans are the objects of the solidarity that is given concrete expression in the third-year tithe, the year of release, in the freeing of slaves and in emergency loans that are interest and pledge free. Also in family law the weaker members are the object of solidarity, especially women.'

[10] See R. Albertz, *Religionsgeschichte Israels in alttestamentlicher Zeit* (Göttingen: Vandenhoeck & Ruprecht, 1992), 539.

By the second half of the fifth century, the situation had once again become desperate for some, perhaps many, families. Nehemiah 5 records the outcry made to Nehemiah, the governor of Judah:

> There were those who said, 'With our sons and daughters, we are many; we must get grain, so that we may eat and stay alive'. There were also those who said, 'We are having to pledge our fields, our vineyards, and our houses in order to get grain during the famine'. And there were those who said, 'We are having to borrow money on our fields and vineyards to pay the king's tax. Now our flesh is the same as that of our kindred ... and yet we are forcing our sons and daughters to be slaves, and some of our daughters have been ravished; we are powerless, and our fields and vineyards now belong to others'. (Neh 5.2–5)

We are told that Nehemiah ordered the nobles and officials responsible to stop charging interest on loans and to repay the interest paid, as well as restoring the houses, fields and vineyards that had been acquired.

It has been observed that the actions of Nehemiah seem to imply the enforcement of the year of release as described in Deut 15.1–7. It has been argued by some (e.g. Kippenberg[11]) that the Jubilee Law in Lev 25 was the later response to the crisis in Nehemiah's time. Whether or not this was so, and whether or not it was ever enforced, the Jubilee is another of the 'structures of grace' in the Old Testament. It decrees that if an Israelite needs to sell land, or cannot maintain himself, or needs to sell himself as a slave, then any fellow-Israelite has certain duties towards him: to buy the land, or to let him live with him as an alien, or to employ him as a hired servant. It is forbidden to enslave a fellow-Israelite, although non-Israelites may be enslaved. When the Jubilee year comes, all debts are cancelled, all land is returned to the original owners, and all Israelites who are dependent on their fellows can return to the lands that were once theirs and be once more free. The Jubilee has been described as a reworking of Deut 15.[12] We

---

[11] H. G. Kippenberg, *Klassenbildung in antiken Judäa* (Göttingen: Vandenhoeck & Ruprecht, 1982) (2nd ed), 62ff.
[12] Otto, *Ethik*, 255.

notice the same use of the term 'brother' in order to transcend family and genealogical limitations (again, gender-free translations such as the NRSV obscure this), while the whole set of ordinances is grounded in the fact that God freed the Israelites from Egypt and gave them the land of Canaan (Lev 25.38) and that the Israelites are the servants or slaves (*ᵃvadim*) of God whom he brought up out of Egypt. Because Israelites are slaves to their heavenly Lord they cannot be slaves of human masters. God did not deliver them from one form of human oppression so that they could become the victims of other forms of human oppression.

Conclusion

With the material before us it is possible to conclude that anyone who wishes to reflect theologically on the family in the Old Testament, or who wishes to use what is said about the family in the Old Testament in order to draw lessons for today's society cannot do this at the level of the letter. The family in ancient Israel was a natural social mechanism that developed initially to meet particular circumstances. It was often polygamous, especially in its leading families and in the pre-exilic period, and it could be the context for rivalry, jealousy and even fratricide. It was far more advantageous to men than to women. Although it tried to generate mechanisms such as blood revenge, and the responsibility of the *mishpachah* to support the smaller family units if their members fell on hard times, it was often powerless in practice to prevent the incursion of the state and of powerful landowners or merchants into its sphere of interest, with the result that families became debt-ridden and lost their land and freedom. Anyone who would want to suggest that the Old Testament family as just described should in some sense be a model for the family today could only do so by means of a highly selective and superficial use of the text.

What is really important is that theologically-driven efforts were made to counteract the forces that undermined the family. These included most notably the 'Bruder-ethos' of Deuteronomy and of Lev 25. Also, substantial attempts were made to improve the position of women. These attempts were grounded in the compassion of God and the need for that compassion to be actualised in inter-human relationships, in the solidarity of God with 'my people', and in the redemptive action of God in freeing the Israelites from slavery in Egypt. These 'structures of grace' transcended family ties, but were not intended to abolish the family; rather to support and sustain it. If the Old Testament says anything to us today, it is that we need to devise theologically-driven 'structures of grace' appropriate to our situation that will sustain those aspects of family life which, from a Christian perspective, we deem to be most valuable, and which may be most under threat from the state and powerful interests. This is not something that biblical scholars or theologians can do, without the expertise of lawyers or sociologists. The sort of questions that have to be asked are the following. What is the effect upon children of the break-up of marriages? What sort of strains are put upon families by the need for both partners to earn substantial salaries in order to pay for a mortgage? What style of family life is appropriate if the aspirations of women are to be met to combine a career with raising a family? How should housework, whether done by a male or female, be regarded in relation to paid employment? These are all new questions which are not envisaged in the Bible and yet which demand a solution in terms of 'structures of grace'. If the Old Testament is instructive, it will be by way of example rather than precept.

3

The Household Rules
in the New Testament

James D. G. Dunn

Any reflection on a Christian theology of the family is bound to take into account the testimony of an important sequence of passages which appear in the New Testament and other early Christian writings across the sixty or so years from about AD 60. These passages, which have become identified by Luther's term, *Haustafeln,* consist of household rules, that is, rules for the regulation of family and household relationships. They therefore give promise of shedding some light on the importance of the household and its good ordering during this important, formative period for Christianity and for Christian ethos.

1. *A common concern*

The passages in view are Col 3.18–4.1, Eph 5.22–6.9, and 1 Pet 2.18–3.7, where a regular structure is most evident, and 1 Tim 2.8–15, 6.1–2, Tit 2.1–10, Did 4.9–11, Barn 19.5–7, 1 Clem 21.6–9, Ignatius, *Pol* 4.1–5.2 and Polycarp, *Phil* 4.2–3 (see table pp. 44-6). Even a cursory reading of them raises a number of important questions and issues which will occupy us for the rest of this essay. But some initial scene-setting observations may be helpful.

First, the passages demonstrate how common was the concern in second and third generation Christianity that the Christian household should be well ordered. They demonstrate also how regularly this concern focused on a basic three-fold relationship – between husband and wife, father and child, master and slave. Only in Colossians is the three-fold structure quite clear, though

The household rules in early Christianity

Col 3.18–4.1

[18]Wives, be subject to your husbands, as is fitting in the Lord.

[19]Husbands, love your wives and do not become embittered towards them.

[20]Children, obey your parents in everything, for this is pleasing in the Lord.

[21]Fathers, do not provoke your children, that they may not lose heart.

[22]Slaves, obey in everything those who are your masters in terms of the flesh, not with eye-service, as menpleasers, but with sincerity of heart, fearing the Lord. [23]Whatever you do, put yourself wholly into it, as to the Lord and not to human beings, [24]knowing that you will receive from the Lord the reward of the inheritance. The master you serve is Christ. [25]For the wrongdoer will be paid back for the wrong he has done, and there is no favouritism. [4.1]Masters, grant your slaves what is just and fair, knowing that you also have a master in heaven.

Eph 5.22–6.9

[21]Be subject to one another out of reverence for Christ. [22]Wives, (be subject) to your own husbands as to the Lord…

[25]Husbands, love your wives, as Christ also loved the church…

[6.1]Children, obey your parents [in the Lord], for this is right…

[4]And fathers, do not provoke your children to anger, but bring them up in the discipline … of the Lord. [5]Slaves, obey those who are your masters in terms of the flesh, with fear and trembling, in sincerity of heart, as you obey Christ, [6]not with eyeservice, as menpleasers, but as slaves of Christ … [7]serving with enthusiasm as to the Lord and not to human beings, [8]knowing that whatever good each has done, he will receive the same again from the Lord, whether we are slaves or free.

[9]And masters, do the same to them. Stop threatening them, for you know that both of you have the same Master in heaven, and with him there is no favouritism.

1 Pet 2.18–3.7

[3.1]Likewise, wives, be subject to your own husbands, so that, if some disobey the word, they might be won through the conduct of their wives, without a word… [7]Husbands, likewise, live together in accordance with knowledge, as to the weaker sex, paying her honour as also to those who are fellow heirs of the grace of life …

[18]Slaves, be subject to your masters with all fear, not only those who are kind and gentle but also those who are harsh. [19]For it is grace if, because conscious of God, someone endures pain in suffering unjustly…

The household rules in early Christianity

1 Tim 2.8–15, 6.1–2
²·¹¹ Women likewise must be serious ...

¹² Let deacons be married only once, and let them manage their children and their households well. ...

⁶·¹ Let all who are under the yoke of slavery regard their masters as worthy of all honour...
²Those who have believing masters must not be disrespectful to them...

Tit 2.1–10
³ Likewise, tell the older women to be reverent in behaviour, ...
⁴ encourage the young women to love their husbands, to love their children, ⁵ to be self-controlled, chaste, good home workers (οἰκουργούς), kind, submissive to their husbands, so that the word of God may not be discredited.

⁹ Tell slaves to be subject to their masters and to give satisfaction in every respect; they are not to talk back...

The household rules in early Christianity

Didache 4.9–11

[9]You shall not withhold your hand from your son or from your daughter, but you shall teach them the fear of God from their youth. [10]You shall not command your slave or female servant, who hope in the same God, in your bitterness, lest they cease to fear God who is over both.

[11]You who are slaves should be subject to your masters, as to God's representative, in reverence and fear.

1 Clement 21.6–9

[6]...let us instruct the young in the fear of God, let us lead our wives to that which is good. [7]Let them exhibit the lovely habit of purity...
[8]Let our children share in the instruction which is in Christ...

Barnabas 19.5–7

[5]You shall not withhold your hand from your son or from your daughter, but you shall teach them the fear of God from their youth.... [7b]You shall not command your slave or female servant in bitterness, who hope in the same God, lest they cease to fear God who is over both....

[7a]...You shall be subject to your masters, as to God's representative, in reverence and fear.

Polycarp, *Philippians* 4.2–3

[2]Next (teach) also our wives to remain in the faith given them, and in love and purity, tenderly loving their husbands in all truth, ...and to educate their children in the fear of God.

Ignatius, *Polycarp* 4.1–5.2

[4.3]Do not be haughty to male and female slaves; but do not let them be puffed up, but let them rather endure slavery to the glory of God, that they might obtain a better freedom from God....

[5.1]Speak to my sisters that they love the Lord, and be content with their husbands in flesh and in spirit. Likewise command my brothers in the name of Jesus Christ, to love their wives as the Lord loved the church.

even there the elaboration of the instructions to the slaves disrupts the simpler format. Elsewhere there is substantial elaboration at particular points, and the three-fold pattern is often lacking. Nevertheless, the repeated appearance of explicit teaching on just these three sets of relationships throughout this period indicates just how important these relationships as such had become in Christian ethics.

Second, it is obvious that no standard pattern is being simply transmitted here, no established traditional catechesis being mouthed 'for good form' as it were. It may be the case that Colossians provided something of a model for the rest; most scholars think that Ephesians has largely drawn on Colossians at this as at other points. And Barnabas has evidently drawn on Didache, or vice-versa, or both have drawn from a common source. But the evidence hardly allows us to postulate a standardised or already well established formula – a piece of baptismal catechesis being the most common suggestion.[1] The important point, however, is that the same motivation and set of values shine through the diversity of form and content, underlining once again just how concerned were these early congregations that their shared Christian life should provide guidelines for everyday relationships.

Third, the three-fold pattern, however irregular, reminds us of the characteristic structure of the family and household of the time – husband and wife, children and slaves. This we may imagine was the typical pattern of the time and is presumably what is in mind in references to 'houses' elsewhere in the NT – 'the house of Stephanas', 'Cornelius with all his house', 'the house of Lydia', 'Crispus with his whole house', and so on (1 Cor 1.16; Acts 10.2; 16.15; 18.8). It is interesting that close family relatives are not mentioned, even though in some houses no doubt dependent female relatives were part of the household (cf. Mk 1.29–31). On the other hand some women, presumably of independent means, ran their own households, for example, Lydia (Acts 16.15) and Nympha (Col 4.15); and widows are treated separately from the household form (as in 1 Tim 5.3–16; cf. Ignatius, *Smyrn* 13.1) or have their own household (1 Tim 5.14; Ignatius, *Polyc* 8.2).

---

[1] See e.g. E. G. Selwyn, *The First Epistle of St Peter* (London: Macmillan, 1947), 363–466.

Fourth, the patriarchal character of the times is clearly evident. Subjection was expected of wives to their husbands. Instruction and discipline of children were primarily the father's responsibility. And slaves were thought of as having masters, but not mistresses. This, of course, simply reflects the law and custom of the time, particularly *patria potestas,* according to which the head of the family (*paterfamilias*) was the only full legal person and had absolute power over the other members of the family, including the power of life and death.[2] Even single women and widows, however independent *de facto,* would technically come under the responsibility of the senior male member of the family.

Finally we should note the prominence of slaves within the ancient household. We should not assume that only the very well-to-do had slaves. A third or more of those living in major cities may have been slaves; as in Victorian England, even modest prosperity made it possible to retain a personal servant. Nor should we assume that slavery was already thought of as immoral or necessarily degrading (it took the slave trade to bring this insight home to Western 'civilisation'). It was simply the means of providing labour at the bottom end of the economic spectrum (originally from the ranks of defeated enemies, but now mainly through birth to slaves). To sell oneself as a slave was a device of last resort for someone in debt, and slaves of important masters could exercise significant influence themselves.[3] The point to be underlined for us here, however, is the fact that such personal slaves were regarded as part of the ancient household.[4]

In short, the household rules of second and third generation Christianity assume the givenness of the household, its three-fold structure, and the headship of the senior male figure.

These, however, are simply preliminary observations, providing a platform from which we mount more specific enquiries. We

---

[2] See *Oxford Classical Dictionary,* 'patria potestas'.

[3] See particularly D. B. Martin, *Slavery as Salvation: The Metaphor of Slavery in Pauline Christianity* (New Haven: Yale University Press, 1990).

[4] On slavery in the Greco-Roman world see e.g. the concise treatments of M. I. Finley, *Oxford Classical Dictionary,* 994–6, and S. S. Bartchy, *Anchor Bible Dictionary* 6.65–73. Valuable documentation has been collected by T. Wiedemann, *Greek and Roman Slavery* (London: Crook Helm, 1981). For more detailed and wide ranging studies see W. W. Buckland, *The Roman Law of Slavery* (Cambridge: Cambridge University Press, 1908), and W. L. Westermann *The Slave Systems of Greek and Roman Antiquity* (Philadelphia: American Philosophical Society, 1955).

will have time for only three. First, where did the first Christians get these household rules from, and how distinctive were they in the ancient world? Second, why did such rules become so prominent in Christian teaching in this period? And finally, is the teaching they contain of continuing value in Christian social ethics?

2. *Whence the* Haustafeln?

In the great wave of research into early Christianity's religious milieu, which marked the beginning of the twentieth century, it was quickly recognised that there were many parallels with the Christian texts. The initial impulse was to argue that the household rules were slightly Christianised versions of Stoic material,[5] though, as is the way with scholarship, that thesis was duly countered by the argument that the codes were more Hellenistic Jewish in character with only minimal Stoic influence.[6] However, in the past fifteen years or so the argument has been virtually settled (or should be regarded as so). This is due to the recognition by several scholars in close succession that the model for the Christian household rules, insofar as there is one, was that of *oikonomia*, 'household management'.[7] The case, particularly as set out by David Balch, is impressive.

In the classic definition of Aristotle, the household was the basic unit of the state.[8] As part of good ordering, therefore, it was

[5] M. Dibelius, *An die Kolosser, Epheser, und Philemon*, revised by H. Greeven, HNT 12 (Tübingen: Mohr, ³1953), 48–50.

[6] J. E. Crouch, *The Origin and Intention of the Colossian Haustafel* (Göttingen: Vandenhoeck & Ruprecht, 1972).

[7] D. Lührmann, 'Wo man nicht mehr Sklave oder Freier ist: Überlegungen zur Struktur frühchristlicher Gemeinden', *Wort und Dienst D* 13 (1975), 53–83, here 76–80; also 'Neutestamentliche Haustafeln und antike Ökonomie', *New Testament Studies* 27 (1980–81), 83–97; K. Thraede, 'Zum historischen Hintergrund der "Haustafeln" des NT', in *Pietas*, B. Kötting FS, ed. E. Dassmann and K. S. Frank (Münster: Aschendorff, 1980), 359–68, followed by K. Müller, 'Die Haustafel des Kolosserbriefes und das antike Frauenthema: Eine kritische Rückschau auf alte Ergebnisse', in *Die Frau im Urchristentum*, ed. G. Dautzenberg et al., QD 95 (Freiburg: Herder, 1983), 263–319, here 284–90; and especially D. L. Balch, *Let Wives be Submissive: The Domestic Code in 1 Peter*, SBLMS 26 (Chico: Scholars, 1981), Part I.

[8] On 'The Household in the Hellenistic-Roman World' see particularly D. C. Verner, *The Household of God. The Social World of the Pastoral Epistles*, SBLDS 71 (Chico: Scholars, 1983), 27–81.

necessary to deal with its basic relationships – 'master and slave, husband and wife, father and children' (*Pol* I 1253b 1–14).[9] That these became common concerns in thoughtful society is sufficiently clear from a variety of examples: (1) Dio Chrysostom, who lived through our period, has left a fragmentary oration on the theme itself (*oikonomia*), covering the same three relationships (LCL 5.348–51);[10] (2) from the preceding generation, we have Seneca's description of one department of philosophy as concerned to 'advise how a husband should conduct himself towards his wife, or how a father should bring up his children, or how a master should rule his slaves' (*Ep* 94:1);[11] and (3) from one generation further back, Dionysius of Halicarnassus praises Roman household relationships using the same three pairs (interestingly enough in the order of Colossians), and deals with duties of wives before those of husbands, and those of children before those of fathers, as again in Colossians, the most complete of the Christian examples (*Roman Antiquities* 2.25.4–26.4).[12]

Given the importance of the subject, it is hardly surprising that similar concerns were often voiced in diaspora Judaism. So, for example, Pseudo-Phocylides, a kind of Jewish Wisdom poem probably composed sometime in the last century BC or first century AD, winds up with sections on marriage and chastity and on family life (*Ps Phoc* 175–227):

> Love your own wife, for what is sweeter and better than whenever a wife is kindly disposed toward (her) husband and a husband toward (his) wife.

> Do not be harsh with your children, but be gentle. And if a child offends against you, let the mother cut her son down to size...

> Provide your slave with the tribute he owes his stomach. Apportion to a slave what is appointed so that he will be as you wish.

> Do not brand (your) slave, thus insulting him.

---

[9] Balch, *Wives* 33–4.
[10] Ibid., 28–9.
[11] Ibid., 51.
[12] Ibid., 55.

Philo, the Alexandrian Jewish philosopher, an older contemporary of Paul's, in the disputed extract, *Hypothetica* 7.14, envisages the male as instructor in knowledge of the laws in the same threefold relationship, as husband to wife, father to children, and master to slave. And both he and Josephus, the Jewish historian writing in our period, find it natural to link treatment of marriage laws and the upbringing of children in exposition of the fifth commandment (Philo, *Decal* 165–7; *Spec Leg* 2.224–41; Jos. *Ap* 2.199–208).[13]

Study of such parallels, however, should be sufficient to warn us once again of one of the standing dangers of a 'form-critical' approach, that is, of assuming there was in the ancient world an original or pure form, from which our examples have been derived or from which they have deteriorated.[14] In this case it is the danger of speaking as though there was in the ancient world an established form of 'household rules', from which the Christian forms have been derived. In point of fact the Colossian code is itself the 'purest' form! And in the passages just cited the household rules are often simply part of a more widely ranging code of social behaviour. Rather we should speak of common preoccupations among ethical and political thinkers of the time which naturally included a focus on the theme of the good ordering of the household and its constituent parts.

We may say, then, that the framework for the Christian codes is provided by the traditional concern for 'household management'. However, within that framework we can take seriously the features which caught attention in the earlier discussion. Thus in reference to the most compact of the Christian *Haustafeln*, we can also speak of the characteristically Stoic features to which Dibelius drew attention – two in particular.[15] The *anēken* of Col 3.18 ('it is fitting') reflects the typical Stoic idea that one's best policy, indeed one's duty, is to live in harmony with the natural order of

---

[13] See particularly Crouch, 74–90.

[14] L. Hartman, 'Some Unorthodox Thoughts on the "Household-Code Form"', *The Social World of Formative Christianity and Judaism*, H. C. Kee FS, ed. J. Neusner et al. (Philadelphia: Fortress, 1988), 219–34. I suspect the mistake derives from a misapplication of the sociological category of the 'type', itself an echo of the Platonic idea or ideal form.

[15] Dibelius, 46, 48–9; J. Gnilka, *Der Kolosserbrief*, HTKNT 10/1 (Freiburg: Herder, 1980), 211–12, 220.

things.[16] And *euarestos* in Col 3.20 and Tit 2.9, 'acceptable, pleasing', can likewise be designated a conventional value (cf. Epictetus, 1.12.8 and 2.23.29). On the other hand, in contrast to the Stoics, there is no argument in our passages based on natural law or on reason.[17]

There are also clearly Jewish features, of which three in particular stand out in the Colossian code. First, we may note the extent of the concern for the weaker members of the three pairings. As Schweizer in particular has observed, the exhortations are addressed not only to the male, the adult and the free; the female, the child and the slave are also addressed directly, as equally members of the assembled congregation.[18] Second, the actual format (address, instruction, motivation) is typically Jewish; we may compare, for example, Sir. 3.1 – 'Listen to me your father, O children; act accordingly, that you may be kept in safety'.[19] And, third, in the expanded section addressed to slaves there is repeated use of Jewish motifs – 'sincerity of heart, fearing the Lord ... you will receive from the Lord the reward of the inheritance ... the wrongdoer will be paid back for the wrong he has done, and there is no favouritism'.[20]

At the same time, again limiting our observations to the most compact Christian model, Col 3.18–4.1, we have to take note of the clearly distinctive Christian features: principally the seven-fold reference to 'the Lord', that is, Christ – 'as is fitting in the Lord' (3.18), 'this is pleasing in the Lord' (3.20), 'fearing the Lord' (3.22), 'as to the Lord' (3.23), 'you will receive from the Lord' (3.24), 'you serve the Lord, Christ' (3.24), 'you have a lord in heaven' (4.1). It should be noted that these do not function as a separate part of the code (duties toward God). Rather they

---

[16] H. Schlier, *TDNT* 1.360 and 3.437–40.

[17] W. Schrage, *The Ethics of the New Testament* (Philadelphia: Fortress/Edinburgh: T. & T. Clark, 1988), 248–9.

[18] E. Schweizer, 'Die Weltlichkeit des Neuen Testamentes: die Haustafeln', *Neues Testament*, 194–210, here 201–3; also 'Traditional ethical patterns in the Pauline and post-Pauline letters and their development (lists of vices and house-tables)', *Text and Interpretation*, M. Black FS, ed. E. Best and R. McL. Wilson (Cambridge: Cambridge University Press, 1979), 195–209, here 201–3.

[19] Gnilka, 214–5; see also Crouch; E. Lohse, *Colossians and Philemon* (Philadelphia: Fortress, 1971), 154–7; and Verner, 86–9.

[20] See e.g. Müller, 273–5; J. D. G. Dunn, *Colossians*, NIGTC (Grand Rapids: Eerdmans/Carlisle: Paternoster, 1995) on these phrases in Col 3.22–25.

provide the motivation and orientation of the whole;[21] this in contrast to some who think the Colossian household code has been only 'vaguely christianized'.[22] There is even the possibility of dependence on some tradition of Jesus' own teaching: the command to obey parents perhaps reflecting not just the fifth commandment, but also Jesus' endorsement of it (Mk 7.10; 10.19), and the concern for children perhaps reflecting the episode of Jesus rebuking those who would prevent children being brought to him (Mk 10.13–16).[23]

So our answer to the first question becomes about as clear as the evidence permits. Whence the *Haustafeln?* Clearly the Christian *Haustafeln* do not express a distinctively Christian concern. The concern evident in the Christian texts cited at the beginning of this section was a common concern to the Christians because it was a common concern more widely shared. That is also to say the Christian *Haustafeln* cannot be regarded as a distinctively Christian creation. However, neither would it be accurate to say that the Christians simply took over a traditional or contemporary form. Rather we have to say that a shared concern came to expression in a form common to different traditions in the Graeco-Roman world. The same applies to some of the content of the rules and to some of the values expressed. In this area of social ethics we may say there was a shared system of values which provided motivation as much for Stoic as for diaspora Jew as for Christian. At the same time, the influence of Jewish ethics and values seems to be the stronger, and the Christian motivation with reference to the Lord pervades the whole. Just what this means for our own evaluation of these household codes is a question to which we must return.

---

[21] O. Merk, *Handeln aus Glauben. Die Motivierungen der paulinischen Ethik* (Marburg: Elwert, 1968), 220–4; Schweizer, 'Weltlichkeit', 199–201; Gnilka, 226; J.-N. Aletti, *Saint Paul Épitre aux Colossiens*, EB (Paris: Gabalda, 1993), 249–50; usefully tabulated in Müller, 268.

[22] J. L. Houlden, *Paul's Letters from Prison* (Harmondsworth: Penguin, 1970), 209–11; R. Yates, *The Epistle to the Colossians*, EC (London: Epworth, 1993), 79.

[23] See L. Goppelt, 'Jesus und die "Haustafel"-Tradition', in *Orientierung an Jesus*, J. Schmid FS, ed. P. Hoffmann (Freiburg: Herder, 1973), 93–106 (particularly 99–100); Schweizer, 'Traditional', 202; J. Ernst, *Die Briefe an die Philipper, an Philemon, an die Kolosser, an die Epheser*, RNT (Regensburg: Pustet, 1974), 233–4; P. Pokorny, *Colossians. A Commentary* (Peabody, MA.: Hendrickson, 1987), 182.

3. *Why the* Haustafeln?

Why should such codes be introduced at this period in Christian beginnings? They do not appear in Pauline letters before Colossians, usually dated at the very end of Paul's life or shortly thereafter. But from then on almost every Christian letter-writer seems to see the need to include a *Haustafel* in his paraenesis. Why?

Earlier reflection on this question made much of the delay of the parousia and the need to combat a (potentially) anarchic enthusiasm.[24] The assumption, on the one hand, was that Christians had been on tip-toe expectation about the Lord's coming for thirty or forty years and found the disappointment of their hope a shattering experience which occasioned a radical transformation of theology and praxis. In this form the hypothesis founders on the absence of any clear evidence in its favour; at most we can speak of a piecemeal modification of tradition and adaptation of perspective in our literature. The assumption, on the other hand, was that more or less all congregations in the Pauline mission were like the church in Corinth – despite, once again, the absence of any clear evidence in favour.

An alternative and more modest answer is that the *Haustafeln* of Colossians and subsequent Christian writings indicate a growing awareness that Christians had to counter suspicion that they were socially disruptive. In a context where foreign religions were often viewed with suspicion, the very fact that wives and slaves embraced Christianity might well seem *ipso facto* to be a threat to good order – particularly if equality between the sexes and between masters and slaves was a quasi-confessional element (Gal 3.28), if women were being encouraged to take active part in the leadership of the Pauline churches (e.g. Rom 16.1–2, 3, 6, 7, 12), and if slaves could regard their masters as 'brother' (Phm 16). In such a situation the apologetic requirement to demonstrate responsible household management could very well be-

---

[24] Cf. e.g. Dibelius, 48–9; Crouch, 146–51; G. E. Cannon, *The Use of Traditional Materials in Colossians* (Macon, GA: Mercer University, 1983), 125–8. The same hypothesis was a fundamental element in the influential thesis that the presence of such material in second generation Christian literature is a sign of 'early catholicism'; see e.g. my *Unity and Diversity in the New Testament* (London: SCM, [2]1990), 345–6.

come irresistible.[25] Less positively expressed, we could talk simply of a second or third generation recognition among Christians that they were stuck with the world and society as it was and had to be content to live within it. In other words, they were settling for and settling down to a more conformist ethic.[26]

Where this would begin to 'bite' on the concerns behind these essays would be if this 'settling for life within the status quo' included a transition from or even turning away from the earliest phase of the Christian mission, more marked, perhaps, by breach with families.[27] As is well known, Jesus' call to discipleship included a degree of disparagement of traditional family ties: 'Who are my mother and my brothers? ... Whoever does the will of God...' (Mk 3.31–35); to follow Jesus meant turning one's back on the obligations of family (Matt 8.21–22 / Luke 9.59–60); the disciple must 'hate' father and mother and wife and children (Luke 14.26 / Matt 10.37). But is there a danger here of too quickly drawing a theological and social corollary from Jesus' evangelistic and hyperbolic rhetoric?[28] As already noted, the affirmation of the fifth commandment is firmly rooted in the Jesus tradition. Nor should we speak glibly of a transition from the earliest Pauline mission to the second generation. For the household unit (*oikos*) was a central feature of the Pauline churches from the first (Acts 16.15; 18.8; 1 Cor 1.16; 16.15; etc.); Paul's assertion of the equality in Christ of man and woman, slave and free is already qualified by the reaffirmation of the dependence of the wife on her husband in church (1 Cor 14.33–36), and by his positive evaluation of the status of slavery; and Paul's own counsel of quietist conformity to the reality of state power in Rom 13.1–7 is well known.

Even so, we can well understand that socially responsible Christian leaders, like their Hellenistic Jewish and Stoic counterparts, would wish to consider not merely how individuals should conduct themselves, but how Christian commitment to 'the

---

[25] So particularly Balch, chs. 5–6.

[26] E.g. M. Y. MacDonald, *The Pauline Churches: A socio-historical study of institutionalization in the Pauline and Deutero-Pauline writings*, SNTSMS 60 (Cambridge: Cambridge University Press, 1988), 102–5.

[27] Lührmann, 'Haustafeln', 91–3.

[28] For further discussion see S. C. Barton, *Discipleship and Family Ties in Mark and Matthew*, SNTSMS 80 (Cambridge: Cambridge University Press, 1994).

Lord' should affect the primary unit of community, the house-hold. It is equally understandable that such concerns should become more prominent as congregations became more estab-lished. After all, their meeting place continued to be in the houses of their more well-to-do members, where other members of the family and slaves would be present (as clearly already in Colossians, where children and slaves are directly addressed). And over a period of time questions about how relationships between the three groups should be ordered were bound to arise, as already by implication in 1 Cor 7 and Philemon. The emergence of structured teaching regarding the threefold rela-tionships of a typical household should therefore occasion no surprise or require any special or unexpected stimulus; it was simply bound to happen.

Whatever the reasons behind the appearance of the house-hold rules as a feature of second generation Christianity, the theological rationale expressed within and by means of the *Haustafeln* is clear. For by including such teaching within more general Christian paraenesis the writers give a clear message about the importance of the household and its proper regulation as an integral part of Christian responsibility. To become a member of the new family of Jesus (using the earlier imagery of Paul, as in Rom. 8.16–17, 29) did not justify neglect of household responsibilities, whether the believer belonged to a Christian or a non-Christian household.[29] The relationships within the family and household were themselves part of Christian vocation and indeed, we may say, were the first place where responsibility to the Lord should come to expression and be put to the test. Discipleship begins in the home.

Moreover, the importance of good household management stretched two ways for these Christians. On the one hand, since, as already noted, the earliest churches were all 'house churches', the model of a well ordered household could serve also as a model of the well ordered congregation. The association is already made in 1 Timothy: an *episkopos* and a *diakonos* should each manage his own household well (1 Tim 3.2–5, 12); likewise

---

[29] But Christian families are evidently in view in the passages cited at the beginning, and not the situation of divided loyalties, as in 1 Cor 7.12–16 (Aletti, 250).

the enrolled widow (5.4). This overlapping space, both household and house church, of course, had already created the
possibility of some dissonance and tension between roles: what
was 'fitting' and 'acceptable' within the 'neither male nor female' ethos of the house *church,* might be at odds with what was
deemed 'fitting' and 'acceptable' within the house*hold.* Something of this undoubtedly lies behind tensions in Paul's teaching
about the role of women and wives in the gatherings of the
Corinthian church (1 Cor 11.2–16; 14.33–36).[30] At the same
time, it underscored the continuity between family responsibility
and church responsibility. The two should not be at odds, or
should we say, not normally be at odds; on the contrary, the one
should feed into, reflect and indeed enhance the other. Responsibility to and for one's household was (normally) an integral
part of one's responsibility to and for the church. 'If anyone does
not provide for his relatives, and especially for his own family, he
has disowned the faith and is worse than an unbeliever' (1 Tim
5.8).

The importance of good household management for these
Christians also stretched the other way – as a witness to wider
society. The *Haustafeln* of the ancient world were attempts to
codify the rules which had been found most effective in promoting social welfare and stability. The fact that the Christians used
similar household codes would thus indicate to their neighbours
that they too shared the same concern for society and its good
order. It would attest clearly to any suspicious outsiders, or even
government spies, that Christian discipleship was not disruptive
but rather supportive of society's basic structure.[31] The theological logic is the same as that which we find earlier in Paul,
particularly Rom 12.14–13.7 – viz. that good citizenship can be an
effective force or stage in witness-bearing, both facilitating com-
munication with the rest of society,[32] and making possible an
apologetic and evangelistic impact which should not be lightly
discounted (cf. 1 Cor 7.16; 1 Pet 3.15–16).

[30] S. C. Barton, 'Paul's Sense of Place: An Anthropological Approach to
Community Formation in Corinth', *New Testament Studies* 32 (1986), 235–46.

[31] W. A. Meeks, *The First Urban Christians: The Social World of the Apostle Paul*
(New Haven: Yale University Press, 1983), 106; MacDonald, 108–9, 113–14.

[32] Pokorny, 177–80. See also B. W. Winter, *Seek the Welfare of the City: Christians
as Benefactors and Citizens* (Grand Rapids: Eerdmans, 1994).

In answering our second question, then, 'Why the *Haustafeln?*', we should avoid oversimplifying or tendentious answers. There were no doubt several answers, of different weight and prominence in different stages and places in the whole process. But insofar as we can say that the common presence of *Haustafeln* across such a spread of Christian literature indicates a common concern, we can also say fairly confidently that that shared concern included the concern for well ordered households as an integral part of being the church and of effective witness to the wider community.

4. *In critique of the* Haustafeln

Finally, what critique of the early Christian household codes is appropriate at our distance from them? Three in particular call for some consideration.

One is the somewhat maverick view of J. T. Sanders who is so impressed with the similarities between the Christian codes and the teaching elsewhere in the Graeco-Roman world that he can find no effective difference, and consequently he condemns the teaching of the *Haustafeln* as 'indistinguishable from the world'.[33] He seems to assume that a Christian writer, by definition, must have wanted to encourage his readers to be ethically different from all others. So he is puzzled when he finds that believers were being urged *not* to be different at this point, but to live fully in accord with high social ideals, widely esteemed as such by other ethicists of the time.[34] The 'in the Lord' perspective and resource were different, but the goals were shared.[35] But why should that be thought of as somehow an embarrassment to Christians? What is this fanciful ideal which imagines that to be Christian is to be sharply distinct on all points of social and ethical concern from everyone else? The fact that others share their high standards of family responsibility and social behaviour, and vice-versa, should be an encouragement to believers and easily containable within a theology of providence or 'general grace'.

[33] J. T. Sanders, *Ethics in the New Testament* (Philadelphia: Fortress/London: SCM, 1975), 73–6, 79–80.
[34] Cf. particularly Müller, 304–10, 318.
[35] W. Schrage, 'Zur Ethik der neutestamentlichen Haustafeln', *New Testament Studies* 21 (1974–75), 1–22, here 9.

In contrast to Sanders, the point of significance which emerges from the Christian household codes is the exhortation *not* to denounce or overthrow everyday relationships, in a Cynic-like disowning of society and its structures, or in an attempt at distinctiveness at all costs. On the contrary, the counsel here is precisely to live responsibly within the pattern of everyday relationships, not to discount or abandon them. As several commentators have noted, 'The purpose of the *Haustafeln* is to subject the life of Christians to the Lordship of Christ within the institutions of the secular world',[36] an ethic which Schnackenburg calls 'healthy worldliness'.[37]

The more common critique is that the *Haustafeln* express a high degree of conformity to the structures of contemporary society which ought to have been radically questioned – a compromise too far with conservative social tradition,[38] with what might now be described as 'conventional middle class morality' (*bürgerliche Ethik*),[39] 'a sanctification of the *status quo*',[40] or even an increasing 'paganising' of the Christian ethic over the period spanned by the Christian household codes.[41] The critique is directed particularly against the patriarchalism expressed in the Christian *Haustafeln* ('Wives be subject to your husbands...' – Col 3.18; etc.), 'the patriarchal pattern of submission'.[42] By reasserting the model of patriarchal dominance in the *home,* where also Christians came together as *church,* the household patriarchal order also became the model for church order. In previous decades a similar criticism was levelled against Paul's failure to attack the institution of slavery.

Now it is quite true that the *Haustafeln* take for granted and work within the accepted structures of the day. As we noted at the

---

[36] Schrage, 'Haustafeln', 21–2; also *Ethics,* 252–7, here 252; Schweizer, 'Traditional', 203–4.

[37] R. Schnackenburg, *Die sittliche Botschaft des Neuen Testaments. Band 2: Die urchristlichen Verkündiger* (Freiburg: Herder, 1988), 81, using Schweizer's phrase, itself drawn from W. Zimmerli.

[38] Lührmann, 'Haustafeln', 94.

[39] S. Schulz, *Neutestamentliche Ethik* (Zürich: Theologischer, 1987), 567–71.

[40] A. J. M. Wedderburn (with A. T. Lincoln), *The Theology of the Later Pauline Letters* (Cambridge: Cambridge University Press, 1993), 57.

[41] Schweizer, 'Traditional', 204–7; critiqued by Thraede, 367.

[42] E. S. Fiorenza, *In Memory of Her: A Feminist Theological Reconstruction of Christian Origins* (London: SCM, 1983), ch. 7, here 262.

beginning, the basic fact of family life throughout the Mediterranean world was that the household was essentially a patriarchal institution, with other members of the household subject to the authority of its male head (*patria potestas*). The assumption that the wife should be subject to her husband is thus just what we find elsewhere, for example, in the nearly contemporary Plutarch's *Conjugal Precepts* 33, or in an Egyptian love charm.[43] So too with slavery, the concern of the early Christians, as with the better philosophers of the day, was simply to ameliorate its harsher features rather than to end slavery as such.

But how realistic or justified is the criticism of conformity to prevailing social and ethical patterns – in effect of a socially and theologically spineless conformity to the world? Hindsight and the superior wisdom of the post-Enlightenment European is not a very good base for a criticism which attempts to censure first-century ethics. Slavery only became a moral issue with the Slave Trade; and the wife only became an equal partner in law with her husband in the nineteenth century (many would say she is still not fully an equal). The fact that our moral sensibilities have been sharpened over a span of two millennia should not give us licence to find fault with those who, two millennia earlier, did not share our enlightenment. On the contrary, the fact that it took our cultured society so long to reach such conclusions should make us humble in the face of those who had to live moral lives and to make ethical decisions within (what we now regard as) a much less enlightened mind-set.

Moreover, how well informed as to the circumstances of the ancient world is such criticism? For example, the *patria potestas* affected primarily the woman as wife; whereas, as noted earlier, the widow or single woman of means could hold important posts in business or society or religion.[44] Or again, while the antithesis between freedom and slavery was an axiomatic ideal in Greek thought, the reality was that the slave of a good master was often better off than the freedman, and that the freedman under the universal system of patronage was often in a more disadvantaged

---

[43] *NDIEC* 1.33–6, where Sarapammon seeks help from the underworld powers to secure the love of Ptolemais that she may be 'obedient (same word) for the rest of my life'.

[44] See e.g. P. Trebilco, *Jewish Communities in Asia Minor*, SNTSMS 69 (Cambridge: Cambridge University Press, 1991), ch. 5.

position. Many contracts of manumission (*paramonē* contracts), for example, specified conditions and continuing obligation to the former master, now patron, which restricted the former slave's freedom considerably.[45] A critique of the first Christians for being socially conformist could only be justified if it was properly informed about the conditions of the time.

Not least we have to ask, how realistic is such criticism? It is all too easy to idealise a text like Gal 3.28 in a historically unrealistic and therefore unfair way. Perhaps we need to remind ourselves that there were no traditions of liberal democracy in the world of the Roman Empire. It was not even conceivable for someone like Paul to think of exercising political influence. Certainly it was open to Christianity to adopt a more radical critique of society (like the Cynics), or to abandon society (like the Qumran Essenes), or to pursue utopian dreams by encouraging slave rebellions – all of which would almost certainly have resulted in the demise of Christianity within a few generations. In fact, however, no programme for a new society was drawn up – not even one for the kingdom of God on earth. Instead we may say that Christianity recognised that it had perforce to live within an inevitably flawed and imperfect society and sought to live and witness within that society by combining the proven wisdom of that society with commitment to its own Lord and the transforming power of the love which he had embodied. If we can envisage first century Christianity having a choice between revolution and transformation from within, then we have to say that Christianity chose the second.

These considerations, however, only pose with all the sharper effect the third and final issue – the question of how these texts, or at least the first five above, can continue to function as Scripture. In recent years the issue has been felt most poignantly and expressed most forceably by feminist writers. How can a twentieth-century European wife hear the command to be subject to her husband in everything (Eph. 5.24) as the word of God? The balancing exhortation to husbands to love their wives as Christ loved the church (5.25) only exacerbates the problem since it reinforces the teaching that the husband is to his wife as

[45] For examples of *paramonē* contracts see e.g. Wiedemann, 46–9 and *NDIEC* 4.98–9.

Christ is to the church, a christological underpinning of the patriarchal marriage pattern (5.24–25).[46] Similar questions arise, we should recall, with regard to Paul's ambivalence on the freeing of slaves (1 Cor 7.20–24; Phm), where we would tend to assume that freedom from ownership by another must be regarded as an axiomatic right and as a virtually absolute good.

The issue, of course, raises much wider hermeneutical issues, into which we can hardly enter here. Nor should we forget that these are just further examples of how 'hard texts', for example prayers for the destruction of enemies in the Psalms, can function as Scripture. But what has already been said points to an important element of an answer – viz. the importance of reading the text in question with as full as possible an awareness of the social context and constraints and presuppositions of the time. The problem arises when we read such texts as Scripture without thought of the context of their time of writing. The problem arises here when we try to make the household codes into timeless rules which can be simply transposed across time to the present day without addition or subtraction. But such rules can no more directly be transferred to the different circumstances of today than can the rules, say, of Susannah Wesley (mother of John and Charles Wesley) for bringing up children. No more can we read Paul's counsel to Christian slaves as a manual for shopfloor ethics. What a fundamentalist or biblicist might regard as an honouring of Scripture in this way is actually an abuse of Scripture – precisely because these are historical texts and must be appropriated as such, whatever other factors are involved in the appropriation. And if that makes the church dependent on its teachers, then that simply underlines the importance of teaching in the contemporary church, of a training for ministry which helps provide that teaching, and of the provision of teaching tools readily accessible to the house group or Bible study leader.

To conclude. We cannot fairly evaluate the *Haustafeln* of early Christianity unless we appreciate how much they were condi-

---

[46] Fiorenza, 269–70. The issue is posed in broader terms e.g. in L. M. Russell, ed., *Feminist Interpretation of the Bible* (Oxford: Blackwell, 1985), Part III, and A. Thatcher, *Liberating Sex: A Christian Sexual Theology* (London: SPCK, 1993), ch. 2.

tioned by and adapted to the situation of their times. That was presumably why they were so prized: because they drew on the riches of moral insight and experience over many centuries, Greek as well as Jewish; because they were so practical and realistic in the circumstances of the times; because they provided the basis of a Christian lifestyle within what we would regard as a characteristically cruel and harsh society; and because they enabled a Christian witness even in the face of such cruelty and injustice. They thus provide a paradigm for the way in which Christians perforce have to live within social conditions often inimical to the gospel. The norm they provide is not necessarily the specific command or injunction, but the sensitivity to what was appropriate and practical and right and witness-bearing within the social constraints of the time – their 'healthy worldliness'. Above all we may say, it is the orientation and motivation indicated in the repeated references to the Lord in the Colossian code in particular ('in the Lord', 'fearing the Lord', 'to the Lord', 'serving the Lord') which provided the orientation, motivation and enabling for this early Christian family ethic, and which still provide the fixed points for a continuing Christian ethic in this as in other spheres of ethical concern.

4

Children and Childhood in the New Testament

James Francis

Any theological discussion about the subject of the family has to take into account the significance of children, and an exploration of the theme of children and the imagery of childhood in the New Testament will serve as a resource in that discussion.

In recent years New Testament scholarship has become increasingly aware of the social context of the Mediterranean world, so much so that any treatment of the subject of children in New Testament perspective cannot be undertaken without reference to the social values of that world. Such values are characterised by a sense of the self in its predominantly public aspect whereby status played a significant role and people were required to recognise their place in a stratified social hierarchy. This was a society in which sensitivity to public honour, the avoidance of shame and the recognition of right conduct in its social approval were especially meaningful. A succinct contrasting summary would be that if we today might accord satisfaction to a job well done, in the ancient world satisfaction was a job well recognised.[1] Thus the social institution of the family or the group becomes the predominant focus of loyalty. This contrasts to some extent with our modern world where the concepts of childhood as a social category and even the child as an individual are relatively recent. As Neil Postman describes it:

---

[1] B. J. Malina and J. H. Neyrey, *Calling Jesus Names: The Social Value of Labels in Matthew* (Sonoma, CA: Polebridge Press, 1988), Table 1, 146. See also J. D. M. Derrett, *Jesus's Audience* (London: Darton, Longman & Todd, 1973), 34–6; T. R. Hobbs, 'Crossing Cultural Bridges: The Biblical World', *McMaster Journal of Theology* vol. 1 no. 2 (1990), 1–21.

Childhood is a social artifact, not a biological category ... if we take the word 'children' to mean a special class of people between the ages say of seven and seventeen, who require special forms of nurturing and protection, and who are believed to be qualitatively different from adults, then there is ample evidence that children have existed for less than four hundred years... The idea of childhood is one of the great inventions of the Renaissance, perhaps its most humane one. Along with science, the nation state, religious freedom, childhood as both a social principle and a psychological condition emerged around the sixteenth century.[2]

As a means of exploring the theme of children and childhood in the New Testament we shall begin by outlining some aspects from the social background. We shall then consider the recorded sayings of Jesus about children, survey some perspectives of childhood as a metaphor for discipleship, and conclude by noting the possibility of the transformation of some patriarchal values connected with children and childhood.

1. *Childhood and the social background of the New Testament*

Where children are mentioned in the New Testament this tends to be within the everyday pattern of daily life. This was a world characterised by a structure of extended family, and where children represented stability and perpetuity (Matt 22.23–28 and par.). That Peter's mother-in-law lived in his house (Mk 1.30) suggests that parents continued to be involved with children and their families, and Lk 11.7 reflects the common custom whereby

---

[2] N. Postman, 'The Disappearance of Childhood', in *Conscientious Objections* (New York: A. Knopf, 1988), 147–61, here 148. On childhood in the ancient world see: H. I. Marrou, *A History of Education in Antiquity* (London: Ward, 1952); W. Barclay, *Educational Ideals in the Ancient World* (Grand Rapids: Baker, 1974); T. Wiedemann, *Adults and Children in the Roman Empire* (London: Routledge, 1989); J. F. Gardner and T. Wiedemann, *The Roman Household: A Sourcebook* (London: Routledge, 1991); B. Rawson, *The Family in Ancient Rome* (New York: Cornell University Press, 1986); P. Ariès, *Centuries of Childhood* (London: Jonathan Cape, 1962). See also G. Krause, ed., *Die Kinder im Evangelium* (Stuttgart/ Göttingen: Klotz Verlag, 1973).

the whole family slept together in a single-roomed house. It was also a world characterised by gender stereotyping where the role of the woman was defined in terms of child-bearing (1 Tim 2.15; cf. 4 Macc 14.13–15.5), and the gender of the child was associated with that of the appropriate parent, father with son and mother with daughter. Thus the divisions in the family at Matt 10.35; Lk 12.53 imply a domestic role for daughters, and a phrase such as 'like father, like son' may underlie the christology of Matt 11.27; Lk 10.22 (cf. Jn 1.18). Again the fact that a number of different terms[3] are used to cover the range of childhood reflects an awareness of the child in its social setting. The principal words for 'child' are the following: *brephos* as baby or infant; *pais* which covers a range of meanings – as child (from the perspective of age, including, Matt 2.16, a young child), or as son (from the perspective of descent), or as slave or servant (from the perspective of social position, cf. *paidiskē* as maid or slave-girl); *paidion* as a diminutive of *pais* as a very young child, and also as a term of affectionate address by a teacher to his hearers or readers; *paidarion* as a further diminutive, though not indicative of extreme youth (Gen 37.30; Joseph as a *paidarion* is seventeen (v. 2) and hence a lad); *teknon* as child from the perspective of origin or descent and as an address in terms of lineage in a metaphorical sense; *teknion* as a diminutive of *teknon*; and *nēpios* as infant or minor, with associations of either immaturity or being unlearned. Such a diversity of vocabulary is not, however, related to an understanding of the precise stages of a child's development and this in turn suggests that the child is really only generally understood as an adult in the making. Significantly, the mention of a child's age at Mk 5.42 links at a stroke two life-stages of toddler and commencement of adulthood.

In this cultural setting of the early Mediterranean world emphasis was placed upon the obligation which was owed within the social group and therefore upon the related accompanying value of obedience. For example 1 Timothy says 'if anyone aspires to the office of elder ... he must manage his own household well, keeping his children submissive and respectful in every way' (1 Tim 3.1,4). In the tables of household duty at Col 3.20 and

---

[3] For a full list see H. R. Weber, *Jesus and the Children* (Geneva: World Council of Churches, 1979) 52–53.

Ephes 6.1–3 obedience is the key requirement of children as a way of interpreting the Torah commandment to honour one's father and one's mother. And in the narrative of the beheading of John the Baptist (Mk 6.14–29; Matt 14.1–12) it is a daughter's filial obedience to her mother (Mk 6.24; Matt 14.8; *korasion* – as diminutive, 'little girl') which discomfits her father, and to save face (v. 26) he grants her request. An echo of this distinctive value associated with childhood may also be found in the presentation of Jesus' own obedience to God as his heavenly Father (Mk 14.36, cf. Hebrews 5.8) in the acceptance of his destiny.[4] Jesus' quotation of Deuteronomy 8.3 in the Temptation narrative (Matt 4.4; Lk 4.4) that 'man does not live by bread alone' is, according to Deuteronomy 8.5, an expression of filial obedience, and this is emphasised by the fact that it is the Spirit who places Jesus in the way of his testing (Matt 4.1; Mk 1.12; Lk 4.1). We may also note how the cry of dereliction in Mk 15.34 is given added poignancy by this one recorded instance of Jesus' failure to address God as Father,[5] whereby shame is expressed in a sense of the abandonment of all kinship. However, the centurion's verdict (v. 39) affirms Jesus' obedience (recalling 1.11 and 9.7), and thus points to the honour which the community of faith will accord him through his cross.

The emphasis on obedience in a patriarchal society betokens two things. First, obedience is an important expression of group loyalty whereby an individual's behaviour represents and affects the whole group, and especially in the case of children, the honour of the family (Deut 21.18–21, cf. Sirach 3.2–16). The value of obedience as a key aspect of childhood in the context of group loyalty (a value which significantly, of course, is viewed from an adult perspective – 'everyone who loves the parent loves

[4] See J. Pilch, '"Beat his Ribs while he is Young" (Sir 30.12): A Window on the Mediterranean World', *Biblical Theology Bulletin* 23 (1993), 101–13. On Jesus' address to God as Father see J. Barr, '"Abba, Father" and the Familiarity of Jesus' Speech', *Theology* 91 (1988), 173–9 and '"Abba" Isn't "Daddy"', *Journal of Theological Studies* 38 (1988), 28–47.

[5] At Lk 23.46 'Father' is prefixed to a Psalm quotation, which makes its absence here notable. Whilst Wisdom 14.15 attributes the origins of idolatry to a father's primal grief over an untimely bereavement which leads him to make an image of his child (an adaptation of the theory of Euhemerus that idolatry arose through the worship of dead heroes), the church discerned in the death of Jesus as God's child the way of honour and righteousness.

the child', 1 Jn 5.1; cf. Lk 1.17) is to be seen in the tensions between Jesus and his family (Mk 6.4; Jn 7.5). It is also reflected in Jesus' parable of the two sons in Matt 21.28–32 where honour and shame are an inherent part of the responses given to the father (cf. Matt 5.16). Similarly in that other parable of two sons and their father (Lk 15.11–32) the prodigal's conduct would have reflected upon the honour of the family, hinted at obliquely in the complaint of the older son (vv. 29–30) A debate about kinship and family honour also underlies the conflict in Jn 8.37–44 (especially v. 41; cf. Mk 6.3).

Second, since obedience is not thought to arise naturally then discipline is to be inculcated from childhood. So, referring again to 1 Tim 3.4, the emphasis on the verb 'keeping' is present continuous – 'keeping his children submissive and respectful in every way' betokens a sense of watchful discipline. Indeed Hebrews 12.7–11 (echoing Prov 3.11–12) provides a cameo of the discipline which a father (as a *good* father) must provide for his children – 'for what son is there whom his father does not discipline ... we have had earthly fathers to discipline us and we respected them ... all discipline seems painful rather than pleasant but it yields the peaceful fruit of righteousness to those who have been trained by it.' In so far as Judaism did not have a predominant view of the innocence of the child,[6] the educative purpose of discipline reflects a view of human nature which Jesus himself may have accepted. Thus human nature is of itself in need of correction – 'What comes out of a man is what defiles a man. For from within, out of the heart of man, come evil thoughts...' (Mk 7.20–23). Whilst this particular catalogue of faults is representative of adulthood, it occurs in the context of an argument which includes the duties of children to parents (Mk 7.10). But such discipline is not to be overly harsh – so fathers are 'not to provoke their children' (Ephes 6.4; Col 3.21).[7] Whilst discipline is necessary as a corrective to innate human tendencies, the social group or the family can only be strengthened if such discipline is constructive rather than destructive. So a

---

[6] See A. Oepke, *Theological Dictionary of the New Testament*, vol. 5 (1967), 646; H. R. Weber, *Jesus and the Children*, 74–76.

[7] Contrast Sirach 30.1–13. In Proverbs and Sirach parenting advice is addressed to sons. For Sirach daughters were a particular source of worry (42.9–14).

(good) father will care for his children – 'What man of you, if his son asks him for bread, will give him a stone? Or if he asks for a fish, will give him a serpent? If you then, who are evil, know how to give good gifts to your children, how much more will your Father who is in heaven give good things to those who ask him' (Matt 7.9–11). The necessity for good parental care, whilst it is here given metaphorical significance concerning prayer, is also recognised elsewhere in the New Testament as an important duty (2 Cor 12.14; 1 Tim 5.8).

The particular value of obedience places the child in proximity (evident in Ephesians and Colossians) to two other groups of whom obedience is also required, namely wives (at Matt 14.21 children are listed with women) and slaves (cf. Gal 4.1ff). Thus wives are to be obedient to their husbands (Ephes 5.22; Col 3.18, cf. 1 Pet 3.1ff;), and slaves are to be obedient to their masters (Ephes 6.5ff; Col 3.22ff, cf. 1 Pet 2.18ff). In recalling the varied vocabulary of childhood we may note that in the Graeco-Roman world 'child' was the standard way of addressing a slave (cf. Jn 6.9, lad – *paidarion*, with its possible reference to 2 Kings 4.42–44 where (v. 38) Elisha's *paidarion* is a servant). 'Yet another dehumanising device was the habit of addressing, or referring to, male slaves of any age as "boy", *pais* in Greek, *puer* in Latin… We must rid our minds of the warm overtones of the word "child" in this connection. Aristophanes (*Wasps* 1297–8, 1307) once invented an etymology of *pais* from *paiein*, "to beat", and that was not the only one of his jokes to point to hard reality.'[8] Such a perspective reflects a view of the adult male as central and children, women and slaves as marginal to that predominant male centrism. (At Matt 18.25 wife and children are part of the man's possessions.)

Because children are thought of as essentially adults in the making, childhood tends to be contrasted with adulthood. At root a child is thought of as weak in mind, that is, deficient in 'logos', *nēpios* (Latin *in-fans*) as literally a non-speaker. Just like barbarians, children, with their faltering speech, are non-participant in the adult rational world. Echoes of this outlook appear in

---

[8] M. I. Finley, *Ancient Slavery and Modern Ideology* (London: Chatto & Windus, 1980), 96. See also T. Wiedemann, *Adults and Children in the Roman Empire*, 22. It is interesting to note that the rare word '*hupogrammon* / example' at 1 Pet 2.21, concerning advice to slaves, recalls the practice of the 'tracing' of letters for children to write over or copy.

the New Testament, e.g. Paul at 1 Cor 3.1ff likens his readers to babes in their lack of understanding (cf. Hebrews 5.13), and at 1 Cor 13.11–12 adulthood is contrasted with childhood as the stage of entering into maturity of understanding (cf. also Ephes 4.14).[9] Again, at Rom 2.19–20 Paul describes the Jewish teacher as 'a guide to the blind, a light to those who are in darkness, a corrector of the foolish, a teacher of children', and at Gal 4.1ff Paul likens his readers' state prior to their faith in the gospel to that of children (here for him the equivalent of a slave state).[10] On the other hand the very aspect of the child as simple in the sense of non-rational, and therefore as an innocent untutored voice-piece through whom the divine might speak or be discerned, may be reflected in the voices of the children who echo in the temple the greeting of Jesus' entry into Jerusalem (Matt 21.15–16 and Psalm 8.2), in the metaphorical contrasts between the wise who fail to understand and the infants who do (Matt 11.25–26; Lk 10.21–22), and in the way in which children could even be under divine protection (Matt 18.10, a feature also perhaps of the dreams of Joseph and of the Magi in Matthew's Infancy Narrative). Thus the intuitive spontaneity of a child's response may actually provide an insight into the divine purpose. We should also not overlook the fact that although the culture of the ancient world was not child-oriented, whereby it is only by training that the child comes to any significance, yet affection can be shown towards children and the death of children does not go unmourned.[11]

In the New Testament generally, and in the ministry of Jesus in particular, mention of children and of childhood occurs in relation both to actual children and to the child as a metaphor

---

[9] T. Wiedemann suggests that Paul here may be echoing a definite stage in a child's life when games and toys were set aside, as reflected in many so-called 'dedication poems', *Adults and Children in the Roman Empire*, 153.

[10] In view of the foregoing it may be that the preferred reading at 1 Thess 2.7 is 'gentle' rather than 'babes'. See B. R. Gaventa, 'Apostles as Babes and Nurses in 1 Thessalonians 2.7' in J. Carroll, ed., *Faith and History: Essays in Honour of Paul W. Meyer* (Atlanta, GA: Scholars Press, 1990), 193–207.

[11] See T. Wiedemann, *Adults and Children in the Roman Empire*, 25ff, 84ff; H. R. Weber, *Jesus and the Children*, 11–12; R. B. Lyman, 'Barbarism and Religion: late Roman and early Medieval Childhood', in L. deMause, ed., *The History of Childhood* (London: Souvenir Press, 1976), 75–100, here 80–81. Cf. 4 Macc 15.4 'O how may I express the passionate love of parents for children...?'

or image of faith. These contexts reflect the way in which the child within a social group is important as a locus for the handing on of the group's values and beliefs, and the way in which, in representing the future, the child both inherits and comes to own the whole life-tradition of the group. In this process of handing on and receiving, which is part of the very nature of discipleship, we may say that the child as person draws attention to what is transmitted, and the child as image draws attention to how what is transmitted is to be received and acted upon.

2. *Childhood and the teaching of Jesus*

In the teaching of Jesus[12] there are two passages which relate to actual children and in relation to whom some teaching is given and lessons drawn. In Mk 9.36–37 (Matt 18.2, 4–5; Lk 9.47–48) Jesus himself places a child in the midst of the disciples and makes a point about the nature of discipleship, and in Mk 10.13–16 (Matt 19.13–15; Lk 18.15–17) children are brought to Jesus for a blessing.

With reference to the first passage, the whole pericope from 9.33-37 is in two parts, vv. 33–34 dealing with the disciples' argument about true greatness, and vv. 36–37 concerning the reception given to a child. What connects them is v. 35 as a logion about the first and the last (recollecting that *talya* in Aramaic also means both servant and child). In this the attention shown to the least and the last in the form of a child becomes the criterion of discipleship, since the child is made, or is claimed by Jesus to be, the fully representative symbol of himself and of the whole mission of the Kingdom of God. The very presence of the child is the answer given to the disciples' question, and thus the one most likely to be overlooked, the one considered the least, is the one from whom one must learn about the way of the Kingdom.

---

[12] See H. R. Weber, *Jesus and the Children*. Also J. Légasse, *Jésus et L'Enfant* (Paris: Gabalda, 1969) and 'L'Enfant dans L'Évangile', *La Vie Spirituelle* 122 (1970), 407–21; S. C. Barton, 'Jesus – Friend of Little Children?' in J. Astley and D. Day, eds., *The Contours of Christian Education* (London: McCrimmon, 1992), 30–40; H.–H. Schroeder, *Eltern und Kinder in der Verkündigung Jesu* (Hamburg-Bergstedt: Herbert Reich, 1972); J. D. Crossan, *The Historical Jesus. The Life of a Jewish Mediterranean Peasant* (San Francisco: Harper San Francisco, 1991) 265–302; 'Kingdom and Children', *Semeia* 29 (Chico, CA: Scholars Press, 1983).

Indeed the child becomes thereby the actual envoy of the Kingdom. This is emphasised in Mark by the warm welcome which Jesus gives (v. 36b), and in Luke's version of the story (Lk 9.47) by the way Jesus places the child 'at his side' rather than 'in the midst'. In the Graeco-Roman world it would have been unusual for an adult to think that he or she might learn anything from a child, though in Judaism a child could have exemplary significance for faith.[13] The phrase 'in my name', meaning 'for my sake' (Mk 8.35, 10.29, 13.9), would suggest an emphasis on receiving the child not because he or she is already a believer (contrast 9.42; Matt 18.6, cf. Rom 14.13, in its developed meaning of 'little ones') but because this action is what I (i.e., Jesus) desire. This would in turn connect this story with the subsequent one of Jesus' blessing of the children and his welcome of them. But whereas the emphasis in Mk 9.36–37 is upon Jesus' own identification with the child in describing the meaning of discipleship, Jesus' welcome of children in Mk 10.13–16; Matt 19.13–15; Lk 18.15–17 affirms their identification with him in the blessing of the Kingdom. It is likely that this second episode has a certain climactic significance in Mark, in that it recalls three earlier episodes where Jesus healed children (Mk 5.21–24 and 35–43, Jairus's daughter; 7.25–30, the daughter of a Syrophoenician woman; and 9.14–29, the healing of a demon possessed boy). Thus the welcome by Jesus of children is the culmination of that wider aspect of his ministry. But since this episode is also part of a larger teaching about discipleship within the section 10.1–31 as a whole, the particular logion of v. 15, 'whoever does not receive the Kingdom of God like a child shall not enter it', undoubtedly recalls the lesson about the significance of children for discipleship already given at 9.33–37. As the children (presumably Jewish children – contrast 7.27) are brought to Jesus for a blessing we need not suppose that it was necessarily women (mothers) who brought them (cf. Mk 9.17; Deut 1.31), since the masculine plural is used of the indeterminate 'they/them'. Nor were the children necessarily babes in arms, though

---

[13] Psalm 8.2 (quoted at Matthew 21.16); cf. 'From the breast of (their) mothers, sucklings made signs with their fingers to their fathers and said to them: "He is our Father who gave us honey to suck out of the rock, and gave us oil from the flinty rock"' (Targum Yerushalmi Exodus 15.2).

Luke makes the point about age with the phrase 'even infants', perhaps in keeping with his own interest in the least and the smallest. Here Jesus, in blessing the children, echoing the blessing of Ephraim and Manasseh by Jacob in Genesis 48,[14] affirms the intention of those who brought the children and declares their covenanted inclusion in Israel in common with rabbinic teaching.[15] Why precisely the disciples proved unwelcoming remains unclear. Various reasons have been advanced, e.g. because they thought children were insignificant (forgetting so easily the lessons of 9.36–37), or that Jesus was too busy, or because they were officious (cf. 2 Kings 4.27), or because they wanted to guard against any idea of superstition.[16] The rebuke of the disciples is, presumably, addressed to the adults rather than to the children. Their opposition, however, is in stark contrast to Jesus' welcome, a welcome which not only meets but, notably, surpasses the expectations of the adults themselves who bring the children. Thus Jesus takes them up in his arms (a verb used only twice in the New Testament, and significantly the other use is at Mk 9.36 in the story of the child in the midst), and he affirms that to such (which, whatever else, must include the actual children), belongs the Kingdom of God. The emphasis of the story, however, falls not only upon the children themselves, but upon an understanding of God's free grace. It expresses the nature of God's unconditional love whereby without questions of qualifications or conditions these children, and by implication all who are equally without merit or desert, receive the Kingdom of God and are ranked equal with Jesus himself. The point of the story is not simply that Jesus chooses to recognise the children but that he affirms their entitlement to be recognised, such is the nature of God's unconditional love.[17] There are two things which combine here. Looked at from the point of view of the child the emphasis

---

[14] See J. D. M. Derrett, 'Why Jesus Blessed the Children (Mk 10.13–16 Par.)' *Novum Testamentum* xxv 1 (1983), 1–18.

[15] See P. Billerbeck and H. L. Strack, *Kommentar zum Neuen Testament aus Talmud und Midrasch* (Munich, 1922–28), 786.

[16] So J. D. M. Derrett, 'Why Jesus Blessed the Children', 11.

[17] 'God embraces them, presses them to his heart and kisses them, thus bringing them into the life of the world to come' (Seder Elijahu Rabba 17, quoted by H. R. Weber, *Jesus and the Children*, 19).

falls on reception, that is upon the fact that Jesus receives the children. But looked at from the point of view of the adults (parents) the emphasis is also upon their sense of duty (cf. Lk 2.22),[18] of discharging an obligation which they felt towards their children in wanting to bring them to this particular person. Jesus then affirms this responsibility, and translates a sense of obligation to the children into a reciprocal welcome which (by his enfolding of them) expresses the nature of God's grace for children and parents, a welcome which not only meets but also exceeds their expectations. Both stories, of the child in the midst and of Jesus' welcome of the children who are brought to him, point to the significance of God's free grace. As that grace is not related to merit so it may be met with in all, especially amongst the least and those of no esteem (the recollection of a feature of Israel's own experience of God e.g. Deut 7.7–8; Hos 11.1–4; Ezek 16.3–8; Ps 74.21).

3. *Childhood and discipleship*

The declaration of God's free grace, however, has its consequences, and in both of these episodes where Jesus meets with children there is an interweaving of interest, as we have seen, in the child in its symbolic significance. The metaphorical significance of the child in representing the least is connected directly to the believer's own understanding of discipleship in its status (Lk 22.26 'let the greatest among you become as *the youngest*'). Again the object lesson drawn from the representative significance of the child establishes a pattern of discipleship which sets particular store by pastoral care for 'little ones', that is, the least, irrespective of age (Matt 18.5; Lk 9.48). The logion 'whoever does not receive the Kingdom of God like a child shall not enter it', which has become attached to the story of Jesus' welcome of the children (Mk 10.15; Lk 18.17, cf. Matt 18.3; Jn 3.3–5), also serves to focus childhood as a metaphor of discipleship (taking 'like a child' as a noun in the nominative case).[19] If the Kingdom

---

[18] Cf. Paul's aphorism 'for children ought not to lay up for their parents but parents for their children' (2. Cor 12.14).

[19] For discussion see H. R. Weber, *Jesus and the Children*, 27ff; J. D. M. Derrett, 'Why Jesus blessed the children', 14; E. Best, *Following Jesus* (Sheffield: JSOT

belongs to children then it is but a step to say that the Kingdom also consists of the childlike. We may also recall the ambiguity of Mk 10.14b whereby the Kingdom may 'belong to such' or, it could equally be, 'consists of such'. Moreover, if 'to receive' can also mean 'to welcome',[20] then Jesus' glad reception of the children in its contrast to the reluctance of the disciples places an emphasis upon the correct attitude of the believer. It becomes a sign of true faith to be able to welcome (to receive) the Kingdom with spontaneous joy.

To explore what it means to receive as a child receives[21] has led the church into many varied interpretations of childhood in its metaphorical significance.[22] One of the earliest interpretations (cf. Isa 11.6–8) centres upon the idea of innocence (including that of sexual innocence as reflected in the Gospel of Thomas), and is elaborated in the early Church Fathers' notion of being untainted.[23] But in Mark and Luke at least the emphasis seems to be on a sense of glad and wholehearted acceptance as a child receives a gift. On the other hand, in Matthew[24] the slightly

Press, 1981) 107–8 and also 'Mk 10.13–16: The child as model recipient', *Disciples and Discipleship: Studies in the Gospel According to St. Mark* (Edinburgh: T.&T. Clark, 1986), 80–97; M. Black, 'The Markan Parable of the Child in the Midst', *Expository Times* 59 (1947–48), 14–16; F. A. Schelling, 'What Means the Saying about Receiving the Kingdom of God as a Little Child?', *Expository Times* 77 (1965–66), 56–8.

[20] J. I. H. McDonald, 'Receiving and Entering the Kingdom: a Study of Mk 10.15', *Studia Evangelica* VI (1973), 328–32, here 329.

[21] J. I. H. McDonald, 'Receiving and Entering the Kingdom', 331ff interprets the distinction between 'receiving' and 'entering upon' in terms of two stages involving a progression linked to the teachability of the child. However, the emphasis is perhaps not so much upon the gap between receiving and entering as upon the attitude of the heart whereby childlike reception is the way by which one enters.

[22] See T. R. Hobbs, 'Crossing Cultural Bridges', 16–18 for a survey of interpretations; J. Jeremias *The Parables of Jesus* (London: SCM, 1963), 190–1.

[23] See H. C. Kee, '"Becoming a Child" in the Gospel of Thomas', *Journal of Biblical Literature* 82 (1963), 307–14; C. Harrison, 'The Childhood of Man in Early Christian Writers', *Augustinianum* 32.1 (1992), 61–76.

[24] For discussion whether the Matthean form ('unless you turn and become like children') is earlier than Mark/Luke see H. R. Weber, *Jesus and the Children*, 24–5; J. Dupont, 'Mattieu 18.3', in E. E. Ellis and M. Wilcox, *Neotestamentica et Semitica: Studies in Honour of M. Black* (Edinburgh: T.&T. Clark, 1969), 50–60; H. Stock *Studien zur Auslegung der synoptischen Evangelien im Unterricht* (Gütersloh: Bertelsmann, 1959), 175–201. The Matthean 'turn' does not refer, at least in its present setting, to an initial religious conversion (and is not, therefore, by implication the same as 'born again' in Jn 3.3) since it is addressed to the disciples who are already believers. The logion in Matthew more appropriately

different version 'unless you turn and become like children you will never enter the Kingdom of Heaven', whilst it removes any ambiguity in favour of the child as a metaphor of the self, places a particular emphasis on humility (Matt 18.4) – not that children are naturally humble but childlikeness betokens a sense of dependency and the recognition of need. To be like a child is to be humble enough to recognise dependency, that is, one's absolute need of the gift of the Kingdom. We may compare Psalm 131 where a similar sense of childlike trust and humility combine – 'O Lord my heart is not lifted up ... but I have calmed and quieted my soul, like a child quieted at its mother's breast; like a child that is quieted is my soul' (cf. Gospel of Thomas 22: 'these infants being suckled are like those who enter the Kingdom'). But Matthew's version with its language of 'turning' may also contain the idea of leaving behind, literally the turning away from, the conventional value perceptions of adulthood,[25] as the corollary to the trustful dependency which is at the heart of the metaphor. The status of childhood, therefore, has a radical edge in that this is dependency upon God and not upon the patriarchal tradition of teachers (Matt 11.29). The consequence of a thanksgiving that God the Father has revealed to babes what is hidden from the wise and understanding (Matt 11.25) is an exhortation to 'call no man your father on earth, for you have one Father who is in Heaven' (Matt 23.9) which continues, significantly, three verses later (in words which echo 18.4) 'he who is greatest among you shall be your servant; whoever exalts himself will be humbled, and whoever humbles himself will be exalted'. (We may also note how the authority claimed by Jesus at 11.28–30 is transposed at 23.10 to the church's faith in Christ, cf. 28.18–20.) The virtue of humility, therefore, is a key value of discipleship, but this does not imply (as the image of the child usually does in Wisdom discourse) deference to the received traditions of others (cf. 5.21–48). Matthew's sense of childlike-

relates to the context of a realisation about, and a change of heart in connection with, the criterion of true greatness. For the view that Matt 18.3 is related to Jn 3.3 see B. Lindars, 'John and the Synoptic Tradition: a Test Case', *New Testament Studies* 27 (1981), 287–94; and also R. Cameron, 'Sayings Traditions in the Apocryphon of James', *Harvard Theological Studies* 34 (Philadelphia: Fortress, 1984), 66–8.

[25] See J. N. Sevenster, 'Education or Conversion: Epictetus and the Gospels', *Novum Testamentum* VIII (1966), 247–62.

ness as a state of what one might call radical humility is not, however, too far removed from the interpretation of Mark and Luke[26] whereby, in a like dependency upon God, one may receive his gift of the Kingdom in absolute trust and with joy.

There are two further instances of Jesus' observation of children with an object lesson drawn from them, that of the children in the market place (Matt 11.16–19; Lk 7.31–35) and that of the children crying out in the temple (Matt 21.15). The parable of the children's game,[27] an example no doubt of just one of those childhood pastimes to be set aside on entry to adulthood (cf. 1 Cor 13.11), does not contain a criticism of the children that their game had failed (since guess-work is part of the game itself), nor does it necessarily serve as an example of foreboding which a children's game could sometimes have for adults,[28] but points to a lesson which is to be drawn from observation of the game. A comparison is made between the game as a whole and the present generation, the significance being that 'this generation' has failed to understand the mission of both John the Baptist and Jesus. Luke in particular, in his use of two separate words for children (at 7.32 and 7.35) emphasises the point. Whilst at verse 32 *paidia* denotes actual children (that is, in distinction from adults) *teknia* in verse 35 denotes origins and descent, and thus discipleship is a matter of proving to be Wisdom's children in discerning the significance of both missions (cf. Mk 11.30). A similar point lies behind that other logion (found only in Matt 21.15) in Jesus' observation of the children crying out in the temple (in recollection of Ps 8.2). It is they, ranked as they are

[26] On the significance for Luke of the child as a pattern of discipleship see J. Kodell, 'Luke and the Children: the Beginning and End of the Great Interpolation (Lk 9.46–56; 18.9–23), *Catholic Biblical Quarterly* 49 (1987), 415–30; S. Fowl, 'Receiving the Kingdom of God as a Child: Children and Riches in Lk 18.15ff', *New Testament Studies* 39 (1993), 153–8.

[27] On this see W. Cotter, 'The Parable of the Children in the Market-place, Q (Lk) 7.31–35: an Examination of the Parable's Image and Significance', *Novum Testamentum* xxix (1987), 289–304; J. M. Suggs, *Wisdom, Christology and Law in Matthew's Gospel* (Cambridge, MA: Harvard University Press, 1970), 31ff. Also H. R. Weber, *Jesus and the Children*, 1ff and F. Mussner, 'Der nicht erkannte Kairos (Matt. 11.16–19; Lk 7.31–35)', *Biblica* 40 (1959), 599–612; J. Jeremias, *The Parables of Jesus*, 160–2; N. Perrin, *Rediscovering the Teaching of Jesus* (London: SCM, 1967), 119–21.

[28] See Wiedemann, *Adults and Children in the Roman Empire,* 150ff, 178ff.

with the marginal (21.14), who have true wisdom (v. 16 babes-*nēpioi*, cf. 11.25 babes-*nēpioi*), reflecting those themes in Matthew's understanding of children which we have already noted.

Whatever be the nuances of the recorded sayings of Jesus, the linking of the child to the activity of God in His Kingdom represents a particularly unforgettable image. It contains a radical message in the reversal of the usual relationship of adult to child and represents a sharp re-evaluation of the pivotal social value of honour. It is not merely the learning of a lesson from the child but a turning around to adopt the way of a child both in ready trust and dependency as the only way into the Kingdom, and in identifying with the weak and the dispossessed as itself the way of the Kingdom.

The metaphorical significance of childhood also develops in a variety of other ways in the church. Positively, childhood as an image comes to represent the needy, the 'little ones' who are specifically members of the church (Mk 9.42; Matt 18.6–14, cf. Acts 20.35) and even a particular group, that is, itinerant missionaries of the church (Matt 10.42; 25.40, 45; Mk 9.41) who might well be open to a sense of their own vulnerability (cf. 1 Cor 2.3). Or again, childhood continues to function extensively as a metaphor for learning in expressing the relationship of pupil to teacher as child to parent (e.g. Mk 10.24b; 2 Cor 12.14; 1 Tim 1.2; 1 Jn 2.1).[29] Again, the relationship of childhood to sonship is a particular feature of imagery in the Fourth Gospel and the Johannine Epistles. In the Fourth Gospel Jesus alone is referred to consistently as the Son of God and believers, through regeneration, are the children of God. As children of God, as 'little children' (Jn 13.33), they are to love one another, which hallmark of the Christian community becomes a focus of particular significance in the Epistles. Again childhood in its symbolism of hope and new beginning (as in Isa 9.6 cf. Luke 2.12–4) becomes associated with imagery of birthing as a new creation, whether in elaboration of the pupil–teacher relationship (Gal 4.19, echoing Gen 1.28a 'be fruitful and multiply'), or more widely in relation to the travail and birth pangs of the messianic age (Jn 16.21; Rom 8.22; 1 Thess 5.3; Rev 12.2, cf. Isa 26.16–19 and 66.7–14).

---

[29] See J. D. M. Derrett, *Jesus's Audience*, 142–50.

Negatively, however, the child continues to portray, as in the ancient world generally, a sense of childishness contrasted with maturity. The predominant context of the image of childhood as childishness is that of learning in the transmission of the community's values and beliefs. It corresponds to the teacher–pupil relationship referred to above, but whereas childhood there in its beneficial connotation refers to a relationship viewed from the perspective of the teacher, childhood as childishness is viewed from the perspective of the recipient's own responsibility for an adequate understanding and grasp of faith. This is borne out by the fact that the pejorative use of the child metaphor concerns vocabulary representative not of descent (*brephos* or *teknon*) but of age (*nēpios* or *pais*).[30] Thus childhood as a state of immaturity is frequently contrasted with a proper role model of discipleship (1 Cor 3.1, 13.11, 14.20a; Gal 4.1, 3; Ephes 4.14 (cf. James 1.6); Heb 5.13,[31] cf. Isa 3.4, 12; Eccl 10.16; Wis 12.24; 15.14[32]). It is noteworthy, however, that the metaphorical significance of childhood in a pejorative sense finds no place in the teaching of Jesus.[33]

4. *Childhood and the transformation of the values of patriarchy*

Nevertheless the church in the light of Jesus' message and the interpretation of the gospel not only mirrored its social world but

[30] See A. Oepke, *Theological Dictionary of the New Testament*, vol. 5, 642, and also the comment above on Lk 7.35 in the discussion of the parable of the Children in the Market-Place.

[31] In this pejorative use the image can elaborate itself into a contrast of diet between milk and solid food (1 Cor 3.1ff; Hebrews 5.13ff, cf. 1 Peter 2.2). See J. Francis, '"Like Newborn Babes" – The Image of the Child in 1 Peter 2.2–3', *Studia Biblica* iii (1978), 111–17 and '"As Babes in Christ" – Some Proposals Regarding 1 Cor 3.1–3', *Journal for the Study of the New Testament* 7 (1980), 41–60.

[32] Childhood as an image of childishness is reflected in Rabbinic thought, e.g. M. Aboth 3.11: 'R. Dosa b. Harkinas said: Morning sleep and midday wine and children's talk and sitting in the meeting-houses of the ignorant people put a man out of the world.'

[33] The poignant image of Jerusalem's children whom Jesus longs to gather as a hen would gather her brood (Matt 23.37; Lk 13.34) echoes a sensitivity expressed in a similar image of a bird and its chicks in Classical Greek tragedy. See G. M. Sifakis, 'Children in Greek Tragedy', *Bulletin of the Institute of Classical Studies* 26 (1979), 67–80, here 68–9.

worked creatively upon it. The theme of children and childhood may allow us to glimpse a number of points of transformation.

1. It is on the basis of Jesus himself as a son, obedient to his Father in the mission of the Kingdom, that there emerges a pattern whereby the obligations of family life, and of a child's obligations to its parents in particular, are both affirmed and transformed. Thus Jesus upholds the fifth commandment (Mk 7.10 and par., cf. Jn 19.26), but declares that there is both a subordination (Matt 10.34–39; Lk 12.51–53; Mk 13.12, cf. Jn 7.5) and a widening (Mk 3.34–35) of family ties in the mission of the Kingdom. This is presaged in Lk 2.41–51 where the intimation of Jesus' ministry of the Kingdom in obedience to the call of God as Father is nurtured through his own childhood obedience to his parents (2.51, cf. Jn 6.42),[34] and is reflected in the way in which, as we have seen, Jesus welcomes the parents with their children in the course of his mission. It is also recalled at Lk 11.27–28 (cf. 23.28–29 and par.) where what is, perhaps, a standard acclamation for an obedient son ('blessed is the womb that bore you and the breast that you sucked') widens the sense of family identity (via a traditional metaphorical link between food and learning) with reference to discipleship. Such a paradox as this is not to be resolved on the basis of a choice between whole-hearted affirmation of family responsibilities or the abandonment of them (there could even be, for the church, a reaffirmation of family ties, Acts 1.14), but on the basis of the way in which the believer, as a child of God, must set all aspects of life in the context of faith. In the social context of the family in Jesus' day that implied, of course, a certain radical critique of normative patriarchal structures.[35]

2. In the tables of household duty it is significant that it is the duties of the subordinates, as it were, which are always mentioned

---

[34] The development of infancy narratives about Jesus in e.g. The Infancy Gospel of Thomas and other apocryphal gospels is concerned less with Jesus as a model of discipleship and more with a precocious display of power by the remarkable Christ child. See H. Koester, *Ancient Christian Gospels* (London: SCM, 1990), 303–14.

[35] See D. Jacobs-Malina, *Beyond Patriarchy: The Images of Family in Jesus* (Mahwah, NJ: Paulist Press, 1993); K. Rahner, 'Ideas for a Theology of Childhood', *Theological Investigations* vol. VIII (London: Darton, Longman & Todd, 1971), 33–50.

first. In this we might just detect the influence of a wider perspective based upon that logion of Jesus which echoes the metaphorical significance of childhood, 'let the greatest among you become as the youngest' (Lk 22.26). Moreover it was in the intimacy of a household (Mk 9.33) that Jesus gave his teaching about the child and true greatness. Thus the particular exemplary significance of the child might have had continuing relevance in the (house) church's influence upon the household in interpreting the meaning of subordination.

3. In 1 Cor 7.12ff. Paul urges that a marriage between a believer and an unbeliever should continue in its validity. Significantly Paul concludes that the believer sanctifies the marriage with reference to the children of the marriage who are already also part thereby of the covenantal purpose of God (v 14). Whether Paul thought that the children were actually part of the membership of the church remains uncertain (though we may note 2 Tim 3.15, 'from infancy' – *apo brephous,* where the church obviously taught its faith to children, even very young children), but he simply accepts that faith is efficacious. That the children are considered to be holy may again be an echo of that unmerited love of God which in its covenantal significance underlay Jesus' blessing of the children who were brought to him.

4. At 1 Cor 13.11 and Gal 4.1ff, whilst Paul acknowledges a distinction between childhood and adulthood, the distinction is no longer controlled by social convention but by the experience of faith. Thus in the case of the former, a state of childhood in its immaturity is the condition of all existence (including adult existence) prior to the Parousia, whilst in the case of the latter, a state of childhood describes existence before the conferring of sonship in the gospel. Here the use of metaphor in what constitutes childhood and adulthood changes according to insights generated by faith and which transcend any particular social distinction.

5. We have already drawn attention to the church of Matthew with its understanding of childhood in the message of Jesus as a critique of the patriarchy inherent in wisdom tradition (summed up at Matt 23.9–10). The language which Paul uses of being a father to his children, whilst it reflects the role of *paterfamilias* in the household of the church (1 Cor 4.15; 1 Thess 2.11), nonetheless also shows flexibility in its use of family imagery. For example, the role of Paul's readers understood as children can make Paul

widen the metaphor from that of father to mother or wet nurse (1 Cor 3.1–2; 1 Thess 2.7; Gal 4.19). At 2 Cor 11.2 the church is his daughter, and at 2 Cor 12.14 he describes his relationship with the Corinthians not as father to children but, quoting an aphorism, as *parents* to children (where *goneis* is normally used when the reference is to both father and mother). This expansion of social metaphor around the image of the child reflects not so much Paul's personal authority as a father in a family but his own apostolic responsibility to Christ for the family of the church. That is to say, he is himself under authority as an apostle. This is reflected in the way in which Paul's varied metaphors change a notion of social hierarchy as, for example, in images which imply social equality rather than superiority (brothers, fellow-workers), and even express his social inferiority (1 Cor 4.11–12). It may be no accident that Paul's language sometimes corresponds closely to the gospel sayings of Jesus which explicitly reverse contemporary values by calling the least the greatest (cf. Mk 10.42–45 with 1 Cor 9.19; 2 Cor 1.24, 4.5) and which reflect the metaphorical significance of childhood in Jesus' teaching. Thus the idea of *paterfamilias,* in the social context of the day, may not be wholly adequate to the way in which Paul explores the nature of authority in the metaphorical use of childhood and parenthood.

6. Beyond the New Testament era (unless Mk 9.37 and 10.14 are thought to contain a reference to baptism), the development of infant baptism in the church surely also meant the crossing of another frontier in marking the full acceptance of the child within the Christian community. Here was a rite which accepted the child not as an adult before its time, nor as marking progression from childhood to adulthood, but which made the child for its own sake a full member of the community. Of course what this acceptance might signal for the child remained predominantly theoretical. Progress in respect for children and a decline in harsh treatment was slow.[36] But the influence of Christianity in recognising children as full members of the church in baptism

---

[36] See R. Lyman, 'Barbarism and Religion', 77ff; T. Wiedemann, *Adults and Children in the Roman Empire,* 176ff; G. Clark, 'The Fathers and the Children', in D. Wood, ed., *The Church and Childhood,* Studies in Church History Volume 31 (Oxford: Blackwell, 1994), 1–27.

(and indeed, with Judaism, as belonging to God from the womb – Ps 139.13–16, cf. 2 Esdras 8.7–14) helped to mitigate sexual abuse and infanticide – 'thou shalt not corrupt boys ... thou shalt not murder a child by abortion nor again shalt thou kill it when it is born' (Epistle of Barnabas 19, c. AD 130[37]).

Such instances as these, though oblique, may suggest a process not so much of adaptation to, but transformation of, the early church's social world. The early church had only the language of its social world upon which to draw, but it used this creatively to fashion a community in which service begins to transform the conventional nature of relationships based upon status and honour. Behind this we may detect something of the radical significance given to children by Jesus in the honour which he accorded them in the gift of the Kingdom and the significance he drew from them for discipleship.

Conclusion

To sum up, we can say that the New Testament understanding of children and childhood in its literal and metaphorical significance reflects much of the social outlook of its day. Children are part of the community of faith and receive the content of faith as this is passed on to them, with an especial emphasis being placed on the value of obedience. But there are also new insights which have the potential, at least, of transforming the role of the child in its social context. In so far as Jesus spoke of children as recipients in their own right of God's free grace in the gift of the Kingdom there is an emphasis placed not so much on what has to be transmitted to the child in its socialisation into community as potential adult, but upon the honour which a child should receive in and of itself.

And in the metaphorical significance of the child as an image of discipleship, whilst the New Testament shares a cultural critique of childishness, a remarkable emphasis is placed on childlikeness whereby it is not only the role of the child to be taught by the adult but that the adult may learn

---

[37] In this development the story of the Slaughter of the Innocents in Matt 2.13–18 was also influential – see R. Lyman, 'Barbarism and Religion,' 90ff.

lessons of faith from the child, and indeed must become as a child in trustful dependency and in the discovery of God in the marginalised. In particular such a mode of discipleship begins to work creatively within a range of social contexts by embodying a sense of service without servility in its openness to God. Such discipleship can both transcend, where necessary, the obligations of family, and also more generally be the basis of affirming the family. In this, not least of all, the person of Jesus himself becomes a role model in both his own childhood and childlikeness, through whose faithful obedience the Kingdom of God is brought near.

To be sure, our modern understanding of childhood is different from that of the ancient world. In the history of the awareness of childhood the church has been an agent both of change and of conformity, contributing to, and yet at times doing little for, the improvement of the lot of children. To this extent the full significance of the child in Jesus' teaching remains a vision for the church to realise. But in striving to realise that vision the church will learn new insights into the purpose and the pattern of its mission in the world. Where those insights are most especially to be learned in the contribution of the understanding of childhood to family may well be in a rediscovery of the role of power in human relationships. It is this theme which takes its course through the social context of the New Testament world in its oblique references to childhood as a predominantly marginal state within a patriarchal culture, which comes to a startling reappraisal in the teaching of Jesus about the powerless and the Kingdom of God, and which, as it imprints itself upon patterns of discipleship, shows the church occasionally seeking to transcend, and not merely to reflect, the culture of its day. Since power is part of all human relationships it is also an inherent part of relationships within the family (whatever precisely is meant by that term) in all its nurturing significance. The literal and metaphorical understanding of children and childhood in the New Testament has much to tell us of the role of power in this particular context where so much of who we are is shaped and fashioned, and where our imaging of the divine is also formed.

5

The Silent Majority: the Family in Patristic Thought

Carol Harrison

The family is not a subject the Fathers of the church turned to very often. When they did it is more often than not to depict the trials and tribulations of marriage and children in contrast to the serene, undisturbed life of the celibate ascetic; to make it clear that while marriage is a good, it is a relatively low one in the scale of perfection: virginity far excels it. Worse still, the majority of the Fathers regarded marriage and sex as part of Adam's punishment, as a result of the fall: 'For where death is, there is marriage', wrote Chrysostom.[1] Peter Brown's widely read and influential study of this central feature of patristic thought, *The Body and Society: Men, Women and Sexual Renunciation in Late Antiquity* (Columbia University Press, 1988), leaves the reader in no doubt that for most of the Fathers marriage and family life were definitely a second best, preferably to be avoided, and certainly not the place for the leaders, heroes and saints of the church.

Our subject is therefore not an easy one: it lurks, rather apologetically and shamefacedly, the result of weakness and compromise, in the dark shadow cast by the glorious ideal of virginity. It must necessarily be sought in a rather negative, roundabout way: we are told what is wrong with marriage, why one should refrain from sex, why children are to be avoided, but rarely, very rarely, find any mention of the positive aspects of family life. We obviously need to ask why this is the case – why the

---

[1] *On Virginity*, XIV, 6.

ascetic ideal was so prominent in the early church. But it seems to me that this is an unsatisfactory way of making a first approach to our subject. Having suggested why the family is not a central concern in patristic thought, I would prefer to leave such considerations until later and to turn first to the much more well-worked (in fact, rather over intensively worked) field of historical investigations into the nature of the Greco-Roman family. These studies obviously only bring us up to the end of the second century, the period from which we are really beginning our essay, but they provide an invaluable context in which to place Christian notions of family and to appreciate any changes which took place.

The Greco-Roman family and the teaching of the Fathers

No approach is without its problems, however, and here we are again limited by the nature of the evidence: the sheer size and diversity of the Roman Empire does not allow for generalisations; the sources are very much limited to a cultured élite, the wealthy, upper classes of the Roman Empire, for whom documentary and inscriptional evidence exists – in other words to 10–20 per cent of the population who are probably not at all representative of the remaining 80–90 per cent given the very stark distinction between slave and free. Moreover, we only hear from men, from lawyers, doctors, writers, theologians, writing from a male perspective for other men – the everyday life of women and children within a household or family can only be glimpsed, rather inadequately, through what is said on other subjects.

But there is still much that can be said. The Roman conception of family, *familia*, was very much based on the idea of the household or *domus*. It consisted of all those who made up a single household, typically, parents, their children, the children's carers and all other slaves employed by the house together with their children. It might also include lodgers, adopted children, and anyone else who happened to reside in the house for whatever reason. Each household or *domus* was ruled over by a *dominus* or master, usually the *paterfamilias*, the father and head of the family, who had virtually absolute power and authority over its inhabitants (including the right of execution).[2] The household was thought of as part of the natural order, the basic unit of society, upon which the city, and ultimately the state, was built. The joining of male and female, their children and household, were, as Cicero put it, the 'seed-bed' of the state.[3] The *paterfamilias* therefore stood between, and mediated between, the household and the larger society in which it had its place. In essence, the household was a miniature state over which he ruled, its unity and harmony ensuring the well-being of the state. The family was therefore a much wider entity than the nuclear family as we know it today, comprehending a more complex set of relationships, in a broader context, thereby forming an important, if not *the* most important social, economic and political entity in the Roman state. Chrysostom, especially, used these ideas in a Christian context to stress the need for model Christian households, organised according to Christian principles, as little churches making up the wider church.[4] Augustine, in *City of God* XIX stresses the role of the *paterfamilias* in securing peace in the state by maintaining peace by just government of his household according to the rules of the state.

Cicero's definition of the origin of society is also the Roman definition of marriage: 'the joining (*coniugium*) of man and woman'.[5] For much of our period marriage remained a secular event, albeit with a priest's or bishop's blessing.[6] Whilst the Fathers always discouraged second or further marriages, they did not forbid them. They were, however, very reluctant to allow inter-marriage between a pagan and a Christian because of the

[2] Ulpian, *Digest*, 50, 16.195, 'In the strict legal sense we call a *familia* a number of people who are by birth or by law subjected to the *potestas* (power) of one man, e.g., *paterfamilias*...' 2(i). Quoted in J. F. Gardner and T. Wiedemann, *The Roman Household : A Sourcebook* (London: Routledge, 1993), 3.

[3] *On Duties*, 1, 17, 54, 'The origin of society is in the joining (*coniugium*) of man and woman, next in children, then in the household (*una domus*), all things held in common; this is the foundation (*principium*) of the city and, so to speak, the seed-bed of the state (*seminarium rei publicae*)'. Quoted in B. D. Shaw, 'The Family in Late Antiquity: The Experience of Augustine', *Past and Present* 115 (1987) 11. He quotes two similar passages in Augustine (*City of God*, 15.16.3; *On the Good of Marriage*, 1, 1) and notes that such ideas are heavily Stoic in tone.

[4] *Homily 20 on Ephes 5.22–33*. C. P. Roth, *Saint John Chrysostom on Marriage and Family Life* (Crestwood, NY: SVS Press, 1986), 57.

[5] Ulpian, *Digest*, 23.2.1.

[6] Roth, 12.

obvious difficulties and compromises this would set in the way of fulfilling Christian duties and observances. By the fourth century, however, Peter Brown points out that the practice was much more tolerated: Augustine could say that whereas it was regarded as a sin by Cyprian it was now no longer avoided as such.[7] The official line, however, remained unchanged: the Council of Chalcedon in 451 still forbade marriage between a Christian and a non-Christian or heretic unless the latter converted to Christianity (Canon 14).

What was uniformly condemned by the church was the Roman practice of concubinage – a sort of 'common-law' marriage which had no legal status, and therefore entailed no legal rights for the children of such partnerships. Divorce, too, though common in Roman experience, and quite straightforward, in that it simply required notification of intent, was also condemned by the Fathers (and Christian emperors) – with only a few exceptions, for example, in the case of adultery.[8]

The very early age at which people married (the minimum age for girls was 12 and 14 for boys – though the evidence is unclear as to when exactly they did marry) was obviously due to financial, social and political reasons in the upper class families for whom we have evidence, but was perhaps also partly attributable to the very short average life expectancy of about 21 years for adults, and the horrifically high rate of infant mortality and death in childbirth. It has been estimated that each woman would have to bear at least five children to keep the population stable.[9] Despite the high rate of infant mortality, the falling population and attempts by successive emperors to encourage free citizens to have more children with legal rewards or penalties, contracep-

[7] *On Faith and Works,* 21.37 cited in P. Brown, *Religion and Society in the Age of Saint Augustine* (London: Faber & Faber, 1972), 'The Christianization of the Roman Aristocracy', 172.

[8] See G. Clark, *Women in Late Antiquity* (Oxford: Oxford University Press, 1993), ch. on 'Law and Morality', on the double standard between men and women in these matters. She also makes clear just how difficult it was for Christians to change traditional moral customs – in their own lives and in society at large – and how the legislation of Christian emperors, for pagans and Christians, could not, and did not intend to, keep pace with the church.

[9] These figures are found in Gardner and Wiedemann (88) who suggest that a third of children died before the age of 1, less than half survived to 5, only 40 per cent reached 20 and one in ten reached 60.

tion, as well as child selling, infanticide, exposure and abortion are not uncommon in our sources, though it is extremely difficult to say just how and when they were practised. The Fathers were to set Christianity apart in their adoption of a strict code of sexual behaviour, set out in the rulings of church councils,[10] which would not tolerate these practices: contraception was to make one's wife a prostitute, abortion was murder. They repeatedly insisted that intercourse should be for the purpose of conception alone (though tacitly, and even explicitly, acknowledging that this was, in fact, rarely the case: 'Never, in friendly conversation' comments Augustine, 'have I heard anyone who is or who has been married say that he never had intercourse with his wife except when hoping for conception'[11]).

The Fathers have very little indeed to say about children except to urge that they should be lovingly received, brought up with tender care and, most importantly, given a religious education.[12] Oddly, in a religion which has as its centre the relation of Father and Son, we learn almost nothing of the affective bonds between children and other members of the household.

The other main group in the household, which would often far outnumber the nuclear family, were slaves – for them, as Pliny puts it, 'the household is a sort of state, a substitute community'.[13] Until the third century slaves were not allowed to marry – though some masters allowed marriage within their own households. Slave family groupings were therefore very fragile and impermanent and could easily be broken up by sale or separation. Although the roles of slaves in a Christian household is discussed, for example in Book XIX of Augustine's *City of God*, the Fathers did not condemn slavery as an institution and Christian emperors simply legislated to remedy some of the obvious hardships of slave life: Constantine, for example, ruled that slave families should not be broken up – in other words, property rights should not take precedence over the bonds of the family.

---

[10] Peter Brown, *Religion and Society*, 206, cites the example of the Council of Elvira which devotes 34 of the 81 rulings to matters concerning marriage and sexual misdeeds.

[11] *On the Good of Marriage*, 13.15 (quoted by B. D. Shaw art. cit., 44 n. 185).

[12] E.g. Augustine's *Literal Commentary on Genesis* IX, 7, 12; Chrysostom, *Homily 21 on Ephes 6.1–4* (Roth, 67–71).

[13] Letter 8, 16.

Until the advent of Christian asceticism, marriage was very much the only option for a woman. As we have seen, it was arranged very early by the person in whose *potestas* she lived, and was transacted financially by a dowry, over which she retained rights (thereby gaining some degree of financial security and insurance against desertion or bereavement). Despite marriage she usually remained very much a member of her original family, under the *potestas* of her father, and kept her maiden name. Her children, however, were legally under the *potestas* of her husband, and unless freed by Augustus' *ius liberorum* for having produced three or more children, she had no rights over them and could not even act as their guardian on her husband's death, until a later period (and only then if she did not re-marry). The woman's sphere was the private one of the household; the man's, the public one of the city. The Fathers tended to see this division of responsibilities as divinely ordained. As Chrysostom observes,

> In general our life is composed of two spheres of activity, the public and the private. When God divided these two He assigned the management of the household to the woman, but to the man he assigned all the affairs of the city, all the business of the marketplace, courts, council-chambers, armies, and all the rest. A woman cannot throw a spear or hurl a javelin, but she can take up a distaff, weave cloth, and manage everything else that concerns the household... God provided for peace by reserving the suitable position for each.[14]

In an illuminating passage Tertullian lists the excuses helpless males give for getting married and in the process gives us a good idea of the sort of tasks a wife might be expected to perform: taking care of the house, controlling the domestics, keeping an eye on coffers and keys, supervising the spinning, managing the kitchen, sharing cares and responsibilities.[15] He also provides us with a rare and fascinating description of the duties of a Christian in the course of advising against marriage to a pagan (who would hinder their performance). The devout wife visits strangers, calls at hovels, attends evening devotions, spends all night away for

---

[14] *How to Choose a Wife* (Roth, 96–7).
[15] *An Exhortation to Charity*, 12. Cf. Chrysostom, *The Kind of Women who should be taken as Wives*, 4.

Paschal vigils, attends the Lord's Supper, visits prisons to kiss martyrs' fetters, washes the feet of saints and gives them food and drink, offers hospitality to fellow-Christians at her house. She could do none of these, without inviting suspicion, if married to a pagan.[16] But in general the Fathers seem to suggest that a married woman's lot is a highly unenviable one – one to be avoided if at all possible because of the inevitable chronic pain and suffering it entails. Long rhetorical descriptions of the trials of marriage – the *molestiae nuptiarum* – are a recurrent literary theme or *topos* in their works – especially in works on virginity.

It is an odd fact that we learn more about the Father's attitude to marriage and family life through treatises advising, or urging the reader to adopt, the ascetic life of a virgin, than anywhere else. In these, the horrors of marriage and family life are depicted in all their appalling reality: the shame and sorrow of infertility, the discomforts of pregnancy, the risks of childbirth, worry about one's children, the drudgery of childrearing and housework, problems with servants, family quarrels, the death of family members, abusive, violent, jealous husbands, constant worry about a husband's fidelity, his health and safety, and finally widowhood.[17] Prefacing a similar catalogue in his *On Virginity*, Gregory of Nyssa comments, 'If only, before experience comes, the results of experience could be learnt... then what a crowd of deserters would run from marriage into the virgin life'.[18] Marriage, in effect, becomes servitude.[19] Indeed, since divorce is not allowed to Christians, it is worse than slavery: slaves at least have the chance of buying back their freedom whereas, as Chrysostom observes, the Christian couple are like fugitive slaves whose legs have been shackled together: if they wish to move at all, they are forced to limp together.[20]

---

[16] *To his Wife*, II, 4.

[17] See D. Amand and M. Ch. Moons, 'Une Curieuse Homélie Grècque sur la Virginité' *Revue Benedictine* 63 (1953), 211–38; Augustine, *On Holy Virginity*, 5. See E. A. Clark, *Ascetic Piety and Women's Faith: Essays on Late Antique Christianity* (Lewiston, NY: E. Mellen, 1986), 261 n. 140 for references to lists of *topoi* on this theme.

[18] *On Virginity*, 3.

[19] Ibid.; Jerome, *Letter xlvii to Pammachius*, 14.

[20] *On Virginity*, XXVIII, 1. Cited by E. A. Clark, *Ascetic Piety*, 'Introduction to Chrysostom: On Virginity; Against Remarriage', 245.

And what of relations between the two enslaved individuals? Having warned people off marriage, or at least exhorted them to virginity, the Fathers could not close their eyes to the silent majority: the vast majority of their congregations who were indeed married men and women with families, suffering the very trials they so vividly depict. It is very difficult to assess just what the married couple's expectations of their union would be. Law codes and funerary epigraphs reveal something of the standard virtues expected of a woman: devotion, modesty, thrift, chastity, fidelity, hard work, reliability, a ready acceptance to remain at home, a good mother. Hardly romantic ideals, but then this could scarcely be expected, nor was it sought, in arranged marriages. The highest expectation and greatest achievement for a married couple seems to have been *concordia*, or harmony, an expression of the ideal harmony of society.[21]

Both Chrysostom in the East and Augustine in the West emphasise that Christian marriage is founded on friendship, fellowship, and a certain equality between the partners. Both make the point that God created Adam and Eve together, that they belong together and thus fulfil each other, forming the first unit of human society. Augustine writes, 'Since every person is part of the human race and human nature is something social and has in itself the power of friendship as a great good, God willed for this reason to create all humans from one person, so that they might be held fast in their society not only by likeness of descent, but also by the bond of relationship. Thus the first tie of natural human society is husband and wife.'[22] He describes the married couple as those who are 'joined one to another side by side, who walk together, and look together where they walk'.[23] In the light of such passages Elizabeth Clark refers to a 'socially

---

[21] There is much artistic evidence for this in, e.g., marriage rings and belts. See G. Vikan, 'Art and Marriage in Early Byzantium', in *Dumbarton Oaks Papers* No. 44 (1990), 145–63.

[22] *On the Good of Marriage*, 1 (translation by E. A. Clark). Chrysostom writes, '...in the beginning woman came forth from man, and from man and woman other men and women proceed. God ... did not, on the one hand, fashion woman independently from man, otherwise man would think of her as essentially different from himself. Nor did he enable women to bear children without man; if this were the case she would be self-sufficient... The love of husband and wife is the force that binds society together...' *Homily 20 on Ephes 5.22–33*.

[23] *On the Good of Marriage*, 1. Cf. 3 and 9.

oriented' or 'companionate' view of marriage, which comple-
ments the more dominant and well-known sexual/reproductive
picture of marriage in Augustine's thought.[24] He develops such
a view most especially in relation to the marriage of Mary and
Joseph, which was a marriage even though there was no sexual
relation between the partners. Mary and Joseph are called husband and wife because 'intercourse of the mind is more intimate
than that of the body'.[25] In *On the Good of Marriage* he makes it
clear that it is not the 'voluptuous connection of the body', as he
puts its, but the 'pledge of affection of the soul' that makes a
marriage.[26]

A marriage of minds, based upon mutual affection, is also the
ideal that underlies Chrysostom's exegesis of Ephes 5.22–33: if a
husband expects obedience from his wife, as the head expects
obedience from the body, then he should love his wife as Christ
did his body, the church: he must be prepared to suffer, and even
die, for his wife – and even then, he is doing no more than
Christ.[27] A wife is, he writes, 'one's partner for life, the mother of
one's children, the source of one's every joy [she] should never
be fettered with fear and threats, but with love and patience ...
what sort of satisfaction could a husband himself have, if he lives
with his wife as if she were a slave, and not with a woman by her
own free will?'[28] Augustine is inspired to similar reflections in
commenting on the First Epistle of John and, with Chrysostom,
he urges that, like Christ, a husband should seek to sanctify his
wife, to make her holy and without blemish,[29] to be the agent of
her salvation.[30]

The Fathers held that marriage was sacramental, in the sense
that it was a human institution that disclosed profound truths
about the Christian faith. It is on such texts as Ephes 5 and
Gen 2, the creation of Eve from Adam's rib while he slept, likened

[24] 'Adam's Only Companion: Augustine and the Early Christian Debate on
Marriage', *Recherches Augustinienne* (1986), 139–62.
[25] *Against Faustus*, XXIII, 8 (quoted by Clark, art. cit., 150 n. 32). Cf. *The
Harmony of the Gospels*, II, 1, 2; II, 1, 3.
[26] *On the Good of Marriage*, 12. Cf. Sermon 51, 13, 21.
[27] *Homily 20 on Ephes 5.22–33* (Roth, 46).
[28] Ibid. (Roth, 47).
[29] Ibid. (Roth, 56).
[30] Augustine, *On the Good of Marriage*, 11.

to the blood and water which issued from Christ's pierced side at his death,[31] that their teaching hinges.[32] Sacramentality also meant indissolubility, and distinguished the church's teaching from Roman divorce law – most especially, it got rid of the double standard whereby the actions of an adulterous husband would be overlooked but an adulterous wife punished. Perhaps more importantly, it set the church's understanding of marriage apart from secular perceptions: Christian marriage was a mysterious bonding of two individuals, a holy, sanctifying union of mutual love, friendship, respect and self-giving. The behaviour of the Christian couple was therefore also distinctive: their household, as we have seen, was to become a little church, characterised by simplicity, sobriety, faithfulness. The couple should pray, fast and attend church together, take communion together, discuss the meaning of the prayers and readings,[33] instruct and encourage one another, sing psalms to one another, give alms, have no secrets from one another and have no fear about fulfilling their Christian duties.[34] 'How beautiful then,' Tertullian observes, is 'the marriage of two Christians, two who are one in hope, one in desire, one in the way of life they follow, one in the religion they practice.... Nothing divides them, either in flesh or spirit'.[35] Leaving their parents they became one with their partner, forming a new relationship which immediately became more powerful than their long-established familiarity with their own families. Even sex and children can take on a sacramental character in this context: 'How do they become one flesh?', Chrysostom asks. 'As if she were gold receiving the purest gold, the woman receives the man's seed with rich pleasure, and within her it is nourished, cherished and refined. It is mingled with her own substance and then she returns it as a child! The child is the bridge connecting mother and father, so the three become one flesh, as when two cities divided by a river are joined by a bridge, and here that bridge is formed from the substance of each.'[36]

---

[31] E.g. Chrysostom, *How to Choose a Wife* (Roth, 93–4).

[32] Augustine, *On Marriage and Concupiscence*, I, 10.11; *On the Good of Marriage*, 17, 21

[33] Chrysostom, *Homily 20 on Ephes 5.22–33* (Roth, 61).

[34] Tertullian, *To his Wife*, 9 – a long passage describing the beauty of Christian marriage.

[35] Ibid.

[36] Chrysostom, *Homily 12 on Colossians 4.18* (Roth, 76).

All this is what we might expect the Fathers to say if we did not know them better; I have dwelt on these very positive notes because, although they are not sounded very often, and are usually drowned out by exhortations to virginity, they are most definitely there when the Fathers come face to face either with their own wives, as in Tertullian's case, or with their married congregations, as is the case with Chrysostom and Augustine.

Marriage and virginity

But I have delayed long enough: we must now ask directly, why the emphasis upon sexual renunciation and the very negative attitude to marriage, sexuality and the family which this engenders? The first point to make is that respect for asceticism was general in late antiquity. The 'high moral ground' meant not the gentle slopes of decency, as nowadays, but the commanding heights of asceticism which Christianity occupied and exploited in the sense that the ascetic life secured an unquestioned *authority* for its practitioners which it was difficult to attain in any other way in ancient society. (Though this is not to suggest that individual Christians would see their asceticism in this way – rather that asceticism, undertaken for other reasons, carried with it an authority which perhaps then encouraged and furthered its growth in popularity.) If one seeks further, one often finds the conviction that unity is true reality and the manifold a declension from it: in these terms the single state affirmed solidarity with unity over against marriage and reproduction. This is of a piece with the short answer to our question we find in the Fathers, that before the fall, in their original state of paradisal perfection, Adam and Eve were either a virginal couple[37] or sexless:[38] there was no marriage, no intercourse, no children – these are all a result of the fall and symptomatic of man's fallenness. 'Where there is marriage, there is death';[39] intercourse and children are measures to counter man's loss of immortality at the fall[40] – they are a sort of solace for man's loss

[37] E.g. Jerome, *Against Jovinian*, I, 16.
[38] Gregory of Nyssa, *On the Making of Man*, 12.9, quoted by P. Brown, *Religion and Society*, 294.
[39] Chrysostom, *On Virginity*, XIV, 6.
[40] E.g. Gregory of Nyssa, *On Virginity*, 12.

of virginity,[41] a concession to his weakness.[42] Why else was Eve created, but that God foresaw that she would cause Adam to fall, and 'for the sake of human reproduction, woman had to be added to the man',[43] as Ambrose puts it. If Adam had simply needed a companion, then God would of course have created another man, observes Augustine as something self-evident.[44] What would have happened in Paradise if Adam and Even had not fallen is obviously a matter of pure speculation, especially since God foresaw the fall, but some of the Fathers do comment either that Adam would have reproduced in some sort of non-sexual way,[45] or that God could have created other human beings in the same manner as the angels and archangels;[46] marriage and the family are not envisaged – with a few notable exceptions to which I will return later.

The Fathers vary in the degree to which this very dark picture of marriage and the family penetrates their thought. What I propose to do in the next section of this essay is work through the spectrum of opinion, from the gloomiest and darkest view to glimmerings of a more positive, even if defensive, outlook on the family.

Marriage and the family

There were a few (heretical) sects which rejected marriage and the family outright: the Encratites (from *enkrateia* – continence) held that continence was a means of overcoming the bondage of the present age and that marriage to Christ's spirit excluded ordinary marriage;[47] the Montanists similarly believed that continence brought down the gift of Christ's spirit; Marcionites also thought that it liberated a person from the present age and would bring about its end; Gnostics and Manichees saw it as avoiding involvement in evil, created matter and as freeing the divine

[41] Chrysostom, *On Virginity*, XIV, 5.
[42] Ibid. XV, 2; Methodius of Olympus, *Symposium*, 3, 10.78–13.89, quoted by Peter Brown, *Religion and Society*, 185.
[43] *On Paradise*, X, 47.
[44] *Literal Commentary on Genesis*, 9, 3, 5; 9, 5, 9.
[45] Maximus the Confessor, *Ambigua*, 41.
[46] Chrysostom, *On Virginity*, XIV, 6.
[47] See Peter Brown, *Religion and Society*, 90–1.

spark in man. Escape from the present and union with God are the common features of these extreme sects.

The majority of the Fathers are more moderate and Eusebius of Caesarea's delineation of 'two ways' in his *Proof of the Gospel* is characteristic of their thought and worth quoting here:

> Two ways of life were thus given by the Lord to His Church. The one is above nature and beyond common human living; it admits not marriage, childbearing, property nor the possession of wealth... Like some celestial beings, these gaze down upon human life, performing the duty of a priesthood to Almighty God for the whole human race... And the more humble, more human way prompts men to join in pure nuptials, and to produce children, to undertake government, to give orders to soldiers fighting for right; it allows them to have minds for farming, for trade and for the other more secular interests as well as for religion.[48]

Marriage and the family are not rejected here, but set alongside a life of asceticism and celibacy as an alternative 'way' – a marriage in the flesh as opposed to one in the spirit, as Gregory of Nyssa puts it.[49] We are left in no doubt as to which is the superior way, the way of the élite, but the way for lesser mortals, that of the silent majority, married and belonging to a family, is acknowledged and accepted. But it is most definitely a lower way – how low depends on who one reads, and in what context. Jerome is well known for his invective against Jovinian who had dared to interpret the Song of Songs in relation to Christian marriage and to suggest that marriage is, in fact, on a par with virginity. For Jerome a first marriage is a regrettable weakness – its only purpose being the conversion of other members of the household, the education of a new Christian generation and the production of Christian ascetics;[50] second marriage is only one step from the brothel, like a dog returning to its vomit. Jerome's views were obviously felt to be extreme by his contemporaries and we see him attempting to moderate or defend them in letters

[48] *The Proof of the Gospel* 1.48 (in W. J. Ferrar, trans.) quoted in Peter Brown, *Body and Society*, 205.

[49] *On Virginity*, 20.

[50] *Epistle* 107, 1 (cited by A. Yarbrough, 'Christianization in the Fourth Century: The Example of Roman Woman', *Church History* 76 (1945), 162).

written to a certain Pammachius. He points out that he is no
Marcionite, Manichee or Encratite, he does not condemn marriage even though he does not praise it, rather it is like wood and
pottery, in contrast to gold and silver in a household: it is of lower
value but still necessary.[51] What *he* has said about marriage is no
more or less favourable than most Latin authors. 'Read them' he
urges 'and in their company curse me or free me'.[52] And of course
a comparative reading supports him.

Most Fathers would, however, add procreation and the controlling of lust to the purposes of marriage: it 'makes us chaste
and makes us parents', as Chrysostom puts it.[53] But then they
usually add that procreation, which, in the beginning, necessitated the creation of Eve[54] and justified the Patriarchs' taking of
a number of wives,[55] is now no longer necessary. This was either
because, like Tertullian, they thought the end to be near –
Christians, 'for whom there is no tomorrow', need no longer be
concerned about posterity[56] he observes – or because hope in the
resurrection makes the desire for children superfluous. Now
that, as Augustine comments, 'there is a vast crowd from all
nations to fill up the number of the saints', what was at first a duty
for man – the begetting of children – is no longer necessary and
is at best a healing remedy for those who are sick[57] – in other
words to control lust. It is in this context that one can appreciate
the Father's frequently reiterated observation that marriage is
good but virginity is better. Spiritual relations and the fruits of the
spirit are infinitely preferable to physical relations and their
fruits – it was to these spiritual relations that Jesus referred when
he asked in the Gospel, 'Who is my mother? Who are my
brothers?'. Now that marriage and the family are no longer
necessary, the number of the saints having been made up, the
resurrected life promised, the individual who is not weighed

---

[51] *To Pammachius*, XLIX, 1.
[52] Ibid. XLIX, 17.
[53] *Sermon on Marriage* (Roth, 85).
[54] Augustine, *Literal Commentary on Genesis*, 9, 3, 5; 9, 5, 9.
[55] Augustine, *On the Good of Marriage*, 19; 21.
[56] Tertullian, *Exhortation to Chastity*, 12. Cf. Augustine, *On the Good of Marriage*,
32.
[57] *Literal Commentary on Genesis*, 9, 7, 12; *On the Good of Marriage*, 5–6. Cf.
Chrysostom, *On Virginity*, 19, 1–2.

down by the chains of lust is free to seek the paradisal existence of Adam and Eve unfettered by the cares and troubles of a family.

What is significant and interesting for our purposes is that when the Fathers describe and celebrate the spiritual life, the life of virginity and asceticism, it is more often than not in language and imagery derived from marriage, sexual intercourse and the family.[58] Not only is the church the Bride of Christ and Christ her Bridegroom, the Virgin is Christ's wife and lover; He is her husband and unites himself to her in a spiritual marriage bond. The spiritual fruits of this union are 'the offspring of devotion', born of the spirit. In a letter to the virgin Eustochium, Jerome goes so far as to refer to her mother as the 'mother-in-law of God' in virtue of Eustochium's marriage to Christ. The marriage is described in highly charged erotic language taken from the Song of Songs: Eustochium flies to Jesus her lover and united with him cries 'Many waters cannot quench love, neither can the floods drown it'.[59] The monastic life is also often perceived in familial terms and indeed fulfilled many of the functions often attributed to families. The brothers or sisters had a father or mother superior, for example, and a nun might be betrothed by her mother Abbess to her Bridegroom, Christ.[60] The household and the life of the virgin ascetic also often overlapped in the case of a daughter (or even a son) who remained at home, under the protection of her father (who is in one text referred to as 'priest of the Most High'), to dedicate her life to virginity.[61] In this way, either as a solitary or in a larger community, women freed themselves from the constraints of family and child-bearing and attained a significant degree of freedom and independence in a society largely under male control. Whether this was a deliberate protest against patriarchy, as some feminist critics might have us believe, is another matter. In any case, it is worth noting that although, for many of the Fathers, the family represented man's fallen condition, it can also be used as a paradigm for man's

[58] E.g. *On the Good of Marriage*, 21; *On Holy Virginity*, 2.11; 48; 55; Gregory of Nyssa, *On Virginity*, 20; Jerome, *Letter 22* to Eustochium.

[59] *Letter 22*, 41 – quoted by E. A. Clark, *Ascetic Piety*, 'Devil's Gateway and Bride of Christ: Women in the Early Christian World', 28–9.

[60] See Alice Mary Talbot, 'The Byzantine Family and the Monastery', in *Dumbarton Oaks Papers* No. 44 (1990), 119–30.

[61] On this subject see D. Amand and M. Ch. Moons, art. cit. n. 17 above.

highest calling and achievement, underlining the fact it was thought to be a good, albeit a lower one; not something to be ultimately rejected in favour of asceticism, but something to be transformed.

Indeed, it is in their reaction against various extreme forms of asceticism that the Fathers can be seen defending marriage and the family. In the early centuries it fell to theologians such as Clement of Alexandria to counter the Gnostics. Their hostility to creation, which they regarded as the work of an alien, evil, creator God, and their consequent extreme asceticism, distancing themselves from the body and matter as much as possible, and especially from intercourse which would only serve to propagate more evil matter, undermined the Christian notion of a creator God responsible for a fundamentally good creation. Clement defends the goodness of marriage and procreation by, in the first instance, redefining celibacy or continence. He stresses that 'it does not pertain just to sexual desire, but to everything that the soul wickedly desires when it rests discontent with the basic necessities'. True celibacy, then, is a matter of controlling our desire, and is therefore equally applicable to married and unmarried. So, someone who wants to marry, he observes, must discipline himself in continence, 'so that it is not desire he experiences for his wife, whom he ought to love, and so that he may beget children with a decorous and temperate will'.[62] Both the married and the unmarried should attempt not to yield to lesser things and to serve God in their different ways: the married man takes care of wife and children, and for Clement this is a much greater testing ground than celibacy: 'True manhood is shown', he comments, 'not in the choice of celibate life; on the contrary, the prize in the contest of men is won by him who has trained himself by the discharge of the duties of husband and father, and by the supervision of a household'.[63] Gregory of Nyssa also suggests a similar redefinition of virginity, when he talks of it, not as sexual abstinence, but as singleness of heart and mind, or disengagedness of heart and mind – this is obviously easier for someone who leads a celibate life than for one caught up in the cares of married life, but insofar as a married person can attain

[62] *Miscellanies*, III, 7, 8. Cf. III, 1, 4.
[63] Ibid. VII, 12, 70.

this he too is attaining 'virginity'. Chrysostom puts this succinctly in a homily on 1 Cor 7 ('those who have wives should be as if they had them not'): '...virginity does not simply mean sexual abstinence. She who is anxious about worldly affairs is not really a virgin. In fact, he [that is, Christ] says that this is the chief difference between a wife and a virgin. He does not mention marriage or abstinence, but attachment as opposed to detachment from worldly cares.'[64] The point to be stressed here is that the antithesis between continence and marriage is not as total as it might first appear in the Fathers and that sex, in this instance, is not the main issue.

Marriage is given perhaps its most positive evaluation against the Gnostics' fourth-century successors, the Manichees. Sex comes to the fore again here, in Augustine's defence of sex and marriage as part of God's original creation and not as a result of the fall. Although at first Augustine interpreted the command of God in Genesis to 'increase and multiply' in a spiritual sense, rather than in reference to human intercourse, Elizabeth Clark suggests[65] that he was moved to temper these early ascetic leanings by the debate between Jovinian and Jerome already mentioned. Jovinian had attacked extreme ascetics such as Jerome by calling them Manichees, and Augustine could see that Jerome had indeed gone too far in his denigration of marriage. An 'earthier', more literal interpretation of Genesis, in which marriage is seen as part of man's original condition, even in Paradise, served Augustine to counter this extremism and defend *himself* against charges of remaining a Manichee (he had been one for almost ten years before his conversion). What this means is that Augustine (almost alone among the Fathers) taught that Adam and Eve were a married couple: Eve was created for the purpose of procreation, and when God blessed them he said 'Increase and multiply and fill the earth and subdue it'. So, although Scripture says that it was after their expulsion from Paradise that sexual intercourse and children happened (Gen 4.1), Augustine

---

[64] *Homily 19 on 1 Cor. 7* (Roth, 41).
[65] See her thesis outlined in 'Heresy, Asceticism, Adam and Eve: Interpretations of Gen 1–3 in the Later Latin Fathers' in *Ascetic Piety*, 353f. Also 'Adam's Only Companion: Augustine and the Early Christian Debate on Marriage', *Recherches Augustinienne* (1986), 139–62.

writes, 'I do not see what could have prohibited them from honourable nuptial union and the bed undefiled even in Paradise... so that without the tumultuous ardour of passion and without any labour and pain of childbirth, offspring would be born from their seed.'[66] If this had happened, he comments, there would be no death, rather, all the inhabitants of paradise would have remained in the prime of life until the determined number was complete, when they would be transformed into spiritual bodies. Offspring would have been desired, not as remedy against death, but as companions for life.[67] In this, we are given a rare glimpse of human society, based upon marriage and the family, as part of the original and intended human condition and part of its ultimate destiny. In terms of the Fathers' thought world, there is probably no better defence of marriage and the family, or higher evaluation of it, than this.

I would like to mention one other, less well-known Western theologian in this context – a Roman priest commonly known to us under the name of Ambrosiaster – since in many respects he foreshadows the very positive teaching of Augustine we have just outlined. He too was probably reacting against what he perceived to be the unacceptably extreme ascetic stance of various individuals in the Roman Church, such as Jerome, and probably represents a current of Christian resistance to asceticism among the socially conservative and theologically traditional Roman Church in the last few decades of the fourth century, which is also present in two authors whom Jerome had occasion to write against in this context, Helvidius and Vigilantius[68] and which will later be seen in Jovinian. In his little-known treatise, *On the sin of Adam and Eve (De Peccato Adae et Evae)*, he puts forward a number of arguments to defend marriage and childbearing which one cannot help but think give voice to the otherwise largely unarticulated views of the 'silent majority' of married Christians with children who were seeking to lead a life in society.

---

[66] *Literal Commentary on Genesis* 9, 3, 6. Cf. *City of God*, XIV, 26.

[67] Ibid., 9, 9, 14.

[68] In his *Against Helvidius and Against Vigilantius*. I am indebted to D. J. Hunter's excellent article in *Harvard Theological Review* 82.3 (July 1989) entitled, '"*On the sin of Adam and Eve*": A little-known Defence of Marriage and Childbearing by Ambrosiaster', to which I refer the reader for a detailed analysis of Ambrosiaster's arguments.

Christianity was an intrinsic part of late antiquity and the first part of this essay attempted to set the Fathers' attitude to the family firmly within this context. We saw that they shared the common late antique regard for asceticism and celibacy. In seeking to elucidate their ideas we have been forced to listen to an élite minority which rather tends to drown out the voice of the silent majority of married Christian people. But we have found that various things can be heard above the deafening clamour for virginity, and even within it, it is in the language of love and marriage that the Fathers advance the ascetic, virgin ideal.

And what, finally, might a Christian theology of the family learn from the Fathers? We have seen that the diversity of their views makes a single Patristic theology of the family impossible. If we were to extract what seems of enduring relevance and importance it would be the views of those for whom virginity is above all singleness of mind and heart, rather than sexual abstinence, and for whom marriage is a sacramental relationship, one of equality, fellowship and friendship, witnessing to man's original nature and his ultimate destiny as a social being, created to be part of society, and to marriage as the basic social relation from which all else derives and in which all coheres.

6

The Family, Marriage and the Upbringing of Children in Protestant England

Anthony Fletcher

The sixteenth-century European Reformation has come to be seen by historians as related to a transition towards a stable patriarchal society.[1] Central to this was the church's advocacy of marriage for all, an implicit rejection of the long tradition which distrusted sex. The Reformation therefore involved a reconsideration of the place of sexuality in family and social life. Yet, at the same time, men retained their fundamental presumption that patriarchy was the order of creation. So marriage was to be seen as a relation of hierarchy. I shall start by considering the contribution of Puritan advice book writers on this theme in the early seventeenth century. Later in the essay I will expand the discussion to include analysis of their views upon the upbringing of boys and girls. My central concern is with the relationship between religion and gender codes, in prescription and practice, in early modern England.

Husband and wife

The English conduct book writers, themselves from the first generation of married pastors, saw it as their task to model the patriarchal family afresh for this new world. It was entirely predictable that they should do so. In the Puritan circles in which

---

[1] L. Roper, *Oedipus and the Devil: Witchcraft, Sexuality and Religion in Early Modern Europe* (London: Routledge, 1994), 37.

107

they moved there was constant talk about the godly household. Its premise was that the family could only exist as a hierarchy. Its main features were the absolute authority of the male head, the subordination of women and the disciplined upbringing of children. Its purpose was that it should act as a bedrock of evangelisation. 'If ever we would have the church of God to continue among us', wrote Richard Greenham, 'we must bring it into our households and nourish it in our families.'[2] 'The family is a seminary of the church and commonwealth', declared John Downame, 'and as a private school, wherein children and servants are fitted for public assemblies.'[3] Samuel Ward traced all 'scandals and enormities' in the commonwealth to parental neglect of religious education and discipline of children and servants.[4] 'First reform your own families and then you will be fitter to reform the family of God', Edmund Calamy told MPs in a sermon of 1642. 'You are like to see no general reformation till you procure family reformation', warned Richard Baxter in a treatise of 1655.[5] Classical ideas, transmitted by sixteenth-century humanists, certainly contributed to this spiritualisation of the household. William Perkins cited Aristotle as his source for the image of the family as the 'seminary of all other societies' which, righteously governed, was 'a direct means for the good ordering both of church and commonwealth'.[6] But the main impetus came from a moral ethic that is distinctly Protestant. The Reformation was at the same time a religious movement and a social movement. Gender relations, it has been shown persuasively, were at the crux of it in the German city of Augsburg. So too were they in the conception of moral and religious reform propagated by English Puritan divines. Lyndal Roper's conclusion that a 'politics of women's role in marriage and the household' was a key to the successful implementation of the German Reforma-

---

[2] Cited in C. Hill, *Society and Puritanism in Pre-Revolutionary England* (London: Secker & Warburg, 1964), 443.

[3] Cited in J. Morgan, *Godly Learning* (Cambridge: Cambridge University Press, 1986), 142–3.

[4] Cited in M. Todd, *Christian Humanism and the Puritan Social Order* (Cambridge: Cambridge University Press, 1987), 100.

[5] Cited in Hill, *Society and Puritanism*, 444–5.

[6] Todd, *Christian Humanism*, 96–117.

tion can be applied equally to the Reformation in England in the decades between the 1560s and the 1650s.[7]

It was in the 1620s and 1630s that the market for advice literature was at its height and that the genre really came into its own. This was when Nehemiah Wallington, that quintessential London Puritan artisan, went to buy his copy of William Gouge's *Of Domestical Duties*. He was recently married and was feeling the weight of 'the charge of so many souls'. 'Every one of us', he recorded in his diary, 'may learn and know our duties and honour God every one in his place where God has set them'. The articles for his family 'for the reforming of our lives', which he later drew up, were signed by his three servants and his apprentice as well as by his wife. Here, prompted by Gouge's work, was the holy household in action.[8]

The central texts of this period are, in chronological order of first editions, William Whateley's *A Bride Bush* in 1616, Gouge's *Domestical Duties* in 1622, Matthew Griffith's *Bethel* in 1633 and Daniel Rogers's *Matrimonial Honour* in 1642. Gouge and Griffith are the two most comprehensive writers in their treatment of all aspects of the management of the household including control of servants as well as children. Both books are 528 pages in length. Gouge's account was by far the more popular of the two since it avoided excessive biblical quotation and was well arranged, with a table of contents, index and cross references. New editions appeared in 1626 and 1634 and the text also appeared in Gouge's *Works*, which itself went through four printings. Whateley confined himself to the relationship between husband and wife and dealt with this more deeply and more thoughtfully than anyone had done before. His hard practical sense and use of personal experience shines through on every page.[9] This was the man whose vigorous preaching during his ministry at Banbury earned him the title of the 'roaring boy'. His book was a 'direction' for

[7] L. Roper, *The Holy Household* (Oxford: Oxford University Press, 1989), 5.

[8] P. S. Seaver, *Wallington's World* (London: Methuen, 1985), 79.

[9] L. B. Wright, *Middle-Class Culture in Elizabethan England* (Chapel Hill: University of North Carolina Press, 1935), 220–3; C. L. Powell, *English Domestic Relations* (New York: Russell & Russell, 1972; orig. 1917), 136–8. It is worth noting that Roger's *Matrimonial Honour*, though not published until 1642 was completed by the end of 1634: T. Webster, 'The Godly of Gosher scattered: an Essex clerical conference in the 1620s and its diaspora' (Cambridge PhD thesis, 1992), 307.

the married, specifying the duties of each partner and if these duties were followed, he promised, they would help some who, neglecting them, found marriage 'a little hell'.[10]

Male authority, in the account given by the conduct books, was based both on God's direction and on nature. 'Thy husband is by God made thy governor and ruler', wrote Whateley. Female inferiority was simply the result of 'God's appointment in the ordering of higher and lower places'.[11] Her husband was the woman's head, said Gouge, and 'by virtue of his place carrieth the very image of Christ'.[12] Gataker quoted liberally from Scripture about women's inferiority and made extensive reference to the Fall: 'woman was an instrument to draw the man on into evil', he reminded his readers.[13] Wing stressed the huge penalty still to be paid by women: 'The time was when it was natural to your sex to be so excellent but she that first enjoyed it destroyed it, altering the property and losing the prerogative belonging to you all; you must therefore go to that God who made her so good to make you anew because now you are so bad.'[14]

The clerical prescriptions were also suffused with the notion of the Great Chain of Being: 'All advancement in place', insisted Whateley, 'doth carry with it a bond to more virtue than that which is called for of them which are set in a lower room.'[15] 'A man must entreat his wife with gentleness and softness', Henry Smith told his readers, 'not expecting that wisdom, nor that faith, nor that patience, nor that strength in the weaker vessel which should be in the stronger.'[16] It was not that every man was mentally and emotionally stronger than every woman: male and female characteristics were seen to overlap within individuals. But the Fall was the proof of women's ultimate flaw, a basic imperfection from which only men could save them. This was why a woman's 'affecting mastership', as Gataker put it, in the home was so very dangerous: 'a course that bringeth commonly disgrace and contempt upon both parties yea utter ruin oft of the

---

[10] W. Whateley, *A Bride Bush* (1623), preface.
[11] Whateley, *Bride Bush*, 192.
[12] W. Gouge, *Domestical Duties* (1622), 269.
[13] T. Gataker, *Marriage Duties* (1620), 8–9.
[14] J. Wing, *The Crown Conjugal* (1620), 62.
[15] Whateley, *Bride Bush*, 30.
[16] H. Smith, *Preparative to Marriage* (1596), 53.

family and of their whole estate'. A woman must 'learn to know her place and her part and to fashion her mind and her will, her disposition and her practice accordingly,' Gataker's admonition continued, 'yea though she be herself of a greater spirit and in some respects of better parts.'[17] Whateley drew upon the physical makeup of male and female bodies as further evidence of what God and nature intended. The print of government appeared in man's 'very face which is more stern and delicate than the woman's'. Men should 'not suffer this order of nature to be inverted'.[18]

The duties of submission were reverence and obedience. Reverence was a matter of words, gestures and behaviour. Whateley, citing biblical precedent, criticised excessive familiarity. Shortened names like Tom, Dick, Ned and Will were fine for servants but a woman should call her husband husband.[19] Gataker too disliked 'gross terms' used in too familiar a way. This concern with the style in which husband and wife related to each other was a question of example. In the 'little commonwealth' of the household they were set in authority together over children and servants. But the young, learning their social duty, needed to see that the head of the household was firmly in control. A wife's duty, explained Gataker, showed itself in a willingness 'to be directed and advised by him for her self, her attire, her behaviour, her carriage, her company, the marshalling and managing of domestical affairs'.[20] When it comes to work and the actual running of the home, all the writers assume there will be a partnership but the partnership is clearly to be an unequal one. The conventional roles are several times set out, emphasising the distinction between tasks indoors and out of doors. Man and wife, Henry Smith tells them, should see themselves like the cock and the dam: 'the cock flyeth abroad to bring in and the dam sitteth upon the nest to keep all at home'. This is what God ordered, he reflects, what the 'nature, wit and strength' of the two sexes fits them for.[21] Whateley was highly practical about it all.

[17] Gataker, *Marriage Duties*, 10–11.
[18] Whateley, *Bride Bush*, 97–8.
[19] Whateley, *Bride Bush*, 97–8.
[20] Gataker, *Marriage Duties*, 14–16.
[21] Smith, *Preparative to Marriage*, 43.

They should each in their own sphere 'be content to unite their pains for their profit', he believed. Husband and wife should be 'as two oxen that draw together in one yoke'.[22]

Such hints as the conduct books contain about real partnership in day to day domestic management are vitiated time and again by warnings about the necessity for obedience and recommendations to husbands about the manner in which they should give reproof when they found it necessary. Wives, one is left feeling, are given little room for discussion or questioning of decisions without appearing shrewish. In so far as a problem with bad husbands is recognised at all, the only advice is to accept the situation with stoic resignation.[23] But there is an assumption that the women of the house will not always come up to scratch. Dod and Cleaver suggested rewarding 'good and dutiful' behaviour and showing patience when a wife was 'shrewish and wayward' so that 'she wax not worse'. Husbands should reprehend their wives as seldom as possible but 'admonish her often'.[24] Gouge, taking a similar line, called for mildness in reproof, stressing the weakness of those under the husband's authority: 'glasses are tenderly handled, a small knock soon breaks them'. 'Sweet and pithy persuasions' should be mixed with the husband's precepts. A wife's reputation should be protected by ensuring that her ignorance was not proclaimed before children, servants or strangers. Gouge found continual chiding too common a fault in husbands and he thought it necessary to lecture them on the body language they displayed in giving reproof. 'His authority over her and eminency above her may not make him forget the near conjunction and union between them', he declared. At the same time he was scathing about some husbands who, forgetting the gravity and sobriety that attached to their household role, were for ever, with their wives in their laps, 'colling, kissing and dallying with them'. This showed 'more lightness, fondness and dotage than true kindness and love'.[25] Wing was rather harsher than either of these writers, seeing a place for a mild kind of punishment. It was proper, in his view, for a man to humble his wife when he was justly angry by depriving her

---

[22] Whateley, *Bride Bush*, 83–4. See also, S. Amussen, *An Ordered Society* (Oxford: Oxford University Press, 1988), 43–4.

[23] E.g. Gouge, *Domestical Duties*, 317–23.

[24] J. Dod and R. Cleaver, *A Godly Form of Household Government* (1614), sig. L4.

[25] Gouge, *Domestical Duties*, 374–92.

for a while of 'some favours and kindness which formerly she hath more freely enjoyed'.[26]

The conduct book writers knew their whole Bibles inside out. Whereas their fiercest patriarchal strictures by and large took their source from the Old Testament, they were at the same time able to propound a doctrine of mutuality in marriage which was based upon a close reading of St Paul's epistles, particularly Col 3.18–20, and Ephes 5.21–33. We need to summarise the findings of the latest biblical scholarship about these household tables as a basis on which to assess the modernity of the Puritan prescriptions. New Testament scholars are not agreed about the origins of these codes of relationships between people in a household, but it is likely that Paul was drawing upon ethical material inherited from his Jewish heritage. The basic argument is that the wife's duty is submission and the husband's is love. The Ephesian household table pursues an analogy between two different kinds of relationships, that between husband and wife and between Christ and the church. It has been argued that what Paul was seeking to do here was set out a new approach to marriage which would effectively reform the patriarchal structure of his day: 'husband and wife are called to a mutual self-giving that is to be total and rules out the idea that one member is superior to the other'. This is not to say that the husband's headship is questioned. The argument in Ephesians subtly portrays a difference in the way submission and service are rendered by husband and wife. The gender roles are not interchangeable.[27]

Several of our writers explored the nature of the love men should show their wives, and the duties it involved, at some length. What is loving, said Wing, should be the rule of their actions. Their love 'must be the most dear, intimate, precious and entire that heart can have toward a creature'. It must be immeasurable and its manifestations 'must be universal in everything'.[28] Dod and Cleaver stressed the point that Paul made to the Ephesians about a husband's respect for his wife's personhood.

---

[26] Wing, *Crown Conjugal*, 47–8.

[27] B. Witherington III, *Women and the Genesis of Christianity* (Cambridge: Cambridge University Press, 1990), 147–62.

[28] Wing, *Crown Conjugal*, 44–6.

'The husband must let his wife perceive and know that for the good opinion that he hath of her', they wrote, 'he doth love her simply and faithfully and not for any utility or pleasure.' She was not to be treated either as a drudge or as a sex object.[29] It was just as much the husband's duty to please his wife as vice versa, asserted Whateley: 'what force obedience hath to tie the wife unto it, the same hath love to tie the husband'. They should care for each other's health, watch themselves against destructive suspicions and jealousies, keep each other's secrets and protect each other's credit.

The Puritan clerics, one is left feeling, go so far with St Paul. There is an authentic desire to reform patriarchy in early Stuart England by an insistence upon the husband's duty to love. Yet they do not go by any means all the way with him. None of them grasped or properly expounded the implications of his analogy of the marital relationship with that between Christ and his church. The fact is Paul was too radical for these conservative men. The sticking point, which prevented them opening their minds to a proper mutuality, was their conviction that women were inferior. This in turn reflected the imprisoning effect of their interpretation of Genesis. He has to begin with the wife's duties rather than the husband's, avowed Gataker in his sermon for Robert and Dorothy Cooke, because it is right to begin with the duty of the inferior partner. 'The wife's duty is as the base or ground that the husband's duty is built upon,' he declared, 'it is that that must draw duty and respect from the husband.' Within a few minutes of quoting his text, Gataker was reading it in a sense which did little justice to Paul's intentions.[30] Gouge had the same problem. For all his stress on how 'tender respect and provident care' will show a man's high account of his wife, his sense of how things are and should be remained inviolate: 'her place is indeed a place of inferiority and subjection yet the nearest to equality that may be, a place of common equity in many respects, wherein man and wife are after a sort even fellows and partners'.[31]

There is no question that all these writers valued the physical and intimate aspect of marriage very highly indeed. They took

[29] Dod and Cleaver, *A Godly Form of Household Government*, sig. L6; Witherington, *Women and the Genesis of Christianity*, 161.

[30] Gataker, *Marriage Duties*, 5–6.

[31] Gouge, *Domestical Duties*, 360–1.

their cue from a wholly traditional notion of 'due benevolence', which appears prominently in sixteenth-century tracts such as Bullinger's *The Christian State of Matrimony*, but they made much more of this notion than catholic or humanist writers had done.[32] The starting point was Paul's counsel to the Corinthians that it is the husband who has rights over his wife's body and the wife who has rights over the husband's. 1 Cor 7.4 was much cited.[33] The Puritan writers gave an account of sex that was entirely positive.

Aware that their readers might expect guidance on the matter, several of the divines gave advice on how much sex was enough. There were no particular limits, said Whateley, what mattered is the spontaneity of desire by one or the other partner. Foreplay – 'mutual dalliances for pleasure's sake' as Whateley put it – was perfectly acceptable when this enabled a spouse to satisfy a partner's need for sexual satisfaction. Emphasising the dangers of natural desires being left to 'tend to unruliness', Whateley enjoined 'the temperate enjoyment of God's ordinance as for a man to drink when labour or other occasion hath made him thirsty'. The rule was for a couple to have intercourse sufficiently regularly that desire 'may not be troublesome to them in the duties of religion and their callings'.[34] Whateley, Rogers and Gouge all promulgated a doctrine of moderation in sexual pleasure which confirms their functional view of intercourse.

What is remarkable about all this is that it shows the Puritan clergy cutting through the weight of Augustinian objection to sexual pleasure with apparent ease and rejecting the whole gnostic Manichean strain of Christianity, which stressed the inherent sinfulness of the flesh. Following St Paul's precepts in 1 Corinthians, there is a notable lack of reference to intercourse being solely or primarily for the purpose of procreation. Indeed their whole account is close to that of St Paul as this is now read by biblical scholars. Like Paul they saw sexual desire as a force to be reckoned with, confined its expression to marriage and interpreted sex in marriage in terms which were at the same time

[32] H. Bullinger, *The Christian State of Matrimony* (1541). See K. M. Davies, 'Continuity and Change in Literary Advice on Marriage' in R. B. Outhwaite, ed., *Marriage and Society* (London: Europa, 1981), 73–4.

[33] E.g. Gouge, *Domestical Duties*, 224; Dod and Cleaver, *A Godly Form of Household Government*, sig. K7.

[34] Whateley, *Bride Bush*, 18–20.

egalitarian and patriarchal. Their anti-catholic polemic brought them in their account of sex to a point somewhere near that of Paul's when he abandons the notion of female inferiority through a concept of sexual self giving.[35] There are times when the sexual union is seen in spiritual terms. 'By nuptial conjunction', preached Gataker, 'being joined to him as his wife she becometh not only part of his flesh as taken from him but sworn flesh conjoined with him ... here reciprocally the wife is part of the husband and the husband is part of the wife, both parts of the same flesh because both making but one flesh'.[36] But mostly the language remained more earthy than this. They only go so far with Paul. Yet we may imagine they went far enough for their message to be a liberating one for their women readers.

Husband and wife were seen as equal in the sight of God, so when it came to spiritual duties the conduct book writers had the delicate task of defining an unequal partnership between spiritual equals.[37] Again a distinction between the public and private aspects of their domestic life is evident. Whateley saw prayer and singing psalms together as means towards the cementing of the souls of the married.[38] Gouge put emphasis upon the mutual duty of helping forward the growth of grace in the other.[39] Rogers advised spouses regularly to hear the word, receive the sacrament and frequent prayers in each other's company. They should also in private 'confer, read, pray, confess and give thanks'.[40] In these respects there could be an approach to a reality of spiritual equality. But in the hall or parlour it was different. Male authority had to be plainly demonstrated in the conduct of family worship, with a wife standing in only if the household head had to be absent. With the gathering of children and servants to hear the Bible, pray and be catechised, the holy household of early Stuart England achieved its most emblematic form.

---

[35] Witherington, *Women and the Genesis of Christianity*, 161, see also A. West, 'Sex and Salvation: A Christian Feminist Bible Study on 1 Cor 6.12–7.39', in A. Loades, ed., *Feminist Theology* (London: SPCK, 1990), 72–80.

[36] Gataker, *Marriage Duties*, 32.

[37] Amussen, *An Ordered Society*, 46–7.

[38] Whateley, *Bride Bush*, 49.

[39] Gouge, *Domestical Duties*, 240–2.

[40] Rogers, *Matrimonial Honour*, 128–9.

The upbringing of children

The core of early modern thinking about the child was that he was a being lacking in self control, which came slowly in adolescence and early adulthood as reason and emotional maturity were established. Proverbs equated children with animals, fools and lunatics. Contemporaries drew upon animal similes from the Old Testament: the young were 'like wild asses and wild heifers' or 'like a young colt, wanton and foolish, till he be broken by education and correction'. 'What wast thou, being an infant', asked Lewis Bayly, 'but a brute having the shape of a man?'[41] Lacking the defences of the adult, the child was prone to evil, 'even', said William Gouge, 'as rank ground is subject to bring forth many weeds'. The crux of the argument, put most didactically by Puritans, that parents should beat their children, was the need to free them from evil. John Robinson, pastor on the *Mayflower*, said that the 'natural pride' of children had to be 'broken and beaten down'.[42] Citing Proverbs chapters 20, 22 and 23, William Gouge described beating children as 'physick to purge out much corruption which lurketh in children and as a salve to heal many wounds and sores made by their folly'. Matthew Griffiths based the case for chastisement of the young on the dictum in Proverbs that 'folly is bound up in the heart of a child'.

The upbringing of children, in Gouge's view, was a highly demanding task requiring constant application of admonition and correction, for 'the apprehension of children is fickle and their memory is weak'. 'If they be but once or seldom or slightly instructed', he warned, 'that which is taught will soon slip away and do little or no good.' This was why the inculcation of piety was the only sure basis for a proper Christian life, for piety held

---

[41] Citations from K. Thomas, 'Age and Authority in Early Modern England', *Proceedings of the British Academy*, 52 (1976), 218; M. MacDonald, *Mystical Bedlam: Madness, Anxiety and Healing in Seventeenth-century England* (Cambridge: Cambridge University Press, 1981), 43. See also C. John Sommerville, *The Discovery of Childhood in Puritan England* (Athens, GA: University of Georgia Press, 1992), 189.

[42] Cited in P. Collinson, *The Birthpangs of Protestant England* (London: Macmillan, 1988), 78.

the whole structure of moral adulthood in place. Piety, declared Gouge, was

> the best thing that a parent can teach his child for as reason maketh a man differ from a beast and as learning and civility maketh a wise and sober man differ from savages and swaggerers, so piety maketh a sound Christian much more to differ from the most civil and well ordered natural man that can be.[43]

They share a common programme of parental duty which can also be found in outline in works such as William Ames's *Conscience with the Power and Cases Thereof.* It can be summarised as nourishing children until they are independent; nurturing them in the fear of God with good discipline; instructing them in God's ways; providing training for an honest calling and arranging a fit marriage. Parents should take all the provident care they could for their children's temporal and spiritual good.[44]

Three aspects of this programme deserve our attention: the demand for outward marks of deference and obedience, the religious education of the young, and the control of their behaviour by admonition and beating. So far as the first is concerned, Dod and Cleaver, Gouge and Griffith all required silence in the presence of elders and 'no stout answers', uncovering the head, bending the knee, standing in the presence of elders, rising before them and bowing as appropriate. Dod and Cleaver emphasised the general importance of teaching children 'how to behave themselves decently in their going, in their speaking and gesture of their bodies'.[45] They defined a spiritual upbringing as one in 'fear and nurture of the Lord, shamefastness, hatred of vice and love of all virtue'.[46] All the conduct book writers emphasised the importance of inculcating the habit of reading the Bible and of attendance at church as soon as children could 'sit reverently or fruitfully'. Dod and Cleaver were particu-

---

[43] Gouge, *Domestical Duties,* 545, 551, 558, 560; M. Griffith, *Bethel* (1633), 366.

[44] John Morgan, *Godly Learning: Puritan Attitudes towards Reason, Learning and Education 1560–1640* (Cambridge: Cambridge University Press, 1986), 150. For a general account see L. L. Schucking, *Puritan Family* (London: Routledge & Kegan Paul, 1989), 56–95.

[45] Gouge, *Domestical Duties,* 436–43.

[46] Dod and Cleaver, *A Godly Form of Household Government,* sigs Q1, R3.

larly concerned about an early start in the first principles of religion:

> so soon as by age they are able to perceive and understand the same that they may (as it were) suck in godliness with their mother's milk and straightways after their cradle may be nourished with the tender food of virtue towards that blessed life ... so soon as the child can begin to speak his tongue should be employed to glorify God ... by learning some short catechism containing the principles and grounds of Christian Religion.

Gouge stressed the importance of an early start in sabbath observance and in teaching the significance of special observances such as the 5 November commemoration and fasts marking occasions of plague. There was a good deal of criticism of parents who were seen as slack in these duties. Gouge thought many parents taught their children 'prophaneness, pride, riot, lying, and deceit'; some, he believed, not only neglected catechising but did not even teach the Lord's Prayer, the Creed and the Ten Commandments; many set a bad example by swearing, drinking and playing unlawful games. Griffith was scathing about parents who pleaded they could not rule their child: 'this may be so indeed but where lies the fault? Is it not because thou did'st pamper him being young? Or not bend him while he was pliable?' 'Wild beasts may be tamed and wild colts by custom be brought to the saddle and are content to be led by the bridle', Dod and Cleaver advised parents who made excuses for themselves.[47]

Robert Schnucker's systematic analysis of twenty-two sources for attitudes to discipline, ranging from conduct books to commentaries on relevant biblical passages, sermons and catechisms, all published between 1560 and 1634, reveals much general consistency in the rules laid down about the beating of children. We should note that none of this material shows any signs at all of gender distinctions and it is taken for granted that a mother's disciplinary powers are equal to those of the father, though he was normally expected to take the initiative. She must support him in questions of punishment, as in other matters, whatever

---

[47] Gouge, *Domestical Duties*, 546–51; Dod and Cleaver, *A Godly Form*, sig Q3.

her private doubts. In the first place, physical correction should only be applied when verbal reproof failed to have effect. How hard a child was beaten should depend on his or her age, temperament and state of physical and moral development. The use of wisdom in discipline was strongly enjoined with warnings in many cases about excessive violence. A parent should never act in anger for, as Robert Cleaver put it, 'he that commeth to reform in anger shall hardly keep a measure in rebuking or chastising'. Every writer insisted that a clear explanation of the offence should precede punishment and when God's express command-ment had been broken, as in cases of swearing, lying or stealing, this should be made evident.[48]

Reading these texts, for all the limitations that were imposed, one cannot but conclude that Puritan clerics believed that all children would need to be beaten at some time and some more than others. Is it not right that they should be? asks the father in Thomas Becon's *Catechism* and the model son replies: 'Yes most lawfully. For moderate correction is as necessary for children as meat and drink.'[49] The buttocks, according to Bartholomew Batty, were specially created by God to receive just correction in childhood without serious bodily injury.[50] William Gouge insisted that a child was 'much more sensible of smart than words': children were kept by this correction 'in filial awe'; 'as trees well pruned and ground well tilled they will bring forth pleasant and abundant fruit'. 'Stripes and blows', he declared, were 'a means appointed by God to help the good nurture and education of children.' It was, he showed with ample scriptural citation, 'by the Holy Ghost both expressly commanded and also very often pressed'.[51] Levin Schucking described Gouge's system of punishment as 'pietistic' in char-acter. It was more than this, for it was also ritualistic: father and child were bound in a collusive bending to God's decree, the one acting in love and lifting up 'the heart for direction and blessing' as he took up the rod, the other bowing the head to

[48] R. V. Schnucker, 'Puritan attitudes towards childhood discipline, 1560–1634', in V. Fildes, ed., *Women as Mothers in Pre-Industrial England: Essays in Memory of Dorothy McLaren* (London: Routledge, 1990), 108–16.

[49] Schucking, *Puritan Family*, 74–5.

[50] Fildes, *Women as Mothers*, 117.

[51] Gouge, *Domestical Duties*, 560–1.

receive the stripes inflicted as the physic to purge corruption. Richard Baxter, in the same frame of mind, would have the child read the passages of Scripture on the strength of which the beating was to be given and kneel after it was over to entreat God to 'bless and sanctify' its effects.[52]

So what of practice? The outward marks of deference recommended by the Puritan clerics were almost certainly only shown by children in a minority of strict Puritan households, like that of the widowed Lady Alice Wandesford, where in the 1640s we are told the children knelt daily after the morning Bible reading to receive her blessing.[53] Gouge admitted that he knew this practice was in decay in the homes of members of his Blackfriars congregation and sought to reinforce it by showing its lawfulness in Scripture.[54] John Aubrey reminisced about gentlemen in middle age who used to stand 'like mutes and fools bareheaded before their parents', which suggests that prescription in this area was probably at a loss in the face of changing custom.[55]

So far as the spiritual upbringing of children in the household is concerned, we have the vivid examples of leadership by those Puritan patriarchs and clerics who, following the model of the advice book writers, sought to inculcate godliness through household religion. Lay exemplars of this pattern included Sir Nathaniel Barnardiston in Suffolk, John Bruen in Cheshire, Sir James Harrington in Rutland, Thomas Scott in Kent and Sir Christopher Wandesford, who as Master of the Rolls in Ireland during the 1630s held family prayers three times a day at 6.00 am, 10.00 am and 9.00 pm. Barnardiston's care for his children's souls, Samuel Clark recorded, showed itself in 'a constant and serious study for their education in the most exact and strict way of pure and paternal religion'. His spiritual counsels were designed towards stirring them up 'to a strict watchfulness over themselves and a close walking with God'.[56]

---

[52] Schucking, *Puritan Family*, 74.

[53] L. Stone, *The Family, Sex and Marriage in England 1500–1800* (London: Weidenfeld & Nicolson, 1977), 155, 171.

[54] Gouge, *Domestical Duties*, 443.

[55] Stone, *Family, Sex and Marriage*, 171.

[56] J. T. Cliffe, *The Puritan Gentry: The Great Puritan Families of Early Stuart England* (London: Routledge & Kegan Paul, 1984), 69–70; R. C. Richardson, *Puritanism in North-west England: A Regional Study of the Diocese of Chester to 1642* (Manchester: Manchester University Press, 1972), 91–2.

So if the evangelisers failed to bring the vast majority of households to the practice of exacting spiritual exercises, did they at least persuade most parents to beat the sinfulness out of their children? The answer, though our evidence here is thin, must be almost certainly not. 'In the light of all we know about medieval society', writes Shulamith Shahar, 'it is highly implausible to assume that small children were never beaten'.[57] The same goes for early modern society but, since this is a matter which stirs deep emotions both in the one who inflicts the punishment and the one who submits to it, there seems to be a case for assuming that it is the kind of thing we could expect to find record of in the intimate pages of diaries, personal memoirs and autobiographies where it occurred. The record in this respect is in fact thin.

No doubt much good Christian education went on through the elements of religious instruction which were attached to the grammar school regime. Sir Simonds D'Ewes attested to his 'increase in the knowledge of divine truths and practice of piety' at Bury St Edmunds school, which was 'little inferior' to his progress in scholarship while there.[58] But this was not primarily how educationalists of the period thought about schooling or how contemporaries remembered the experience of their youth. For, in an age in which apprehension of disorder was always rife, the school became more than anything else an instrument of discipline, based on coercion and intended to check youthful high spirits with solid and monotonous learning. 'The prevailing grammar school ethic', writes Keith Thomas, 'was one of instinctual renunciation.'[59] Boys were taught self control by working long hours at a curriculum which no-one pretended would have intrinsic interest for them. The early seventeenth-century ballad *A Table of Good Nurture* details the ways in which scholars should learn 'good manners'. Punctuality, care of basic school possessions like inkhorn, pen and book, neat attire, clean language, mild and gentle behaviour to schoolfellows, quietness and obedience, steady application: these were the precepts the master

[57] S. Shahar, *Childhood in the Middle Ages* (London: Routledge, 1990), 111.

[58] Cliffe, *Puritan Gentry*, 79–80.

[59] K. V. Thomas, *Rule and Misrule in the Schools of Early Modern England* (University of Reading, Stenton Lecture, 1975), 8.

sought to inculcate. The coercion of course came in the form of the birchrod, figured on school seals, prominent in representations of the classroom at this time and still occasionally on view, as is one safely put away behind a pane of glass at Roysse's schoolroom in Abingdon. 'Therefore be wary you do not offend', runs the ballad,

> Lest stripes do reward you and make you to say
> Your precepts I'll follow, your words I'll obey.

Those who loitered and were lazy 'shall for their labour be brought on their knee'.[60] 'Your points untie' were the schoolmaster's dreaded words.[61]

Whereas the ties of parental love pulled against home beating, it was the experience of thousands of boys in this period to submit to kneeling before their fellows with their breeches down to receive the birchrod's stripes. Some suffered under masters who were exceptionally cruel; few, one suspects, were as fortunate as Sir Simonds D'Ewes whose 'mild and loving' master went no further than denying bad children a share of the raisins he brought to school for his pupils. Many others, besides John Aubrey who recorded his dreams about them twenty years later, must have remembered these beatings as the chief emotional legacy of their schooldays. For masters needed quite exceptional personal authority, given the kind of learning they were inculcating and the crowded conditions of the schoolroom under their sole charge, to maintain order any other way. Francis Cheynell, in a pamphlet of 1646, called the schoolmaster 'a kind of magistrate'. At home he was a symbol of authority: the standard parental threat was 'your master shall hear of it'. 'At country schools your masters drive you on by fear', noted Richard Baxter.[62] Scripture sanctioned the harsh rule of the birch, which was of course not new but simply a regime that came to hold very many more children, as many more went to school, at its mercy.

The prescriptive advice which underpinned bringing up girls at home ranges from a series of published funeral sermons lauding godly women to a large pamphlet literature which

---

[60] W. Chappell, *The Roxburghe Ballads* (Hertford, 1874), II, 571–2.
[61] R. O'Day, *Education and Society* (London: Longman, 1982), 49–50.
[62] Citations from Thomas, *Rule and Misrule*, 8–9.

counselled females to be 'chaste, silent and obedient'. Popular ballads, such as *The Virgin's ABC,* issued the same precepts in a more accessible format.[63] Surveying the lives of godly women Jacqueline Eales concluded that they were didactic pieces which gave a selective biographical account, invariably portraying their subjects as 'pious, charitable, and the centre of religious life within their homes'.[64] The qualities of womanhood that were enjoined and that amounted to a life of virtue included modesty, courtesy, gentleness, grace, zeal and self control. The message was always strongly scriptural. Thus Katherine Stubs was alleged never to have brawled or scolded: 'she obeyed the command-ment of the Apostle who biddeth women to be silent and learn of their husbands at home'.[65] In the preface to the published version of his 1697 funeral sermon for Elizabeth Dunton, Thomas Rogers drew examples from both the Old and New Testaments to put his subject in context. He commented upon Sarah's 'meekness of spirit' and lauded Rachel as 'pure in her thoughts, honest in her calling and innocent in her life'. The crucial importance of a girl's training in piety was stressed in this genre in several ways.[66] It was a matter of laying proper foundations. Elizabeth Wilkinson 'was observed from her childhood to be very docile, very willing to learn, industrious in reading of and swift to hear the word of God preached'.[67] The mother's role was to set an example and organise a pattern of instruction. Elizabeth Dunton's regime for her girls is described in detail: how she 'guards them against selfwill and peevishness'; how she has one read while others were sewing, bringing useful sayings to the minds of those with their fingers employed; how she catechises them and how she 'teaches them to think of what is good when they lie down and when they rise'. In all this 'a great calmness and quietness' attended her actions.[68]

---

[63] S. W. Hull, *Chaste, Silent and Obedient: English Books for Women 1475–1640* (San Marino: Huntington Library, 1982), 133–43.

[64] J. Eales, 'Samuel Clarke and the "Lives" of Godly Women in Seventeenth-century England', in W. Sheils ed., *Women in the Church,* Studies in Church History 21 (1990), 368–9.

[65] P. Stubs, *A Cristal Glass for Christian Women* (1663).

[66] T. Rogers, *The Character of a Good Woman* (1697), epistle dedicatory.

[67] W. Shiels, ed., *Women in the Church,* 371.

[68] Rogers, *Character of a Good Woman,* 24–6.

Sir Robert Filmer's essay 'In Praise of the Virtuous Wife', written in the 1640s, is a superb summary of the end product that the gentry looked for in the education of their girls. His discourse revolves around two passages from Proverbs – 12.4: 'a virtuous wife is the crown of her husband' and 31.10: 'who can find a virtuous woman, for her price is above rubies'. Chastity was central to Filmer's conception of virtue but, in his reading, what mattered as much was courage, the self discipline to live virtuously from day to day: 'That courage is true virtue', he declared, 'it appeareth because true virtue is the moderation of the affections by faith and prudence, the one showing what is lawful, the other what is possible and convenient.'[69] By 'moderation of the affections' Filmer means control of the will. Female gender construction in early modern England was exacting: it required girls to deprive themselves of expectations of initiative and independence and to internalise qualities of modesty and humility.

Whereas I have suggested that there was a very wide gap between prescription and practice with regard to the disciplining of young children, there is good evidence that in the matter of girls' general upbringing the two went closely together. For the kind of prescriptive advice which has just been quoted can be closely paralleled with personal injunctions from parents to daughters. Justinian Isham, a deeply thoughtful Northamptonshire gentleman, composed a code of conduct for his daughters Jane, Elizabeth, Judith and Susan, the eldest of whom was nine, after the death of their mother in 1642. His advice began with and laid heavy emphasis upon the girls' spiritual development. His charge was

> first of all to instruct in the knowledge of another Father, the Father and Creator of all things. Him you may learn both in his word and works, as of the latter you are daily eye witnesses, so of the first you cannot be too diligent either readers or hearers. … prayers, meditations and holy treatises I rather commend unto you than knotty disputes; and although your sex is not so capable of those stronger abilities of the intellect, to make you

---

[69] M. J. M. Ezell, *The Patriarch's Wife: Literary Evidence and the History of the Family* (Chapel Hill: University of North Carolina Press, 1987), 132–3.

so learned and knowing as men ought to be; yet be sure to keep your hearts upright and your affections to God unfeigned and there is no doubt but that will be more acceptable unto him than all the wisdom of the world besides.

Isham commended the fair examples 'of their own sex and kindred' that his girls could follow, 'there having been of our house both maids, wives and widows, all of a very virtuous and exemplary life'. He warned against reliance in the most serious business of his daughters' lives, finding a husband, on a fair fortune or a fair face:

> I am sure the internal graces of the mind will be your best and surest portion, both unto yourselves, and unto men of such discretions as I believe you would willingly give yourselves unto. A virtuous woman is a good portion which shall be given as a gift to such as fear the Lord.

He then listed the 'graces and virtues' which Scripture described as 'most proper' for women: 'holiness, chastity, obedience, charity, meekness, modesty, sobriety, silence, discretion, frugality and affability'.[70]

The upbringing of girls, as Linda Pollock has explored the theme, was about teaching them to 'live under obedience'. The phrase comes from a letter of Sir Ralph Verney's to his friend Dr Denton about young Nancy. The female life-cycle was supposed to move from a schooling in deference along the lines outlined here to acceptance of the governance of a husband. The pressure came from what men were looking for. John Evelyn's eulogy of his daughter Susannah on the eve of her marriage is set in the pattern of male expectation. She was a girl, he wrote, who used her talents 'with great modesty'; she was 'exquisitely shaped and of an agreeable countenance'; she is 'a good child, religious, discreet, ingenious and qualified with all the ornaments of her sex'. Edward Montagu was reassured in 1632 that his proposed bride's religion was 'very perfect and her education most modest without exception'. A letter to Peregrine Osborne later in the century sought to persuade him to favour a proposed bride who

---

[70] L. Pollock, *A Lasting Relationship: Parents and their Children Over Three Centuries* (London: Fourth Estate, 1987) 226.

was 'very modestly bred'.[71] The Bible had proved the starting point for the English Protestant gentry to elucidate a concept of femininity that, if it could be driven into the mind at home in childhood by mothers trained in the same mould, offered a secure ideological basis for their permanent patriarchal control of women.

The legacy today

Let me conclude with some brief reflections on the legacy of these developments in the perspective of English history between 1700 and the present day. I have argued that the Protestant church, in its first century and a half, was identified with a set of prescriptions for harsh childhood discipline which parents largely refused to follow. It was also deeply implicated in a system of schooling for boys in which the same kind of prescriptions had much more impact than in the home. Fathers, it seems, by and large supported the schoolmaster's use of the birch and mothers were in no position to protect their offspring from its stripes. Mary Woodforde, wracked by the news that her son and others 'in rebellion' at Winchester were refusing to be whipped in 1687, wrote in her diary 'give them grace to repent and accept of their punishment ... and let them not run on to ruin, for Christ's sake'.[72] The church, I have suggested, also lent its authority to a system of gender training of girls for a restricted and restrictive social role in their adult lives. This allegiance, in these several respects, to a particular pattern of English upbringing, I contend, has been immensely powerful and the results are clearly with us and our society today. There is still a conservative evangelical strain of thought in the church which, based on a pessimistic view of human nature, advocates physical punishment of children. So far as schooling is concerned, it was no coincidence that the first flagellant brothels appeared in London around the 1670s. Thomas Shadwell's comedy *The Virtuoso*, first performed in 1676, contains a scene in which the old

[71] L. Pollock, 'Teach her to Live under Obedience: the Making of Women in the Upper Ranks of Early Modern England, *Continuity and Change* 4 (1989), 244–5, 256.

[72] L. Pollock, *A Lasting Relationship*, 193.

libertine Snarl tells the prostitute Mrs Figgu how he 'loves castigation mightily': 'I was so used to it at Westminster school I could never leave it off since'.[73] The 'English vice' has flourished ever since, though recent reforms in school punishment regimes may spell its decline. But perhaps the most disturbing legacy of all from the biblical teachings which have been considered in this essay concerns the gender construction of girls in a manner which deprives them of the proper fulfilment of their energy, for this has surely been more pervasive in its effects than an inappropriate ideology of punishment. The narrow and inhibiting view of femininity which some seventeenth-century Protestants took authoritatively from the Bible has lain like a pall, in the intervening centuries, across many woman's lives. It obviously contributed to the reactionary position in the recent debates on women's ordination. The church, I believe, has never repudiated a series of dire legacies of certain biblical teachings; it has never spoken out about what has been done to children in the name of Scripture. Perhaps it is about time it did so.

---

[73] I. Gibson, *The English Vice: Beating, Sex and Shame in Victorian England and After* (London: Duckworth, 1978), 12.

7

Chesterton, Catholicism and the Family

Sheridan Gilley

1. *The Catholic family*

Everyone has a view of the family, informed or no, as they are husbands or wives, sons or daughters. The word contains a whole philosophy of things, being like air or water to commonsense, indefinable and indescribable because universal. Again, Catholicism means the universal, and only an exceptional scholarship or stamina could summarise the Catholic family, from St Paul to John Paul. Yet there is a common Catholic picture of the heavenly family and Holy Family, or the Holy Trinity and the earthly Trinity: God the Father and the Spirit in Heaven brooding over Mary and Joseph and the babe in the manger who, as in the Tome of Leo, binds earth and heaven in one. This teaches that God is a divine society or family in heaven as the family is a God-given human society on earth. What God has put together, let no man put asunder, for in the Trinity there is a bound or committed communion, a union of persons in love.

The family is also God-given, because it is rooted in marriage, which 'is by its very nature above human law', and being 'instituted by God, is subject to the Divine law, and cannot for that reason be rescinded by human law'. Marriage 'is natural in purpose, but Divine in origin'.[1] Both marriage and the family derive from God's creation of Adam and Eve, the aboriginal bond of social union, and are thereby anterior to the state and to any other form of society; for, in the words of Pope Leo XIII, God gave marriage as 'from the very beginning a kind of foreshadowing of the Incarnation of His Son', as the union of two natures in

---

[1] 'Marriage', *The Catholic Encyclopedia,* vol. IX (New York: The Encyclopedia Press, 1910), 699.

one person prefigured the union of two persons in one flesh, 'and therefore there abides in it a something holy and religious; not extraneous but innate; not derived from men, but implanted by nature'. Thus even among unbelievers, 'marriage is holy by its own power, in its own nature, and of itself'.[2] And so the family is 'a communion of persons, a sign and image of the communion of the Father and the Son in the Holy Spirit',[3] which corresponds 'more directly to the nature of man',[4] being 'the *original cell of social life* ... the natural society in which husband and wife are called to give themselves in love and in the gift of life. Authority, stability and a life of relationships within the family constitute the foundations for freedom, security and fraternity within society'.[5] And so too, arising from the Fourth Commandment, the family draws on the mutual love and respect that its parts and generations owe to one another.[6]

Yet truths, however tremendous, induce only *ennui* when told as abstractions unrelated to flesh and blood. There is another picture of the family, in the fifteenth-century Guild east window in Holy Trinity Goodramgate in York. The upper lights depict the saints of the Guilds, including St Christopher who, in bearing the infant Jesus, is another Mary and Joseph. The lower lights, however, show the story of St Anne and Joachim, and of the Virgin Mary, Mary Cleophas and Mary Salome, the mothers of Christ and of the brethren of the Lord. In the central light, the Virgin is crowned Queen of Heaven by her heavenly Father, Spouse and Son, and thereby takes this large extended earthly family into the heavenly family.[7] The window, commissioned by a celibate priest, is a tribute to an extended family in a city dominated by celibate priests, but its meaning is again that the family is no merely human institution in its origin or end but receives its crowning and completion in the family life of God.

---

[2] 'Arcanum Divinae Sapientiae', Etienne Gilson, ed., *The Church Speaks to the Modern World: The Social Teachings of Leo XIII* (New York: Doubleday, 1966), 96–7.

[3] *Catechism of the Catholic Church* (Ottawa, Canada: Canadian Conference of Catholic Bishops, 1994), 2205, 452.

[4] Ibid., 1882, 395.

[5] Ibid., 2207, 453.

[6] Ibid., 2219, 455.

[7] *Holy Trinity, Goodramgate-York* (York, 1980), 14.

Catholics believe that, with other matters of faith and morals, the truth about the family is a matter of authoritative teaching; but that this also answers to a human need. Mankind hungers and thirsts for authority, even if only by way of resort to the agony aunt or the latest sex manual; and when they stop believing in Christian authority, they do not stop believing in authority; they believe in any authority. The free spirit may be the most enslaved to an idea; he only escapes from the power of the Pope by falling into the capacious bosom of Claire Rayner. Yet in the modern world, the ultimate truth about authority in moral and doctrinal matters has to be discovered for oneself, as by Gilbert Keith Chesterton, who came to recognise the moral authority of the Catholic Church in family matters by this process of discovery. Chesterton was a Catholic convert who did not inherit a traditional Catholic teaching on the family but embraced it, like Christianity itself, as a kind of wild poetry. Moreover he defended the family, not from the high ground of revelation, but as a form of mystical commonsense, learned from hard experience and not from family inheritance.

The subject needs such a grounding in a time and place, because in any period the family will carry features of one time and place and no other. Catholic families have been slave and free, peasant and aristocrat, Roman and medieval, feudal and mercantile and proletarian, extended and nuclear. Even the cement which binds them, that marriage is a sacrament with the six others, was only decided in the Middle Ages, and was only defined at the Council of Trent. The sacramental view of marriage is rooted in Christ's presence at Cana and in St Paul's comparison of marriage with the love between Christ and his church.[8] Again, the church has insisted on the indissolubility of marriage from the first, following Christ's reversal of the law of Moses on the point.[9] But the Catholic Church has to ground her teaching in her social and political setting, and when the papacy became concerned about the family in the reign of Pope Leo XIII, in response to the spread of civil marriage and divorce, his encyclical on marriage, *Arcanum Divinae Sapientiae* of 1880, appeared as one in a series of papal utterances on social, pastoral

[8] Eph 5.25–26.
[9] Matt 19.8.

and political problems, most famously the letter *Rerum Novarum* of 1891, condemning both unregulated capitalism and secular socialism and defending both property rights and the right to a living wage as rights of the family. Modern Catholics tend to exalt Rome's teaching on social justice and ignore her teaching on sexual ethics; or exalt her teaching on sexual ethics and ignore her teaching on social justice. But in this, Rome is very like the Anglo-Catholic tradition of my youth, now dead, alas, which combined traditional teaching on faith and morals with Christian Socialism. The great Anglo-Catholic Bishop Gore was equally horrified by modern capitalism and modern contraception. Chesterton was the double product of Gore's kind of Anglo-Catholicism and of Leonine Roman Catholicism, in that his understanding of the family arose out of his passion for social justice.

2. *Chesterton, religion, ethics and the Edwardian cultural crisis*

Chesterton was born in 1874, and his convictions were matured by the time that he came to write *Heretics* and *Orthodoxy,* in 1905 and 1908, presenting his apologetic for traditional Christianity as an enormously exciting private adventure. His family background was vaguely Unitarian, and Chesterton's upbringing assumed the rejection of religious authority and tradition. The essential elements in his vision came out of a two-fold crisis, one personal and one public. The personal crisis occurred in his adolescence and darkened the heavenly happiness of his childhood, from which he emerged with a strong belief in Original Sin. Chesterton thought his private predicament had been compounded by the artistic and intellectual worlds of the late Victorian England of his youth, 'like one long afternoon in a rich house on a rainy day',[10] the England of Whistler, Beardsley and Wilde, rich, cosmopolitan and amoral, in which the pampered guests felt free to doubt everything, even the distinction between right and wrong. This mental revolution had the curious conservatising effect of destroying the possibility of rebellion by

---

[10] G. K. Chesterton, *The Victorian Age in Literature* (London: Williams & Norgate, 1913), 217.

relativising the moral difference between oppressor and oppressed. To Chesterton, early Victorian England had been revolutionary because it had convictions. The late Victorian agnostics like Huxley fatally weakened those convictions, and so kyboshed all fundamental change, and 'with bowed gigantic backs, bore up the throne of the Archbishop of Canterbury'.[11] Doubt was the best ally of despotism. Moral subjectivity was no more than an ideology for tyrants. No one can change the world if he is always changing his mind about what it ought to be. All revolutionaries are dogmatic believers.

Thus Chesterton's thought goes back to the first principles of recognising reality and the existence of the moral order. Yet this commonsense was also a poetic recovery of a proper mysticism, that the way to see things is with the eyes of childhood in the wonder of their novelty and strangeness. The point about the ordinary, which is as true of morals as of matter, is how extraordinary it is; the unborn child dreams of impossible landscapes covered with green hair, grass, under a fixed fire hanging in the sky. This poetic vision amounted to a particularist sacramentality about both creation and man. From the love of the particular comes patriotism, the love of neighbourhood as well as of country, and there is a logical transition from the discovery that all matter is miraculous to asserting the same of all men:

> But now a great thing in the street
> Seems any human nod,
> Where shift in strange democracy
> The million masks of God.[12]

We are the masks of the God in whose image we are made, an infinity of human variations on that one divine primaeval mystery.

> When we really see men as they are, we do not criticise, but worship; and very rightly. For a monster with mysterious eyes and miraculous thumbs, with strange dreams in his skull, and a queer tenderness for this place or that baby, is truly a

---

[11] G. K. Chesterton, *Orthodoxy* (London: John Lane, 1909), 195.
[12] 'Gold Leaves', G. K. Chesterton, *Collected Poems* (London: Methuen, 1933) (henceforth cited as *CP*), 329.

wonderful and unnerving matter... It is the fact that every face in the street has the incredible unexpectedness of a fairy-tale.[13]

Chesterton imbibed the ideals of liberty, equality and fraternity from his heroes Whitman and Stevenson, Dickens and Browning, but in 1908, when he wrote *Orthodoxy*, he gave these a foundation in dogmatic Christianity, on the ground that 'there are only two kinds of people, those who accept dogmas and know it and those who accept dogmas and don't know it'.[14] Democracy is founded on a dogma. All men are brothers, because all have the same heavenly Father. All men are equal, because all men are brothers. All men are equal, because all are sinners. All men are equal, because all can be saints. 'The basis of Christianity as well as of Democracy is that man is sacred'.[15] 'There is no basis for democracy expect in a dogma about the divine origin of man'.[16]

Chesterton's discovery of democracy was also the discovery of tradition, the democracy of the dead, of giving one's ancestors a say in one's destiny, and of the concomitant preference for the popular or people's wisdom embodied in traditional folklore and fairy tale to academic learning. Marriage is the oldest of all fairy tales, in which boy and girl fall in love and live happily ever after. A depraved modern world makes 'fairy tale' a synonym for lie rather than for fundamental truth, but this particular fairy tale, for Chesterton, was the profoundest truth about his own life. He fell in love with a Bohemian and artistic young lady, Frances Blogg, and married her, and they lived happily ever after. She confirmed him in his romantic view of women and the married state; on their wedding day, after the ceremony, he bought her a glass of milk in the shop where his mother had bought him a glass of milk as a child, and purchased a revolver to protect his bride from danger. Like the knight errant of old, he was armed to fight for his lady. The same veneration for womanhood was to enter his devotion to the Virgin Mary. Such chivalry, deriving

---

[13] G. K. Chesterton, *Heretics* (London: John Lane, 1905), 56–7.

[14] Maisie Ward, *Gilbert Keith Chesterton* (London: Sheed & Ward, 1944), 189.

[15] G. K. Chesterton, *Vox Populi, Vox Dei*, 265; cited by Ian Boyd, 'The Legendary Chesterton', in Michael H. Macdonald and Andrew A. Tadie, *G. K. Chesterton and C. S. Lewis: The Riddle of Joy* (Grand Rapids, MI: Eerdmans, 1989), 65.

[16] G. K. Chesterton, *What I saw in America*, cited by P. J. Kavanagh, 'Chesterton Reappraised', in D. J. Conlon, ed., *G. K. Chesterton: A Half Century of Views* (Oxford: Oxford University Press, 1987), 353.

from the world of the troubadours, has coloured Catholic Christianity ever since, and was common in Chesterton's own day. In legend, Hilaire Belloc walked from New York to San Francisco to claim his bride-to-be from a nunnery. Going the three thousand miles on foot made an epic and romance of a journey which could have been tamely travelled by train.

Fairy-tales are always popular, and Chesterton's thought has been called 'a radical populism'.[17] His writings were directed to the popular mind of the time, in which he filled the office of general Christian apologist taken on by C. S. Lewis after him. As John Coates has argued,[18] Chesterton's thought was a response to the Edwardian cultural crisis. In the opening of his poem to his childhood friend E. C. Bentley, he recalled the world of his youth:

A cloud was on the mind of men, and wailing went the weather,
Yea, a sick cloud upon the soul when we were boys together...
But we were young; we lived to see God break their bitter charms,
God and the good Republic come riding back in arms;
We have seen the city of Mansoul, even as it rocked, relieved –
Blessed are they who did not see, but being blind, believed.

This is a tale of those old fears, even of those emptied hells,
And none but you shall understand the true thing that it tells–...
Between us, by the peace of God, such truth can now be told;
Yea, there is strength in striking root, and good in growing old.
We have found common things at last, and marriage and a creed,
And I may safely write it now, and you may safely read.[19]

Chesterton associated marriage with his recovery of mental health; marriage and the Creed had been found together.

The Edwardian crisis was partly political. Chesterton's earliest politics were socialist, but he was estranged from secular socialism by the class determinism of socialists like Robert Blatchford

---

[17] Margaret Canovan, *G. K. Chesterton: Radical Populist* (New York and London: Harcourt Brace Jovanovich, 1977).
[18] John Coates, *G. K. Chesterton and the Edwardian Cultural Crisis* (Hull: Hull University Press, 1984).
[19] *CP*, 109–11.

who denied human freedom. Equally opposed to liberty was the socialist exaltation of the state, which Chesterton saw as bent on destroying the freedom of the individual and the subsidiary institutions of club, voluntary association and family. Again, secularist socialism was associated with so-called free love, as a communism in goods was sometimes identified with a community in women. Last, Chesterton was driven into anti-socialism by his friend and sparring partner, the Fabian socialist George Bernard Shaw; Shaw and Chesterton made their careers out of amiable public debates attacking each other. Shaw was a teetotal vegetarian Puritan, who loathed poverty because he loathed the poor and wanted to abolish them. Chesterton loved the poor and wanted to preserve them by taking them out of their poverty. Especially he loved them for their pleasure in good beer, beef and tobacco, which he saw as virtuous and Shaw saw as vicious, like the Victorian Archbishop of York, William Connor Magee, who preferred England free to England sober. Chesterton's opposition to Shaw on moral and family issues was also that of the radical populist to the élitist Puritan; and of the intellectual democrat to the intellectual snob.

In his socialism, Shaw was not a typical member of the Labour Party, who was more likely to be a Primitive Methodist than an evolutionary pantheist. In 1900, the Labour Party was not very socialist and was the little brother of the Liberals; and Chesterton's estrangement from political liberalism after 1910 had to do with the party's increasing corruption by Lloyd George, as the creature of big business, and as the proponent of what Chesterton's friend Hilaire Belloc called the Servile State.[20] The Servile State would grant certain benefits like old-age pensions, and in return, all labour would be state-directed and controlled. Belloc converted Chesterton to an alternative system, distributism, a kind of middle way between capitalism and communism, equally anti-capitalist and anti-communist, which involved dismantling the factory system, perceived to underlie every social ill, and increasing the ownership of property through the creation of small workshops and the encouragement of small tradesmen and craftsmen and peasant farmers. For the distributists, the landed peasant was the property

[20] Hilaire Belloc, *The Servile State* (London: T.N. Foulis, 1912).

owner *par excellence,* unalienated from his place of work and the fruit of his own labour, in a permanent community living the rhythms of the seasons in the natural world, with stable traditions, a proper patriotism and the practice of the arts and crafts; and of course, with stable families.

3. *Chesterton, society, politics and the family*

Distributism coloured the newspapers which Chesterton edited, the *Eye Witness,* the *New Witness* and *G. K.'s Weekly,* and his thought about the family arose in the context of his social doctrine. Thus he wanted women out of the factories and offices and back into the home because he wanted men out of the factories and offices and back into the home. It was his disciple Fritz Schumacher who coined the phrase that 'Small is beautiful', and it well expresses his leading idea. 'It is the negation of property that the Duke of Sutherland should have all the farms in one estate: just as it would be the negation of marriage if he had all our wives in one harem'.[21] One wife is more than enough for any man, for any woman is a creature of infinite possibilities. The serial monogamist who is always remarrying can never know any of his wives more than superficially. Like the supercapitalist who can never enjoy all his property, he wants more than his proper share. It is one of the crimes of Innocent Smith, the hero of Chesterton's novel *Manalive,* that he is always eloping with women. It turns out that he is renewing the excitement of his marriage by re-eloping with his wife.

The roots of Chesterton's Social Gospel lie in the neo-medievalism of Carlyle and the anti-industrialism of William Morris. Its religious content came partly from the Roman Catholic Belloc, a sometime Liberal MP and afterwards the party's greatest enemy, while 'distributism' derives from *Rerum Novarum* and its commendation of 'that justice which is called *distributive* – toward each and every class alike'.[22] Chesterton was only, however, received into the Catholic Church in 1922, and his early setting was more Anglo-Catholic than Roman, partly through his

[21] *What's Wrong with the World* (London: Cassell, 1910), 48.
[22] Gilson, *The Church Speaks to the Modern World,* 223.

Anglo-Catholic wife Frances, partly through his friend, the Anglo-Catholic Rev Conrad Noel, who officiated at his marriage. Noel was appointed by a mistress of Edward VII, the Countess of Warwick, to the East Anglian rural living of Thaxted, where he made his parish church notorious as the capital of Anglo-Catholic communism with morris-dancing, an altar to John Ball, the leader of the Peasants' Revolt, and the hammer and sickle flying in the nave. Chesterton spoke regularly to one Anglican body, the Christian Social Union, while another, the more militant Church Socialist League, gave rise to the Guild Socialism which had much in common with distributism.

This, then, was the background to Chesterton's thought about the family, which has an extraordinary consistency between his works *What's Wrong with the World* published in 1910 and *The Outline of Sanity* of 1926. He defended the family, as a popular institution, against an intellectual élite which despised it. He looked at marriage, and saw that most wanted it enough to enter it. The enemies of the traditional family, on the other hand, were the intellectual 'spawn of Nietzsche'[23] who thought like Shaw in terms of the remaking of man as superman, and refused to recognise the limits and boundaries set up for human behaviour by the general character of mankind, and the distinct and particular characters of men and women.

Chesterton's initial defence of the family is that man is a creative animal. Where 'God is that which can make something out of nothing', man 'can make something out of anything',[24] that is, where God's creativity is without limits, man's pleasure lies in creation within limits, with making the best of what he has. The poet respects the shape of his poem. Michelangelo discovers the possibilities of his block of marble. Ordinary men, who cannot write sonnets or sculpt statues, can make a house and garden. In this, 'Property is merely the art of the democracy. It means that every man should have something that he can shape in his own image, as he is shaped in the image of Heaven.'[25]

And so too, the family is the one anarchist institution and free society that the ordinary man and woman can create for them-

[23] G. K. Chesterton, *Eugenics and other Evils* (London: Cassell, 1922), 101.
[24] *What's Wrong with the World*, 46.
[25] Ibid., 47.

selves. The home is the one place in which the individual can be truly free; in which he can please himself, as he cannot please himself in a restaurant, by eating his meal if he so wishes on the floor; in which he can show the wildest unconventionality: 'the founding of a family is the personal adventure of a free man'.[26] And like any form of free expression the family means stickability, the business of getting through the hardship which must be a part of making it. For the difficulty of marriage is that in every pleasure there is a point of pain or tedium to be survived; to attain to the delight of reading Virgil, the student has to go through the agony of learning Latin, though constantly tempted to give up. Human vows, laws and contracts are ways of surviving this point of surrender. Like the sculptor confronted with the block of marble, the marriage-maker makes do with his materials. Above all, marriage must mean overcoming the basic difficulty, the natural incompatibility of man and woman, for 'a man and a woman, as such, are incompatible'.[27] There would be no point in their union if they were the same. The successful marriage plumbs the deep-sea riches of the differences between them. 'Every marriage is a sort of wild balance; and in every case the compromise is as unique as an eccentricity.'[28]

> Our God who made two lovers in a garden,
> And smote them separate and set them free,
> Their four eyes wild for wonder and wrath and pardon
> And their kiss thunder as lips of land and sea;
> Each rapt unendingly beyond the other,
> Two starry worlds of unknown gods at war,
> Wife and not mate, a man and not a brother,
> We thank thee thou hast made us what we are...
>
> Make not this sex, this other side of things,
> A thing less distant than the world's desire;
> What colour to the end of evening clings,
> And what far cry of frontiers and what fire
> Fallen too far beyond the sun for seeking,
> Let it divide us though our kingdom come;

[26] *Eugenics and other Evils*, 10.
[27] *What's Wrong with the World*, 54.
[28] *The Superstition of Divorce*, 66.

With a far signal in our secret speaking
To hang the proud horizon in our home.[29]

No marriage is all wine and roses. But its success depends on difference, on distinctions, on horizons, on a division of labour, on unlikeness of roles. Chesterton thought that women's place was in the home, because he had the highest view of the labour of the home, because almost the only work worth doing was in the home. Nothing was more important than the nurture and bringing up of children; and no work was more opposed than home work to the narrowness of the modern specialist, which included most modern men:

> To be Queen Elizabeth within a definite area, deciding sales, banquets, labours and holidays: to be Whiteley within a certain area, providing toys, boots, sheets, cakes and books, to be Aristotle within a certain area, teaching morals, manners, theology, and hygiene; I can understand how this might exhaust the mind, but I cannot imagine how it could narrow it. How can it be a large career to tell other people's children about the Rule of Three, and a small career to tell one's own children about the universe?... No; a woman's function is laborious, but because it is gigantic, not because it is minute. I will pity Mrs. Jones for the hugeness of her task; I will never pity her for its smallness.[30]

Chesterton therefore thought that woman's work is the real and indispensable work of the world, and not the world of public employment to which so many in his own day were aspiring. Hundreds of thousands of women cried out that they would not be dictated to, and became stenographers. His song of the crèche is full of pity for the working mother and the child in the public nursery. The child speaks:

> I remember my mother, the day that we met,
> A thing I shall never entirely forget;
> And I toy with the fancy that, young as I am,
> I should know her again if we met in a tram.
>   But mother is happy in turning a crank
>   That increases the balance at somebody's bank;

[29] 'A Wedding in Wartime', *CP*, 66–7.
[30] *What's Wrong with the World*, 132–3.

And I feel satisfaction that mother is free
From the sinister task of attending to me.

They have brightened our room, that is spacious and cool,
With diagrams used in the Idiot School,
And Books for the Blind that will teach us to see;
But mother is happy, for mother is free.
    For mother is dancing up forty-eight floors,
    For love of the Leeds International Stores,
    And the flame of that faith might perhaps have grown cold,
    With the care of a baby of seven weeks old.

For mother is happy in greasing a wheel
For somebody else, who is cornering Steel;
And though our one meeting was not very long,
She took the occasion to sing me this song:
    'O, hush thee, my baby, the time will soon come
    When thy sleep will be broken with hooting and hum;
    There are handles want turning and turning all day.
    And knobs to be pressed in the usual way;
    O, hush thee, my baby, take rest while I croon,
For Progress comes early, and Freedom too soon.'[31]

This is not an attack on women working but satire on the repetitive, mechanical, exploitative character of modern work; the feminist argument was that because men were enslaved by the kind of work they did, women should be enslaved as well. Indeed in the claims of the women's liberationists of his time, the suffragettes and such, Chesterton saw a female surrender to male values. 'All we men had grown used to our wives and mothers, and grandmothers, and great-aunts all pouring a chorus of contempt upon our hobbies of sport, drink and party politics. And now comes Miss Pankhurst ... owning that all women were wrong and all the men were right',[32] and that these public things were the only ones worth valuing. In this respect, modern feminism had espoused not merely male values, but male vices. Chesterton did not think such feminism democratic; he asked his wife, his mother and his charwoman whether they wanted the vote, and

---

[31] 'For the Creche: *Form 8277059, Sub-Section K*', *CP*, 101–2.
[32] *What's Wrong with the World*, 154–5.

they all said no. He thought that if women were to be given a vote on whether to be given a vote, they would have voted against it. But democracy means giving people what they want. The ballot was the demand of a minority foisted on a majority; it stood in contradiction to the very democratic principle that it seemed to be upholding.

But then Chesterton did not think that women were by nature democrats: there were three things that no woman could understand, liberty, equality and fraternity. He might have foreseen the ultimate paradox of universal suffrage once introduced, that the female vote was to keep Conservative administrations in power in Britain for most of the twentieth century; that the first woman to take her seat in the Commons was a Tory aristocrat, and one of nature's oligarchs to boot; and that the first woman Prime Minister was to be a Tory. Even in 1910, Chesterton was coming to his view of British politics as an undemocratic sham conflict between two oligarchies of the rich, which the wider franchise would fail to cure, and which the female vote would only reinforce.

For his view of women was that they are naturally autocrats, not democrats. In the private sphere petticoat government is wholly desirable. It is the form of unlimited and loving female tyranny which every child experiences in the cradle and at his mother's knee. And it goes with the loyalty, without limit or condition, which the mother gives her child. Such loyalty is a good within the home; it becomes dangerous in the public sphere when the woman gives this unconditional loyalty to her boss or colleague, and wears herself out in devotion to him, like Lady Macbeth, whose only crime was to want the best for her husband and children.

The threat to the family was, however, essentially a political one. It came partly from the socialism which wanted to replace the family with the Servile State; but even more from the capitalism which denied the family by demanding the women at its workplace; as Chesterton wrote, 'if it be true that Socialism attacks the family in theory, it is far more certain that Capitalism attacks it in practice'.[33] The family 'is the only formation in which

[33] *The Superstition of Divorce*, 76.

the charge of the rich can be repulsed'.[34] The verses above have two villains, the state-run nursery and the Leeds International Stores; and the one stands in the need of the other. 'Capitalism, of course, is at war with the family, for the same reason which has led to its being at war with the Trade Union ... Capitalism believes in collectivism for itself and individualism for its enemies. It desires its victims to be individuals, or (in other words) to be atoms'.[35] This anticipates Mrs Thatcher's remark that there is no such thing as society, though she claimed to believe in the family. But there was for Chesterton an equal and ancillary danger of the Servile State interfering with the family, which is a free and voluntary society: 'the small state founded on the sexes is at once the most voluntary and the most natural of all self-governing states';[36] it is the ultimate refuge against tyranny, and all the powers, of state and society and workplace, which are larger than itself.

Marriage is, moreover, a state freely entered by that most mystical and sensible of all ties, the vow. Chesterton thought that the pre-Christian world had been founded on status: one was pleb or patrician, slave or free. The modern world which came in with Protestantism and capitalism was founded on contract. But Catholic Christendom had been founded on the vow, in which the nun sinks her freedom in a mystical marriage to Christ and the pilgrim promises to die or to reach Jerusalem. Here in the vow is the ultimate in free action, the freedom to acknowledge limitation for the sake of creation, and to sacrifice a freedom freely for some nobler good; the freedom by which any lover, be he priest or pilgrim or bridegroom at the altar, wins the whole world by losing it, and gains a higher life by throwing his life away.

The Protestant world began by dismissing priestly and monastic vows of virginity and ended up by dispensing with marriage ones. The offence of Christianity had not been to exalt virginity. The ancient pagan world had also honoured the virginal ideal, as the sacred vestal flame had been carried before the Roman legions. But Christianity had shown that the vow of virginity was a practical ideal. Marriage was to be exalted because virginity was

---

[34] Ibid., 32.
[35] Ibid., 30–1.
[36] Ibid., 22.

more exalted. Virginity and marriage are different kinds of
fidelity and chastity, within the world of honour and the vow; they
are as difficult as each other; they make sense of each other.

And it was here that Chesterton attacked divorce, the betrayal
of the vow, as a superstition, because it is an irrationality within
the world to which it claims to belong. Belief in divorce implies
a belief in marriage; but it also implies a disbelief in marriage.
There is no point in dissolving the marriage bond if there is no
bond that needs dissolving; but the dissolution is also a destruction. Any couple can simply separate, with the blessing of the
Church, so the only point of divorce is to remarry. But the man
remarrying is involved in a contradiction. He has denied his own
vows of exclusive and eternal devotion to one woman merely in
order to make the same vows of exclusive and eternal devotion to
another. And yet the Church is damned for her narrow-
mindedness in refusing him her blessing to do this: 'the broad-
minded are extremely bitter because a Christian who wishes to
have several wives when his own promise bound him to one, is not
allowed to violate his vow at the same altar at which he made it.'[37]
He is foresworn, but insists on being foresworn again. 'The
modern man wants to eat his wedding cake and have it too.'[38]
Divorce for remarriage paradoxically destroys marriage by destroying the point and purpose of the vow from which marriage
takes its very being. The 'divorce controversy is not really a
controversy about divorce. It is a controversy about re-marriage;
or rather about whether it is marriage at all.'[39] It is a controversy
about a freedom to make an everlasting vow which the would-be
divorcee wants to take away.

The trouble with the modern world's desire for divorce,
according to Chesterton, was that it was not honest enough for
Christianity, but nor was it honest enough for paganism:

If I had been a Heathen,
    I'd have crowned Neaera's curls,
And filled my life with love affairs,
    My house with dancing girls.
But Higgins is a Heathen,
    And to lecture rooms is forced,

[37] Ibid., 108.
[38] Ibid., 107.
[39] Ibid., 124.

Where his aunts, who are not married,
Demand to be divorced.[40]

A truly *carpe diem* pagan would not bother with either marriage or divorce; the real impulse behind the demand for easier divorce was not the desire for liberty but for respectability. The English may not care for liberty but they do care to be respectable. Divorce was designed for Mrs Grundy. But the outcome of widespread divorce and remarriage would be two different standards of morality, and two kinds of person, those who are married and those who are really married. The issue was whether any social order could survive such moral divisiveness.

The threat to the family was also a threat from a new so-called science, Eugenics. The apologists for Eugenics, for the most part a now forgotten generation of doctors, wanted the State to interfere with the freedom of the family to have children by declaring certain individuals mentally or morally or physically unfit to do so, on the ground that their feebleminded or feeblelimbed offspring would be a burden to society. Chesterton wrote a work in opposition to a proposal to enact a law giving doctors this right, pointing out that, generally speaking, children are a lottery, in which the unlikeliest combination of individuals may produce mental or physical defectives.[41] Nor are these necessarily undesirables themselves, and even where there may be an hereditary predisposition to disease, this is hardly a good reason for refusing the right to reproduce; Keats and Stevenson both died young of TB, but mankind must still be grateful to the parents who begot and bore them. More profoundly, Chesterton saw in the argument against the unfit an attack upon the reproductive rights of the poor, and an attempt to impose a medical solution to the social problem of poverty, and indeed among progressives, for whom Nietzschean evolutionary theory demanded the elimination of the unfit, Eugenics was directed against the feckless and overfertile working classes, especially those so-called inferior races like the Irish who produced large families. Chesterton thought of children as the treasure of the poor who have no other; and he came to the Catholic view of the intrinsic value of large families. He also

[40] 'The Song of the Strange Ascetic', *CP*, 216.
[41] *Eugenics and Other Evils.*

called Eugenics Prussianism – a number of its supporters were German – and after his death, the Nazis were to bring the subject into disrepute by mass executions of the mentally and physically disabled. The subject has only returned to haunt us in our own day, with the emergence of a much more scientific genetics now capable of identifying probable abnormalities before conception or in the womb, with the moral dilemmas which this knowledge now creates, in a world in which the disabled look to diminishing public support.

Eugenics was the setting for the 1920s debates over artificial contraception, which was again propagated, especially by an intellectual élite of women rich in everything but children, as a cure for poverty. The poor were poor because they had too many children. They were, moreover, unfit to reproduce; and their numbers were a danger to the rich. Here again, Chesterton saw the 'Birth Controller' at work in promoting the interests of the smaller family.

> He always insists that a workman has no right to have so many children, or that a slum is perilous because it is producing so many children. The question he dreads is 'Why has not the workman a better wage? Why has not the slum family a better house?' His way of escaping from it is to suggest, not a larger house but a smaller family.[42]

Birth control was offered as a substitute for social reform. It was a mechanical solution to an organic problem. This was precisely the Vatican's argument recently at Cairo, that what was needed in the world was more social justice, not more condoms. In fact, the only strength of the poor is now their numbers; they are too numerous not to be feared by a Western consumer culture that places a higher value on its comforts than on its children.

There is, then, a contemporary context of Chesterton's ideas, though his setting is so different from our own. He lived in the twilight of Christendom, when much of Europe was still dominated by traditionally minded peasantries, while the middle classes were still largely attached by instinct and tradition to an older neo-Christian understanding of the family. It would be more

---

[42] G. K. Chesterton, *Social Reform Versus Birth Control* (London: League of National Life, 1927), 7.

difficult to argue now, as Chesterton did, that marriage is an intrinsically popular institution and that ordinary sexual morality carries a democratic authority. He could not have foreseen the widespread rejection of traditional norms since the 1960s, when the popularisation of contraception separated most sexual activity from reproduction and so inaugurated the permissive society. In the West only Catholic teaching tries to maintain that link, and it is rejected by many if not most Catholics. The decline of secular socialism has removed one enemy of Catholic Christianity, even while the lack of an agreed public ethic has made it difficult to define a moral system acceptable to more than a minority. Yet a man can do no more than work for his own time. And in his own time, Chesterton 'fed the immediately pre-1914 reaction against the notion of the unlimited development and progress of a human nature capable of endless alteration, and prepared the way for a body of thought which stressed logic, limits, authority and tradition'.[43] This is a labour that all needs to be done again today, in the changed political and social setting of our own time.

Tolstoy famously began *Anna Karenina,* perhaps the most celebrated modern novel about adultery, by saying that 'All happy families are more or less like one another; every unhappy family is unhappy in its own particular way.'[44] There are, then, all sorts of ways of going wrong; but there is only one way of going right.

[43] Coates, *Chesterton and the Edwardian Cultural Crisis,* 243–4.
[44] Leo Tolstoy, *Anna Karenina,* 2 vols (London: J. M. Dent & Sons, 1949), vol. 1, 1.

PART II

Faith, the Family and
the Modern World

8

Is the Church a Family?

Peter Selby

Is the church a family? Obviously not. You do not have to be an occasional player of *Happy Families* or dogmatically wedded to the nuclear family of mother, father and children to see that the church is not one of them, or even one of the extended variety. There have been congregations where the minister passes the pastorate on to a son (hardly ever, I think, a daughter), including some distinguished examples; but even then while that may make the church a family heirloom it hardly makes it a family.

Nonetheless, there are constant reminders within church life of the prevalence of some notion that the church is, or is supposed to be, a family. Sometimes this appears in a way that is ambiguous: for example it is often not clear whether the words 'Family Service' are merely intended to target a particular clientele, signifying an occasion at which account will be taken of the presence of young children (and therefore what takes place stands a better chance of being understood by the adults than is usually the case and will also ring bells with their childhood memories of church attendance).

Yet an occasion for families easily becomes a family occasion, one where the casual and easy intimacies which are the public face of family life are re-enacted, without too much recognition that family life often also has a less attractive private face. After all, when Sir Nicholas Ridley replied to the standard political jibe that it was time for him to 'spend more time with his family' by saying that that was the last thing he would wish to do, many regarded that not only as an endearing piece of honesty from him, but also as having a ring of truth that could be quite widely recognised. It would also be good if the churches that run occasions for families could at least recognise at the same time the effect of such occasions on those for whom life in families is either not a present reality or had for them been times of profound distress or even damage. Such groups between them almost certainly figure more largely within churches than in the population at large.

More serious are those occasions when family terminology is used for what appears the express purpose of achieving certain feelings or responses on the part of church members. Notices welcoming you to 'our church family', mentions of 'the diocesan family' or even, as I have seen it, 'the worldwide family of the Anglican Communion' are clearly meant to engender feelings of loyalty and belonging in those who read them. They may occasionally succeed in that intention, but their success must be at the cost of debasing the currency of life in families, which those who use the phrases presumably consider important. At the same time such language undermines the significance of those other forms of human membership one of another which are just as full of meaning, vitality and significance for us. Needless to say, words which are so evidently intended to engender a sense of belonging bear an inescapable witness to its absence. Why otherwise do the words need to be brought into so inappropriate a context? Sometimes the reasons for family language become even more sadly obvious, as when attempts are made to commend forms of assessment of church dues by referring to them as 'the family purse'.

In this essay I shall be examining some rather less obvious ways in which the lives of churches tend to be assimilated to assumptions about the family and their effects on the ability of churches to be like churches. Those examples will sometimes be anecdotal, based in my own pastoral experience. I shall then draw from those experiences some conclusions about what might be the real significance for ecclesiology of 'family' vocabulary. Finally, I shall reflect on the significance of those ecclesiological conclusions for the theme of this book, the family in theological perspective.

However, two introductory points are in order, the first methodological, the second by way of a justification for including this essay in this book at all. With regard to method, theological reflection that seeks to begin with accounts of contemporary experience and relate them to our biblical or doctrinal inheritance runs all the risks attendant on any 'theology from below', that the tradition is simply plundered for those insights that will confirm pre-existent perceptions, while other less congenial ones will be bypassed, a point which Stephen Barton makes more than once in his essay. It is not a sufficient response to make the point that there are other risks attendant upon beginning from a traditional standpoint, not least that it is possible to make statements about the church that bear no relation to any church that anyone has ever seen. For there is also the risk that the experience selected as a starting-point will be such as to lead to a conclusion chosen in advance, with counter-experience simply left out of account. This latter point might be particularly telling in my case.

To this point I can only say that we have the experience we have and not the one we do not have, and that if my accounts elicit from the reader some significant counter-experiences, that can only help the process of clarification. And to the more important risk, that of simply using the tradition for the purpose of finding support for prejudices, I would say that I should expect, as some safeguard, to find from the reference back to the biblical or doctrinal tradition insights emerging which were not present within the experience itself or my initial conclusions from it.

This brings me to the need to justify the inclusion of an essentially ecclesiological question, 'Is the Church a family?', among essays about the family in theological perspective. My contention will be that the reference back of the experiences I shall describe to some biblical roots of the use of family language about the Church turns out to shed some unexpected light – that is, to introduce theological perspective – on our consideration of the family, in ways that do not simply emerge from the experiences I shall describe or my own evaluation of them. I hope this will offer some support for the theological method, as well as a contribution to the main purpose of the book. The question in the title may indeed be ecclesiological; but what emerges from the study is more.

The congregation as family

The lives of local churches can on the surface bear a close resemblance to the ethos of many clubs and societies in which the need for maintaining themselves constantly threatens to overwhelm the awareness of the purpose for which they exist. A good deal of energy is consumed in the round of jumble sales, raffles and ever more ingenious sponsored activities so as to keep the financial wolves at bay. Those activities can take on a life of their own that competes with the congregation's more central concern with worship and witness; we can all parallel the story of the row that was occasioned locally when a room in a piece of church property that used to be let out for a whist drive to raise money was found being used for prayer.

The architectural and other heirlooms of the local Christian community have also turned into rather expensive luxuries. They have their own double message and double effect: at one moment they are a source of strength to the worshipping community as well as a witness to the neighbourhood. At another their effect is to divert the consciousness both of congregation and local community from the gospel to which they are intended to witness and become in their own right the focus of loyalties that are remarkably persistent and fierce. In either event their claim on resources can be immense.

Yet an inspection of these club-like features, evident enough in most local Christian congregations, shows that their purpose is maintenance also in a less material and economic sense. That is, they exist also for a secondary purpose of producing a form of community bonding, highly analogous to the bonding that is produced in families by means of shared activity. This can easily come to predominate over the originating fund-raising purpose, just as the fund-raising had in its turn come to predominate over the central purpose of the Christian enterprise.

The evidence for this point emerged quite early on in the process of incorporating modern fund-raising techniques into the life of local congregations. In the early days it was quite common when commending various schemes of regular or committed giving or covenanting to propose in exchange that there would thereafter be no need to conduct the usual round of fund-raising activities, which were presented as being an undesirable thing for a well-run church to be doing and an unnecessary drain on time and energy. Congregations were even told that special collections would be a thing of the past. It was not long, however, before the special collections and fund-raising activities began to return, initially often for purposes outside the maintenance of the congregation, but eventually very much as before.

The impetus for this came in part of course from the constant need to find more ways of raising money; but to a great extent the reintroduction of the sales of work and Christmas draws was the result of resentment felt by members of the congregation at the loss of what they saw as important opportunities for the congregation to experience 'fellowship' and 'get to know one another better'.

'Fellowship' and 'getting to know one another better' were also keynote themes that emerged with great frequency as vital steps forward for congregations to take when they met to reassess their life and work at the parish training weekends with which I was much involved in the 1970s, and are heard with just as great frequency now. It is not a very comfortable experience to question the content of either expression, a questioning frequently heard as hostile, or at least quite unnecessary because 'we all know what they mean'. Yet this defensiveness is, I suggest, a popular form of the 'personalism' which Stephen Barton has cause to question in his essay. It would appear that the virtues of intimacy, and in this case often a somewhat artificial jollity too, have taken far too high a place in the hierarchy of virtues for human well-being. As a result we are in danger of being left with a very impoverished rendering of the *koinōnia* and *philadelphia* which were enjoined upon the earliest Christian communities; neither can be very faithfully reflected without taking seriously the structural and missionary purposes of the Christian enterprise itself, which determine what that fellowship and closer knowledge one of another are really for.

In a series of articles in *MC*, the journal of the Modern Churchpeople's Union, now known as *Modern Believing*, a number of contributors address the phenomenon of clericism. One of them, Carol Smith, particularly raises the issue of the use of 'family' terminology about the local church. She points to the cost that may be involved in making a positive virtue of the way in which people understand family life:

> [Church communities] are claiming that they display some of the characteristics frequently attributed to families (often by the popular media). Families are portrayed as warm, close groups of people, creating environments where all family members, particularly children, feel secure, accepted, and loved. Such families can point us towards an understanding of

the unconditional love of God, so are desirable models for church communities to follow.

> There is nothing wrong with wanting church communities to be accepting environments where members feel secure and loved. Neither is there anything wrong with working to enable them to become like that. But we do need to question whether a loving, secure environment modelling the unconditional love of God is necessarily the impression conveyed by the use of the word 'family'.[1]

So there are grounds for questioning what happens when modern understandings and experiences of family life intrude themselves upon the life of the congregation. From whatever point of view mission is regarded, whether primarily as having to do with drawing our neighbours into an apprehension of the loving purposes of God in Christ or forwarding the justice, healing and peace which might be described as among the key 'values of the Kingdom', these 'intrusions' of processes and beliefs derived from the experience of the nuclear family are on the whole obstructive. Many congregations are so like family networks that it was necessary to ask them, before they undertook programmes of meetings and training which they said were their response to the Decade of Evangelism, whether they really wanted anybody new to come; so evident was it from their body language that their preference was to continue to grow old gracefully together.

The church family: parents and children

My suggestion is that these characteristics of local congregations are very widely present. Their presence is not always pathological. Many communities manage to combine the exaltation of what I have suggested are family virtues within the life of the congregation with strong missionary concerns for their locality, with vitality and openness to the world in their worship, with a seriousness about promoting the understanding and prayerfulness of their members and a non-intrusive awareness of their needs. To the extent that they do, I shall suggest that it is because they have been able to balance the pressure for their congregational

[1] Carol Smith, 'What Price a "Family"?', *MC*, New Series XXXIV. 5 (1993), 83.

life to be assimilated to some of the more cloying features of the modern nuclear family with an engagement with what both Bible and tradition claim to be the purposes for which the church came into being. That is not to say that some of the processes of the modern family are not in fact making themselves felt.

In particular, there is much evidence of the way in which such processes bear upon the pastor's relationship to the congregation, and the extent to which that is assimilated to patterns of family life in which there is a clear division of roles between adults and children. In the article to which I have already referred, Carol Smith draws some uncomfortably accurate parallels between the roles which belong to adults in families and those which belong, whether by custom, by the use of officially sanctioned power, or by processes of collusion, to the clergy. Like the power adults have to determine who is admitted to the family home, clergy exercise the dominant role in decisions about who is to be baptised or confirmed; like adults who decide which books children may read and which television programmes they may watch, the clergy have substantial power over the access of members of the congregation to information about theology and ways in which they can enlarge their understanding of the faith. In families, adults have the major say in how major family events are to be celebrated; in congregations, it is the clergy who in the main determine the pattern of liturgy.

In families the roles of adults are largely given by the power they have legally and financially, long after they have ceased to have the power with which the beginning of life endows them, first to bring into being and then physically to control. In churches, the power of the clergy is largely given by certain institutional, canonical and customary arrangements. But, and this is the point which I am most concerned to make, the power of parents over children extends itself into every aspect of their lives as a result, as psychological and emotional power; and it is this experience of childhood which also allows for the psychological and emotional extension of the power of the clergy over the laity.

More serious is the fact that this analogy between congregation and family also has the effect of preventing such issues of power and authority being confronted in a mature way. The feeling of impending disaster if children confront parents, and the sense, often imparted by their parents, that this will destroy the unity and love within the family, mean that for much of the time children are bound to adopt methods of attention-seeking, manipulation and regression to make their point. The regressive tendencies of many local congregations seem directly reminiscent of this experience: the dysfunctionality is often such that the result of membership of a local congregation will be to demean the person, making him or her less able, mature and capable than might otherwise have been the case.

But how is it for the parents?

It must be stressed here that this is not some general criticism of the behaviour of ministers. There are of course some who would merit such criticism for the way in which they use their power, just as there are also abusive, insecure and tyrannical parents. The point I am making is a structural one, and for the most part that structure is as problematical for the pastor as for the laity. Indeed, the more aware and conscientious the pastor is, the more problematical the structure is likely to become.

It is my experience of operating a rudimentary clergy appraisal system over a period of seven years that the overworkers outnumber the lazy by at least ten to one (and I never found a way of belonging to the minority). This ratio can only increase as numbers of ministers decline and financial pressures grow. The phenomenon is complex, and the roots of it will also go deep into the psyche of the individuals concerned; but at least part of what is at work here is the overdeveloped sense of responsibility which comes the pastor's way as he or she assumes the sense of responsibility for the congregation's well-being. That responsibility may arise from some of the very solemn language of the ordination rite; but it also grows out of the assimilation of the pastor's professional role to that of a parent, the universal provider, sustainer and guarantor of the family's survival and unity. The distress or pain or quarrelling of the 'children' becomes something it is the pastor's duty to resolve; and signs of the 'family's' decline, poverty or loss of respectability becomes a standing rebuke to the pastor's failure. Pastors come to see themselves, furthermore, as having to discharge the functions of a *lone* parent, fathering and mothering as best they can, on scant resources and with minimal support, with many of their lay members only too willing to accept such a division of roles – for in many churches a willingness to be like a child in a family becomes almost an essential qualification for membership.

It is worth adding that in the pastor's relation to the hierarchy a similar dynamic appears to operate. I have a vivid memory of being deputed to represent the bishops at the closing session of a training course for clergy from three Anglican dioceses, so as to enable participants to communicate their learning to the hierarchy. One of the groups chose to present its learning by placing the members' chairs in the centre of the room and then having the one who was directly in front of me back his chair violently into me. There followed the unloading of what felt like two millennia of rage on the part of the clergy against their bishops, an unloading which had all the force of a child's temper and none of the hopeful possibilities of a mature tabling of demands for change and negotiation. If anything was gained it was a clarity for me about some of the lurking and unnamed feelings that I had sensed in numerous encounters, underneath the surface presentation of respect and even deference.

This observation makes it plain that, contrary to what family-oriented perceptions are likely to suggest, a move on the part of the church away from a self-perception as 'family' would not mean the loss of all possibilities of warmth. Most pastors, certainly including myself, experience a great deal of warmth and affirmation from their congregations and colleagues. What working towards alternative self-understandings might offer would be the chance of establishing realistic expectations and boundaries to the roles people carry in the life of the church, in a context where what counted most was the church's function and task in the world and not the incessant carryover of the power of unacknowledged experiences of the nursery. In the next-but-one section I shall give just one example of what such an alternative self-understanding might be and what direct advantages it might bring to the church's performance of its task.

But what goes on in the bedroom?

Before leaving this survey of the consequence of the power of family perceptions in the church, it is important not to leave out the particularly baleful effect they have, paradoxically, precisely on the lives of the families of church members. I have two examples of this general point.

I recall being part of the planning of a major training event involving several hundred people, endeavouring to determine strategy for the years ahead and hopefully therefore enhancing the ability of those present to make an impact in society at large. It was proposed that a letter be drafted and made available from the diocesan bishop describing the event and offering it to those intending to come with a view to their giving it to their employers with a request to be given time off from work. The suggestion was immediately condemned as inappropriate, and the demand made that the event take place at the weekend. The suggestion of an approach to employers may well have been unrealistic; but what was revealing was the complete lack of hesitation about a comparable invasion of people's family time. When this was pointed out it was said that this was a kind of clash we all had to face, and that in any case 'this is a different sort of family time'.

I move from the generality of the effect of the 'family' perception of the church on its members and their families to a particularly acute form of that problem in the effect that 'church-as-family' has on the family life of the pastor. If the congregation has the tendency to assume the identity of the nursery, that can only mean that the parsonage house is pressed into the re-enactment of the function of the parents' bedroom. My reference at an earlier point to the sense in which ministers are pressed into service as parents and indeed *lone* parents needs to be modified to take account of the fact that the majority of non-Roman Catholic congregations are served by a married clergy. That means that while the parsonage house may occupy one role in the unacknowledged fantasy of the congregation, it is also in many cases inhabited by real people who live in real families. The impact of the 'family of the church' on these real families is turning at increasing speed into a tragedy of considerable scale. My own limited experience would itself take up more space than I have, but two examples must serve to represent them.

There now exists, thanks in great measure to some energetic and creative work done by Frank Field MP, an organisation for divorced and separated wives of clergy, known as Broken Rites. When I visited a local branch and discussed the experiences of those women, I have to say that I can remember few occasions on which I have encountered more largely undigested and certainly unresolved quantities of rage. Much of what we discussed concerned the effect on them of hearing that their former husbands – and many of the stories they had to tell were quite lurid – had been after varying intervals reinstated in ministry. There were many aspects to the fury this occasioned in them, but its force seemed to me to be related to a sense of betrayal: they had given enormously of themselves to communities which their husbands had served. Now they had been cast off, despite all the protestations of love and sympathy at the time, and often even official acknowledgment that what had happened was not their fault. The feeling that came over from them and which I suspect lay behind the force of their bitterness, was that their 'children' had decided after all to go and live with 'Dad', and that despite his outrageous behaviour.

My second example is an illustration of the way in which the parsonage and its actual family is invaded by the dysfunctionality of church 'family' as well as other actual families in the community. When a congregation experiences marital break-up or a public kind of difficulty in its pastor's family it often comes as a great shock. When it happens twice they are even more upset; but what about the community's own role in bringing that situation to pass? I recall one example of a place whose architecture expressed vividly the modern ideology of the family, the housing an attempt to recreate the ethos of a village, the whole surroundings a complex of church and school – and vicarage. Little wonder where the dysfunctionality, and there was a good bit of it on the estate and in the congregation too, found its focus. The church as family, the church of families, the church among families communicates its distress in and through the actual families of its pastors. To both examples must be added, of course, the huge pain involved in the requirement to share this great personal distress with your boss, or your spouse's boss; in the totality of life in the church 'family' the roles of 'boss' and 'parent' become very confused.

The church as public company?

This of course would not be the case were the church to see itself not as family but as public company. That would enable, indeed require, the distancing of professional and personal issues, and the creation of structures to enable the tabling of demands and handling of negotiations of which we noticed so marked an absence in a previous section. Criticism of the church's management systems is often met with the defensive assertion that 'we are not a business', on the assumption that we can all agree that that is so, and that being a family is something far better. The situations I have just described are ones where it can easily be shown that for the church to regard itself, and then structure itself, as a business might enable some of its most intractable pastoral difficulties to be better handled.

It might also enable, indeed require, the church to do some things which would actively promote its mission in the world, and I shall give just one example to conclude this part of the essay. I have been party on several occasions to discussions about what should happen in the case of clergy afflicted by disabilities that affected their capacity to do their jobs enough for the congregation to be distressed and the bishop to become involved. In relation to disability the church has a triple problem: it has an inheritance of a theology of 'completeness' in the priesthood, reflected in some of the ancient canons about ordination. This view is no longer part of any official teaching that I am aware of; but its replacement by a more Protestant and functional view of priesthood, backed by a Protestant work ethic, is hardly any more friendly to those with disabilities. Add to that the financial and staffing pressures affecting all the churches, and you have in any case a massive triple whammy affecting the less able-bodied or able-minded in ministry.

The discussions I have had have generally taken the form first of seeing whether there were places to which the person could be moved so that they could manage. That becomes more and more difficult, and so then there is a discussion about invalidity and early retirement. In all this the person concerned is confronted always with their boss-and-parent figure who is supposed to express the ideals and aspirations of the church family towards a person in need; but that in itself conceals the reality that there is here a conflict of interest in which there are no provisions to enable the different 'sides' of the conflict to come to expression. The person may feel unjustly treated, but how can he or she say so in the face of all that kindness and Christian love?

If the church were to see itself as a public company, not only would it have to have mechanisms for enabling such conflicts to come to expression and be resolved; but it would not be long before the law or pressure groups made the point that Church plc had a responsibility to ensure that it was actively recruiting into its employment enough less able-bodied or able-minded people to fulfil its responsibility to the community. Families do not actively want to have one of their members disabled; those who experience that often show heroic courage and great love in dealing with their situation, or even extend their compassion to adopting others in need. But companies have to have policies and structures, a situation which requires planning and lifts the burden of responsibility from individuals.

This reflection was partly prompted by the experience of a friend who visited a local department of a large company where the local authority had placed two people with particularly severe learning difficulties. He was struck by the creativity of the employees he met in seeking to enable the two people concerned to make the maximum contribution they could, but even more by the clarity within the management structure that this was company policy and provision had to be made for the job arrangements to accommodate them. I know that the suggestion that the church should actively recruit into its ministry a quota of people with disabilities would provoke first blank amazement, and secondly the observation – an accurate one as well as an excuse – that the church's structures simply would not enable the putting into effect of such a policy even if it were decided on.

What I also know is that such a policy would be an immensely powerful witness, greater than innumerable acts of kindness to people with disabilities, to the Christ who brought near those who had been far away and who after his resurrection enabled there to be a church for the continuing of that work. This is not of course to say that companies are all wonderful and the church bad, far less to compare a good example with a bad one in order to draw prearranged conclusions. It is to make the point that any word you use about the church, family no less than company, can work for good, and at the same time requires constant reference to what the Bible and the tradition have to say about what a church is intended to be and to do if its good possibilities are not to be overwhelmed by unintended negative effects.

What this section has sought to show is that consideration of the nature of the church as it can be observed in contemporary society does not give much encouragement to the view that seeing it as a 'family' really assists it in its task, and indeed suggests that other ways of seeing it might make it if anything a more effective environment for human flourishing. But what, we must now ask, about the roots of the 'family' ideal in the Bible?

New covenant, new family

The need to make modern translations of the New Testament inclusive in their language has had the result of increasing from next to nothing the occasions when readers will encounter explicit reference to the church as 'family'. *Patria* has often been translated 'family' in Ephes 3.15, and it is now an easier translation to handle than 'fatherhood'. To that verse we shall return. It is the need to find inclusive translations of *adelphoi* that has caused those who represent Christ in the parable of the judgement in Matt 25 to become 'the least of these who are members of my family' (Matt 25.40 NRSV), those *adelphoi* who are with Paul in Gal 1.2 to become 'members of God's family', and the audience of the First Epistle of Peter to be enjoined to 'love the family of believers' rather than 'the brotherhood' (1 Pet 2.17).

These translations highlight the fact that an understanding of the church as a 'family' has its origin in the determination of the New Testament to speak of the human situation in terms of relationship, and of the transformation of that situation by the grace of Christ in terms of transformed relationship. What happens is the breaking open of clan boundaries, so that those who have to be addressed as two groups in Paul's address in Antioch, 'My brothers who are of Abraham's family, and you others who fear God' (Acts 13.26), are able to become newly related as brothers and sisters. The relationship to Abraham is extended so as to belong to 'many nations' through a gracious act of God who is so far unconstrained by clan boundaries as to be able to raise up descendants of Abraham from the stones on the ground (Matt 3.9).

It goes without saying that such language only has meaning if the loyalty that belongs to the family is taken seriously. If you live in a society where family relationships cannot be assumed, or carry no honour with them, then they cannot be used as any kind of idiom of transformation. Jesus' addressing of God as his Father, and his declaration that the God who is his Father is also ours, make sense only in the context of a world where descent matters, and where people are accustomed to claim Abraham as their father. Only then does it make sense to speak of this Abraham as the father of many nations, and of God as Father of all.

That makes it doubly important, however, to recognise that the language of family and kinship is there in relation to church not for the purpose of encouraging some of the attributes which we have seen to be associated with the concept of family in our time. Rather, it is there to emphasise the character of the transformation which has taken place in the relationships which human beings have to each other and to God in the light of God's grace. The repeated address to *adelphoi* is a statement about where the members of the church, whatever their kinship and origin, stand in relation to the saving work of Christ. The effect of the rebirth required of Nicodemus and of those for whom he acts as representative (Jn 3) would be to change his line of descent. So the source of his membership of the community of God's people is changed from human descent to spiritual descent. This is also the effect enacted for all believers when they are baptised into the family of faith, which is God's 'house', that is God's lineage.

This very quickly goes beyond a mere method of explanation, an analogy to help people to understand. Were it just that, it might simply be replaced by other analogies in other cultures. As was suggested at the beginning of this essay, the reference back to the scriptures has a double effect. It does of course illuminate the source of a certain kind of language that the church has come to use, and perhaps to misuse, about itself. We have seen that it does not originate in a desire to commend intimacy, jollity or loyalty, but to offer a transformation of the loyalties and intimacies people naturally have, if they do, into a pattern of living that is intentionally inclusive. Natural loyalties may be determined by the boundaries of kinship, but not so with the new kind of clan God is about creating: 'Whoever does the will of God is my brother, my sister and my mother' (Mk 3.35).

As a result it is possible to speak of the gospel's offer as a form of *huiothesia,* translated 'adoption' and meaning in effect an extension of all the rights that belong to descent by the male line, to an essentially unlimited community of brothers and sisters. What then happens, inevitably, is that the notion of 'family' as the key to membership and to esteem has to take second place to the new community of faith. Suddenly what emerges is not an image by which to convey truth, but a truth that radically changes the image: for the message of Ephes 3.15 is not that by reference to our experience of life in families we are able to understand our relationship with God. It is that our membership of family has to take its meaning and shape from what has emerged about our relationship with God, 'from whom *pasa patria,* all [patrilinear] familyhood takes its name'. In the light of God's fatherhood, and the fraternity and sorority which turned out to be God's human project, family patterns have to be re-examined.

For example, we may well share many of the concerns expressed by Stephen Barton's quotation in his essay from former Chief Rabbi Jakobovits, about the results of the decline of the family, and certainly we should not belittle as from some superior Christian standpoint his concern, and his successor's even stronger concern, that the decline of family loyalty may make the transmission of faith considerably harder than it has been in earlier generations. But we have at the same time to weigh the significance of a different tradition. Where he says, 'I belong to the people who first taught the human race that we were all originally descended from an identifiable father and an identifiable mother…', the Church that emerged from the people who heard that message also heard another, that it emerged in its turn from another primeval pair who were called to leave home and kindred.

The point at which Stephen Barton's essay ended was that the institutions of marriage and the family are not to be disparaged for they are 'in the providence of God and as the Bible testifies so amply ways of giving shape and form to the life for which God has made us'. To that we must add that part of that providence was to provide an idiom for the kind of transformation which God also had in store, a transformation which leads to the conclusion that in some ways families can be valued too much. Against the dire effects of the loss of family belonging as a preparation for adulthood we have to weigh the even more dire effects of the refusal of human clans everywhere to honour their membership of the boundless family that the divine grace seeks to bring into being.

If this should appear as a disparagement of the institutions of marriage and the family, a subordination of them to another institution called church, that is not my intention. It is rather, as I hinted at the beginning, that our journey through some rather negative aspects of the church's appropriation of family language and (even more) of family processes leads to the point where something has to be said about life in families. That message may be hard to express and live out, but it belongs to their essential well-being and that of those who share in them.

Families exist because human beings come together to produce, and then hopefully rear, their young. Nobody who has taken part in that process for better and worse can be in any doubt about how powerful that coming together, that procreating and nourishing can be. But even in the face of that, the church claims to set before its families an even larger project. Having borne children, families are invited to present them for baptism; having fed them, to teach their children to pray; having given them the best upbringing they know how, at the same time to place themselves alongside their children in the community which is subject to God's word and exists by God's nourishment. That is to say, whatever may be the power and responsibility accorded to parents by their strength, their money or their rights, their relationship is actually, and ultimately more crucially, defined as an equality. That equality derives not from our politics or our culture but from our being recipients alike of that *huiothesia* which is God's offer to humankind. Therefore whatever hopes any of us may hold out for our children, the real issue for us is the hope God has in store for us and them alike in the divine family from which ours has to take its name and within which our families, like all our other loyalties, including of course, church loyalties, have to take their place.

This is not in my view in the least remote from the 'crisis facing the family'. In the families of the present day we experience in a most acute way the dilemmas of freedom and dependence, of authority and rebellion, of disintegrating social fabric on the one hand and the power of peer group pressure on the other. We also experience in the same context huge resources of love and loyalty. It is surely crucial to remember – as much in so-called positive as in so-called negative experiences of life in families – that a larger project is in hand even than making our family work. That larger project turns out to contain resources for our life in families too: built around hope, forgiveness and openness. They come with a particular force when it is remembered that those themes derive ultimately from an invitation to us to become people who transcend our descent: we are to become children of God 'born not of blood or of the will of the flesh or of the will of a man, but of God' (Jn 1.13).

9

The Family and the Liturgy

Michael Vasey

This essay suggests ways in which the practice and study of the church's worship can throw light on current Christian reflection on the family. The invitation to include such a contribution is particularly welcome given the common reluctance of analytical theology to see the liturgy of the church as a useful source for theological reflection. Many people are inclined to view liturgical practice as a second-order activity in the church's theological calling, something that can be left to applied or pastoral theologians, or to devotional aesthetes, after exegetes, systematicians, or even sociologists, have completed the serious work of articulating the church's faith. The assumption behind this essay is that liturgical assembly is a primary place where theology – the demanding task of understanding and responding to God – is done. The conviction is finely expressed in one of Aidan Kavanagh's chapter headings where he describes liturgy as 'Church doing World'.[1]

The liturgy created by the people of God's encounter with the good news of Jesus Christ is both an articulation of the gospel in society and also a formative influence on the church's understanding of its calling. In Christian worship one meets the gospel of Jesus Christ in dialogue with human culture. Liturgy is not merely analytical or cerebral; it is a place where the church discovers and acts out a theological anthropology. While the three lines of exploration set out in this paper assume rather than defend these positions, they may also provide some evidence of their validity.

[1] Aidan Kavanagh, *On Liturgical Theology* (New York: Pueblo, 1984), chapter 4.

169

Two ways of organising desire

Modern churchgoers expect to sit together in families. Taken against the wider practice of Christian people, this expectation cannot be taken for granted but invites analysis and reflection. A common practice in the ancient world, in Jewish synagogues, and in the Third World is for men and women to sit separately. Anyone who has worshipped with Christians in India or Africa is likely to have met this pattern. 1 Timothy, whose literary genre I take to be an early 'church order', assumes that men and women form distinct groups in the worshipping gathering (2.8–10). The Didascalia, a third-century church order, describes this aspect of liturgical assembly in greater detail:[2]

> And again, let the lay men sit in another part of the house towards the east ... so that when you stand up to pray, the leaders stand first, and after them the lay men, and then the women too.... And if anyone is found sitting out of his place, let the deacon who is inside reprove them and make him get up and sit in the place that is appropriate for him. For our Lord compared the church to a farmstead: for as we can observe the dumb animals – I mean oxen and sheep and goats – lie down and sit up, feed and chew the cud by species, with none of them separating itself from its own kind ... so too in the church, those who are young ought to sit separately, if there is room, and if not, to stand up. And those who are advanced in years should sit separately too. And let the children stand on one side, or let their fathers and mothers have them close to themselves; and let them stand up. The young girls should also sit separately, or if there is no room, they should stand behind the women.

A Methodist student once protested strongly during a lecture in which I was tentatively defending this non-Western practice. She heard my comments as an objection to the welding together of Christian faith and family life that lay near the heart of her vision of Christian discipleship. When I told Raymond George, the distinguished Methodist liturgist, of the incident he sent me the following quotation from John Wesley:

[2] *The Liturgical Portions of the Didascalia,* ed. Sebastian Brock and Michael Vasey (Nottingham: Grove Books, 1982), 15–16.

Let the persons who propose to subvert the Methodist plan by mixing men and women together in your chapel consider the consequence of so doing. First, I will never set foot in it more. Second, I will forbid any collection to be made for it in any of our Societies.[3]

Behind this clash of expectations lie interesting differences in the way in which desire and gender are acknowledged within the social order. Four strands that contribute to this cultural difference can be identified.[4]

1. Two worlds of gendered affection

In many ancient and non-industrial societies people live out their lives in two gendered worlds which complement each other and which meet and interact at various points. This pattern is obviously part of the Christian monastic tradition but is also widespread elsewhere. An interesting biblical example is the book of Proverbs which is written within a male world of affectionate relationships – reflected for example in the recurring 'my son'. At various points in Proverbs we are given a window into a complementary female world in which women of similar social standing live out a life that seems to be characterised by dignity and responsibility (cf. 5.15ff; 7.4, 5; 8; 9.1–6; 31.1–8; 31.10–31). The sphere of the 'good wife' of Proverbs 31.10ff includes many activities of management and commerce that industrial society locates in a public realm which is theoretically genderless but actually dominated by men.[5] This pattern of two interlocking gendered worlds is also found in the movement gathered round Jesus. It is represented, to the embarrassment of modern susceptibilities, by the all male membership of the Twelve and by the complementary world of the women who followed Jesus (cf. Lk 23.49; 8.1–3).

In such cultures these two worlds are not static realms rigidly separate from each other. They exist in a dynamic relationship

---

[3] John Wesley to the Leaders at Sheffield, 4 September 1780, *Letters* (ed. Telford) *VII.* 32.

[4] A number of points in this section draw on my *Strangers and Friends* (London: Hodder & Stoughton, 1995).

[5] Cf. Ivan Illich, *Gender* (London: Marion Boyars, 1983).

that does not preclude significant areas of overlap. The relationship between the two worlds may be more or less oppressive of individuals or of groups. The existence of these two worlds means that people enter the world of the other gender supported and formed by a network of affectionate relationships with their own gender.

The word 'affectionate' is important. Anglicans meet the mindset of these older cultures in the elaborate wording of the bishop's license for a priest. A public official who may not even know the cleric by sight addresses him in terms of warm affection, 'John by Divine Providence Lord Bishop of Durham, to our well beloved in Christ ... Greeting etc.' Hardly the language that accompanies an electricity bill or a council tax demand! Underlying this public rhetoric is the view that society consists of a network of bonds of affection. Society is held together by bonds of friendship that arise in a wide variety of ways and are characterised by mutual obligation and affection. In medieval society the significance of godparents lay partly in their role in the creation of such bonds.[6] (This may also be the proper context to understand the relationships created by the same-sex liturgical rites discussed by John Boswell in *Same-Sex Unions in Premodern Europe.*)[7] One of the important results of the triumph of the economic arrangement of modern capitalism has been the destruction of this vision of networks of gendered affection and its replacement by a more isolated, competitive and male identity. Particularly in public relationships between men it has led to the formation of an anti-emotional and competitive style of relating. Even the apparent exception of the world of sport often has, as its underlying rationale, the aim of sharpening men's ability to compete.

---

[6] Cf. J. H. Lynch *Godparents and Kinship in Early Medieval Europe* (Princeton: Princeton University Press, 1986); M. Searle, 'From Gossips to Compadres. A Note on the Role of Godparents in the Roman Rite for the Baptism of Children', in *Eulogema,* ed. E. Carr et al. (Rome, 1993). The subject is also being explored by Peter Robinson in his current doctoral work in the Department of Theology, Durham University.

[7] John Boswell, *Same-Sex Unions in Premodern Europe* (New York: Villand Books, 1994), subsequently published in Britain under the title *The Marriage of Likeness* (London: Harper Collins, 1995).

2. Desire and the social order

It is part of the genius of Augustine's great work *The City of God* that he brings the desire of the human heart and the public ordering of society into relationship with each other. He uses the scriptural images of Babylon and Jerusalem to portray human history as the outworking of a dual citizenship. Two loves, the love of God and the love of self, create two human projects that provide the context for all human life. The visible church is not an alternative society turning its back on the world but something more like a resistance movement – a company of people responding to the hidden presence of the love of God while living out their lives within the 'earthly city' that forms the current context for their lives and their obligations to God and neighbour.

This Augustinian vision is often suspected or rejected on the ground of an inherent dualism. Certainly for Augustine himself this probably rests on a number of misunderstandings. One way it is kept from dualism is its treatment of desire. Another lies in the insight of Augustine and his medieval successors that desire itself is mediated and evoked through images that arise within creation. The qualities that draw out the desire that creates and orders society include age (with unfamiliar resonances of dignity and gravitas), strength, beauty and harmony. Each responds to the varied echoes and reflections of the divine beauty that are hidden in creation. Bernard of Cluny's great hymn 'Jerusalem the golden' presents us with his world of thought in which human desire can be evoked by and focused on the beauty and humanity of a political image.

This provides a useful background against which to understand Christian liturgy. Christian worship is a corporate art form which gives temporary and partial expression to the hidden current of the love of God. Classical liturgical forms often anticipate and model the heavenly city. They also inevitably reflect the ambiguity of any expression of desire in the context of human alienation from God:

> In the activity of worship not only are the idols of the day kept at bay, but a renewed desire for God, in a limited and transcendent way, creates glimpses and reflections of true human glory.... The problem, of course, is that these manifestations of love for God cannot trap the movement of the Spirit that

creates them nor are they ever pure. In different eras of the church's life what some have seen as signs of the heavenly city others have seen as the captivity of the church to powers that seek to supplant God. Was the splendour of 4th century worship a celebration of Christian freedom or collusion with imperial power? Is medieval worship and art a hauntingly beautiful testimony to the way a society's imagination can be captivated by Christ or an idolatrous attempt by a powerful institution to grab wealth and power in feudal society? Are the Reformation liturgies the recovery of scriptural Christianity or the instruments of social control by ruthless Tudor monarchs and their greedy courtiers?[8]

3. The goal of erotic love

While modern thought identifies the sharp emotion of desire with the human sexual project, classical thought was wiser to identify *eros* more simply with the strong emotion evoked by an image. Erotic desire does not of itself imply an outworking in affection, relationship, intimacy, or sex. Behind the modern conceptualisation of erotic love lies a precise history.

It is not completely clear where the first cultural articulation of romantic love in European society began to take shape. One of its earliest expressions occurred in the romantic love that often arose between individuals of the same sex within monastic communities; in individuals such as Bernard and Aelred this love is celebrated and taken up into a vision of the spiritual life. Outside the monastic communities the tradition of courtly love focused erotic desire on another man's wife and saw its appropriate expression in chivalry rather than adultery. Another important interpretation is found in Dante, who took the beauty of the young Beatrice as a revelation of the beauty of God reflected in creation and made it the basis of his great theological poem, the *Divine Comedy*.[9] The later medieval church responded to these powerful and disturbing emotions by presenting the love be-

---

[8] Quotation from Vasey, *Strangers and Friends*, 190–1.
[9] Cf. Charles Williams, *The Figure of Beatrice* (1961, reprinted New York: Octagon Books, 1978).

tween a husband and wife in marriage as the proper goal and expression of erotic desire.

This attempt to identify desire with marriage has profoundly reshaped Western culture. An association made in the later Middle Ages was consolidated by two features of the Reformation. The first was the strange alliance that developed between Reformers and the new landed gentry of the Tudor age in their opposition to monasticism. The second was the Reformers' promotion of a new ideal of companionate marriage. The effect of these was to determine the public realm as a place for the articulation of desire or affectionate relationship. It created the familiar world of the middle classes in which the public realm is seen as a place of economic competition rather than public affection. Art and intimacy are then relocated to the domestic realm; instead of building cathedrals, creative energy is directed towards domestic decoration. Intimacy and desire move from the public realm to the home and then to the bedroom. Human intuitions of beauty are identified as being about sex. In the nineteenth century the new sciences of human behaviour rename this human intuition as heterosexual love and confirm the cultural judgement that it is properly directed to marriage. One outcome of this development is the loss of the notion that wealth is held for the community. Another is the destruction of the idea of public art of which liturgy had been an important example.

4. The repackaging of family as humane refuge

Jeffrey Weeks in his book *Sex, Politics and Society: The regulation of sexuality since 1800* charts a final development that shapes the modern conceptualisation of desire. Faced with the cruelty and inhumanity of industrial society, nineteenth century social reformers, including evangelical Christians, responded by creating the notion of the family as a place of humane refuge from the full rigours of the economic market. The idea is already present in the attempts to withdraw children and women from the harsh working conditions of the factories and the mines.

Although this strategy had much to commend it, at a deeper level it should be seen as a counsel of despair. Unable to reassert humanity in the public and economic realm, it was content to identify the home as the place of humane affection. Whereas ancient culture had seen the household as the model and microcosm of society, the effect of this social movement was to repackage the family as the place of refuge. Earlier tendencies were consolidated, with the domestic sphere becoming the place of affection, intimacy – and, as we have recently been realising, abuse.

However well intentioned, this strategy had a number of unintended results. It led to the creation of a domestic sphere immune from the sort of scrutiny normal in societies that operate with more extended networks. In Jewish, Asian or African society children do not belong exclusively to the parents but rather to a wider affectionate community. Again, within working class communities the proffered image of the family was adopted but refashioned to fulfil a different social role from that envisaged by its middle class advocates.[10] Proposed as a way of relating personal life to the public institution of the church, it was reworked in these communities and given a more tribal character that effectively became an alternative to the church's claim to authenticate desire and affection.

The strategy also had serious results for men in industrial society. The majority of men were forced to subordinate affection and desire to the harsh realism of the new economic order. Men who were unable to accept the scripts on offer attempted to forge alternative identities – of which the modern gay identity is an important instance – and did so at considerable cost. The impact of this strategy on adolescent males has been particularly serious. At a time in their life when other societies would be affirming the artistic and civic elements of desire, the adolescent male of Western culture is forced to deny desire as the condition of acceptance and belonging in the public realm.

Baptism and marriage

The rites of baptism and marriage provide important places in which the Christian community discovers and forms its understanding of human life.

---

[10] Jeffrey Weekes, *Sex, Politics and Society* (London: Longman, 1981) 32–3, 57–95.

1. Process

Pastoral experience, historical study and anthropological reflection have together led contemporary liturgical study to recognise that liturgical rites need to be related to the human processes that they acknowledge and promote. The key to understanding many of the liturgical rites of the Western Christian tradition is to see that their current form arises from the collapse of an extended ritual process into a single transactional moment. For example, the traditional burial liturgy of many cultures is a process lasting about 40 days that begins with the approach of death and ends at the conclusion of an initial period of mourning. At its heart this liturgy is an accompanied journey in which the community walks with the person who is dying and their immediate family through the experience of death and loss. This notion is still present in the processional use of the psalms provided by Cranmer in the funeral liturgy of the Book of Common Prayer. In the case of funerals, the triumph of the motor car, with the isolation of moving anonymously through traffic, has further lessened any sense of the corporate and extended character of liturgical engagement with death; instead of a ritual that symbolises the *journeys* of death and bereavement, people become the passive recipients of the action of an alien officialdom.

Similarly, the ordinary marriage rite of the Western church includes two sets of questions addressed to the couple. The first set was originally the betrothal that would have taken place a considerable time before the marriage. Not only were the two parts of the present rite once separated in time; they will have been part of a more extended process that included the wedding feast and the blessing of the marriage bed.

In recent years some churches have begun to recognise that certain rites which look like single solemn transactions presided over by an ecclesiastical official are better seen as an extended social process marked at significant points by corporate liturgical celebrations. The first major initiative in this direction occurred in 1972[11] with the publication by the Roman Catholic Church of a revised baptismal rite under the title the *Rite of the Christian*

---

[11] An English translation authorised for use in England and Wales was adopted in 1987.

Initiation of Adults (RCIA). The initial inspiration for this rite arose from Catholic missionary experience in Africa and from an attempt to respond to profound secularisation in parts of France. This rite not only takes seriously the human processes involved in a journey to faith, it also creates a context in which the baptising church accepts its responsibility to support and learn from those coming to faith. (The recently published report *On The Way* makes proposals for the adoption of a similar approach in the Church of England.)[12]

Following the RCIA the Roman Catholic Church has adopted a new *Order of Christian Funerals* based on similar principles.[13] Since then the Pastoral Liturgy Committee for the Catholic Bishops' Conference for England and Wales has nearly completed work on a new *Order of Christian Marriage* which attempts to recognise that the establishing of a marriage is a process that takes place within a community.[14] This rite has now been accepted by the Bishops' Conference. (Before it can come into use the Government has to be persuaded to facilitate legislation to change the wording of the marriage vow, and confirmation of the rite has to be received from Rome.) The new Roman Catholic rite will allow the reintegration of experience and liturgy in the establishing of marriages. Although there is plenty of evidence for continuing nostalgic conservatism in the celebration of marriage, this rite will at least open up the possibility of couples relating their developing relationship within the community to an understanding of Christian faith.

The current practice of a single marriage service encourages the notion that marriage is a status into which people enter and which is conferred by church or state. It would be truer to older practice to see marriage as a developing human process negotiated within a community.

2. Pragmatism

Baptism and marriage are both rites of passage. The sort of

---

[12] *On the Way: Towards an Integrated Approach to Christian Initiation* (London: Church House Publishing, 1995).

[13] *Order of Christian Funerals* (London: Geoffrey Chapman, 1990).

[14] Christopher Walsh, 'The Revision of the Marriage Rite', *Liturgy* 10/5 (1986) 180–202.

Reformed theology represented by the Thirty-Nine Articles speaks of baptism as a sacrament and of marriage as a 'state of life allowed in the scriptures' (Article XXV). There are, of course, many difficulties with the term 'sacrament'. Even before the expanded use of the word found in modern theology there was a conflict between those who identified the essence of sacrament in its derivation from the Good News of Jesus Christ, and those who saw its essence in a symbolic and embodied character. Another difficulty with the traditional categories of Word and Sacrament is that they easily set up a series of contrasts: Bible *against* Eucharist; concept *against* symbol; cerebral *against* ritual. The introduction to the new constitution recently adopted by the Joint Liturgical Group attempts to avoid these polarisations by speaking of 'four elements' that 'provide a God-given framework to Christian worship: ordered worship on the first day of the week; the public reading of scripture with exhortation and teaching; the welcome of new Christians in baptism; and the celebration of the eucharist'. This formulation recognises that while these elements differ from each other they carry with them the gospel and need to be embodied by the community that receives them.

Perhaps a better way of making the distinction attempted in Article XXV would be to say that some liturgical rites arise out of the givens of the Gospel corporately received, and others arise out of human processes corporately received. Interesting evidence of the difference between the two occurs in the ethical section of some New Testament letters. Thus Colossians 3.5–17 roots the ethical injunctions of the passage in the identity conferred in baptism, whereas the verses that immediately follow, with their specific address to wives, husbands, children, fathers, slaves, masters accept the social roles prevailing in the culture. Baptism is a given of the Gospel that creates a theologically significant identity; the institutions of the household have no theological imperative other than the ordinary processes of human society. For the modern reader the most obvious evidence of this social pragmatism is the way in which these 'household codes' accept the institution of slavery.

The evidence of the early liturgical tradition is that marriage comes into the second category; it is a human process being celebrated and supported within the community. There is disagreement among liturgical scholars as to the character and origin of early Christian marriage rites. Kenneth Stevenson has argued against K. Ritzers' scepticism about an early explicitly Christian marriage rite[15] and points, for example, to the following passage from Tertullian as evidence that marriage liturgy was an aspect of ecclesial life by the third century:

> How shall we ever be able adequately to describe the happiness of that marriage which the Church arranges, the Sacrifice strengthens, upon which the blessing sets a seal, at which the angels are present as witnesses, and to which the Father gives his consent?

The earliest forms of marriage liturgy do not consist, as modern people might imagine, of an exchange of promises but simply of prayers. In essence, as the argument of 1 Timothy 4.3–5 itself might suggest, they are a sort of grace – the acknowledgement and reception by prayer of an aspect of life. In ancient collections such prayers are included alongside such rites as prayer after birth, prayer for fertility, prayer for rain, the blessing of seed, prayer after a boy's first haircut, and so forth. Marriage in Roman culture was effectively the entrance of the woman into recognised and independent legal status.[16] This is reflected in the enduring Western tradition that the heart of the marriage rite is the blessing of the bride. Even modern Western liturgical rites struggle to assert in the choreography or the wording of the nuptial blessing that the event is of equal significance for the husband.

3. Praise

Modern Western theology regards the essential act that makes a marriage as the promise that the couple make to each other and which is witnessed by an ordained minister and the assembled company. This reflects a later development in the Western liturgical tradition, namely the exchange of vows which, particularly in forms derived from the Sarum rite, have gripped popular

[15] Kenneth Stevenson, *Nuptial Blessing* (London: SPCK, 1982), 13–21. See also the discussion in Boswell, chapter 5.

[16] *Documents of the Marriage Liturgy*, ed. Mark Searle and Kenneth W. Stevenson (Collegeville, MN: The Liturgical Press, 1992), 5, 6.

imagination. The introduction of this exchange in the marriage rite occurred in the eleventh century as part of an attempt to regulate marriage more carefully out of concern both for property and consanguinity, and also to prevent forced marriages.[17]

The older liturgical tradition, represented by the apocryphal book of Tobit (7–9) and the continuing practice of the Eastern churches, locates the act of marriage in a prayer of praise. In the case of Tobit and the continuing Jewish tradition this prayer of praise is offered by the husband or family member. In the Orthodox tradition the blessing of the marriage is reserved to the priest.

These two traditions have two different tendencies. At its core the later Western marriage rite is the support and clothing of a promise, whereas in the earlier tradition it is the celebration and receiving of a gift. The natural outworking of the later Western practice is to locate the heart of marriage in the *will*; the stability of marriages is made to depend substantially on the shifting ground of human resolution. The Jewish and Eastern tradition understands marriage as a *gift*. Marriage is seen as an aspect of human life, with its own inherent potentialities and responsibilities, that comes to us from the hand of the creator. Furthermore, marriage is then seen simultaneously as a gift to the couple and to the community; it carries blessings and responsibilities for both.

The inclusion of the community in the reception of the gift of marriage finds faint echoes in various marriage rites. Two forms of marriage blessing prepared for the forthcoming Joint Liturgical Group's rite for interchurch marriage will attempt to embody this insight more directly. They take a responsive form: the couple begin the praise that 'receives' the marriage and this is taken up first by representatives of their natural community and then by the ordained ministers.

The 'Family Service' movement

What are often known as Family Services have become an important part of the landscape of worship in the Church of England in the last thirty years. In many places they are the best attended

---

[17] *Documents of the Marriage Liturgy*, 148, 149.

services in a parish. Their essential elements are a lively more informal style, accessible music and vivid illustrated teaching. These elements may stand on their own or form the first part of a Eucharist. More recently a certain nervousness about the title Family Service has emerged and the search is on for a more inclusive term; people often speak of 'All Age worship'. The Church of England has recently authorised a framework for such services under the title *A Service of the Word*.[18]

Discussion of these services often focuses on whether they should be seen as a bridge to the regular worship of the church or whether they represent a distinct third strand within Anglicanism. Thus a report from the Chelmsford diocese concludes that these services should be seen as 'another strand of Anglican worship'.[19] An important chapter by Bryan Spinks in the Liturgical Commission's *The Renewal of Common Prayer* is entitled 'Not so Common Prayer: The Third Service'.[20] The term 'the Third Service' derives from the 1872 'Shortened Services Act' which made explicit provision for the minister to provide liturgical worship on Sundays alongside the ordinary provision of the Eucharist and the 'Office' services of Morning and Evening Prayer. There is plenty of evidence that since the Reformation English Christianity has not found these two services a sufficient liturgical diet. Early examples are to be found both in the Dissenting Tradition and in the preaching service of Methodism. Within the Church of England at different periods both the Oxford Movement and the Evangelical Movement have appealed to the authority of the Book of Common Prayer while exercising considerable creativity in devising forms of worship that appeal to those who would find Eucharist or Office inaccessible.

Since the early Middle Ages the Church of England has often accepted the role of being the regulator of the domestic and sexual lives of ordinary English people. This pattern can be seen in the relationship of the early medieval church to the emerging

---

[18] *A Service of the Word and Affirmations of Faith* (London: Church House Publishing, 1994) reproduced in *Patterns for Worship* (London: Church House Publishing, 1995).

[19] Diocese of Chelmsford, *For the Family* (London: 1987), 4.

[20] Michael Perham, ed. *The Renewal of Common Prayer* (London: Church House Publishing/SPCK, 1993).

authority of the king, in the desire of the Puritans to 'instruct the magistrate' and discipline the church, and in the reforming programme of the religious middle class in the nineteenth century. One result of this is that the 'third strand' of worship regularly adopts a style designed to make worship accessible to people who find it hard to identify with the church as an institution in society.

An important book by the American Methodist James White called *Protestant Worship* surveys the developing practice of nine traditions of Protestant worship.[21] One of the strands that he discusses is the Frontier tradition which emerged in the Mid-Western rural culture of the USA. This Christian tradition responded to the dispersed character of this society by creating a religious culture focused on summer camps and revival meetings. Distinctive features of the Frontier tradition include its easy and emotional style and its evangelistic use of music. Part of the interest of James White's book lies in his argument that many of the more classic Protestant liturgical traditions have adopted aspects of the Frontier tradition. Although the 'third strand' of English worship had no original links with this Frontier tradition it is easy to see that many of its modern forms are now indebted to it.

One element in the success and importance of the Family Service movement is its relation to an aspect of modern culture which has not received sufficient attention in the churches, namely the collapse of the classic evangelistic strategy of the West.[22] Since the rise of the monastic movement the primary way in which Western society has gained a knowledge of the Bible has been through schools run and financed by Christians. One of the last expressions of this was the Sunday School movement whose founders saw it not as a bridge into church life but as providing basic education for the deprived poor.[23] This long tradition of service had the effect of giving the Bible an integral place in society's canon of knowledge. In Britain its collapse began in 1870 when the state began to build schools and fund education

---

[21] James White, *Protestant Worship: Traditions in Transition* (Kentucky: Westminster/John Knox Press, 1989).

[22] Cf. *On the Way*, 56–7.

[23] Rosemary Nixon, *Who's the Greatest? A Study of the Sunday School in Contemporary Society* (London: National Society, 1985), 14–21.

and was considerably hastened by the explosion in scientific knowledge which pushed religion to the edge of the curriculum. The Family Service movement needs to be seen in part as an attempt to engage with this cultural marginalisation of the Bible by providing people with lively and accessible ways into Scripture. One of the recurring tensions in the movement arises between those who see its heart as music that promises and promotes intimacy and those who see it as a corporate celebration and appropriation of Scripture. A Jewish example of the latter is the exuberant and corporate reading of the book of Esther at the feast of Purim. One way of understanding the Christian calendar is to see it precisely as a well ordered communal celebration of the main narratives of Scripture.

The Family Service movement can be seen to stand in a long and important tradition within English Christian worship. However, in its contemporary forms it is profoundly shaped by those developments of Western society which have sought to identify intimacy and desire with the domestic sphere of the family. The link created by this association explains some of the serious ambiguities of the movement. The image and emotional tone of family as intimate refuge both attracts and disables the worshipper. Its power as refuge makes it harder to see the public world as a place where humanity and intimacy are also to be sought, where desire can properly be expressed, and where the Spirit of God is active. It excludes those for whom the modern form of the family does not provide viable access to affection, intimacy and domestic support. It fails both men and teenagers by its lack of a political vision of the city (the *polis*) as a place where desire for God and the true character of human glory are to be celebrated.

An important recent development has been the rise of forms of alternative worship which take as their starting point not the intimacy associated with the family but the desire and aspiration of young people between the ages of 15 and 25.[24] While these alternative liturgies exist in conscious dialogue with more classic liturgical forms, they distance themselves from the more sentimental and domestic piety of the Family Service movement and its various offshoots. These alternative movements deliberately take as their starting point people who are most excluded by the

[24] Pete Ward, *Worship and Youth Culture* (London: Marshall Pickering, 1993).

culture's identification of desire and domesticity. A church which wishes to recover again a whole and political vision of the city of God will need to listen with some humility to what emerges in these congregations.

Conclusion

This essay has tried to explore ways in which the study of liturgical processes or events can throw light on some current debates or movements within the life of the church. Categories and concepts that are often taken for granted – the intimacy and holiness of the modern family, the links between particular social patterns and creation, the invisibility of the community in individual life decisions, the place of the will in marriage, the sense that same-sex gendered affection is hostile to the stability of the household – are called in question. Modern liturgical reform often finds that the tradition has hidden within itself resources for addressing or bypassing the polarisations of modern debates and for uncovering pastoral strategies that address the fragmentation of modern social patterns or the cultural marginalisation of the human desire for God. The new – or strictly, more ancient – categories implicit in the liturgical tradition can, no doubt, be harnessed to very different strategies for responding to the current crisis of the family. Whether people opt for 'conservative' or 'radical' approaches to social policy, my own conviction is that priority needs to be given to public worship that treats God as the primary goal of human desire, and to a style of community life that is based on public affection, and extends courtesy, honour and constancy of commitment (faithfulness) to all.

10

The Role of the Family in the Formation and Criticism of Faith

Jeff Astley

'Home is the place where, when you have to go there,
They have to take you in.'

— Robert Frost, 'The Death of the Hired Man'.

Introduction

The phrase 'formation and criticism of faith' is being used here as synonymous with the more familiar 'Christian education'. I understand 'Christian education' very broadly. Primarily it designates those formative learning experiences that lead to changes 'in a Christian direction' in a person's attitudes, values, beliefs, emotions, skills and dispositions to act and experience. These changes are often described as the results of 'Christian nurture' or 'Christian formation'. But Christian education may also be said to include educational processes that make Christians more self-critical of their religious beliefs, attitudes, values, emotions and actions. Indeed many would argue that Christian education is not truly *education* if it does not incorporate such a *critical* educational element.

In this essay I shall follow the suggestions of James Fowler and others that faith is also to be construed very broadly, as designating the almost universal human activity of creating / finding meaning, and of knowing, valuing and relating to that which is taken to be meaningful, in commitment and trust. *Religious* faith, on this account, differs from other species of faith primarily in having specifically religious objects or contents: on Fowler's analysis, religious centres of value and power in which we believe, and religious master stories by which we live our lives. Fowler's researches are concerned with the development of the *form* of this faith, rather than with its *content*.[1]

Parents (and to some extent siblings) occupy first place within the ranks of what social scientists have taught us to call our 'significant others', and the family that contains them is routinely described as having as two of its primary functions the emotional support and socialisation of children. On my broad definitions of education and Christian education, the family is of its very nature an educational entity. It is not surprising, therefore, that it has become a commonplace of discussion in religious education to assert that the family is a major contributor to the religious and moral formation of the child.[2]

The notion of bringing up a child with a definite religious, moral or political world-view has sometimes been castigated by liberal educationalists as inevitably indoctrinatory. But others have defended the parents' right to provide stability and coherence through determining the primary culture of the young child, recognising that even liberal education involves or presupposes an early initiation or socialisation stage additional to the development of rationality and critical openness. Accounts of religious nurture that seek to escape the charge of its being (pejoratively) indoctrinatory often argue that faith is not the enemy of autonomy and that critical education always presupposes formative education.[3]

[1] James W. Fowler, *Stages of Faith* (San Francisco: Harper & Row, 1981); *Becoming Adult, Becoming Christian* (San Francisco: Harper & Row, 1984); *Faith Development and Pastoral Care* (Philadelphia: Fortress, 1987).

[2] Such claims are supported by many empirical studies: see Kenneth E. Hyde, *Religion in Childhood and Adolescence* (Birmingham, AL: Religious Education Press, 1990), 224–37, 254, 262–3, 315, 328–3; Leslie J. Francis and Harry M. Gibson, 'Parental Influence and Adolescent Religiosity', *The International Journal for the Psychology of Religion*, 3 (1993), 241–53.

[3] See John M. Hull, *Studies in Religion and Education* (Lewes: Falmer, 1984), Part IV; Elmer J. Thiessen, *Teaching for Commitment* (Montreal and Kingston: McGill-Queen's University Press; Leominster: Fowler Wright, 1993), 221–32; T. H. McLaughlin, 'Parental rights and the religious upbringing of children', in Jeff Astley and Leslie J. Francis, eds., *Critical Perspectives on Christian Education* (Leominster: Fowler Wright, 1994); Jeff Astley, *The Philosophy of Christian Religious Education* (Birmingham, AL: Religious Education Press; London: SPCK, 1994), ch. 5.

Nurturing meaning

As Edward Farley has noted, Horace Bushnell's classic volume on *Christian Nurture* was not about intentional cognitive education[4] but focused rather on the processes of child-rearing that constitute the Christian *paideia* (rather than *didaché*): the expression in the parent-child relationship of God's love and work of discipline. 'Nurture or cultivation', Bushnell argued, involves the 'Christian life and spirit of the parents' flowing into the child and blending with his character so as to 'beget their own good within him'.[5] This is largely a non-verbal, non-explicit matter. With regard to our children, he insisted, 'We preach too much, and live Christ too little.'[6] As one commentator on the role of the family in Christian formation has put it: 'Parents educate usually not by teaching but by parenting.'[7]

James Fowler has concentrated on the family in a number of essays on faith development. The family, he claims, 'uniquely and indispensably' attempts to meet various 'ontic needs' – his term for needs that are essential to both our being and our well-being. These are:

(i) the need for communion and valued 'place' (particularly important for the very young child, but carrying over into later years and our continuing need for a 'home');

(ii) the need for the development of agency and responsible autonomy (as we move towards separateness and develop the ability to stand alone in the context of an assured return to communion);

(iii) the need for assurance of meaning and for participation in rituals of shared meaning and orientation (the family mediating our first 'social construction of reality' and providing the repeated actions and words that allow children to participate in a shared loyalty of values); and finally and most fundamentally,

[4] Edward Farley, 'The strange history of Christian paedeia', *Religious Education*, 60 (1965), 339–346.

[5] Horace Bushnell, *Christian Nurture* (1861 edition, reprinted Grand Rapids, MI: Baker Book House, 1979), 30.

[6] Bushnell, op. cit., 61.

[7] Kieran Scott, 'The family, feminism and religious education', *Religious Education*, 75 (1980), 337.

(iv) the need for bodily sustenance, shelter and sexual identification, which themselves serve as sacramental media for our
other ontic needs.[8]

Need (ii) will be considered below, under the heading of
'individuation and interdependence'. I wish to concentrate
here, as Fowler does, on (iii) – our need for meaning – recognising that 'the meaning of one's life is derived to a large degree
from one's relationship to the lives of one's parents and one's
children'.[9]

Fowler's view of faith is of a relationship both to the perceived
conditions of our existence and to our companions-in-faith: we
compose our image of our ultimate environment through our
commitment to centres of value and power, and we do this 'in
interaction with communities of co-interpreters and
co-commitants'. He describes the family unit as an ecology of
faith consciousness. A *Christian* family, he writes, is 'an ecology of
consciousness whose principle of coherence and meaning centres on God as disclosed in Jesus Christ'.[10] The human family
promotes the development of human faith; the Christian family
nurtures a faith with a particular Christian content and focus.

Dependable, structured parenting is crucial at the early faith
stages for proper human and Christian development. At Fowler's
pre-stage of *primal faith* our ultimate environment consists of our
mother's face, arms and breasts. Erik Erikson has described the
first task of the ego at this stage as the firm establishment of
'enduring patterns for the solution of the nuclear conflict of
basic trust versus basic mistrust in pure existence'. This is the
basis for the child's developing sense of identity. Parents must be
able 'to represent to the child a deep, an almost somatic conviction that there is a meaning to what they are doing'. The parental
faith that supports this emerging trust has as its institutional

---

[8] James W. Fowler, 'Perspectives on the family from the standpoint of faith
development theory', in Jeff Astley and Leslie Francis, eds., *Christian Perspectives
on Faith Development* (Leominster: Fowler Wright; Grand Rapids, MI: Eerdmans,
1992), 320–6. Cf. Fowler, 'Faith development through the family life cycle',
Catholic Families: growing and sharing faith (Network Paper 31) (Rochelle, NY:
Don Bosco Multimedia, 1990), 4.

[9] Robert N. Bellah et al., *Habits of the Heart* (Berkeley, CA: University of
California Press, 1985), 82.

[10] Fowler, 'Perspectives on the family', 337.

safeguard – at least in principle – organised religion. Thus, according to Erikson the clinician, there are 'many who are proud to be without religion [or rather "vital faith"] whose children cannot afford their being without it'.[11]

For Donald Evans basic trust (whose elements are assurance, receptivity, fidelity, hope and passion) is the foundational 'attitude-virtue' underlying both religion and morality. Other valued attitudes, each of which is described as an integral part of human fulfilment and a goal of human life, are humility, self-acceptance, responsibility, self-commitment, friendliness, concern and contemplation.[12] The family may also be said to be the most important context for the first development of all these attributes, which are themselves built on the basic trust that develops during this earliest stage of faith.

The next stage of *intuitive-projective faith* is one in which reality is perceived by the infant as a scrap-book of impressions, not yet ordered and related together by sustained logical thinking. At this faith stage long-lasting images are laid down that provide the raw material for our rather chaotic, and certainly uncontrolled, imaginative construction of reality. The symbols and sacraments of family and Christian life are very important to children at this stage, and these faith-images will stay with the child and be reworked as he or she matures and changes.

In later childhood, at the stage of *mythic-literal faith*, our ability to think more logically and causally, and to unify our experience will help us to order reality, to separate fact from fantasy, and particularly to capture life and meaning in concrete stories. Stories now become very important to us and we may note that the family, like any true community, is structured by story. In *Habits of the Heart* Robert Bellah *et al.* claim that real communities are 'communities of memory' because they have a history, and indeed are 'constituted by their past'. Significantly, they claim that the stories that communities retell about themselves contain 'conceptions of character, what a good person is like, and the virtues that define such character'.[13] The family is patently one

[11] Erik Erikson, *Childhood and Society* (London: Granada, 1977), 224–5.
[12] Donald Evans, *Struggle and Fulfillment* (Cleveland: Collins, 1979), 172–84.
[13] Bellah, et al., *Habits of the Heart*, 333, 335, 153; cf. 139–40.

such community, having its own stories or formative myths that help to bind it together.[14] These are particularly significant at faith stage 2.

At stage 3, the stage of *synthetic-conventional faith*, abstract thinking has fully developed and there is a new capacity for interpersonal perspective taking. Relationships are now perceived to be all-important, and I am now most likely to swim with the 'faith current'. My early adolescent meaning-making is therefore largely at second hand, derived in bits-and-pieces from the world-views of others, including my parents but also (particularly) my peer group. But as yet I know not what I do in my faithing. So it is no use my parents criticising me for being so influenced by others, for not thinking for myself, or for being so conventional an adolescent – despite my desperate attempts to prove my unconventionality. The processes of my faithing remain largely hidden from me.

Fowler lays particular stress on the problems that may be caused in families – as in congregations – when 'the modal level' of faith development (i.e., the expected level or image of adult faith at which the group aims)[15] remains at this conformist faith stage 3, a stage at which individuals are very concerned to live up to the expectations of their significant others, their very selfhood being constituted by their roles and their relationships within their circle. Critical and analytical thought is not yet welcomed at this stage, and we shy away from argument and controversy about faith. It is only in the stages beyond stage 3 that the intention of Christian faith for adult commitment is properly captured.[16] Without a real 'climate of developmental expectation', Fowler contends, faith communities – including families – 'collude with one of the aspects of original sin, namely, the refusal to grow – the effort to evade or avoid the pain of growth'.[17]

---

[14] See John H. Westerhoff, *The Christian Family* (London, Ontario: Huron College, 1982), 19.

[15] Cf. James W. Fowler in Doris Blazer, ed., *Faith Development in Early Childhood* (Kansas City: Sheed & Ward, 1989), 144; *Stages of Faith*, 294; 'Perspectives on the family ...', 342–3.

[16] Fowler, 'Perspectives on the family ...', 341.

[17] James W. Fowler, 'Practical theology and the shaping of Christian lives', in Don S. Browning, ed., *Practical Theology* (San Francisco: Harper & Row, 1983), 163.

The development to a more autonomous, self-reflective faith can be a traumatic transition and may take several years. Some never make it. If I move to the stage of *individuative-reflective faith* (stage 4) I can step out of my faith current and away from the faith crowd to choose a world-view for myself. Even though I may return, as it were, to the bosom of my faith-family or faith-church, I will never be the same again. The move from stage 3 to stage 4 inevitably involves a psychological *leaving home*, a withdrawal to a vantage point from which I feel that I can make my own decisions. Fowler notes that this move can lead to tragedy if it results in a real departure from the family community, on the grounds that I now perceive it to be incompatible with my new critical self-reflection and autonomous responsibility.[18]

Some adults will later change further as they enter the mid-life stage 5 of *conjunctive faith*. Now more open and responsive to others and their world-views, the person at this stage is also more realistic and humble in his or her cognitions and affections, recognising in particular the interdependent nature of their life. If stage 4 is the stage of narrow Enlightenment rationality, Fowler suggests that stage 5 may reflect a move to a more open post-Enlightenment approach to meaning and truth.[19] Stage 5-ers are not easily accommodated in churches, nor in those families that can only understand and empathise with others who accept the rather rigid demands for conceptual clarity and the resolution of all intellectual and moral tensions that are characteristic of stage 4. However, those who have not yet reached stage 3 are sometimes more welcoming of this 'new found playfulness in faith'.[20]

Individuation and interdependence

The family context is crucial for the child's development of selfhood. Healthy families are no more the enemies of proper adult autonomy than formative (and often non-rational) nur-

[18] Fowler, 'Perspectives on the family ...', 341.
[19] Fowler, 'The Enlightenment and faith development theory', in Astley and Francis, eds., *Christian Perspectives on Faith Development*, 21–7.
[20] Fowler, 'Perspectives on the family ...', 16–17.

ture is fundamentally opposed to critical reflection and the transformation of beliefs. Herbert Anderson argues that the health and vitality of the family is finally determined by a proper balance between the needs and demands of its individual members and those of the whole unit, and thus by 'how its members learn to be separate together'.[21] 'The shaping of human particularity has its beginnings in the context of the family', he writes, because 'it is not possible to be an individual except in relation to community' *and* because the possibility of community presupposes separateness ('there is no intimacy without identity').[22]

On this account, learning the delicate balancing act of being separate together is therefore the fundamental educative role of the family. In the family the child becomes uniquely himself or herself, and the adults (who start further along the road of individuation) also grow as individuals. In faith development terms a large part of 'being ourselves' is a function of being allowed to think, feel, relate, and commit ourselves in ways that are appropriate to *our* particular faith stage. Families must encourage and allow this plurality of ways of being and of being in faith.

But individuation must be balanced by interdependence. The family is our first experience of community, 'where we are first schooled in the art of group living'.[23] Hence it is the place where the self learns not to be selfish: where it learns the attitudes, dispositions and skills of sharing, responsibility and altruism at a deep, because unreflective, level. Of course young children have to be selfish in order to survive. At an early stage they inevitably tend to see members of their family almost exclusively from an egocentric viewpoint, in terms of their own relationships with them. Only later can they see other members of the family 'as people in their own right, and themselves as having the responsible task of taking account of others'.[24] This development is encouraged first, and its lessons learned – or not learned, within the family.

[21] Herbert Anderson, *The Family and Pastoral Care* (Philadelphia: Fortress, 1984), 15, cf. 12.

[22] Ibid., 60, 62, cf. 67.

[23] Ibid., 45.

[24] Jeff Astley et al., *How Faith Grows* (London: National Society, 1991), 63.

The family has its own developmental history which is influenced by (but does not reduce to) the faith development of its members.[25] From early on in their relationship both parents and children must learn to cope with the little bereavements of letting go, but the stage of the 'emptying nest' will particularly demand of them all the resources that they can derive from the lesson that, in C. Day Lewis' words,

... God alone could perfectly show –
How selfhood begins with a walking away,
and love is proved in the letting go.[26]

Christian maturity, it may be argued, demands a recognition of the importance of interdependence *and* of the necessity of letting go – not only in relationships, but also of status, strength, power, freedom and self-contained, extreme autonomy. To become a parent is already to have to let go of some of these attributes. It is to have discovered the centrality of *kenosis*, the truth that equality with God is not a matter of grasping or holding on to ourselves but of 'giving and spending oneself out', of giving up power and possessiveness and letting others be.[27]

Modelling

Among the various processes proposed by psychologists for moral development, one of the most potent would appear to be

[25] See Betty A. Carter and Monica McGoldrick, eds., *The Changing Family Life Cycle* (Boston: Allyn & Bacon, 1989), 15. Cf. Anderson, *The Family and Pastoral Care*, 36–9, 104; James W. Fowler, 'Gifting the imagination: awakening and informing children's faith', *Review and Expositor (Journal of the Southern Baptist Theological Seminary)*, 80 (1983), 198; Fowler, 'Faith development through the family life cycle', 5–9.

[26] C. Day Lewis, 'Walking Away: for Sean'. On the *adolescent's* 'letting go', compare Erik Erikson, *Insight and Responsibility* (London: Faber & Faber, 1964), 90, and Sharon Parks, *The Critical Years: the young adult search for a faith to live by* (San Francisco: Harper & Row, 1986), 55.

[27] C. F. D. Moule, in S. W. Sykes and J. P. Clayton, eds., *Christ, Faith and History* (Cambridge: Cambridge University Press, 1972), 97. Cf. Gabriel Moran, *Education Toward Adulthood* (New York: Paulist, 1979), ch. 2, and Jeff Astley, 'Growing into Christ', in Jeff Astley and David Day, eds., *The Contours of Christian Education* (Great Wakering: McCrimmons, 1992), ch. 21.

the phenomenon of *modelling*.[28] When we are presented with an example of behaviour being displayed by a person we admire and respect, we are very likely to change our attitudes to correspond with those shown by the model. According to Stanley Hauerwas, morality in general 'cannot be separated from moral persons so that it can be learned independent of them, but rather requires learning to be as they are'.[29] The part played by the parental role model, and other authority figures within the family, is surely significant here.

But this cannot be a proper learning of a *Christian* morality if the character being modelled is not truly a Christ-like character. The *imitatio Christi* is our conformation not to the impersonal and impossible ideals of perfection, but to the embodied form of these principles in the figure of Jesus, who is himself gracious enabler as well as demanding preacher and supreme examplar. Christian parents, as Christian submodels ('Be imitators of me, as I am of Christ'), must also portray in their relationships with their children both demand *and succour*. The experience of grace in human relationships, or at least of the 'mutual regard [that] provides an undercurrent for grace',[30] is very important in the child's development. We first learn the empowerment of forgiveness, along with the demands of love, within the family.

Faith formation in the family is not all in one direction. One of the significant features of intergenerational education is said to be that adults can learn from children and young people, as well as vice versa. In the Gospels the child is not presented primarily as the one who receives instruction, but rather as the model of discipleship for adults.[31] In my view, among the better explanations of why many adults become 'more religious' when they have children are (i) that they are daily confronted with the demands of being God themselves (like God, parents create,

---

[28] See A. Bandura, *Principles of Behavioral Modification* (New York: Holt, Rinehart & Winston, 1969), ch. 3; Nicholas Wolterstorff, *Educating for Responsible Action* (Grand Rapids, MI: Eerdmans, 1980), ch. 6.

[29] Stanley Hauerwas, 'Character, Narrative, and Growth in the Christian Life', in James Fowler and Antoine Vergote, eds., *Toward Moral and Religious Maturity* (Morriston, NJ: Silver Burdett, 1980), 445.

[30] Romney M. Moseley and Ken Brockenbrough, 'Faith development in the preschool years', in Donald Ratcliffe, ed., *Handbook of Preschool Religious Education* (Birmingham, AL: Religious Education Press, 1988), 121.

[31] See Hans-Ruedi Weber, *Jesus and the Children* (Geneva: World Council of

sustain, provide, guide, reveal, inspire, and so on); and (ii) that they have undergone to some extent a revolution in their system of valuing, insofar as they have come to esteem most highly a person who, in the world's eyes, has no status, power or possessions – that is, a child.

A further point is that children teach us about ourselves. As we respond to the child-without we are often helped to recognise the child-within, and that allows us to be more accepting of ourselves and to empathise more fully with the behaviour of other children-within-adults. True adult maturity demands such a recognition, and living with children is a cheaper alternative to psychotherapy as a way of achieving it!

Learning the language of faith

It is generally agreed that the child's 'theology', or at least the basic lineaments of his or her image of God, is powerfully influenced by the interpersonal interaction between parent and child and 'at least partially constructed of ideal parental images'.[32] But there are more general points that may be made about the family and the learning of religious ideas.

Drawing on Wittgenstein's 'pedagogical turn' in philosophy and his insistence on the social context of meaning and the public nature of the rules of language, many have acknowledged that religious concepts too are learned within the Christian community, including the home. What counts as their correct use is thus embedded in the language of believers.[33] Through listening to the religious language of their parents and observing its context in their behaviour (their actions and their expressions of emotion), children will learn – for good or ill – the family's theology.

Churches, 1979), ch. 4; Ian Stockton, 'Children, church and kingdom', *Scottish Journal of Theology*, 36 (1983) 87–97; Stephen Barton, 'Jesus – friend of little children?', in Astley and Day, eds., *The Contours of Christian Education*, ch. 2.

[32] Moseley and Brockenbrough, 'Faith development in the preschool years', 110, cf. 115. Cf. Ana-Marie Rizzuto, *The Birth of the Living God* (Chicago: University of Chicago Press, 1979), *passim.*; David Heller, *The Children's God* (Chicago: University of Chicago Press, 1986), ch. 7; Hyde, *Religion in Childhood and Adolescence*, chs. 3 and 4.

[33] Dean M. Martin, 'Learning to become a Christian', in Astley and Francis, eds., *Critical Perspectives on Christian Education*, 184–90.

What needs to be learned eventually is the correct depth grammar of religious concepts: including what sort of a reality and nature God has (and how God is not another thing or even person); what religious believing or religious service is and what it is not; what God's presence or God's action or God's reward is and what it is not. Children learn to be Christian in one important sense by learning to speak and think as Christians, and 'it is through the attitudes and disposition and activities of Christians that their language gets its meaning'.[34] A particularly sharp example here is that of prayer. Through hearing, sharing and practising prayer children learn 'how to pray', a feat that involves learning the contextual grammar of prayer, of talking to 'the one I am with when I am with *nobody*',[35] including what it means to say that God has heard and answered my prayers. The affective context of this learning is also highly significant.[36]

Formative and critical education

Of course, many remain suspicious of religious formation, arguing that it is essentially a conservative process of passing on a family (or a church's) culture-tradition. As such it allows little room for the liberating call to freedom or for the critical evaluation and indeed overturning of the past that they regard as of the essence of the gospel of the Kingdom, and perhaps of education itself. If formation involves passing on Grandma's furniture, *critical education* encourages us to make our own judgements about this inheritance, and then to rearrange, reconstruct and even jettison at least part of it. While explicit Christian formation focuses on the Christian tradition and how it shapes and forms the learner, critical Christian education is more learner-centred and encourages a reformation and critique of the tradition in the learner's own terms. This may be a 'rational critique' of the cognitive content and implications of Christianity, informed by a liberal educational tradition and the analytical and evaluative skills of Western philosophical method. In the hands of others, however, it may be presented more as a

---

[34] Gareth Moore, *Believing in God* (Edinburgh: T. & T. Clark, 1988), 147.
[35] Ibid., 190.
[36] Cf. Martin, 'Learning to become a Christian', 190.

social, moral and political critique involving the 'conscientisation' of the learner. In this latter form critical education can embrace liberation approaches such as feminism that challenge the *miseducative* dynamics of the family, its stereotypical assumptions and its barriers to human fulfilment, calling for a critical re-examination of relationships within and outside the family, including political, economic and ecological relationships.

Although the family is fairly universally fêted as the primary locus for faith formation, its positive role in critical Christian education is less often noted. I should like to make three comments relevant to that role.

First, while formative enculturation might appear to be the enemy of transformative, liberating education, everything depends on what tradition is being passed on. According to John Westerhoff, for whom Christian education is primarily intentional enculturation, the fact that the Christian gospel is itself a transforming, liberating thing means that the Christian learner who is effectively formed by it *will be* critical of other aspects of the Christian tradition as well as of the anti-gospel values of the world. 'Catechesis', he writes, therefore 'implies more than conserving', and transformation is a part of formation.[37]

Second, critical education itself requires the formation in the learner of appropriate critical attitudes, values, dispositions and skills that are essential for taking a 'critical stance' and exercising a 'critical outlook'. Now there is certainly a tension between formation in particular values and beliefs and helping people learn the critical, reflective skills and attitudes that will enable them to critique such values and beliefs, and possibly to jettison some of their traditional cargo in order to make room for other, foreign goods. Parents need to bear this tension so as to exercise a mature balance between on the one hand encouraging 'settled convictions, deep-seated virtues and profound loyalties', and on the other facilitating a critical openness to other viewpoints, other evidence and other minds.[38] I suspect that this style of

[37] John Westerhoff, 'Religious education and catechesis', in M. C. Felderhof, ed., *Religious Education in a Pluralistic Society* (London: Hodder & Stoughton, 1985), 62–3.

[38] B. G. Mitchell, 'Indoctrination', Appendix B to The Bishop of Durham's Commission, *The Fourth R* (London: National Society and SPCK, 1970), 358.

education demands a particular sort of intellectual and personal maturity on the part of parents.

Third, we may note that in a plural world not only do we need to educate our children into an awareness of plurality; we also need to help them to cope with the 'vertigo of relativity' that such awareness often brings, and to give them the attitudes, dispositions and skills to decide for themselves among the competing values of the wider society.[39] Purely formative education that eschews any critical dimension will not create citizens who will easily cope with the world outside the walls of the nursery of faith. Fundamentalist homes and schools seem often to be unaware of this problem. In the real world our children need a faith that can cope with other faiths (in every sense of the word 'faith'). They also need a sense of identity, self-confidence and ownership of their own value-system. But they need in addition the continuing support of a home they can go back to even after they have changed. We have after all created and nurtured them *to be themselves*.

A wider community?

Families can fail, of course, while remaining powerful educational contexts. Failing families teach the wrong lessons, nurturing distrust, insecurity and selfishness. Paradoxically, they may sometime fail by succeeding too well, in encouraging family love for instance. Charity, as self-giving love, certainly begins at home, but it is only when the family teaches openness to the stranger – the non-family and non-kin – that we can be sure that charity will not end there.[40]

Nevertheless, the family remains our first and society's primary expression of community. In this role, however, it needs strengthening by wider, non-familial expressions of community, 'other sources of intimacy and socialization' which possess some of the family's 'seriousness, depth, and permanence'.[41] For

[39] Cf. Anderson, *The Family and Pastoral Care*, 45–67; Peter L. Berger, *The Social Reality of Religion* (Harmondsworth: Penguin, 1967), 186.

[40] Cf. Anderson, *The Family and Pastoral Care*, 46–8.

[41] Moran, *Education Toward Adulthood*, 93, 95. Cf. Anderson, *The Family and Pastoral Care*, 57.

Christians this second, wider home should ideally be provided by the *congregation*: a relatively small group of people, meeting weekly to speak, sing and act out together their beliefs and values in story and ritual.[42]

Many have argued on more theological grounds for a complementary church community to ensure proper Christian education. Without it, they claim, there is a danger of the family becoming just an agent for the surrounding (more or less secular) society,[43] the values of the gospel being diluted and domesticated to fit the family hearth and its household gods. Thus, in addition to denying the claim that 'the kind of character developed by the family is sufficient to sustain [even] the moral demands made by marriage and family',[44] Hauerwas argues that giving the family the primary role in moral formation is to idolise it. Rather, parenting in a Christian perspective is to be regarded as a responsibility of the whole Christian community and, correlatively, 'the first family of every Christian ... is the church', wherein we learn fidelity and love in a community that is sustained by a faithful God.[45]

But these high-flown words may mask the rather grim reality of many a local church. Just as the family needs a *good* church to support its role of Christian formation (and criticism), so the church needs to acknowledge the broader and more fundamental educational – and perhaps religious – goals of the family.

Interestingly, Hauerwas himself acknowledges that one of the positive features of the family in the formation of Christian character is that it often contains people who have not *chosen* one another as worthy objects of love and faithfulness.[46] We did not, after all, choose our parents or their other children. True Christian fidelity and love, which involve more than mere emotional attachment, need this sort of community in which to grow. For Hauerwas, however, this is provided primarily by the *church*.

[42] Westerhoff, *The Christian Family*, 14; but contrast Moran, *Education Toward Adulthood*, 101.

[43] C. Ellis Nelson, *Where Faith Begins* (Atlanta, GA: John Knox, 1967), 37–8, 117.

[44] Stanley Hauerwas, 'The family as a school for character', *Religious Education*, 80 (1985), 273, 280–1.

[45] *Ibid.*, 278, 281. Cf. Westerhoff, *The Christian Family*, 5–14.

[46] Hauerwas, 'The family as a school for character', 283, cf. 281.

But one might be forgiven for commenting that many congregations are themselves very much groups of like-minded, self-selected individuals. These groups sometimes prove to be very selfish institutions concerned primarily with their own well-being, and voraciously devouring the individuality of individuals and the fragile value-systems of small families. Examples of this abound, from authoritarian house churches robbing parents of their proper role in religious and moral nurture, to those polite congregations that destroy the family life of their clergy with or without their connivance.

Parents do indeed need support in their vocation of faith education, but I wonder whether the church is always able, and willing, to provide it. As with Christian education generally, the church needs to indulge less in the seductive pleasures of condemning the failures of other institutions and individuals. What is required on its part is more humble self-criticism of its own practices, testing them against the fundamental criterion of whether or not they serve to create and form persons and communities that may properly bear the name of Christ.

11

Right Relations: Forgiveness and Family Life

Anne Borrowdale

Ask people what makes family relationships work, and the willingness to forgive will be high on the list. Clearly forgiveness is a good thing, like 'community' or 'the love of God'. But as with those words, it requires a lot of unpacking if it is not merely to be a pious, sentimental and ultimately empty solution to the problems families face. For within the real, complex dynamics of family relationships, forgiveness can have different meanings in different contexts. It has to relate to the nature of the offence which has been committed. In this paper, I look at the different things, or sins, in families which require forgiveness, at whether forgiveness itself therefore needs to take different forms, and at what the issue of forgiveness in family life says about our theological understanding.

There are at least four levels of offences within families which might be said to need forgiveness. The distinction between them is far from clear cut in practice. The same offence will have different meanings in different families, and judgement is needed as to how those involved are to react. Moreover, both offences and forgiveness are frequently parts of a process. However, I distinguish between these different levels for the moment, because it does help to unpack the issue, even though we need to move on from it.

1. 'The flowers will grow again next year'

At the first level, there is what might be described as the rough and tumble of family relationships. These are things which do not have a lasting significance. Recently, my children and hus-

band have been playing football in our garden, and what should
be a border of tulips and grape hyacinths is a line of broken stems.
I have tried saying 'mind the flowers', but have now given up
bothering. What is actually important is that they are enjoying
one another's company; the flowers will grow again next year.
There are an awful lot of offences in families which are of this
nature. We have arguments, we hurt one another, siblings bicker,
granny picks a fight, but it passes. Tomorrow, or by Christmas,
we'll be friends again. The damage to relationships is superficial.
The flowers will grow again next year. At this level, what we need
is a 'letting go' of the offence. A couple may exchange angry
words when they get lost in the car, but in the end they arrive. To
make an issue of it is to spoil the whole day, why not just let go,
we were stressed, but it's over now. In such a situation, it may be
better to go to bed angry, and wake up in the morning having
forgotten, than to talk about the problem and perhaps give it an
undue importance. A child shouts and slams the door as they
leave for school. Is the parent to hold onto that all day, confront
the child on their return, insist on an apology? Or can it be let go,
since they have probably forgotten and it will only further
fracture the relationship to go back to it?

Obviously there are things which matter, that must be dealt
with, but at this level I am concerned with the things that really
are not worth making an issue of. This particularly arises with
parenting of dependent children. A wise parent knows that
children need what Marguerite Kelly calls 'a healthy balance of
attention and benign neglect'.[1] Parents often feel that they
should be intervening in every area of a child's life, telling them
what to do, and think of this as discipline. Yet it is not the parent's
job to run a child's life for them, but to enable them to become
responsible for themselves. Often, the natural consequences
which follow from a particular act are enough to bring about
altered behaviour. Forgiving childish mistakes, and even letting
some deliberate wrong-doing pass, may be what is required. Of
course there may need to be acknowledgement that something
wrong has been done. 'I'm sorry' and 'That's alright' usually
need to be said. But we can resist the temptation to go on about
it with: 'You always …'.

[1] M. Kelly, *The Mother's Almanac* (New York: Doubleday, 1989), 64.

Similarly, with adults in family relationships, there is room for a great deal more 'letting go' of offences. It is easy to become calculating, to remember real and imagined offences. This may be something the older generation finds easy – when there is more time to sit and brood, and adult children may be too absorbed in their own lives to remember Mothering Sunday. Resentments can easily build up between partners too. But it is not simply a matter of urging them to forgive one another. At issue may be the fact that forgiveness is only going one way. One partner, often for psychological and historical reasons the woman, feels it is their job to smooth things over, constantly to let things go. But this is not healthy for the person who can always get away with things, or for the one who always forgives but feels that their needs are never taken account of. Mutuality is essential. In terms of parents and children relating, this means the willingness for parents to admit they were in the wrong, and for children to feel able to express their sense of grievance, as well as the other way round. It's worth adding that some people, by nature of their personality, find it much easier to let go than others. Some people do keep things in their hearts, perhaps unknown to anyone else, brooding on grudges. Others can shout appalling things one minute, and have quite forgotten the next. Appreciating how the other operates in the world is an essential part of developing good relationships.

Also at this level, there can be acceptance that irritation, and some irrational behaviour, are a normal part of family relationships. Indeed the picture we sometimes have of the Holy Family, with a sweetly smiling patient mother, could not possibly equip children for life! We should not even characterise all over-reactions or arguments as sin – learning to live with a certain amount of parental fallibility is an essential ingredient if children are to be able to cope with the world. We must avoid acting out of a belief that conflict is sinful, that in an ideal family, people do not argue. The damage that has been done, especially within Christian homes, by this viewpoint is substantial, leaving family members unable to deal with strong feelings of anger or to handle conflict. Yet any group of people living intimately together will experience difference and conflict. The essential point is that they should learn to deal with that conflict in such a way as to keep a right relationship between them.

How does this relate to Christian ideas about forgiveness? It is one meaning of the word. The Greek *aphesis* is about letting go, refraining from exacting the lawful penalty, putting something out of mind. Paul uses the term *charizesthai*, of God making us a present of our sins, letting us get away with them. This is not the whole meaning of forgiveness in divine or human terms, but it is part of it. Certainly when the temptation is to be too rigorous in exacting penalties from those who have offended against us, to remind ourselves to let go is to reflect how God frequently behaves towards us. If God were to pounce on humanity for every sin, where indeed would we be? The form of our relationship with God, like the form of the relationship within families, can hold these sort of offences.

2. Negligence, weakness and deliberate fault

At the first level, forgiveness is a simple, though not necessarily easy, matter. It is about a generosity of spirit that refuses to hold any offence against the other, lets it go, allows it to pass. That level shades into the next, because things that ought to be trivial come to stand for significant problems in a relationship – it is not just that he is cross because she failed to navigate in the car, but because she is useless at everything. The child who slams the door treats everyone and everything in the home with contempt. The difference is that whereas in the first instance we are talking about things that disturb but do not unravel the fabric of right relations, here we are talking about things that do seriously disrupt, things which cannot just be allowed to pass, the sins we commit against other family members through negligence, through weakness, through our own deliberate fault, and some- times also through ignorance, though there are further ques- tions about what kind of responsibility we can take for that. Here, the wrong done has to be acknowledged and things put right through repentance, some form of restitution and/or punish- ment, and forgiveness. Such acts will not be forgotten, but they are ultimately forgivable. Whereas it would be understandable for a child to say 'I will never forgive my father for abusing me throughout my childhood', it would be an over-reaction if a child said 'I will never forgive you for slapping me in front of my friend', for example. Remembrance does not preclude forgiveness, and it would not be satisfactory merely to say 'forget it', for the significance has to be recognised.

Though these kind of offences disrupt right relations, tearing them apart for a while, they can be repaired. The fabric is torn, but it can still contain the needs of family members. We are still talking here about families which are 'good enough', places where there is a fundamental commitment to the well-being of family members, and where ultimately there will always be acceptance and forgiveness. Andrew Stanway comments that children need 'to be loved consistently, for themselves alone and not on the condition that they be something special or different from what they really are. This kind of love can withstand even quite bad parenting in other ways because it gives a child a sense of worth and stability that will last a lifetime'.[2]

If parents are constantly critical, always believing the worst of children, this has a bad effect on children's sense of worth. The willingness to forgive wrongdoing enables children to believe themselves forgivable, worth something, and capable of making new beginnings. The fostering of forgiveness works here because it is not all one way – parents and spouses acknowledge that they offend and need forgiveness too.

How does all this relate to Christian forgiveness? It is not so much a 'letting go', as if the offence has never happened, but a recognition of what has happened and acknowledgement that punishment or restitution must happen as a result. The repairing of right relations at this level often requires that a penalty follow from the wrong-doing, either as a result of natural consequences taking their course, or because a punishment is inflicted. Adults dealing with children are more likely to impose a punishment – stopping pocket money, grounding, and so forth. The key considerations should be that the penalty is a just and proportionate one – in my book *Reconstructing Family Values*,[3] I speak of a 'just smack' theory, which parallels the 'just war' theory.

There are clear resonances with general thinking about justice and the criminal justice system here. Much of what is said in Christian literature about child-rearing does see the family rather in these terms. The parent is the authority figure, who must

---

[2] A. Stanway, *Preparing for Life* (London: Viking, 1988), 134.
[3] A. Borrowdale, *Reconstructing Family Values* (London: SPCK, 1994).

punish and pardon the offences of children for their own good. Physical discipline is emphasised, rather as the 'short sharp shock' may be in discussions of law and order – and indeed there can be a common right-wing agenda involved in discussions of both crime and parenting. But I would want to suggest that if there are parallels here, the better way is to emphasise restorative rather than retributive justice. Howard Zehr, for example, points out that for retributive justice, 'Crime is a violation of the state, defined by lawbreaking and guilt. Justice determines blame and administers pain in a contest between the offender and the state directed by systematic rules.' But for restorative justice, 'Crime is a violation of people and relationships. It creates obligations to make things right. Justice involves the victim, the offender, and the community in a search for solutions which promote repair, reconciliation and reassurance.' Biblical justice points us towards the future, and is concerned about people and community, admitting the humanity of those who offend as well as those who are offended against.[4]

This does apply where the offence happens between adults, but it takes a different form, because it less easily parallels the idea of an authority figure pardoning an offence. Many people are not good at expressing their anger or hurt at an offence, but the ability to express anger and hurt is important here. With the first level, minor conflict and anger are part and parcel of family life. Here, anger is part of acknowledging the intensity of the wound. Forgiveness does not come cheap. Wildung Harrison in an important essay entitled 'The power of anger in the work of love' argues that Christians have come close to killing love because they have seen anger as a deadly sin. But anger is a 'feeling-signal that all is not well in our relation to other persons or groups or to the world around us. Anger is a mode of connectedness to others and it is always a vivid form of caring.' And where anger is hidden or goes unattended, 'the power of love, the power to act, to deepen relation, atrophies and dies'.[5]

Harrison discusses this in a wider context, but it is relevant here. The danger is of speaking of forgiveness too readily, and

---

[4] See H. Zehr, *Changing Lenses: a new focus for Crime and Justice* (Ontario: Herald Press, 1990).

[5] B. Wildung Harrison, 'The Power of Anger in the Work of Love', in A. Loades, ed., *Feminist Theology: A Reader* (London: SPCK, 1990), 206.

thereby denying and smoothing over conflict. For a number of historical and psychological reasons, women may feel under particular pressure to give way in relationships, to put up with husbands mistreating them or having affairs, and then to forgive and receive them back again. The idea of tough love has been mooted in such contexts, where people are shown that there comes a point where the most loving thing is to refuse to keep on forgiving, to take a stand. Generally, the one who has offended needs to accept the anger directed at them, the one offended against needs a chance to express their anger, or perhaps grief, and both need to know that this does not threaten the fabric of relationship. Forgiveness, in this context, becomes, not some pious hope, but something gritty, rough-edged, an act of will, a recognition of pain, a genuine gift.

It is worth noting in passing the examples given by Brian Frost in *The Politics of Peace*[6] of the way that forgiveness can operate powerfully in public and political life. Think of South Africa, or of the powerful effect of the late Gordon Wilson's forgiveness of his daughter's IRA murderers in Northern Ireland. A human willingness to let go can set God free to act. As Arendt put it: 'Forgiving ... acts anew and unexpectedly, unconditioned by the act which provoked it and therefore freeing from its consequences both the one who forgives and one who is forgiven.'[7] By contrast, the refusal to forgive, however understandable, locks both victim and offender into a bitter, endless nightmare. As Conway puts it in *Adult Children of Legal or Emotional Divorce*,[8] the basis for forgiveness is not the intensity of the hurt, but the need to let go of the burden a person carries because of what was done to them. Gandhi once observed that if we all live by an eye for an eye, the whole world will be blind. Forgiveness, says Conway, does not mean letting the other person off the hook of responsibility, but taking the hook of pain out of your mouth.

3. The fabric falls apart

The third level of offence within families is where extreme hurt

---

[6] B. Frost, in *The Politics of Peace* (London: Darton, Longman & Todd, 1991).
[7] H. Arendt, quoted in Frost, *ibid.*, 201.
[8] J. Conway, *Adult Children of Legal or Emotional Divorce* (Eastbourne: Monarch, 1990).

has been caused, for example by physical, sexual or emotional abuse. We are used to focusing on the terrible impact of this happening to a child, but it should not be forgotten that domestic violence against women, and to a much lesser extent against men, is a widespread problem, and that elderly people are sometimes abused by those who care for them. The fact that such things happen within families, the places where we hope to feel safe and trustful, exacerbates their effect. People have suffered the pain not only of the abuse, but of a betrayal too. Forgiveness here takes on its own dimension and, in particular, cannot be separated from the need for justice.

A great deal of attention has been given in recent years to abuse and its consequences. Theologians are addressing these issues, but in popular Christian literature there is a tendency to underplay the destructive aspects of family life, for this seems to threaten the notion of the family as a divinely ordained building block for society. Forgiveness may be advocated strongly as an essential part of Christian family life, without fully recognising the problems with it at this level. Secular literature, on the other hand, may strongly denounce forgiveness as destructive to a person's development. It is equated with a denial of the offence, dangerous because it impedes the expression of anger and delays or prevents healing.

Hilary Cashman discusses this in her book *Christianity and Child Sexual Abuse*,[9] and notes that there can be no forgiving and forgetting of crimes of abuse, since abusers need treatment and children need protection – forgiveness must be allied with justice. Future relationships between family members will always be conducted in the light of what has happened. Cashman points out that there is a distinction between repentance and remorse. Abusers may well feel sorry for what they've done, but unless they repent and really change their behaviour, this has no meaning. Right relations will never be entirely re-established, but there has to be 'rightness' in the sense of justice. At this level, we are in the realms of criminal offence, and it cannot be discussed merely in terms of forgiveness. The sorry tales of the way churches have often dealt with cases of abuse indicate that this is not always recognised. The values required include confrontation and

---

[9] H. Cashman, *Christianity and Child Sexual Abuse* (London: SPCK, 1993).

denunciation of injustice, care for the victim, and appropriate treatment for the offender – making them accountable. Forgiveness and absolution may need to be withheld until conditions have been met, if permanent change is to happen.

Perhaps one reason why Christianity has been slow to recognise this is that the model of forgiveness with which we operate is to forgive as Christ forgave us, to reflect the forgiveness of God the Father in our human or family relationships. Thus the parent stands for God, forgiving the sins of the child, and men may be encouraged to relate to their wives as Christ loved the Church. The image of love in both cases is powerful, but it is ultimately an unequal one. It avoids engagement with the fact that parents and husbands sin themselves, that often they are the ones who need to be forgiven. It is not the case that the one who has most power in the relationship is to be magnanimous to the one who has least, or that the small offender must appease the almighty offended one; but that the powerful offender must change their behaviour. Instead, we find ourselves mapping that notion of free, generous forgiveness onto a situation where a victim is required to accept the evil done to them.

We see Peter in the New Testament asking Jesus how many times he must forgive his brother, and receiving the answer 'seventy times seven'. But surely Jesus' answer would have been different if Peter had been seven years old and asking how often he should forgive the adult brother who beat him daily? Surely the answer there would be to denounce the abuser, 'Better for him that he should have a millstone fastened round his neck and be cast into the sea, than that he should cause one of these little ones to stumble'? It may well be that the idea that human beings should forgive one another as Christ forgave them is a metaphor which should not be taken too literally. But traditional Christian talk of forgiveness very often does reflect this power relation and prevents a proper recognition of the victim's experience. One way of moving on from this may be to ask whether there is any sense in which we, small and vulnerable humanity, have to forgive God. Perhaps a God who relates to humanity as a parent must accept the limited understandings and pronouncements through which human beings attempt to control and define God. Perhaps God accepts the vulnerability which comes with being misunderstood.

It is not always easy to say at what point harsh treatment becomes abuse. Perhaps asking how repairable the damage is gives one answer. It could be argued that it is a matter of treating what happens in families in the same way as if they happened elsewhere – in a school, residential home, or on the street. There should be no protection in saying: 'But it's my own child, my own parent, I have a right to treat them as I do.' Nonetheless, there is a difference, because of the prior relationship. A child wants the abuse to stop; but they also often want their family to remain intact. This abuser is still the only father they've got, it may be difficult for them to see the person as the enemy (which in itself makes expressing feelings of anger more difficult). An adult looking back on an experience of abuse may also recognise the pressures which drove their abuser – and issues of responsibility and blame arise. One solution suggested (which might apply to all the levels I've described) is that we might hate the sin, but love and therefore forgive the sinner.

Yet this solution is not entirely satisfactory: to be told I hate what you do but I love you seems to divide a person from their acts in a way that is unhelpful. Oppenheimer's discussion of loving and liking in *The Hope of Happiness*[10] is useful here. She talks about what it means to love and forgive our enemies, and whether it is reasonable to say we can love but not like them. In extreme cases – say the Nazi, the oppressor – we cannot possibly talk about liking but, says Oppenheimer, what does love mean if it does not include liking and partiality? God's love for us is not a matter of loving everyone as if they were all the same, but loving each of us in our uniqueness. It may be more honest to say that we cannot talk about liking *or* loving yet, but that just refraining from hating is a start, and 'we leave them in God's hands, knowing that His love can encompass them where ours at present cannot.... if one day we come to love them, it will be by seeing them with different eyes. A real forgiveness to come is better than a sham forgiveness imagined. Even the conquest of bitterness is a beginning.'[11] The Christian demand is beyond what we can easily achieve, but there is a realism here which connects with what Harrison says about anger and love. We may not be able to act rightly yet, but at least

[10] H. Oppenheimer, *The Hope of Happiness* (London: SCM, 1983).
[11] Ibid., 129.

feelings have been given a place in the enterprise and not denied by too easy a reference to love and piety.

Right relations are not restored at this level by distinguishing between love for the sinner and hate for the sin. There may be more help in reflecting on a distinction between sin and evil, such as that suggested by Mary Potter Engel. She differentiates between evil and sin for perpetrator and victim of abuse. Evil is found in the structures of oppression which are larger than individuals, distort our perceptions, and make it hard for us to do good. Sin is found in our individual acts which create or reinforce the structures of oppression. It is not, she says, that victim and perpetrator are equally to blame. Victims have not committed the sin of abusing others, but they have been affected by the systems of evil, which may have lured them into complying with their victimisation. Perpetrators need to be held accountable for sinful actions. Speaking of evil structures to them is not helpful, for it allows them to escape their responsibility for what they have done.[12] Both victim and assailant are invited to new life, says Pellauer, 'Neither are bound in inexorable laws to live as doers of evil or sufferers of its consequences.' Forgiveness enables the victim to say this will no longer dominate their life, they can let go and move on.[13]

4. *A state of sin*

The second and third levels of offence relate to particular acts. I also want to add a fourth, which may be a feature of these other levels but needs attention by itself too. It is something about a failure to be, rather than specific acts of omission or commission. It is summed up by the agonised cry of the child or spouse: 'You were never there when I needed you.' One example of this in families is where children are subject to poor parenting, not through deliberate acts, but because parents do not know any better. This is something psychoanalyst Alice Miller writes passionately about, calling it 'the unintentional persecution of

---

[12] M. Engel, in M. Engel and S. Thistlethwaite, eds., *Lift Every Voice* (New York: Harper and Row, 1990), 318ff.
[13] M. Pellauer, *Sexual Assault and Abuse* (New York: Harper and Row, 1987), 102.

children by their parents, sanctioned by society and called child-rearing'. Children have their needs and feelings overridden, the emphasis is on punishment rather than understanding, and so on, she says. But 'it is not a matter of assigning blame to individual parents, who, after all, are themselves victims of this system, but of identifying a hidden societal structure that determines our lives'. A different sort of forgiveness is required here. For Miller, it involves naming the problem, not ignoring it simply in order to protect parents. Parents cannot expect to be perfect, and they too are victims of their childhood and child-rearing ideology. But adults need to express their rage at being failed.[14]

Many criticisms can be made of Miller's work, but she does raise acutely the question of how far parents can be blamed for the damage they cause, and whether it is Christian to refuse to blame them for fear of hurting their feelings. How responsible are parents for what they do in relation to their children, if they have done their best? It is possible for someone to accept responsibility for things for which they are not strictly to blame. It is hard enough to apologise for problems arising from weakness and deliberate fault. But perhaps harder still to accept responsibility for what we do through ignorance, particularly if we felt we were acting in the best way possible at the time. Being able to acknowledge the consequence of actions, to accept responsibility, may be helpful here, and to allow others to express their feelings about what it has done to them.

There are of course also all the external factors which affect upbringing, which I have not had space to discuss here, but which are an essential feature. Circumstances such as unemployment, stress at work, housing problems, debt, or crime, mean both that we commit more offences against one another, and that we have fewer resources within ourselves to put the problems right. Such factors are influential, and yet who can be blamed or forgiven for them?

There is also an issue about people who behave in a certain way because of their upbringing, who may not be able to change. Such behaviour may damage relationships, but what does it mean to forgive someone for being who they are? This is a key issue for men in dealing with their sexism, and white people in

---

[14] A. Miller, *For Your Own Good* (London: Virago, 1987), 194–5.

dealing with their racism. We are not to blame for being formed by the culture in which we grow to maturity, but once we become aware of sexism and racism, we become responsible for repenting of them and doing something about them. It is not a simple matter of confessing one action or thought and receiving absolution, but of constantly challenging those ingrained patterns of thought that we now see to be wrong.

For men in family relationships, problems over gender issues are one factor in the high rate of relationships breakdown between the sexes. Women expect different things from men, and yet how hard it is for men to change, if they have grown up learning particular patterns of relating to women. A man who has grown up in a home where mother waits on the men of the family may want to talk about equality, for example, but in fact easily relapses into treating his wife in the same way.

Does it help here to look at the distinction theology has traditionally made between the state of sin, being in original sin, and sinful acts? Christians are freed from being in a state of sin, and yet do commit individual offences against God and neighbour, sins of omission and commission – Luther's *simul justus et peccator.* One of the emphases in modern Roman Catholic theology asks the question whether the self is fundamentally committed to the life of grace or the life of sin. Actual sin is distinguished from habitual sin. Is this what we want in families? A commitment to the well-being of the family is the framework within which we are to live. Within that, we will find ourselves injuring one another, but these are forgivable injuries, because the overall framework is one of love. The most serious problems arise when that commitment has been lost, or never existed. Instead of an overall right relation within which offences happen, no right relations exist. Something dramatic is required to instate or reinstate them. This is more akin to the idea of God putting humankind into a right relation with God, so that we are then free to live as God's people.

Finally, there is the general problem of the way that we have conceived of God as Father; the one in authority, who disciplines with a firm but loving hand, the one who is all-wise, to be obeyed. We deserve punishment, but rather as a mother might shield a naughty child from the father's disciplinary blow, or intercede, so Christ is seen as coming between us and the punishment we deserve from God. One Christian approach to parenting suggests that children must learn that parents punish them for wrongdoing, so that they can learn to fear and obey God. Is that what God is like? Is that what human parents are like – if the best in human parenting must be a reflection of God? In both cases, what of the glimpse of the father of the prodigal son, refusing to punish, opening his arms wide, and saying the son is valued whatever he has done? If God is like that, what implication might it have for theories of the atonement which see Christ's work entirely in terms of saving humanity from a wrathful father? Further, whatever the intention, when Christ's acceptance of pain and suffering as a victim on the cross is spoken of as the model all should follow, victims of abuse may feel that their role too is to accept pain without complaint.

This discussion inevitably leads to the atonement, and to asking how thinking on it influences how we see forgiveness in family life. I was struck by the connections Lehmann makes in his article on forgiveness in *A New Dictionary of Christian Ethics*.[15] He suggests that the religious reality of forgiveness centres on human offences against the awesome holiness of God, human guilt, and 'the ineradicable human need for assurance that sin against God has been pardoned and right relations between God and humanity have been restored'. God sets aside the enmity between God and humanity through justification; right relations are restored through reconciliation. Forgiveness requires both these things. Lehmann also draws attention to the relation between forgiveness, justice and love. 'In love, God faithfully favors humanity with his presence and grace. In forgiveness, God "sends away" or "pardons" ... human disavowals and violations of this divine initiative. In justice, God's presence in, with, and under the human aspiration and struggle to be human is discerned and experienced in the setting right of what is not right in personal and social interaction.' Lehmann believes that a juridical view of the sacrificial and atoning death of Christ has meant that justification, forgiveness and justice do not intersect as they should. If this is true in theological terms, is it also true in looking at the family – that the sort of forgiveness we talk about does not adequately allow for justice (especially on that third

---

[15] J. Macquarrie and J. Childress, eds., *A New Dictionary of Christian Ethics* (London: SCM, 1986).

level) or justification (on that second level)? We fail to allow for the need for something to be done.

Many years ago, I did an MA on the work of H. A. Hodges who insisted in *The Pattern of Atonement*[16] that Christ's atonement was not a matter of substitution, but of belonging, of relationship: Christ in us and we in Christ. He quotes the hymn lines: 'Look, Father, look on his anointed face, and only look on us as found in him.' Forgiveness, salvation itself, is about the restoration of right relations. There may be a parallel here with the way that where offences are committed within families – at least at the first levels – we look not at the severity of the offence, but at the fact that the person who committed it is someone who belongs to us, and we to them. What the parent, child, or spouse, sees is not the offence, but the relationship.[17]

---

[16] H. A. Hodges, *The Pattern of Atonement* (London: SCM, 1955).

[17] See in general, L. Gregory Jones, *Embodying Forgiveness* (Grand Rapids, MI: Eerdmans, 1995). Though not available at the time of writing, this book discusses at a much deeper theological level the concerns I touch on here.

12

A Preferential Option for the Family

Jon Davies

Introduction

We can perhaps agree with Stephen Barton[1] that there are sound reasons for acknowledging that the Bible is not the only place to start in the search for 'good news for human sexuality'. In addition to asking 'what the Bible says', we need also to ask questions such as

> what is our *experience* as men and women in church and society *today*? and what kind of people do we need to be in order to interpret wisely what the Bible says, in a way which is life-giving in the realm of sexuality and gender?[2]

As a sociologist, I welcome this interest in things empirical. Theologians are perhaps not over-inclined to accept the discipline of quantitative data or the careful rigours of statistical inquiry! This is more of a comment than a criticism: different academic disciplines have different definitions as to what is to be regarded as factual, and different traditions as to the significance of such factualities in the development of their profession. I do, however, feel very strongly that the empirical tradition of sociology (which seeks to turn arguments about opinion into discussion about facts) is a tradition which has much to recommend it when the topic under discussion is in part at least a matter of public policy and great public concern. This is undoubtedly the

---

[1] S. C. Barton, 'Is the Bible Good News for Human Sexuality? Reflections on Method in Biblical Interpretation', *Theology and Sexuality* 1 (September 1994), 42–54.

[2] Ibid., 52 (my emphasis).

case with the family, an institution central to both public and private fates and futures.

Further, as a sociologist with a serious concern for theology, I feel obliged to point out that an *experiential* location for theological exegesis can only too easily become a form of *ad hominem* argument, as indeed is the case with any form of 'the sociology of knowledge'. In the chaos of competitive 'truths' which can (*can*, not *has to*) follow from such an exegetical standpoint, it becomes rather easy to ignore the views of those whose experience is different on the grounds that the cheerful deployment of pluralism will ensure a fair hearing for all – and, besides, it's all relative ... We end up, if not too careful, in the quagmire of the hermeneutics of suspicion.

My own position is quite clear. On many issues to do with the family, we now have a range of reasonably well-established facts which carry reasonably clear normative prescriptions. In essence, these fact-derived prescriptions tend to support conservative family values and to contra-indicate further experimentation in domestic arrangements.

I am convinced that the empirical data we have on the family in contemporary society indicate that neither society as a whole nor the poor in particular benefit from its progressive dismantlement: and that any 'preferential option for the family' (to use a Liberation Theology phrase) requires a firm and loving restatement of the necessity of family life for children, for the poor and for society as a whole. The poor have many problems. It is hard to see how any of these can be made less onerous by breaking down their family lives. No hole that they are in is made anything but deeper by practices or encouragements to take their family life less seriously. Amongst these encouragements are the examples, by word or by action, of the better-off opinion-formers of our society, for whom the social and economic costs of domestic and sexual experimentation are so much easier to bear.

A theology, or indeed a sociology, which ignores the empirical data showing how much damage is being done is a theology or a sociology indifferent, in consequence if not in intent, to the miseries of thousands and tens of thousands, and to the destabilising of society. In what follows I will concentrate on what is happening to our children, who tend to be relatively invisible in the adult-concerned language of the great mass of social and socio-theological commentary. Stephen Barton's essay quoted above makes no mention at all of children; and Adrian Thatcher[3] is concerned mainly to minimise the role that children have always had in the Christian discussion of sexuality and gender. The very fact that academic or socio-theological discussions about 'sexuality' or 'family' can be pursued by ignoring children or by relegating them to some separate or separable area of life is in itself evidence of how far sexuality has become something to be seen as an adult-only matter.

I should perhaps stress that what is happening to children is part of the broader development of postmodern society, as it surely if somewhat erratically demolishes, in the name of liberation, all the old restrictive roles and moralities of traditional society. One of the major preoccupations of postmodernism is to confer upon as many adults as possible the full range of freedoms hitherto restricted either to élites or selected political or gender groupings. The post-modern world is almost entirely preoccupied with adults.

The journey from tradition

Where, as men and women in church and society, have we come from and where, as men and women in the church, are we today?

We live in a society which has a marked antipathy to the centuries-old tradition in which, in familial as in all other aspects of the pilgrimage towards the virtuous life, men and women sought *first* to know what the rules of good (or godly) conduct were, and then, *secondly*, to so organise their personal and public life as to ensure that both they and as many people as possible were trained in or made to conform to those rules. The first 'Archbishop of Canterbury', Augustine, exemplifies (or perhaps introduces) this tradition when, at the outset of his mission to the barbarians of what is now Kent, he wrote back to His Holiness the Pope asking for detailed rules on sexual and familial matters: what, for example, was the appropriate rule for people who had erotic dreams in their sleep? Should men be allowed Holy Communion if they had not washed after intercourse with their

[3] A. Thatcher, *Liberating Sex: a Christian Sexual Theology* (London: SPCK, 1993).

wives? His Holiness Pope Gregory provided answers, given as *the* answers, canonical, true, fixed.[4]

In the Catholic centuries, *and* later under Protestant authorities, this underlying premiss, of the existence and availability of authoritative rules of conduct, providing a definite institutional setting for sexual and procreational matters, remained the essential foundation of sexual ethics, no matter how, in detail, some aspects of the ethics varied.

So strong was the normative power of these rules that, at every social level, and by tradition, education and by legitimate coercion, it was held to be perfectly proper to identify *and to punish* all those who transgressed them. In secular and religious courts, in the endless surveillance of the parish confessional, and in the day to day regulatory potency of intimate kinship and community life, our Christian ancestors elaborated and enforced a set of sexual and familial rules around which Christian virtue was defined and defended against all the wiles and temptations of both inner and outer demons and temptations.

Christianity was compulsory: and this strict attitude applied to both the ordinary laity, those 'without the gift of continency' for whom sex within marriage was condoned, and for the clergy, the celibates, whose life was seen as expressing a higher sexual ethic, but one which was also rigorously policed: celibacy meant chastity – as indeed did marriage. Godly rules were enforced within the monastery and chapter-house just as rigorously as in the parish.

This entire system, the two sexual trajectories, was grounded on a second major premiss, viz. that children were important. In the adult-only world of the celibate, this premiss revealed itself straightforwardly enough – by an insisted-upon childlessness: either two parents or no children. For the other adults, marriage may indeed have been seen as the answer to lust, but overwhelmingly as *an institution providing the best way to bring up children*: that was what sex was for, and before and after the formal marriage ceremony, Christian societies sought to ensure that children were brought up within a fixed and predictable institution, within which adult appetites took second place. Sex was meant to

---

[4] See Bede, *Ecclesiastical History of the English People* (Harmondsworth: Penguin, 1990), 77–89.

produce children: children were not to be born outside of marriage. Adults were following the Godly Rule when they put their children first. Those who put God first – the clerical celibates – were allowed neither children nor sex. Those who 'had to' have sex had to do so within the context or 'confines' of marriage, and to do so in order to have children. This view of society is well presented in the Book of Common Prayer, which provides a 'Guide to Life' for all stages of the parental and juvenile life cycles.

History is littered with evidence of the vicissitudes of this system. Medieval poems and ballads and, later, novels and histories show how fragile was this repressive and restrictive accomplishment. Indeed, at the end of the eighteenth century, and in the early decades of the nineteenth, it seemed clear to contemporary observers that there was yet another breakdown in both private and public morals. The Victorian reaction was so strong, and was so influential until the late 1950s, that commentators today are apt to see the entire Christian family and sexual system as actually originating under Victoria – 'Victorian values' – forgetting perhaps that it has a much longer pedigree than that!

Whatever the case, it is clear that the 'Victorian' set of attitudes to sexual and familial matters is now a thing of the past. The modern pilgrim seeks to know not the Rules which, because they apply to everyone, apply to him, but the many and varied paths to freedom *from* rules, a freedom for activities and pursuits which are valued precisely because they are idiosyncratic rather than collective. Lest idiosyncrasy be seen as selfishness, the freely chosen erotic and procreative lifestyles of today are justified with such terms as 'authentic', or 'liberated' or 'happiness'. Lest selfishness be seen as loneliness, there is a great emphasis on 'relationship' and on 'relating' 'persons' to 'persons'.

This modern or post-modern view of inter-personal life-strategies is well symbolised in the change of title of one of the United Kingdom's main 'family agencies': from 'The Marriage Guidance Council' to 'Relate'. In the earlier title, the word 'guidance' implies the existence of a clear objectively-best way of doing things, those things being 'marriage', as is equally clear. 'Guidance' also implies the existence of an authoritative source of wisdom on such matters, a 'Council', by which seekers for help would be told what the Good Rule was, and then guided to it, by people who knew best. 'Relate,' on the other hand, by transforming what is normally a verb into an open ended, object-less cross between an injunction, an invitation and a passivity, confers virtue on any and all persons so engaged: it is a word quite incapable of moral evaluation. This clearly suits the modern, secular mind, characterised above all by the desire to privatise, as a matter of dogma, all those sexual and procreative activities regarded, in the not so distant past, as being prototypically in the public domain and subject to public regulation. Health Minister John Bowis, for example, addressing the 25th Gay Pride march and party in (ironically enough) Victoria Park, London, said:

> I do not believe loving or sexual feelings are mental aberra-tions to be suppressed whether they are heterosexual, homo-sexual or bisexual. I do not believe society should be judgmen-tal about what, for an individual, is a fact of nature – whether that nature was fashioned or developed in the genes or in the environment.[5]

It is not as if these freedoms are to be exercised as a purely private choice, as might be justified under classic liberal free-market doctrine, in which choice is 'free' when the *costs* as well as the benefits are borne by the chooser. There is a kind of one-way or reversed collectivism at play in the modern attitudes to sexual expression and sexual repertoire-deployment: Minister of Health John Bowis, for example, went on to describe those in the public sector (he was referring to the staff of the Health Service) who demonstrated 'prejudice' against lesbian and gay people as being properly the object of the new complaints procedures of the Health Service. This degree of social control was not, how-ever, to be universally applied, as

> The key theme of the (Patient's) Charter is respect for indi-viduals – giving them information, enabling them to make choices, respecting privacy and dignity, and responding when things go wrong ... the attitude of the public is changing as more and more people recognise the richness that lesbian and gay people add to society ... More and more gay people are prepared to be open about their sexual orientation and make known their requirements for appropriate health and social services. In the future we will see a more openly ageing gay

population who will require services as elderly people, geared to their specific needs.[6]

While some groups (the aging gay population in this case) have 'requirements', there is no expectation here that the opinions of the NHS staff will be similarly respected: their opinions are, after all, 'prejudices', and anyway they are, as public servants of a history-reversing, prejudice-reversing state, obliged to do what they are told. There is also an odd set of futurologies at work here, amongst them the insistence that gays and lesbians (who at the very least are likely to have lower birth rates than heterosexuals) will legitimately, and practically, be able to call on the younger generation (other people's children?) to fund whatever general and specific health needs they may have. John Bowis is at least making a positive case for gays and lesbians. Freed from ancient repressions, they can (he says) contribute to society as a whole. Nigella Lawson, commenting on the Bishop of Birmingham's expressed view that married couples should have children or risk the wrath of God, said that there is no (longer?) public interest in the having of children: 'we no longer have to procreate to survive', she wrote, and love and marriage might well be damaged by babies:

> If love means anything, or is to have any endurance, then it must be felt for someone in the present, not in some putative, babied future. And those who marry just to fructify tend to find decay can set in sooner than they expected.[7]

Minister John Bowis and journalist Nigella Lawson may well find this new range of freedoms unproblematic. No doubt gays and lesbians are happier, relating, than they ever have been. The old restrictive rules, under which their sexual relationships would have been severely punished, are, properly enough, now seen as justifying a special call on the collective purse. Neither, if Ms Lawson is any guide, do we need a new generation of children! Such comments may be rational optimism: and they clearly confer benefits and freedoms upon whole 'new' sectors of the population. One is, though, entitled to wonder how long such liberty will last if procreation simply comes to an end!

[6] Ibid.
[7] Nigella Lawson, *The Times* (27 June 1995), 17.

No theologian with any sense of responsibility whatsoever, and alive to repeated worries and fears in society and church, can ignore the very serious arguments which indicate that whatever may have been gained in the realm of 'freedom to relate' for one or more sections of society can perhaps be seen as entailing a diminished freedom to flourish for others; and that amongst those are some of the most vulnerable of society's members: children. Readers will please note that I am not, for example, saying that gay rights have been and can only be achieved at the expense of children. But I am saying that a culture now so indifferent to its children carries serious risks for a steady erosion of the rights and well-being of all.

The next section of this paper reviews some of the empirical data which 'tell us where we are today' on this matter. In the empirical data which follow, I find it necessary to offer a couple of comments on the uses of statistics, as they are often misunderstood.

First, where a statistic relates to the whole of society, it is generally safe to assume that the poorer sections of society will experience a disproportionate share of the misery: so that, for example, figures indicating that 'for all groups divorce creates a housing problem' will tend to mask the fact that this effect will be most pronounced for poorer people. Wealthy or wealthier people are usually more able to cope with things such as single parenthood or divorce, whereas the poor tend, in these as in most other social experiments, to 'pay' more.

Second, generalised statements about, say, the effects on children's educational performance of divorce, in which a non-divorcing group is compared with a divorcing group, are nearly always *statements of probability* of outcome, not of guarantee of outcome. Thus for example a statement such as 'children from broken homes are most likely to get into trouble with the police' means neither that *all* children from such homes get into such trouble, nor that *no* children from intact families get into trouble with the police. The statement means what it says, that children from one kind of home have a greater probability of getting into and causing trouble than the children from another. Such a careful use of statistics would, for example, enable us to avoid a misleading comment such as this:

The argument that 'if children are born to partners in such a union [the author has in mind pre-marital sexual liaisons or living together] it will be to their detriment', draws on the likelihood that children born in secure homes where both parents live are more likely to thrive. But this is by no means universally true and the confident, almost complacent assumption that children are automatically disadvantaged if their parents have not been through a ceremony is easily falsified by common-law marriages which work and Christian marriages which do not.[8]

The 'complacency' is really in the clear message that being married or not doesn't matter. The author of this comment clearly knows about probabilities, which he calls 'likelihood', a much weaker phrase, but in creating a straw man ('universally true'!) is able to avoid the clear conclusion of probability statements, which in this case is simply this: if you wish to increase the number of distressed children, then increase the number of children born into unmarried or cohabiting unions. There are no guarantees in any form of human institution. But to ignore the clear message, even when the underlying logic of probability statements is known, is irresponsible in that it will encourage people to do things which they should not. The figures we will now present show as clearly as such figures can that the society in which we live has embarked upon a social experiment which is resulting in extra and avoidable human misery.

Relating to children

Martin Richards[9] states that the children of divorcing parents tend to show a period of disturbed behaviour, either acting up or disruptive or depressive or anxiety-ridden, that this behaviour may last through the entire divorcing experience, that such children leave school with fewer educational qualifications, and that they have less chance of going to university. The effects of divorce, writes Richards, may well persist into adulthood, with lower occupational status and lower income, earlier marriage and earlier divorce, and increased psychological problems. There is, in fact, a general picture of downward social mobility.

---

[8] Thatcher, *Liberating Sex*, 98.
[9] Martin Richards in M. Maclean and J. Kurczewski, eds., *Families, Politics and the Law* (Oxford: Clarendon Press, 1994), 306ff.

Monica Cockett and John Tripp[10] compared two groups of children: (a) those who were normally resident in a family that had been 're-ordered' (the authors' word: 'refragmented' is clearly the better word) because of the departure of one parent since the child's birth and (b) children who were normally resident with both their biological parents, termed 'intact families'. In the event, the first category could also be subdivided into lone parent families, step-families and re-disrupted families. Throughout, the data establish the clear superiority of the intact families, with two resident biological parents, as the best way of bringing up children. The various forms of 're-ordered' families felt 'worst off', they experienced more financial difficulty, they experienced greater health problems, with parental ill-health both affecting the health of their children and giving those children concern for parental pathologies such as heavy smoking or drinking. The intact families had higher levels of overall satisfaction with family life. They shared (in ways which they found satisfactory) in family tasks, had organised family outings, events and rituals, and experienced the different needs of each parent and the children as a positive rather than a negative force. Single-parent families, step-families and re-disrupted families were, overall and on practically every measure of social pathology, more miserable and less settled. As one step-family put it: 'There has been constant turmoil since the divorce and remarriage, constant stress'.[11] Children's self-esteem was affected by family troubles, their educational performance was affected, the experience of family discord and rows affected their lives in practically every sphere, domestic violence was more common in every type of family other than the intact family; and support from or contact with *grandparents* was as disrupted as the relationships with parents and siblings.

The overwhelming impression from findings such as these is that referred to in the quotation immediately above: any form of family life other than the intact family carries with it a concomitant increase in tension and stress. In 1994 the Family Policy Studies Centre held a conference in London on 'Crime and the

---

[10] Monica Cockett and John Tripp, *Family Breakdown and its Impact on Children, The Exeter Family Study* (Exeter: University of Exeter Press, 1994).
[11] Ibid., 10.

Family'. Reviewing the literature, Professor David P. Farrington said that:

> Poor parental supervision or monitoring, erratic or harsh parental discipline, parental disharmony, parental rejection of the child, and low parental involvement in the child's activities (as well as antisocial parents and large family size) were all important predictors of offending.[12]

He reported on Kolvin's work on children growing up in Newcastle, showing that marital disruption (divorce or separation) doubled the risk of offending for males; and on McCord's work, which attempts to break down the single category of 'broken home', showing that in *some* kinds of broken homes there is a *weaker* association with criminogenic outcomes. Farrington commented that 'it is not so much the broken home which is criminogenic as the parental conflict which often causes it',[13] a view rather ignoring the point that divorce and separation are themselves so intrinsically wrapped up in conflict. Norman Dennis's work[14] which reviews a series of longitudinal studies, adds to a battery of findings which (to say the least) make it very difficult to ignore the proposition that family breakdown and various forms of social pathology go hand in hand.

Robert Whelan, in *Broken Homes and Battered Children*, demonstrates as conclusively as it possibly can be that in the very 'opaque' area of study of child abuse, including child murder, the risk is highest (sometimes spectacularly so) the further the family pattern diverges from the married relationship of two natural parents. The 'alternative' families (natural mother alone, natural mother and father substitute, natural father alone, natural father and mother substitute, and others such as children living with relatives) which contain a minority of the nation's children provide the majority of cases of child abuse.[15] In the terrible practice of child murder, Whelan shows:

[12] D. P. Farrington in C. Henricson, ed., *Crime and the Family* (London: Family Policy Studies Centre, 1994), 9.

[13] Ibid., 11.

[14] N. Dennis and G. Erdos, *Families Without Fatherhood* (London: IEA Health and Welfare Unit, 1993).

[15] Robert Whelan, *Broken Homes and Battered Children: a study of the relationship between child abuse and family type* (Oxford: Family Education Trust, 1994), 16.

the striking gap between the traditional family based on marriage and all other types. Households of cohabiting natural parents show a risk factor eighteen times greater than natural married parents. The natural mother with a live-in boyfriend represents a risk eight times greater than a mother and step-father.[16]

What is important is the consistent appearance of the two-parent family as a comparatively safe type for children, carrying a relatively low risk of abuse, and the equally consistent appearance of those households headed by lone mothers or by mothers living with other men in the comparatively risky categories.[17]

Jack Dominian and his co-authors may perhaps be allowed to summarise what is now a very solid mass of evidence showing that children are better off being brought up by their two natural parents, married to each other. The quote below restricts itself to the effects on children of divorce; and while there are certainly differences in outcome for children of single-parent, never-married households, and of step-households and of re-ordered households, and of various permutations of these, the general truth stands and bears repeating: children are better off being brought up by their married natural parents. Dominian says:

Children of divorced parents carry a higher risk of physical and psychological ill-health from the time of parental separation well into adult life. Children under five years at the time of their parent's divorce are particularly vulnerable. Children of divorced parents are between two and five times more susceptible to psychiatric illness. There is conclusive evidence that relationship instability is transmitted between generations with those whose parents divorce being more likely to divorce themselves.[18]

Divorce begets divorce and a related career of marital disharmony, across the generations. Jesus insisted that we put children

---

[16] Ibid., 32.
[17] Ibid., 23.
[18] J. Dominian, et al., eds., *Marital Breakdown and the Health of the Nation* (London: One Plus One: Marriage and Partnership Research, 1991), 29.

first. We don't. Somewhere in the long processes of cultural change we have come to see 'the family' as being constituted primarily to relate the sexes (rather than, overridingly, the generations) to each other. Given 'sex', then monogamy becomes insufficient and relationships become fragile and fractious – not least when there are children around. The kind of libertarian philosophies and theologies which either cause or legitimate the deconstruction of family life are philosophies and theologies which see the world as full of adults, and of adults who have a pressing appetite agenda to attend to, not least because those agendas have been too long ignored. In such a sexualised, mature world, children are a problem.

Come unto me?

We are dealing with 'the children problem' in three ways. First, we are (and Nigella Lawson is no doubt pleased) simply stopping having them. While the number of children born to a 'Western' family has been declining for nearly two hundred years, there has been 'a spectacular fall in the fertility rate since the 1960s'.[19] The European Union has a fertility rate of 1.54 births per woman in 1990, as compared with a rate of 2.61 in 1960, and a required replacement rate of 2.1 births per woman. This change has a variety of explanations, but amongst them is the postponement of the age of having the first child (26.7 in 1990, 24.2 in 1970) as well as having fewer children. The deconstruction of the family is a contraceptive device. It may well be that, as Nigella Lawson blithely says (see above), we don't need children as the world as a whole is overpopulated: but that overpopulated world will in all probability need the continuing viability of a confident, wealth-creating European Union, not a European Union in which a precarious, declining and ageing population can see no use for its wealth other than to hang on to it, and in which a small, indigenous, young, working population sees nothing but unfair taxation in whatever residual obligation it may feel to 'look after' the elderly, the sick or the children of other people. Neither internally, nor externally, does the rapid decline of the populations of the European Union make sense.

[19] N. Cronin, ed., *Families in the European Union* (London: Family Policy Studies Centre, 1994), 9.

Second, we can deal with the problem of disrupted family life by regarding all children as a 'public good', as economists say, or by 'nationalising' them, as politicians might say. Some theologians and some moral philosophers might well feel that there is something selfish in the exclusivity of 'parents and *their* children', and that communal nurturance is a good thing. Whatever the range of opinion, we are already well on the way to collectivising children. Single parent households, for example, are massively dependent on 'the state' (i.e. on the taxpayers) for housing and publicly-sourced income. Divorce seriously damages the family budget. Working mothers generate demands for 'nursery' and pre-school provision: in France, Italy and Denmark, over 80 per cent of children aged 3–5 are accommodated by some form of public childcare provision, and the figure for all the other EU countries, apart from the UK and Portugal, is above 50 per cent, nearing 60 per cent.[20] Under the guise of 'community care', and even of Christian versions of such an ethic, such a shift in the costs of having children, or at least in the costs of having to bring them up (there generally being little but ease and pleasure in the business of having them – especially for men) might well be what is on the democratic agenda in the years ahead.

There may, of course, be some difficulty in persuading an electorate with a low tax tolerance that it should be keen to pay for other people's pleasures, and it could well be that the nature and scale of the public childcare system would therefore be such as to be chronically underfunded and as such, amongst other things, to be able to pay wages at a level only too likely to attract some dubious child 'care' workers, of a type not unknown today. 'Realists', however, may be correct in thinking that there is now no turning back to the days of no divorce and low outside-of-marriage birth-rates.

This might then take us to a third method of dealing with children, once they have already been much reduced in number and taken onto the public payroll: this is to steadily move to a position of regarding children as being full beneficiaries of that tradition of possessive or appetitive individualism which has been so radical a liberator of adult men and, more slowly, adult women. The enfranchisement of teenagers in 1966 symbolised this process: various 'Children's Acts' of the mid and late 1980s

[20] Ibid.

built on this, conferring some form of autonomous legal status on ever-younger children. A very clear echo of this is to be found in the Exeter Family Study referred to above. The authors conclude their work with a series of recommendations which would extend the 'public parenting' role of the state:

> We recommend that the core educational curriculum for all children should be adapted to include components that address social and philosophical issues of modern life with particular reference to issues of personal relationships and family life. An important part of this curriculum would be the acknowledg-ment of the pluralistic nature of modern life and the exploration of the many forms of family in which children find themselves. Normalisation of this experience, with recognition that families commonly do not have the traditional form *that children still believe to be the norm,* would enable teachers and others to address these issues. This would allow children to feel better about themselves so that the resulting improvement in self-image might break the cycle of underachievement that affects many of these children.[21]

Such a formulation imposes *upon children* (together, to be sure, with their nursery and primary school teachers) the task of dealing with the problems given to them by a resolutely hedonistic adult world. It is not as if the authors of this recommendation can see much to favour in what is happening to the family. They do not appear to think that 'the cycle of underachievement' is a figment of some reactionary mind. They state quite bluntly that

> There is no disagreement that children involved in family reorganisation (*sic*) are disadvantaged in a number of ways: poorer self-esteem, more difficulties in their daily lives with health, school performance, friendships and behaviour, increased long term likelihood of lower socio-economic grouping, associated with reduced educational and vocational qualification, increased likelihood of early and shorter-lasting personal relationships with sexual partners, with the associated increased risk of birth outside marriage and breakdown of their own marriages.[22]

[21] Cockett and Tripp, *Family Breakdown,* 65. Emphasis added.
[22] Ibid., 61.

Children 'educated' to cope with such a world are being asked to do things that very few adults could manage. The argument from 'realism', that this is the world they live in anyway and they had better get used to it, provides a steadily self-legitimating excuse for ever-larger numbers of narcissistic adults. As the moral and practical centrality of monogamous parenthood is, in and by a public educational system, denied, we will see the attempted production of ever-larger numbers of children denied their proper period of innocence and expected to behave 'as adults', that being the most convenient opt-out for the 'adults' who produced them. These children (and bear in mind that they will have to be introduced to these thoughts at very early ages) will be pressured to behave as 'responsible' adults before they have had time to be children, and to do so in order to 'adjust' to a world of infantilised adults.

Towards a fission society

The logical end of the pursuit of individualism is solitariness, either in practice (26 per cent of European Union families live on their own[23]) or in spirit, as the absence of clear rules makes each 'relationship' so problematic and unpredictable as to sensibly invite conditional partnerings and relationships. David Riesman some years ago described this society as one grounded in morale rather than morality and composed of 'adult self-exploiting peer-groups'.[24] Riesman on balance seems to have welcomed this new society: and no doubt there is, and will continue to be, a very large amount of excitement and creativity in such relationships; and the evidence we have on the morbidity and mortality results of such practices for mature adults – both single and divorced men and women drink more than married men and women, go mad more often, and so forth – *can be held to be nothing but their problem: a matter of adult choice.* The same cannot, clearly, be said about children, although in some combination of the three 'child-management' tactics discussed above may be found at least a plausible solution. It is my belief that the destruction of the family

[23] Cronin, *Families in the European Union*, 3.
[24] D. Riesman, *The Lonely Crowd* (New Haven: Yale University Press, 1964), 157. The book was first published in 1950.

is causing suffering: the facts seem to me to be as powerfully clear and true as any such facts can be. A church, a Christian community which contributes to this suffering is behaving sinfully. We may with some sense of purpose borrow Janet Martin Soskice's quote about women, and ask readers to insert 'children' for 'women' in the appropriate places:

> What we must also ask ourselves as Christians, women as well as men, is, Has our Church made things any better, or have we colluded in silencing the already half-voiced, and in making the problems of women, 'just women's problems'? Bodies are being broken day after day in linked wheels of poverty, prostitution, sexual abuse and domestic violence. How can we map these on the broken and risen body of Christ?[25]

The 'map' that I find to hand is the Book of Common Prayer, which in its Calendar and sequence of rituals and prayers provides a *vade mecum* for adult living and childrearing. In quoting the Fifth Commandment the Book of Common Prayer reasserts the essential, and essentially practical, view of family life, that it is a matter, crucially, of transactions between the generations, between the young and the old, between those whose life is beginning and those whose life is beginning to end, in creativity, with the advent of the new life with which they have been trusted. Modern reconstructions of 'the family', be these theological or sociological or philosophical, assume always and predominantly the interests of adults: the adult is the centre of their system. There is clearly nothing wrong with that; and there is equally no doubt that the bigotry of centuries presents us with too many broken bodies and too many diminished adults. It is relatively easy, and a considerable temptation, not always resisted, to present 'the family' as the source and prime mover of all this hurt and bigotry. The greater challenge is to construct a theology which insists on the primacy of the family as the agency certainly for the bearing and nurturance of children and, associated with that, for the most profound and spiritual expressions of sexual and serious love between adult men and women.

As 'men and women in the church and society today' we must face up to the fact that the family is *not* a privileged institution in

---

[25] Quoted in Barton, 'Is the Bible Good News?', 52.

the world we live in. Adrian Thatcher's concern for 'the danger that a strong emphasis on marriage can eclipse all other possible sexual relations'[26] is simply *not true* for today. There is now little interest in virginity; divorce is being made steadily easier; marriage is fiscally and in terms of social security highly disprivileged; on some projections the proportion of children born outside of marriage will reach nearly 70 per cent by the first decade of the next century; and recent changes in the licencing of places of marriage underline very firmly that the ceremony itself has become part of the entertainment industry. No parent bringing up children today could possibly think that there is a danger of them being overwhelmed by virginity or of rushing or even walking into marriage! It is perhaps not surprising that on BBC Radio 4's, 'Sunday' programme, 9 July 1995, Cardinal Hume could express the view that one argument for a celibate clergy was the evident difficulties of contemporary married life: celibacy is easier! It may well be that in an adult-only world none of this matters, and that the Christian tradition and agenda can cheerfully be invoked to regard all non-procreative sex as of equal status in the eyes of God, and that children can be dealt with in some permutation of the three strategies described above. A steady look at the 'society in which we live today' should show to all but the most resolutely, adamantly and smugly blind how wrong this is – in fact, and in the light of Christian teaching.

---

[26] Thatcher, *Liberating Sex*, 92.

13

Ideology, Power and the Family[1]

Alan M. Suggate

The need for meaning and institutions

The focus of this essay is on the wider social context of the family. Brigitte and Peter Berger stress that the ideas, values and norms operative in a society are crucial factors in the socialisation process; they determine what kind of human beings inherit the future of the society. They go on, 'Identity is very closely related to the overall framework of meaning within which the individual can make sense of his life ... Modernity has let loose a variety of processes that weaken or undermine such frameworks of meanings – mostly by relativising them ... Yet a society cannot survive without a widely shared moral consensus.'[2]

Ideas, values and norms are embedded in institutions. Indeed, as the Bergers say, 'Human beings could not survive without institutions ... If it were not for institutions, the world would have to be reinvented every day – an impossible idea ... Children need a world to grow into. It follows that any programme of radical deinstitutionalisation is futile ...'[3] The Bergers write this with special reference to the family itself, but it equally applies to those other institutions which form the context of the family in society. We have to keep reviewing the institutions of society and asking how they can better support family life.

An ideology has been defined by Julius Gould as 'a pattern of beliefs and concepts (both factual and normative) which purports to explain complex social phenomena with a view to

---

[1] The author thanks Fr Dominic Kirkham for the information and advice he has kindly given.
[2] Brigitte and Peter Berger, *The War over the Family: Capturing the Middle Ground* (Harmondsworth: Penguin, 1983), 161f.
[3] Ibid., 159f.

directing and simplifying socio-political choices facing individuals and groups'.[4] But it is not simply a set of ideas which is used to generate policy. It is also an instrument for the exercise of power by one group in relation to others. Hence it is often used in a pejorative sense by those who feel themselves threatened or oppressed.

In this essay I consider two British ideologies of the twentieth century which have certainly been concerned with power. Both have recognised and promoted the capital importance of the family. The first is ethical socialism, the second ethical capitalism (observe how I strive to avoid tendentiousness!). The first is best represented by William Temple and R. H. Tawney, and I shall concentrate on Tawney. The obvious representative of the second is Mrs (now Lady) Thatcher. So far as possible in a short essay I will consider the debate between them and give hints of a possible way forward.

Tawney's ideology of ethical socialism

Tawney, like almost all socialists of his day, assumed the centrality of the family, and it can be said that his whole endeavour was to create the conditions in society which would best enable the family to flourish and fulfil its role in society.

His significance lies partly in his full recognition of the importance of the wider social and institutional context of families. Like Temple he stressed the importance of social groups intermediate between the individual and the state. The expansion of state activity which he sought was to be geared to supporting the family, the school, the trade union, and so forth.

In *Poverty as an Industrial Problem* (1913) he drew attention to the way in which social studies had moved away from focusing on this or that individual poor person in their search for explanations of poverty, and concentrated much more on social forces and institutions. He himself singled out the organisation of industry. He drew on Seebohm Rowntree's investigation of poverty in York in 1900, where it was revealed that over 15 per cent of all wage earners were living in primary poverty. In other

[4] Quoted by J. Philip Wogaman, *Christians and the Great Economic Debate* (London: SCM Press, 1977), 10.

words, a major factor in poverty was the abysmally low level of wages. Wages could not be abstracted from the whole way industry was organised. Tawney pointed to a factory where the hours and pay of the workforce had been severely cut, yet at the same time shareholders had received a dividend of 22 per cent and vast sums had been transferred to the firm's reserves. Tawney was also concerned not simply with those who were in actual poverty, but with the huge numbers who were living on the margins of poverty, vulnerable to the economic fluctuations of boom and slump.[5]

His chief aim therefore was to find ways of jacking up the standard of living for whole classes of people, so that they had much greater security, and could lead healthy, independent and self-respecting lives. Part of this jacking up entailed the provision of more and regular income. Tawney called it economic resisting power. He was an enthusiast for the new Trade Boards, which succeeded in introducing higher basic levels of pay in certain industries. In so doing they confounded the view that this would ruin the industry. Not only was this not so, but the standard of work in the factories went up and also the whole quality of life in the area as families and the local economy benefited.[6]

Tawney's aim was never simply pecuniary but always also moral, grounded in Christian concepts of what was due to human beings simply as human beings. Like Temple he supported better quality schooling (with a higher school leaving age) so that the young especially could develop their personalities and skills and thus play a responsible role in the life of their country. He also argued with characteristic vigour and wit for improved health care, stressing the relative cheapness of collective provision over against each person fending for himself. No man by taking thought, he wrote, can add a cubit to his stature, but a country can add an inch to the height of its children and a pound to their weight, if it so wills, by collective provision.[7]

Tawney was thus a firm supporter of the beneficent potential of state intervention. Yet this was to be directed to the ultimate aim of the welfare of communities, and at the heart was the

[5] *Poverty as an Industrial Problem* (London: The Ratan Tata Foundation, London School of Economics, 1914), 11, 14.

[6] Ibid., 15f.

[7] R. H. Tawney, *Equality* (London: Allen & Unwin, 1931), 139.

welfare of families. Study of the wider conditions in which poverty arises did not imply that the personal factor was unimportant – indeed, his assumption was that most people do respond to favourable conditions.

> If any group of people have ... adequate economic resisting power, they may usually be relied upon themselves to protect the weaker members of the group against the principal accidents of life; whereas if they have not, merely to supplement their immediate needs ... [is] positively maddening, [since they] want not to be given their living by someone else but to earn it under fair conditions for themselves.

Such resisting power enables a class

> to build up its own institutions with its own habits and ideals, to interpose a whole network of personal relationships between the individual and either the offensive intrusion of sympathetic outsiders or the bare machinery of bureaucracy ... It is in Lancashire, where labour is protected by factory acts and trade unions, that family life, co-operation, friendly societies, education, social institutions for a hundred different purposes, find their fullest development.[8]

The ethical socialism of figures like Temple and Tawney underpinned the Labour administrations after the Second World War. Indeed, it has been said that Temple's *Christianity and Social Order* was one of the foundation piers of the welfare state. Tawney lived to see the realisation of many of his hopes. Even the Conservative governments which dominated the 1950s and early 1960s, especially that of Harold Macmillan, shared many of the commitments of ethical socialism. It is no accident that it was Edward Heath who wrote a foreword to the reissue of Temple's *Christianity and Social Order* in 1976.[9]

Mrs Thatcher's ideology of ethical capitalism

Yet after Tawney's death in 1962 a new mood began to set in,

---

[8] *Poverty as an Industrial Problem*, 15f.
[9] W. Temple, *Christianity and Social Order* (Harmondsworth: Penguin, 1942). Reissued in 1976 with a Foreword by Edward Heath and Introduction by R. H. Preston (London: Shepherd-Walwyn and SPCK).

which precipitated a new ideology deeply critical of the prevailing consensus, and especially of events in the 1960s and 1970s. Mrs Thatcher and her associates felt a deep revulsion against what they saw as the decline of Britain. Shortly after her election in 1979 Mrs Thatcher was saying that the wanton expansion of the state's responsibilities had been accompanied by a great drop in public spirit.

> The mission of this Government is much more than the promotion of economic progress. It is to renew the spirit and solidarity of the nation. To ensure that these assertions lead to action, we need to inspire a new national mood, as much as to carry through legislation. At the heart of a new mood in the nation must be the recovery of our self-confidence and our self-respect ... The foundation of this confidence has to be individual responsibility.[10]

At the heart of Mrs Thatcher's ideology lay an interlocking set of economic, political, social and moral ideas, which are tolerably well known to most people who have been alive in the last 15 years. As many writers have remarked, this ideology has two strands which in the most obvious sense are contradictory. As Andrew Gamble puts it, 'The New Right has two major strands: a liberal tendency which argues the case for a freer, more open, and more competitive economy, and a conservative tendency which is more interested in restoring social and political authority throughout society.'[11]

The liberalism of the New Right is a restatement of the classical liberal tradition. It considers liberty and the individual to be fundamental values. Market mechanisms are deemed superior in promoting national prosperity within the global economy, because of the alleged greater efficiency of the market in the allocation and use of scarce resources. They also maximise individual freedom through limiting state intervention.

This attitude was reinforced by public choice theory, in which politicians are viewed as rational actors with the primary aim of maximising votes, bureaucrats as instinctive maximisers of their

---

[10] Peter Riddell, *The Thatcher Decade* (Oxford: Basil Blackwell, 1989), 7.

[11] Andrew Gamble, *The Free Economy and the Strong State: The Politics of Thatcherism* (London: Macmillan, 1988), 29.

own budget, prestige and benefits. 'The absence of profit criteria in the public sector encourages its reckless expansion engineered by self-interested rational bureaucrats. This tendency is exacerbated by elections where politicians promise goods and services to voters in order to get elected, ignoring their costs or how the burden of that cost is to be distributed.'[12]

Yet Mrs Thatcher was never a pure libertarian. There is another strand which makes freedom vie with order. Many of Mrs Thatcher's supporters bemoaned the collapse of moral standards in society, and singled out the 1960s as the time *par excellence* when the destruction took place. The transmitter of these standards is the family. The policy of Mrs Thatcher was constantly to emphasise the centrality of the family. Here she took over a traditional theme of One Nation Toryism, though her own understanding of it was coloured by her experience of upbringing in her family in Grantham, and above all by her father's regimen. It is this appeal which has had much to do with the curbing of welfare provision by the state, on the grounds that it erodes the traditional role of the family as a provider of support against hardship.

However much these two strands might be in conflict, both could agree that the enemy within was social democracy, the potential Trojan Horse for communism. Liberals could lament the decadence of social democracy because it was less efficient in economic terms, increased the role of government in society, and weakened people's resolve to show the virtues which were the prerequisite for economic success: individual responsibility and initiative and discipline. The conservatives were more directly concerned about the cultural ravages of social democracy. It extended rights to diverse groups and thereby limited traditional hierarchical and authority relationships.[13] Either way there was the need for strong government to combat threats to society. The joint call was therefore for a powerful government.

The chief threat lay in the army of public sector professionals which had multiplied in the post-war period and now powerfully shaped the public consciousness over what was politically desir-

---

[12] Desmond S. King, *The New Right: Politics, Markets and Citizenship* (Chicago: The Dorsey Press and London: Macmillan, 1987), 11f.
[13] See e.g. King, 8f; Gamble, 58.

able and politically practicable. These enemies of the free society were particularly in evidence in the civil service (both nationally and locally), the unions, the schools and the universities. It is in this context that we must see the ferocity of the conservative attack on the churches, and especially the established church, as they appeared naively to collude with the threats to public and private morality.[14]

How are we to evaluate these ideologies, and what sort of constructive ideas and practices seem best for the future? I quail at the complexities, but try to go to the heart of the matter.[15]

A critique of the two ideologies

Keynesian social democracy had certainly run into crisis by 1970. At the economic level the assumption had been that by technical means the economy could continually be fine-tuned to deliver growth, full employment and low inflation. This in turn assumed the competence of government to manage the economy. The government of Harold Wilson – the most addicted to technique of all post-war governments – failed to confirm the assumption. 'Stagflation' reared its head, and for the ordinary citizen the increasing burden of taxation in such a climate bred disenchant ment. New ideas were required, not only of an economic but also of a political kind.

It had also been assumed that government could achieve desired social objectives by a process of social engineering. Legislation would provide the framework and an army of civil servants – national and local government, bureaucrats and professionals – would carry it out for the benefit of society. The experts however were often not as wise and knowledgeable as was thought. It was also suspected that the interests of the civil servants sometimes took precedence over their clients' interests. Once again new ideas seemed to be required, both political and social.

---

[14] Gamble, 58–60.
[15] In what follows I am much indebted to Paul Wilding, 'What went wrong? Where now?' in Alison J. Elliot and Ian Swanson, *The Renewal of Social Vision* (Edinburgh: Centre for Theology and Public Issues, 1989), 23–9.

It therefore became questionable how far it was possible to reconstruct society along the lines of the radical vision of the age of Temple and Tawney and the post-war Labour government. This mood of disenchantment, even fatalism, unsurprisingly prompted the thought, Is such a vision even desirable? Mrs Thatcher's convictions were sufficiently in tune with the popular mood to secure her election in 1979.

I have mixed feelings about the legacy of Tawney himself. On the positive side, he spent a lifetime elaborating a coherent social philosophy, which wove together social analysis, deep moral convictions about what was due to human beings – to their dignity and their need for community – and concrete policy proposals. It is perhaps the failure of his heirs on the left that they rested on the assumption that the social consensus needed no defence, but would continue for ever. They needed to be much stronger on monitoring the limitations and failures of policies as they became apparent and creatively adjusting them to new aims and objectives. Perhaps it is partly the weaknesses of Tawney which contributed to this failure. He had an immense antipathy to capitalism, which he judged anti-Christian, and thereby probably reinforced the distaste of many on the left for market activity. Perhaps also, along with the Fabians, he overestimated the importance of hard professional knowledge and assumed in other professionals and bureaucrats the same ascetic integrity and moral passion which he showed himself. It was therefore easy to assume that the role of the state could be endlessly expanded in the quest for the floor on which the working class could securely stand and demonstrate their independence.[16]

However, the failure of the left is only a part of the problem. Much more powerful (and I here pick up my earlier quotation from the Bergers) was the continuing impact of the modern world. As society became ever more diverse, in its own internal composition and through contact with the rest of the world, so, even if culture at one level became homogenised, there grew the pressure for the dissolution of common goals and shared stand-

---

[16] The standard (unpublished) thesis on Tawney's Christian social ethics is by John R. Atherton, *R. H. Tawney as a Christian Social Moralist* (Manchester Ph.D., 1979). For an evaluation of Tawney which criticises his utopianism see R. H. Preston, 'R. H. Tawney as a Christian moralist' in *Christianity and the Persistence of Capitalism* (London: SCM Press, 1979), 83–110.

ards. There has been a continual shift away from a substantive view of social justice to a procedural one, where societies are held together by ground rules of behaviour. Friedrich Hayek and John Rawls each in his own way argues for a theory of procedural justice.[17] Rawls in particular was trying to find foundations for society in something more profound than the pragmatic utilitarianism so characteristic of the modern world. By the 1960s this type of utilitarianism was often allied with the view that there are not and cannot be any publicly agreed criteria for morality, and therefore the tendency has been to say that any practice must be accepted as long as it does not harm others. It is surely ridiculous to attribute the propagation of this endemic assumption to left-wing intellectuals alone. It certainly had its philosophical defenders, but it is essentially a sign of and response to widespread cultural forces.

I also wish to argue that there were serious defects in the ideology of Mrs Thatcher and the style with which it was implemented. The ideology has a far inferior account of the human person than Tawney's social philosophy. It has become rather hackneyed to quote Mrs Thatcher's dictum, 'There is no such thing as society; there are only individuals and their families', yet it is very revealing. First, the centre-piece is the individual and his freedom. In line with Hayek, it is primarily a freedom from coercion and a freedom to make choices in order to satisfy the desires and wants the individual may have. On liberal premises there can be no putting of the question whether those desires and wants *ought* to be advanced or not – it is up to the individual to posit his own value system. Mrs Thatcher had to invoke the other strand of the ideology to emphasise the importance of character. But there is a tension here, and given the climate it was no surprise that vast numbers of citizens pursued a possessive individualism. Mrs Thatcher belatedly had to mount a campaign to urge generosity and altruism. This trend to possessive individualism was made all the more virulent by the sharp distinction drawn between the individual and family on the one hand and whatever else may lie beyond on the other. Of course there was

---

[17] Friedrich Hayek, e.g. *Law, Legislation and Liberty*, Vol. II: *The Mirage of Social Justice* (London: Routledge & Kegan Paul, 1976); John Rawls, *A Theory of Justice* (Cambridge, MA: Harvard University Press, 1971).

much that lay beyond in Mrs Thatcher's ideology, but it worked on a quite different basis. The private world was governed by personal choice, the public by impersonal technique – a different technique from Keynesian economics, but technique none the less. Nothing had to impede the free working of the market, and human beings were expected to accept its outcomes as if they were natural, beyond human choice. No critique from the standpoint of human justice was held to be admissible.

This ideology was made all the more stringent in its operation by Mrs Thatcher's very confrontational style. It was a style born not only of conviction but also of fear. Mrs Thatcher had very clear ideas who was for her ideology and who was against – there was no middle course. It was another form of class consciousness – however much the cry was that Britain was becoming a classless society. The protagonists were showered with favours; the rest treated with grave suspicion: denied dialogue, derided and suppressed, as if they were barely citizens of the same country, even enemies within. Powers were accumulated by central government for the defence of the realm and taken away from any lesser grouping which might question or threaten the new radical vision.

The practice of this ideology has, I believe, been one of the major sources of the disempowering of families. The poor have unquestionably been made poorer, both in relative and absolute terms. Legislation has selectively borne heavily on them; for example the Fowler review of 1988 reorganised only one part of the welfare state, and ignored all the others, such as mortgage tax relief. Whilst claiming to deliver the poor from dependency, it made poorer families even more dependent than before – dependent on the vagaries of charity rather than government hand-outs. The number of unemployed rose and remained very high, but the ideology forbade the state to create 'unreal' jobs, even though there was plenty of work that needed doing in society. For many still in work there was growing insecurity and low pay as short-term contracts became commoner and the Whitley Councils (the Trade Boards of Tawney's 1913 paper) were abolished. In the meantime the majority of people in the country grew in affluence, and everywhere there appeared glittering malls to satisfy their desires for more goods. The incessant advertising in the media underlined for the poor that they were not in any effective sense participants in the society produced by the new vision of Mrs Thatcher. It is not in the least surprising that many families were so ground down that they cracked in despair.

It will be clear that I have my reservations about Tawney, even more about the left in the 1960s, and consider the ideology of Mrs Thatcher retrograde, being fundamentally more flawed than Tawney or the left. At this juncture it is essential to generate new ideas. Let me now turn therefore to positive proposals for tackling the impasse we are in. I aim to be both theoretical and practical.

Out of the impasse: a theoretical sketch

In principle we need to break out of both myopic individualism and the divorce of the private and public realms. The aim of a Christian social order for William Temple was the fullest possible development of individual personality in the widest and deepest possible fellowship.[18] We are not first individuals who then choose to relate ourselves to others; we only become persons through those relationships, starting in the family but reaching out into a multitude of associations. These associations are a vital context in which the individual can grow to maturity: they can shape for good or ill, empower or disempower for responsible living. They are not just private and voluntary but also public and statutory.

The task today is to encourage these bodies not only severally to fulfil their tasks but also to work together. There is a great need here to break out of a narrow ideology imposed by central government – whether of the present right or the left of the 1960s – and experiment with a variety of forms of co-operation. A crucial factor here is the recognition of the diversity of local situations and their needs. The accent should go much more on enabling local communities to articulate their own perceptions of living in their locality, their complaints and their aspirations, and on partnership between them and various enabling bodies, whereby the professionals serve the actual needs of the inhabitants. Essential though a procedural notion of justice is in modern conditions, we should not abandon hope of finding a consensus on substantive justice focused on basic human needs. There is a

[18] W. Temple, *Christianity and Social Order* (1942), 74.

good deal of work being done on this concept, for instance by the New Economics Foundation. The Foundation has emphasised that economics should not be treated simply as a technique whose outcomes are to be accepted without reference to social good; rather, economic policy should serve basic needs.[19]

The task of government, local and national, would therefore be to promote such partnerships, according those who have suffered most and been heard least the courtesy of serious attention and genuine participation. It would need to bear in mind that social problems are not necessarily best tackled by focusing on the obvious. You do not sensibly tackle poverty by concentrating on poor people. As Tawney used to say, what to some people is the problem of poverty, to other equally thoughtful people is the problem of riches.[20] Short-term working and redundancy often go with high returns to shareholders. Equally, family breakdown may not be remedied by focusing on broken families. One of the important ways to restore and enhance family life is to give people positive opportunities within wider institutions, both to develop their own talents and to experience the give and take of collaboration for constructive ends. A growing confidence and sensitivity in negotiating relationships – between peers, between the sexes and between generations – is the very stuff of which family life is made.

A case study: a local 'therapeutic community'

Let us take a concrete case. In *The Month* for June 1992 and August 1994 Fr Dominic Kirkham describes the initiatives being taken in Miles Platting, Manchester.[21] Once the heartland of the 'Workshop of the World', it experienced almost total industrial collapse in the 1960s and 1970s. 'With it also went local confidence, purpose and the fabric of society.' There are record highs for unemployment, crime, premature death, suicide, ill-health, single parent families.

[19] See e.g. Paul Ekins, ed., *The Living Economy: A New Economics in the Making* (London: Routledge, 1986).

[20] *Poverty as an Industrial Problem*, 10.

[21] Dominic Kirkham, 'Hope in a city: a better role for the urban church', *The Month*, June 1992, 212–219; 'A view from the wilderness: an inner-city perspective of "community"', *The Month*, August 1994, 331–5.

Writing in 1992, Kirkham sketched a society in chaos and on the verge of collapse:

> Central to the problem of an area such as Miles Platting is the fact that people have increasingly opted out of any civic or parental responsibility for what is happening in the area. As almost entirely welfare dependants they have become used to abdicating all responsibility to 'them' [the Council]. In turn services which have become increasingly short of funds have been either cut back, rationalised, or moved out of the area, leaving an increasing sense of abandonment and dearth.

Clearly there was a crisis in local government. A major issue was the relation of local and central government. Though the Widdicombe Report had declared that local government was government by local communities rather than of local communities, the reality was central government administered locally by local government in an increasingly bitter so-called 'partnership'.

Dominic Kirkham was not only concerned with what could be done, but also challenged by remarks made to him to consider how the church could be involved and what he as a representative of the church could do. His first act was to start a petition to ask for more policing, and the urgency of the situation was reinforced at that moment when a parishioner was stabbed to death at the door of his priory. This underlined the despair and fear which was the underlying reality of people's lives. A meeting was well attended by professional and civic figures – and also by the local people themselves. Kirkham himself became chairman of a succession of meetings where different interest groups talked over common problems, and this led to a range of initiatives – homewatch schemes, victim support, clean ups. But:

> the key fault was that the local people were not themselves involved in the discussion of their issues nor in the initiation of action. What was needed was something of a somersault which would put the professional people in a secondary supportive role and give the burden of decision making and initiation to local people: – as someone commented, professionals should be on tap, not on top.

This led to the formation of the Miles Platting Community Assembly which has initiated, for example, regular playschemes, professional football coaching, a children's club, a gardening service, and a fifty-three seater luxury coach which takes groups out of the area on trips which would otherwise have been quite impossible.

These measures did help to give the local people a sense that they could take steps to influence their own lives for good. The Assembly has gone on to set up two dependent trusts. On the one hand it set up a Charitable Trust, so that it would not be in a state of grant dependency, but have its own reserve of funds to resource new projects. For example it has been able to give a substantial grant to a local primary school to pay for musical instruments and professional tuition. It has also set up a friend-ship club for the lonely and socially marginalised.

However, these initiatives did not really tackle the key factors of deprivation – the chief being unemployment. Long-term unemployment stands at 50 per cent – the highest in the country, and a whole alternative culture and lifestyle had been estab-lished. Thus the Assembly also established the Miles Platting and Ancoats Development Trust as the economic arm of the Assem-bly. The Trust exists to stimulate the sustainable regeneration of the area, to improve the quality of life through the creation of permanent jobs and attraction of new investment, and by ena-bling local people to develop their abilities and self-confidence. It lays particular emphasis on valuing individuals and developing relationships with local residents and public, private and volun-tary agencies. It is dedicated to community profit, not private shareholding, through the generation of income so as to become financially self-sufficient. It aims within three years to provide permanent employment for 250 local residents, raise educa-tional standards, enable the investment of £14m of private and public money into the area, and provide support for 50 local businesses. These targets are well on the way to being realised. A leading light here was Terry Thomas, Managing Director of the Co-operative Bank, who was emphatic that the very first criterion for any proposed new investment would be, Is it in the best interests of the local people? He was scathing about the Canary Wharf project precisely on those grounds.

A test of the Trust is the Victoria Mill Project. The mill is a vast monument to a past industrial age of which the motivating principle was the accumulation of capital for individual profit. The mill is being converted to provide commercial workspace, offices, shops, a community centre and cafe with youth and child-care facilities, and 102 homes. The aim is thus to make it an asset to the community, developed for collective benefit by imaginative community participation. Kirkham's vision is of a 'therapeutic community', one whose members have at their disposal and control the means to take whatever action they think necessary to improve the quality of their life in such a way as to bring fullness of being. Such a community fills the vacuum now existing between the individual and the centralised state, which perpetuates authoritarianism, alienation and irresponsibility.

Kirkham shows the various ways in which the church has been involved in this project. Indeed, he believes that the success of the structure of an Assembly with two dependent Trusts has rested on the foundation of the three local church communities, since virtually all key personnel are drawn from them. The local churches have worked together, pooling their resources, making their premises available for meetings, a credit union and a business. They have also been able to draw on a sense of community and loyalty present within them as the foundation for restoring a wider, public sense of community. The clergy have used their professional standing to articulate local feelings and act as facilitators for appropriate initiatives. Dominic Kirkham is himself Secretary of the Assembly and the two Trusts.

Moreover, the Victoria Mill scheme is being fronted by 'Linking Up', a project sponsored by the Church of England Board of Social Responsibility in response to the report *Faith in the City*. The government has shown an interest in the project through Robert Key, Junior Minister of the Environment, and committed £1.5m to it. 'Linking up' has however stressed the importance of partnership if the local community is to benefit.

Tawney used to remark that the touchstone of a society was the spirit in which it regarded the misfortunes of those of its members who fell by the way.[22] And being Tawney he would instantly link attitudes to institutions. The developments in Miles Platting are not of course 'the answer' to family and social crisis. There are still huge problems in tackling youth unemployment in new imaginative ways which can break through the

[22] R. H. Tawney, *Religion and the Rise of Capitalism* (London: Murray, 1926), 286.

legacy of alienation, often several generations deep. Suspicion and fears linger, and it will require at least a decade of sustainable growth if the community is to become a real therapeutic community. However, a start has been made and the lives and aspirations of a number of parents and families have improved. The developments hitherto are a vivid illustration of what can be done when interested groups, both voluntary and statutory, and especially the local inhabitants, are enabled to work together for the revitalisation of a community and its institutions, and thereby its family life. The inference is that we do not need a fully-fledged ideology, but a broad and experimental movement, rooted in the lives of those who have every justification for despair but are enabled to find hope and transmit it to a wider public.

14

Dympna Revisited: Thinking About the Sexual Abuse of Children

Ann Loades

Introduction

Jean Bethke Elshtain has some pertinent questions to put to those concerned with the 'family debate' overall, in the light of her remark that 'Every political culture has a point at which it threatens to come unglued.' Fault lines may lie beneath the surface, and we prefer not to attend to them, but may be compelled to do so when certain circumstances prevail. For circumstances sometimes prompt attention to particular issues, not least those which 'involve substantive moral imperatives and implicate us in larger, competing visions of social life and possibility'. Given attention to certain issues, we may then find ourselves with a 'crisis' on our hands, but 'who gets to decide what constitutes a crisis in a fundamental social institution?' Or, how does that crisis get placed on the political agenda? And what sorts of remedies may be proposed to end the crisis, or to ameliorate it? What do the questions, the crisis itself, its end or amelioration tell us about 'who we are as people, how we live, and how we choose to see ourselves'? More particularly, how does 'child abuse' come to be constructed as discourse, and with an even narrower focus, how does the sexual abuse of children figure in all this?[1]

The story of Dympna illustrates that deep-seated worries about the sexual abuse of children in one particular form may be long-

[1] Jean Bethke Elshtain, 'The family crisis and state intervention: the construction of child abuse as social problem and popular rhetoric', *Power Trips and other Journeys. Essays in Feminism as Civic Discourse* (Madison: University of Wisconsin Press, 1990), 73–8.

standing in certain cultures. I was recently told by a clergyman that in the village where he was brought up, a definition of 'virgin' was that she was a girl who could run faster than her father. The remark immediately helps us to see the point of Dympna's story, that children may indeed need to 'run for it'. For whilst there are 'fairy-tales' which begin with the death of a beautiful mother, leaving a daughter who is her 'spitting image' to fear suffering at the hands of a jealous stepmother, there are fairy-tales which are alert to another possibility, that a father may want to make his daughter the sexual 'stand-in' for her mother. Eventually the child must flee, heavily disguised, perhaps in animal skins, to work in a scullery maybe (symbol of the sort of place where princesses are not to be expected) until either rescued, or discovered in a Cinderella-like transformation scene by a prince who will marry her and thus protect her from her father. Not a fairy-tale, but a saint's tale, Dympna's story is that of a martyr. Daughter of a Christian mother and of a pagan father (Christian fathers do not behave in certain ways?), she runs from her father, accompanied by her confessor and by the court jester and his wife, reaching sanctuary near Gheel. When the king and his attendants catch up with them, the attendants kill the confessor, but the king must do his own dirty work in murdering his daughter.

Apart from the story, and the relics of the girl and of her confessor, Dympna's memorial is primarily that she has long been regarded as the patroness of the insane, with Gheel associated with the practice of what would now be referred to as 'care in the community', albeit of a genuinely communitarian kind. In his *Lives of the Saints* Butler comments only that popular belief has attached to the murdered pair a story which, with variations, is to be found in the folk-lore of many European countries, and leaves it at that.[2] Just how folk-lore reflects and shapes the assumptions and concerns of societies is a fascinating subject in its own right,[3] but at least we may say that the fact that Dympna's story is not 'authenticated' by the sorts of documents which

---

[2] H. Thurston and D. Attwater, eds., *Butler's Lives of the Saints* (London: Burns & Oates, 1956).

[3] See Wendy Doniger's review, 'Once upon a real time', of Marina Warner's *From the Beast to the Blonde: On Fairy Tales and their Tellers* of 1994, in *London Review of Books* (23 March 1995), 12–13.

would satisfy a historian is less important than what the story reveals to us, as Judith Lewis Herman perceptively points out.[4] In other words, if we want to know why Dympna became important, it is because she represents the real experiences of numberless women or girls, resisting threats even at the cost of life itself. Dympna represents those who feel like 'outsiders' even whilst still within the apparent 'shelter' of their society and their home, because of their experiences there, or of threatened experiences, burdened too with things about which they cannot or dare not speak. And Dympna symbolises acute emotional distress, even 'madness', as a result of intolerable abuse which was in no sense her fault.

We must, however, add that the possible or actual experiences she represents can no longer (if they ever were) be associated only with the behaviour of the 'pagan' rather than of the 'Christian', for the empirical evidence, such as it is, does not support a distinction between the experience of children brought up in Christian as distinct from non-Christian households where sexual abuse, of whatever kind, incestuous or not, is concerned. The word 'household' here simply means the domestic context of a child's upbringing, whether that be the familial home, with or without 'carers' who are genetically a child's parents or genetically related to some degree or other, or 'home' in an analogous sense, that is, a non-familial institution of some kind. Some of these may be church-related, as we have recently discovered to our distress and to our cost.

A new topic on the agenda of Christian ethics?

For Christians, the sexual abuse of children now has a place on the agenda of ethics in a way it has not had before. There are various indications of this, such as the existence of the organisation Christian Survivors of Sexual Abuse (concerned, obviously, with more than the sexual abuse of children) which held its first national conference in York in the summer of 1993. The House of Bishops of the Church of England published in July 1995 its *Policy on Child Abuse*. The Church of Scotland's Board of

---

[4] Judith Lewis Herman, *Father-Daughter Incest* (London: Harvard University Press, 1981), 1–4.

Social Responsibility produced its own report in 1990, now incorporated into a study pack. There are publications available from a number of dioceses, such as *Protecting our Children* from the Diocese of Southwark, July 1994. Those who need to see as well as to read about child abuse may peruse the *ABC of Child Abuse* edited by Roy Meadow for the British Medical Publishing Group, 1993. In these publications, the sexual abuse of children takes its place within the range of abuse. Documents directed specifically at the sexual abuse of children are represented by a publication commissioned by the Roman Catholic Bishops' Conference of England and Wales, published in *Briefing* for 14 January 1993, and looking further afield, by the substantial report of the Canadian Council of Catholic Bishops (CCCB), *From Pain to Hope,* of June 1992.

The Christian response includes invaluable publications from 'survivors' and counsellors of those seeking to negotiate experiences of sexual abuse,[5] and it is in these writings that one is most likely to find attempts to address the contribution which may be made, however inadvertently, to the 'gender constructions' which may help to precipitate the conditions which make the sexual abuse of children possible. There will be some attention given to this latter difficulty later in this essay. It seems, however, both from the 'official' statements from those who bear responsibility for the conduct of those who represent their institutions, whether ordained or lay of either sex, and from the non-official publications, that as yet little attention is being given, in the United Kingdom at least, to enable *children* to discriminate between what may and may not harm them so far as the introduction to their own sexuality is concerned. How this problem may be tackled without introducing children to possibilities many, one hopes, need never fear, whilst empowering them to resist what they do not want or need, must be a major responsibility for all those concerned with their well-being. If Jean La Fontaine is right, what is important to a child's emotional health 'is not whether s/he

---

[5] For example, Tracy Hansen, *Seven for a Secret: Healing the Wounds of Sexual Abuse in Childhood* (London: SPCK, 1991); Hilary Cashman, *Christianity and Child Sexual Abuse* (London: SPCK, 1993); Muriel Green and Anne Townsend, *Hidden Treasure. A Journey towards Healing from Sexual Abuse* (London: Darton, Longman & Todd, 1994); Dan B. Allender, *The Wounded Heart. Hope for Adult Victims of Childhood Sexual Abuse* (Colorado: NavPress, 1990).

knows it is forbidden or not but whether s/he can stop it when s/he does not wish it to go on. The majority of these children are not allowed to say "no".'[6] Children's voices will be unheard when they are not attended to in their own right, so to speak, when they are regarded primarily as the appendages of their mothers whose own voices may also be unheard. This is only to be expected given the extent to which their mothers are regarded, or worse still, regard themselves, as 'childlike' in the worst senses. Children may not be taught to say 'no' because mother cannot say 'no' either, on her own behalf or on behalf of the household's children. Children are failed by not being enabled to refuse sexual intrusion, as well as by failure to protect them from it, or to stop it if once suspected. If 'mother' is not fully regarded, or cannot regard herself, as a person in her own right, it is difficult to see how a child can so perceive herself or himself in a situation of great stress such as is fostered by sexual abuse.

Our indifference to children

To get some sort of focus on the sexual abuse of children we need in Christian ethics and theology to take children seriously. It is hardly likely that we can think through our attitudes to their abuse if we do not normally think about them in any case. Christian tradition (the feast of Holy Innocents included) does indeed provide material for reflection on the subject of church and childhood,[7] but so far as I know, only Stanley Hauerwas amongst contemporary writers on Christian ethics has made the vocation, the calling, to have children a central focus in his theology, though Helen Oppenheimer has now also made a distinguished contribution to the whole matter of 'talking with children about God' which has significant implications for the way everyone, and not just children, may talk about God.[8]

For the most part, theologians have given a great deal of attention to such topics as the moral status of the human embryo

[6] Jean La Fontaine, *Child Sexual Abuse* (Oxford: Polity Press, 1990), 89.
[7] See, for example, Diana Wood, ed., *The Church and Childhood* (Oxford: Blackwell, 1994).
[8] Helen Oppenheimer, *Finding and Following. Talking with Children about God* (London: SCM, 1994).

and the human foetus, and to damaged new-borns, and what can and cannot and should or should not be done for them. Much of this discussion has arguably been conducted with little attention to the social, community, and church dimension of the lives of those children, born or unborn, and of the lives of those who care for them in relation to them. It is as though we have a 'blind-spot' about the lives of children between birth and infancy and the stage of developing post-pubertal sexuality, which then may become another focus of anxiety. Little attention has been given to the value and significance of the lives of those who may or may not flourish in the period between birth and social maturity, and to the abuse which may be present in their lives. Insofar as we do not have children as the focus of our attention, except to the extent that we spend time and energy trying to prevent their conception and birth or to ensure our own procreativity in having them, we are not likely to find ourselves well-equipped for evaluating their abuse, sexual or other. And to the degree that feminist theology and ethics mimics the agenda of ethics as it is commonly practised, this new emphasis in theology will make little difference to the problem.

Betrayal of trust

Like it or not, and whatever tentative response we may give to Jean Bethke Elshtain's questions, we now have to address ourselves to the bitter and unpalatable fact that whereas children should be able to trust those entrusted with their care, all too often it seems that they cannot do so. The problem spills beyond the situation in which the abuse occurs if children turn for 'salvation' to those who represent its possibility, and there meet with inappropriate reactions. Having summoned the strength to 'tell', one may have great difficulty in so doing, since even as an adult one may hardly have the vocabulary to describe or indicate it. At that point, to be met with the injunction to confess one's own 'sins of impurity', or to be told simply to 'forgive' one's abuser, is to experience being offered not 'salvation' but the offer of a further intolerable burden to carry. The former is deeply wounding to someone who must be deemed to be *not* responsible for whatever is happening, even if a child's modesty has been so damaged as for them to have learned inappropriate sexual behaviour, rendering them yet more vulnerable to abuse, assault and isolation. The latter response, the demand for forgiveness, may be even more deadly, precisely because there is indeed truth and salvation in the need to forgive and to be forgiven in order to flourish, and not to be trapped by harm and hurt. Where forgiveness may be placed in the process of recovery from abuse is a topic to which we will return. The sole merit of these identifiable errors is that at least they represent recognition that there is indeed something profoundly wrong at stake here. Those who 'tell' should never be met with denial of the reality of their experiences, for such denial is itself a harm, a betrayal of trust.

There are complications to think about, inevitably. For when a topic is high on the agenda of social and pastoral concern, there may be false accusations, sometimes made by deeply disturbed children, sometimes made out of sheer mischief and malice. For instance, what are we to make of False Memory Syndrome, supposedly engendered by therapists? All we need at this juncture is the acknowledgement that whilst it would doubtless be a mistake to claim that there are never examples of False Memory Syndrome, or fantasies born of desperate need to find some explanation of why someone feels so awful, leading to false accusation, we can hardly proceed except on the basis that these are likely to be exceptional, if the most vulnerable are indeed to be protected.

And we need to dislodge from our working assumptions the 'norm' that children lie and that adults tell the truth, in the matter of sexual abuse at least, for here adults have everything to lose from the exposure of their abusive behaviour. They have everything to gain by truth-telling, however, to the extent that like the rest of us they need to be freed from their own deceptions. The capacity for self-deception is present in our own responses, or lack of them, too, as the history of recognition of the 'battered child' syndrome shows. And then, as the story of Dympna reveals, there may be connections between 'domestic violence' (a phrase which conceals the identity of the *agents*) and sexual abuse of children, as contemporary examples also illustrate.[9] To focus only on incest, if it is the case that the only universal incest taboo is on the mother-son relationship, what are

[9] See, for example, Violence against Children Study Group, *Taking Child Abuse Seriously* (London: Unwin Hyman, 1990).

we to make of those patterns of prohibition in which father-daughter incest is *not* mentioned?[10]

Sexual abuse and our concern for children

We may say with some confidence that discussion of the sexual abuse of children is part of a movement of concern about children that has been developing for some time.[11] What may well be new is *making children's points of view central to our thinking.* Whatever our concern for the abuser her or himself, it is the child whose well-being must have priority. Children must be seen as 'victims', so long as we are clear that this word signals that the abused child is not to blame for what has or is happening, that responsibility lies elsewhere. Equally firmly it needs to be understood that 'victim' status may become dangerous if it is taken to be a permanent mark of identity. Both the vulnerability of being a 'victim' and even more important, perhaps, the strength of being a 'survivor' need to be affirmed, but we might say, transcended *in good time.* They lie on the track of freedom from the hurt and damage, a track at the end of which may lie forgiveness. The well-being of children in respect of their developing sexuality has been expressed in legislation in the past by raising the 'age of consent' from 13 to 16 in 1885, in connection with campaigns to discourage the disposal of children into prostitution. We may note here that prostitution, perhaps mistakenly, is associated not with children in our own societies, but with the nauseating issue of 'sex tourism', since it seems that the spread of sexually transmitted diseases through groups of very young girls and boys in some parts of the world is a direct result of the pressures of international tourism in some of its forms.[12]

The difficulties of expressing concern for children through legislation (recently in the 1989 Children's Act) must to some

---

[10] Mary Noble and J. K. Mason, with Commentary by Gerard J. Hughes SJ, 'Incest', *Journal of Medical Ethics* 4 (1978), 64–70; and see 'Incest and Husbandry', in Howard Eilberg-Schwarz, *The Savage in Judaism* (Bloomington: Indiana University Press, 1990), 128–34.

[11] See, for example, Nigel Parton, *The Politics of Child Abuse* (London: Macmillan, 1985).

[12] See Anne Symons, 'Child Prostitution and Tourism', *Crucible* (Jan.–March 1995), 26–31; Gordon T. Stewart, 'AIDS and the ethics of programmed compassion', *Bulletin of Medical Ethics* 106 (1995), 19–24.

extent be obvious. Childhood is only to some degree an age-
related phenomenon, since human beings develop and mature
in different respects at different rates.[13] So at one level we need
to acknowledge a *continuum* of child-adult sexuality[14] and allow
for the reality of sexual experimentation which is not abusive,
and yet find ways of distinguishing such experimentation from
abusive behaviour, possible for someone 'under-age' in legal
terms. My own pre-judgments on this matter are by now no doubt
clear. Within theology and ethics we do not and should not
expect to think in a value-neutral way, except perhaps at some
level of statistical abstraction. We are trying to talk and think
about what is properly described as maltreatment, the infliction
of undeserved suffering on the young of an entirely avoidable
kind, suffering which may result in a kind of 'soul murder'[15] of
those involved.

Gender issues and the sexual abuse of children

An important shift in public attention to the sexual abuse of
children is to be associated with the BBC's 'Child Watch' campaign of 1985–86, which helped large numbers of people to
begin to attend to the issues. What weight do we give to the
interests of children and why? Who speaks for them if they are too
young to speak for themselves, or if they are not trusted to do so,
and why do we not trust them? How do children tell us or show
us what is happening to them? Do we attend only to their physical
wounds? How do we value 'interference' or 'intervention' by
'professionals' such as medical specialists in paediatric care, or
social workers, for instance? How is such intervention complicated by the gender issues involved if the professionals happen to
be female, attempting to function in a male-dominated environment in which both the alleged abuse and responses to it may be

[13] Brian Corby, *Child Abuse. Towards a Knowledge Base* (Buckingham: Open
University Press, 1993), 70.

[14] See C. K. Li, D. J. West, T. P. Woodhouse, *Children's Sexual Encounters with
Adults* (London: Duckworth, 1990), especially ch. 12 on the question of ethics,
304–16; and John L. Randall, *Childhood and Sexuality. A Radical Christian Approach*
(Pittsburgh: Dorrance, 1992).

[15] Leonard Shengold, 'Child abuse and deprivation: soul murder', *Journal of
the American Psychoanalytic Association* 27 (1979), 533–59.

affected by hypersensitivity to gender issues in some parties and oblivion or indifference to those issues by other parties?

How much value do we place on the expression of adult 'freedom in private' in sexual matters? What indeed do we think about the relative autonomy of domestic groups? Discussion of 'Natural Bonding and the "Right to Rear"'[16] needs to attend to the difficulties of how to resolve emotional ambivalence and conflict, given that these are not always resolved to the benefit of the most vulnerable; and that paternal and maternal interests are not necessarily in harmony with one another. Nor need parental authority be identified with that to be attributed to males rather than to females, least of all when disguised by an appeal to the 'autonomy of the family'.

Ian Hacking may well be right when he says that without the women's movement and 'feminism' there is little likelihood that the idea of child abuse would so quickly have absorbed the notion of the sexual abuse of children,[17] 'gender' adding one more perspective to our understanding of 'domination' (or patriarchy) which includes unequal distribution of access to power resources in money, status, knowledge, experience, language, physical and emotional strength and allocated social power.[18] However, attention to gender issues must not be allowed to oversimplify a complexity of problems. For instance, how much concern about it is an oblique way of expressing acute dis-ease about adult sexual relationships in our societies rather than an expression of deep and genuine concern for children? And despite all the publicity and the discussion, we still have no clear picture of how frequent or widespread the sexual abuse of children actually is. It may involve as many as one third of females before the age of 12, and a quarter of males by a little older. Some abuse begins very early in a child's life – at under a year old, or so it is claimed. We still do not know whether boys are less or more

[16] Mary Midgley, 'Rights-talk will not sort out child abuse: comment on Archard on Parental Rights', *Journal of Applied Philosophy* 8:1 (1991), 103–14.

[17] Ian Hacking, 'The making and molding of child abuse', *Critical Inquiry* 17 (1991), 253–88.

[18] A. Imkens and I. Jonker, *Christianity and Incest* (London: Burns & Oates, 1992), 120; Linda Gordon, *Heroes of their Own Lives* (London: Viking, 1988), 204–49.

frequently abused than girls, given that they are more likely to be left to fend for themselves. Also, they are less likely to 'tell', given a certain fear of the possibility of same-sex orientation. We do not know how many female abusers there are. Much of the attention in the literature is on 'mother' as the non-abuser in the household (who may collude in as well as fail to protect a child from sexual abuse) but the truth may be different. Even if very few women are actually abusers, we may have great difficulty in evaluating the extent of their willing or unwilling complicity in the sexual abuse of children. If, however, women are deemed, as they must be so deemed, to be moral agents, we must ask whether responsibility for children requires the determination and capacity both to stop abuse if it occurs and preferably to prevent its ever happening. As in the matter of domestic violence, women's behaviour may appear to be profoundly ambivalent, when not only their own sexual relationship with an abuser may be at stake, but their negotiation of some precarious economic independence also. It is nonetheless important not to lose sight of the point that just as mothers may batter their children, they may sexually abuse them, although the one thing they cannot do is violate a child by penile penetration. We may have over-investment in father-figures as those who represent the 'rational', the 'control' element in human nurture of the young, but our investment in mother-figures as 'carers', as primarily 'relational' beings, may blind us to truths about them too. In any event, until we know who the abusers are, few may be enabled to become the kind of people who recognise that she or he must not allow her or himself to be in the kinds of situations which make abuse possible. This may have radical implications for a particular household.

Towards definition of the sexual abuse of children

We need to acknowledge here the old and familiar problem that we cannot always recognise or interpret correctly what we see, and that to do either or both may take time, however distressing that is in retrospect. In the matter of the sexual abuse of children we may indeed experience the alarm, distaste, disbelief and denial which may be inevitable in the initial stages at least of trying to recognise what one sees and hears for what it is, and of learning to react appropriately.[19]

If and when a 'problem' has been identified there is still a long way to go beyond clear and unambiguous affirmation that the interests of the child must be paramount. What does one do, if anything, since some modes of intervention may compound the harm? What amounts to full evaluation of a problem and by whom? How is it to be 'managed' if trauma is not to be deepened? We cannot yet be clear about what weight is to be given to 'medical' evidence until there is agreement about how to interpret 'abnormal physical signs' such as to categorise these as 'clinical findings'. Nor can the responsibility to sort out the 'evidence' be left to members of the medical profession alone, partly because we need to avoid 'medicalising' our problems if we can, and partly because we have no reason to suppose that 'medics' can function as our surrogate consciences. Rather, responsibility for the sexual abuse of children needs to be located exactly where it occurs, that is, in the households in which it is practised. Such abuse is about a mode of relating to children in situations where the latter are acutely vulnerable to those whose role in caring for them is betrayed by their instigation, involvement or collusion in abuse.

Above all, we need to be able to distinguish between the properly *sensual* warmth of exchange between human beings, as vital for the well-being of the very young as of the not-so-young, as for the ways in which adults themselves learn to express tenderness for one another, and abuse. Those who care for children need to retain confidence in themselves as 'good enough' (to use a Winnicott-style phrase) for such care. In certain societies, for instance, it may be the case that children are soothed to sleep by gentle 'genital' comfort provided by someone they love and trust. It hardly seems difficult, however, to distinguish this from, for instance, signs of sexual intercourse on 'a non-assaultive and possibly chronic basis', or 'rape with acute forced intercourse', or evidence of sexually transmitted disease.

Depending on how broad the definition is to be, sexual abuse may include not merely 'fondling and touching' of an adult by a

---

[19] See, for example, J. H. Keen et al., 'Inflicted burns and scalds in children', *British Medical Journal* 1 (Nov. 1975), 268–9.

child who has been introduced to a mode of sexual behaviour appropriate between adults, but exposure to or involvement in the production of pornography, the viewing of sexual acts, or exhibitionism.[20] These involve sexuality and are abusive, but the broader the sweep of what is included, the higher the statistics and perhaps the greater our sense of incapacity to respond in an appropriate way. If the interests of children are indeed to be central to our thinking in this matter, however, emotional care for them must include taking them seriously enough to listen to what they find disturbing and unwanted, not humiliating them further by denying what they are trying to say. For a child does not have to be very advanced in years or to have a very extensive vocabulary to say both that someone has hurt or disturbed him or her and who that person is, if, that is, the child can come to trust the person to whom he or she talks and can find the strength not to be terrified by fear of the consequences to tell, or show, what has happened.

If in doubt about the capacity of children to understand, like or object to what is happening to them, we can learn much from the work of Priscilla Alderson and her research on children's consent to surgery. The new European Charter for Children in Hospital includes as its tenth clause, 'Children shall be treated with tact and understanding and their privacy shall be respected at all times.' It is evident that children under three years of age can understand explanations, and that they mind their privacy and dignity being disregarded. They are capable of taking part in making complex and serious decisions about their treatment. And even older adolescents may both need and want close 'mothering' care.[21] We have absolutely no reason to suppose that children do not know when they are being abused in one way or another.

Apparently there is no easy correlation between what happens and a child's degree of trauma, but there are certain indicators of when the sexual abuse of children is likely to be most harmful. These are when the abusive acts involve penetration of the child's

[20] H. Steiner, 'Description and recording of physical signs in suspected child sexual abuse', *British Journal of Hospital Medicine* 40 (1988), 346–51.

[21] Priscilla Alderson, 'European charter of children's rights', *Bulletin of Medical Ethics* 92 (1993), 13–15; and her *Children's Consent to Surgery* (Buckingham: Open University Press, 1993).

body (as in vaginal, anal or oral intercourse or other modes of penetration); where the abuse has persisted for some time; where the abuser is a 'father-figure'; when the abuse is accompanied by force or the threat of it; and where the response of the family is negative.[22] Definitions from a variety of sources pay explicit attention to the *intention* of the abuser, that is, to obtain gratification for the abuser, irrespective of the child's attempts to resist, expressed wishes, or well-being.[23] It is particularly damaging to be made to participate in an activity, feel 'besmirched' by it, therefore guilty for it, when one's own emotional and physical integrity has been violated.

Of the available definitions, we employ here that from the Canadian Council of Catholic Bishops' Conference document, *From Pain to Hope*:

> Contacts or interactions between a child and an adult when the child is being used as an object of sexual gratification for the adult. A child is abused whether or not this activity involves explicit force, whether or not it involves genital or physical contact, whether or not it is initiated by the child, and whether or not there is discernible harmful outcome.[24]

The bishops are clearly trying to avoid entanglement in any appeal to 'no harmful consequences' such as might be advanced by those who want to involve children in sexual activities with adults, claiming that the children learn valuable things about their own sexuality through such interaction and so on.[25] On the matter of 'force', the bishops are implicitly attending to the point that though coercion may include both extremely violent and physically damaging behaviour, it may also be far more subtle. For children may be 'groomed' and seduced into sexual activities, bribed and rewarded, in such a way that their natural affections for those they love or hope to love are deeply confused and then corrupted. The 'price' of what they need, which includes sensual contact with those they love, lots of 'good touch', kisses, hugs and cuddles, and emotional care, should

---

[22] Corby, *Child Abuse*, 125.
[23] La Fontaine, *Child Sexual Abuse*, 191.
[24] Canadian Council of Catholic Bishops, *From Pain to Hope* (Ottawa: CCCB, 1992), 20.
[25] See Randall, *Childhood and Sexuality*, above, note 14.

never include involvement in activities which they dread or fear whilst being compelled to keep them secret (a clue to identifying what is forbidden, and forbidden because wrong). In any case, there should be no 'price' to pay for dependency. Nor should they be precipitated into fear, fear of not being believed, or of not being protected, left in their loneliness until and unless they can be heard and believed by someone they can come to trust in place of the people they should have been able to trust with their vulnerability and have learned that they cannot.

We can as it were thicken out definition of the sexual abuse of children by contrasting material from an essay by Rowan Williams on *The Body's Grace*[26] with passages from the writing of Tilman Furniss.[27] This is deliberately to contrast a 'best' with a 'worst' case scenario to illustrate the symmetry of sexual exchange between adults and the dissymmetry of sexual exchanges between adults and children. For Williams, 'grace' is a 'transformation that depends in large part on knowing yourself to be seen in a certain way: as significant, as wanted'. To be the occasion of joy in another is to be directed to the enjoyment, the happiness of the other, because only as so directed does my body become unreservedly lovable. 'To desire my joy is to desire the joy of the one I desire: my search for enjoyment through the bodily presence of another is a longing to be enjoyed in my body.' All this needs the fidelity and trust in another which can only be developed through time. How could an adult construe him or herself in relation to a child, or expect a child to construe him or herself in relation to an adult, in the terms of Williams' understanding of grace and transformation? We may also want to think about the 'sacramental' aspects of bodiliness in Helen Oppenheimer's terms, of how God gives to human creatures a surprisingly large part in consecrating and adopting one another.[28] How could such consecration and adoption be expressed in an adult's sexual relationship with a child? In the sensual expression of parental love, yes, but not in what we can see is abuse.

[26] Rowan Williams, *The Body's Grace* (London: LGCM, 1989).
[27] Tilman Furniss, *The Multi-Professional Handbook of Child Sexual Abuse* (London: Routledge, 1991), 25f.
[28] Helen Oppenheimer, 'Ourselves, our souls and bodies', *Studies in Christian Ethics* 4 (1991), 1–21.

A worst-case scenario is represented in Tilman Furniss' work in the description of the way in which an abuser may create a certain kind of context for abuse. This context may include silence, a withholding of eye contact (crucial in human interaction from the first moment a child is held in someone's arms at birth), darkness, with entrance and exit rituals creating a physical and temporal 'space' between abuser and child, in which the change to 'abuser' takes place and is reversed at the end of the incident. Gestures, speech, voice and facial expression may all change, and in the course of the abuse the child may experience intense physical stimulation, pain and sexual arousal, anxiety and help-lessness, that is, a combination of intense bodily and physical contact disconnected and dissociated from intimacy, empathy and joy. Whatever else it is, it cannot count as 'love-making' as Williams understands it, or as a manifestation of the body's grace. Quite apart from anything else, grace by definition cannot be coerced or compelled or seduced.

Christian response to the sexual abuse of children

This essay has already ventured to suggest the importance of thinking theologically about the lives of actual children. We would no doubt like to think that Christians can respond con-structively and creatively to the phenomenon of the sexual abuse of children, and draw on their traditions to see what, if any, resources there may be for changing things for the better. Apart from our 'blind spot' about children, we also have to cope with the sheer wariness and uneasiness of Christian attitudes to human sexuality, and its unfortunate 'genital fixation', remote from the giving and receiving of pleasure, let alone of 'the body's grace' in Williams' style.

That said, we could draw not only on the work of Stanley Hauerwas and Helen Oppenheimer, already mentioned, but on the work of philosophers such as Mary Midgley[29] about the importance of children in the human community, as gifts not only to those to whom they are born. We might want to 're-tool'

---

[29] Mary Midgely, *Beast and Man. The Roots of Human Nature* (Brighton: Harvester, 1978), with Judy Hughes, *Women's Choices* (London: Weidenfeld & Nicolson, 1989).

some familiar theological phrases, such as the 'sanctity of life', from their familiar contexts to this new one. The phrase fundamentally has to do with the relationships human beings have with one another and with God. Children, like all other human persons, are precious to God, sacrosanct before God, and have an inherent right to be protected from harm.[30] To remind ourselves of their inviolability is to enable us also to say that no one should have to work and pray for deliverance from the harm of sexual abuse and its legacy in heart, mind or body.

We need not, however, assume that the constructive resources which may be available in the Christian tradition can be freed up, so to speak, without some thorough-going self-critique of that same tradition. Again, the Canadian Bishops have the courage to point up some of the issues here:

> Child sexual abuse flourishes in a society that is based on competition and power and which is undermined by sexual exploitation and violence against women. Contemporary society has shown itself quick to reject traditional values, to be unable to offer new ones, and to be unfair to women and children. The challenge to transform society becomes enormous when we begin to realise the terrible social cost when child abuse is tolerated. Another contributing factor to child sexual abuse is a Church that too readily shelters its ministers from having to account for their conduct; that is often tempted to settle moral problems behind a veil of secrecy which only encourages their growth; that has not yet fully developed a process of internal reform in which the values of familial communion would predominate. Challenges for personal conversion and institutional change are far from lacking. We would like to see our Church take firm steps which would leave no doubt as to its genuine desire to eradicate the phenomenon of child sexual abuse.[31]

The primary focus of attention here is correctly identified as having to do with power rather than with sexuality, except as that is one means of its expression. And as ecclesiastical institutions are at last realising, they must clarify what to do when someone

---

[30] Gordon Dunstan, *The Artifice of Ethics* (London: SCM, 1974), 71.
[31] CCCB, *From Pain to Hope*, 41.

who represents such an institution abuses a child. The problem may be more theologically complicated than even such an exemplary document exhibits, however, in that it may well be the gender constructions of our theological traditions, and not just those of contemporary society, which, however indirectly, sustain and legitimate the sexual abuse of children, insofar as they legitimate certain kinds of relationships based on power. What kinds of theologies support the view that someone does not have to account for their actions, and in effect sanctify the abuse of power?

According to Poling, to give only one example, women's behaviour is circumscribed by the limitations of patriarchy and inequality, whereas men are 'socialized to be dominant in inter-personal relationships, and they are excused for their abusive behaviours'.[32] He goes on to claim that men abuse children because they are not held accountable for their actions, and because they choose to inflict suffering on others. What is being believed about God which licences earthly fathers to behave in this way? This is one area where feminist insistence on the re-evaluation of what it means to address God as 'Father'[33] is too important to be ignored, even if this requires radical critique of familiar doctrines of atonement,[34] Christology or Trinity.[35] It has to be added, however, that women's complicity in the sexual abuse of children needs to be addressed theologically, as part of any project about the re-evaluation of the female and feminine in relation to the divine, and the overcoming of naivety in respect of perhaps characteristically feminine forms of sinfulness.[36]

In tandem with this radical critique must in the meantime run generous attention to those who need help in the process of

[32] James Newton Poling, *The Abuse of Power. A Theological Problem* (Nashville: Abingdon, 1993), 54, 89–90.

[33] Janet Pais, *Suffer the Little Children. A Theology of Liberation by a Victim of Child Abuse* (Mahwah: Paulist, 1991), 62–87.

[34] In addition to Poling, see Debora Kuller Shuger, *The Renaissance Bible: Scholarship, Sacrifice and Subjectivity* (Berkeley: University of California Press, 1994), 89–127.

[35] Rita Nashima Brock, 'And a little child will lead us: Christology and child abuse', Joanne Carlson Brown and Carole R. Bohn, eds., *Christianity, Patriarchy, and Abuse: a feminist critique* (New York: Pilgrim, 1989), 42–61, and Janet Martin Soskice, 'Trinity and "the Feminine Other"', *New Blackfriars* 75 (1994), 2–17.

[36] A discussion begun by Valerie Saiving in her article 'The human situation: a feminine view', *Journal of Religion* 40 (1960), 100–12.

recovery. We return here to our earlier themes of salvation and forgiveness. Salvation here will perhaps be perceived initially in the form of the resilience of hope, that the damage received (if indeed inflicted) need not be the last word. In the first place, people need to know that it is *not* inevitable that the abused become abusers themselves.[37] From that nightmare at least they need release, in the form of reassurance, repeated as often as necessary and essential throughout the process of recovery, not only in the initial stages of being laid hold of by saving grace. Such reassurance may be mediated, for example, by repetition of the Psalms which convince us that no injustice is hidden to God, and by sacramental acts of anointing and healing, again, which may need repetition.[38]

Recovery may be a long process, and may or may not be marked by what can be identified as 'forgiveness'. As we noted earlier, this identifying mark of someone playing their part in the Christian tradition must not be required prematurely or inappropriately of someone recovering from damage of any kind, least of all from sexual abuse. Being able to forgive may be contingent upon the conviction, perhaps entirely novel, that one bears or may come to bear, baptismal glory, and as such need not be bound by the past any more, that one can at least get to the point of not wishing an abuser harm. The process of recovery will not be fostered by misplaced injunctions to 'forgive and forget'. To forget may be vital for survival at some stages,[39] but the track to recovery seems to be through remembering, recalling, giving up denial, believing, digesting, feeling, sharing, letting the hurt surface, letting the hurt show in tears and anger, from all of which may come healing, and at length, perhaps, something recognisable as an appropriate mode of forgiveness. Even then, in matters of the sexual abuse of children, depending on the hurt and

[37] Linda Sandford, *Strong at the Broken Places* (New York: Random, 1990).

[38] See David R. Blumenthal, *Facing the Abusing God. A Theology of Protest* (Louisville: Westminster/John Knox, 1993), 57–189; and Rebecca Abrams and Hugo Slim, 'The revival of oils in contemporary culture: implications for the sacrament of anointing', Martin Dudley and Geoffrey Rowell, eds., *The Oil of Gladness. Anointing in the Christian Tradition* (London: SPCK, 1993), 169–75.

[39] Pamela Cooper-White, *The City of Tamar. Violence against Women and the Church's Response* (Minneapolis: Fortress, 1995), 158. See also Ian Hacking, 'Memoro-politics, trauma and the soul', *History of the Human Sciences* 7:2 (1994), 29–52.

damage, we may have to say that forgiveness has to be left to God, with the human beings involved able only to proffer some pale simulacrum of what forgiveness might mean.

We have referred to the sacrament of healing and to the conviction expressed in the words of the psalmists, but no one can have their childhood back. We are deeply reluctant, as our theology all too often reveals, to believe anything other than that *all* the bad can somehow be recovered in such a way that it can be transformed, made good.[40] There is also a need for a kind of biblical realism conveyed in the story of Tamar (in the 'court history' of David) which reminds us that this is not so, which provides us with at least one reason why this text now has its place in quasi-liturgical contexts where 'survivors' of sexual abuse meet and support one another in moving forward in their lives, learning from the shreds of Tamar's dignity as well as from her tragedy.[41] It is interesting that those who suffer from the legacy of sexual abuse do not seem to have found comparable resources in the re-telling of the incident of the raising of Jairus's daughter or other biblical stories of the raising of children from death. This may mean that they associate the abuse with the tradition, but are as yet deeply ambivalent about the resources on offer for their recovery and future fulfilment, at least so long as there is little engagement with the constructive critique of its doctrines. It is perhaps to their ambivalence that Christians need to turn their attention in the next phase of understanding not simply the sexual abuse of children, but the conditions which may help to precipitate it, as well as to the resources for human flourishing and fulfilment of which the Christian tradition has also been a bearer.

---

[40] Shengold, 'Child Abuse', 539–41.
[41] Cooper-White, *The Cry of Tamar*, 1–14, 24–5, 33–4.

15

Feminism and the Family

Susan F. Parsons

Feminists are not of one mind about the family. This is perhaps obvious to most readers, but is a continual source of interest to me, as I read the increasing diversity and richness of feminist arguments concerning the institution of the family and family relationships. The literature by women about women in the family, throughout history and across cultures, is now considerable, and reveals a broad spectrum of methodology and assumptions and implications which would make a very interesting study in itself. The subject suggested for this essay, 'Feminism and the Family', is therefore far too large for the limitations of space, and far too complex and interesting to be given an adequate treatment here. I propose therefore to pick up just one thread of this fabric of diversity, a fabric into which so many themes have now been woven, and within which there are entanglements and patterns and spaces and knots. I pick one thread of the arguments, in order first of all to examine it singly, secondly to discover what other threads of thinking it may be attached to, and finally to consider its theological meaning.

The thread is shaped around an ethical question, 'Is justice appropriate in our considerations of the family? I make no claim that this is the most important issue raised by feminists about the family. However, there are three good reasons for choosing it:

1. It is certainly a key area of concern as it relates to social policy, economic measures, and legal decisions, that have direct impact upon the lives and welfare of women. In this sense, it is something in which all of us are implicated as we consider the ethical dimensions of our corporate life, not only as a nation, but also in international discussion.

2. This question reveals the confusion of ideas regarding the nature of justice which has increasingly come to characterise a

plural, and perhaps also a postmodern, society. In picking it up, we have hold of a thread which contains in itself the tensions of competing political ideologies and moral frameworks, to which diverse forms of feminist thinking also contribute.

3. It raises some of the most sensitive and important theological matters concerning our human embodiment as women and men made in the divine image. Precisely what constitutes the completion of that image within and between us is a matter that deeply implicates justice, drawing us continually into theological reflection upon the relationship of justice and love and power.

The family and an ethic of justice

Well, even this one thread now seems too large, but let me see if I can highlight some of the main points that emerge as one examines this question, first of all, by considering the arguments of one feminist for whom the answer to it is a resounding, yes. In her book, *Justice, Gender and the Family*, the American political scientist, Susan Moller Okin, presents an appeal for the family to be included in our general understanding of justice, alongside an account of the requirements that this justice would have for family life.[1] As a feminist within the liberal political and philosophical tradition, Okin is dismayed, as her liberal sisters have been for centuries before her, at the ignorance of the family in so many theories of social justice, and at the consequent invisibility of the family in practical applications of theory. She suggests two reasons for this in her introduction. The first is that theories of social justice assume the existence of the family as a realm of purely personal or private matters, quite distinct from the public social world of the wider body politic. The assumption of two spheres is etched quite deeply into western liberalism, and out of an uncritical acceptance of this division, the family has been excluded from its considerations of justice.[2]

The second reason Okin offers is that the use of supposedly gender neutral language in theories of justice serves 'to disguise

---

[1] Susan Moller Okin, *Justice, Gender and the Family* (New York: Basic Books, 1989).
[2] See Jean Bethke Elshtain, *Public Man, Private Woman: Women in Social and Political Thought* (New Jersey: Princeton University Press, 1981).

the real and continuing failure of theorists to confront the fact that the human race consists of persons of two sexes'.[3] The neutrality of language thus hides in theory what is commonly recognised in experience, that men inhabit the world of public affairs, of work and its corresponding responsibilities, of political action and debate, of derivatives speculation, and that this involvement depends upon the hidden work of women within the private realm of the family. Men, and not women, are thus really the subjects to whom theories of justice apply. Okin summarises her criticism by suggesting that unless this division of realms is challenged, along with the differential consequences which it has for women and for men, then theories of justice become themselves deeply self-contradictory. They propose an equality which they implicitly deny. Okin is concerned that unless justice counts women in, and particularly draws in the sphere of marriage and the family, then women's lives will continue to be made vulnerable by this exclusion, and children will have no proper training in the ways of justice as they develop moral and social awareness. The family must therefore become a school of justice, and the just family the essential foundation for a just society.[4]

As Okin understands the matter, challenging the division of the public and private realms is 'the core idea of most contemporary feminism'.[5] Summarised in the rallying cry of 'the personal is political', feminists have made 'the personal sphere of sexuality, of housework, of child care and family life' into issues of public concern, thereby making the family central to the politics and the theory of feminism. This means a number of things in practice, as feminists seek both to challenge and to restructure the unequal gender implications of the public/domestic dichotomy.

1. It means putting onto the public agenda the issue of power. No longer, it is claimed, may the family be romanticised as a place in which power has no hold, for differentials in physical strength, in economic and emotional dependency, and in socially sanctioned authority, all appear in the dailiness of family living,

[3] Okin, *Justice*, 10.
[4] Ibid., 5, 17.
[5] Ibid., 124.

raising issues from domestic violence to sexual abuse to punishment which call out for public attention. A theory of justice needs to be applicable in such matters, and is inconsistent with itself if it leaves them unexamined or considers them irrelevant to the larger social context.

2. Added to this agenda goes a recognition that the public world has shaped and continues to define what the space of the family is. Thus Okin argues, 'to the extent that a more private, domestic sphere does exist, its very existence, the limits that define it, and the types of behavior that are acceptable and not acceptable within it all result from political decisions'.[6] This belies the rhetoric that the state has nothing to do with the family, that the family either preceded the existence of the state, or drops down from heaven into it, and likewise that the state should not interfere with the family. For in marriage and divorce regulations, property rights, legal liabilities, payment for work, and a whole range of related matters, 'the issue is not whether, but *how* the state intervenes'.[7]

3. It becomes a matter of general social concern how it is that children are raised within families, since during our early socialisation we are prepared for social roles as women and men. These roles reproduce the same social practices, status, and responsibilities of the parents and, feminists argue, these must be subject to moral evaluation. Without some independent standard of judgement by reference to which social roles can be assessed as good or healthy or purposive, human beings become slaves of custom, repeating the patterns of the past whether they are helpful or not.

4. The restructuring of the public/domestic dichotomy requires women to be seen and heard as full participants in society, in the workplace, in political bodies, in institutions and groups of all kinds, for it is in these arenas that women's speech may be practised and may gain authority and credibility, as women take their part in public affairs. When women are present and are heard, one may expect a greater measure of justice in the decisions which are taken, since these will now take account of women's experiences and knowledge.

[6] Ibid., 129.
[7] Ibid., 131.

These four feminist applications of justice to the family are important to the extension of justice throughout a whole society, in both its public and domestic spheres. Thus Okin passionately argues:

> If justice cannot at least begin to be learned from our day-to-day experience within the family, it seems futile to expect that it can be developed anywhere else. Without just families, how can we expect to have a just society? In particular, if the relationship between a child's parents does not conform to basic standards of justice, how can we expect that child to grow up with a sense of justice?[8]

Okin draws her own understanding of justice primarily from John Rawls, and it is worth stating what precisely she believes can be derived from his theory of justice, since it is itself the subject of so many feminist challenges.[9] She is impressed by the notion of 'the original position', that heuristic device by which the parties making a decision draw a 'veil of ignorance' over any knowledge of their individual characteristics, personal experiences, or social relationships. Persons are ready to participate in discussions of what is just when they quite simply do not know who they are in the dilemma, and thus have to formulate the guiding principles of justice without any self-interest, and without any linking of how the chips will fall upon them once the decision has been taken. Rawls, she argues, believes that 'since no one knows who he is, all think identically and the standpoint of any one party represents that of all. Thus the principles of justice are arrived at unanimously'.[10] She is struck by the potential of this theory for removing the public/domestic dichotomy and for bringing previously hidden gender assumptions into consideration. The veil of ignorance would also have to fall over the participants' gender, for they would be required to 'think from the perspective of everybody'. The amusing possibilities of this she suggests by reference to a cartoon, in which three elderly robed male judges are depicted, 'looking down with astonishment at their very pregnant bellies', and saying 'Perhaps we'd

[8] Ibid., 135.
[9] John Rawls, *A Theory of Justice* (Cambridge: Harvard University Press, 1971).
[10] Okin, *Justice*, 90.

better reconsider that decision.'[11] If their judgement had been derived from the original position in the first place, no such reconsideration would be necessary.

Okin believes that this approach to principles of justice implicitly contains 'a potential critique of gender-structured social institutions',[12] on the basis of which she argues that

> marriage and the family, as currently practised in our society, are unjust institutions. They constitute the pivot of a societal system of gender that renders women vulnerable to dependency, exploitation, and abuse. When we look seriously at the distribution between husbands and wives of such critical social goods as work (paid and unpaid), power, prestige, self-esteem, opportunities for self-development, and both physical and economic security, we find socially constructed inequalities between them, right down the list.[13]

Her proposals are specifically directed to correct these injustices, through the more even distribution of dull and burdensome tasks within the house, through measures that allow career and household or child-care tasks to be shared, through schooling that aims to eradicate sex-stereotyping, through divorce legislation that ensures the equality of the two post-divorce households, through child-support legislation that enables children to enjoy the standard of living equal to that of the non-custodial parent, and so on. In all of these, women's asymmetrical vulnerability, which is caused by every dimension of marriage and family life as presently constituted, is the primary target, in order that a just future may emerge in which gender simply does not figure at all. Only when gender does not matter in any social institutions and practices will a fully humanist justice have appeared, practised and nurtured within just families.

This answer to the question whether justice is appropriate in our considerations of the family is not an uncommon liberal feminist approach to the matter. It has two outstanding characteristics by which it may be known. The first is an affirmation of the universality of justice, that justice somehow is both a concept and a practice which is universally applicable, and against which

[11] Ibid., 102.
[12] Ibid., 105.
[13] Ibid., 136.

no barriers of cultural custom, historical ties, or ideological conviction can hold. Justice overrides these by its appeal to what is rational and consistent, and by its relentless scrutiny of all practices and institutions in the light of its fundamental principles. Thus in any given society, justice provides the framework within which the family is to be challenged and changed, and to stop short of this institution is not to be consistent with what such a framework requires. Furthermore, between societies justice provides the standards by which we may gather the whole human community into a common life, so that families everywhere become subject to its requirements.

The second characteristic of this approach is its hopefulness, its optimism for human relationships, and particularly for those between women and men, for it understands not only that these can be improved, literally and materially in everyday conditions of living, but also that these relationships can be allowed to blossom into even greater fullness of companionship, once just conditions obtain. Thus Okin speaks of parents who, combining love for each other with a just concern for equality, become the most fully human, and thereby provide the best models of that fullness of humanity for children. And we discover and live out our full humanity when gender matters no more than any other merely physical characteristic.[14]

The family and an ethic of care

Having pulled this thread, we may now begin to notice the other themes to which it is related, and other possible answers that feminists might provide to this question. For there are a number of feminists who challenge the description of justice upon which Okin depends, and who therefore cannot accept its appropriateness in considerations of the family, for it removes precisely the distinctive moral reasoning for which the family may be the most suitable environment.

The work of Joan Tronto is helpful in this respect, for in her book, *Moral Boundaries*, she seeks to discover a political argument

---

[14] Ibid., 171.

for an ethic of care in which the terms of justice are challenged.[15] The notion of justice upon which liberal feminism depends has been a manifestation of the profound influence of Kant upon modern moral and political thinking, and Tronto suggests that it has been this influence which has resulted in the setting up of a boundary, a boundary marking the special zone of moral thinking. Since Kant, she argues, we have come to believe that a moral theory 'should arise not out of the concrete circumstances of any given society, but out of the requirements of reason. Moral theory, above all, must be from "the moral point of view", which means from a standpoint of disinterested and disengaged moral actors.'[16] The person who thinks morally is thus the one who 'is detached and anonymous, willing to surrender special connections and circumstances when necessary to achieve a rationally justifiable account of morality'.[17] This marking of the boundary has the effect of consigning other human realities, like emotions and feeling, or local customs and habits, to a lower order of things in which they are judged to be 'non-rational and idiosyncratic'.

When this is combined with another boundary marking the special zone of public life as distinct from the private world of friends and family, we have lines drawn around human reality in a number of areas that are particularly exclusive of women. Tronto's argument is not that the detached rational ethic of justice be given full reign over the whole of human life, but rather that to give due attention and support to an ethic and a politics of care will explicitly enhance the importance of the non-rational private domain, thereby implicitly challenging the drawing of the boundaries in this way. Whereas Okin's approach allowed the wider society to question the family, this one turns the tables.

Feminists' descriptions of care may be shown to have roots in an alternative Western moral tradition which became identified particularly with women and with the domestic sphere in response to the emergence of a global consciousness. Thus by the eighteenth century, the emphasis upon moral sentiments, and the importance of those with whom one shared more immediate social life, both diminished, in favour of a concern for a universal

---

[15] Joan C. Tronto, *Moral Boundaries: A Political Argument for an Ethic of Care* (London: Routledge, 1993); see particularly her discussion of Rawls, 167.

[16] Tronto, *Boundaries*, 9.

[17] Ibid., 9–10.

political order in which all persons, even those quite distant from us, were participants. In this context, Tronto argues that approaches to moral issues became genderised, such that the universalistic abstract approach became identified with man's way of reasoning, and the particularist immediate approach with woman's, with its special locus in the sentimental family. The separation of domesticity from production completed the division, and resulted in what Tronto calls the demise of the moral sentiments.

What she acknowledges to be difficult is to give special emphasis to an ethic of care in this kind of historical and political context, for several dangers are lurking around such a project. A number of feminists have argued that women's nature is especially centred on the ability to care, based on their unique embodiment which allows the bearing and feeding of children. From this naturalistic base, women are believed to have special capacities for nurturance, for attending to the needs of others before their own, and for giving special concern to the health of the relationships in which they are involved. What is dangerous here for women is the loss of a critical distance from which their work might be evaluated as good for them, and as a result, the inability of this affirmation of care definitively to challenge the boundaries of moral and political life as they are presently drawn.[18]

At the other extreme, there are repeated calls for the restoration of the family, from feminists and anti-feminists alike, which claim that the extension of family values and relationships throughout the whole of life would be the solution to our problems. These utopian visions, which include expectations ranging from the cessation of all warfare to a proper respect for authority, are attempts to make the family itself into a political ideal, thus drawing the world into one big happy family.[19] Once again this, as Tronto argues, imports wholesale whatever prevailing and historically-shaped notions of family abound within the wider culture, and misses in its simplistic paean to the family the much more radical implications that an ethic of care might have for the reshaping of society.[20]

[18] Ibid., 158–61.
[19] Ibid., 169–70.
[20] Ibid., 172.

Tronto suggests several of these political implications. Care is to be understood, not as 'a parochial concern of women, a type of secondary moral question, or the work of the least well off in society', but rather as 'a central concern of human life'.[21] To draw caring activity into the centre of living is to affirm that care is a political concept, and that the provision a society makes for caring work should be taken as a central indication of its adequacy as a society. This does not mean simply to look for ways of propping up the work of care presently being done, invisibly and in isolation, by women, by the poor and the powerless, nor does it mean merely to support what is being done in private families in caring for the elderly, young, and sick. Much social provision has been viewed in just those terms, and has thereby confirmed the moral boundaries that are proving to be not only exploitative, but actually dehumanising, and has indeed even used those boundaries as a buttress against any more dramatic social changes. This does mean that to emphasise care 'requires a shift in our values', putting onto the political agenda the issue of child care provision as a social responsibility, the matter of payment for the productive work of carers in order that its status be elevated, assessment and limitation of the care needs of those in full-time employment, the use of care-receivers' lives as the basis for social policy concerning them, a consideration of the distribution of caring tasks, and the involvement of care-givers in policy-making. In all of these ways and more, care can become a central part of political life, leaving the family to its 'necessarily private and parochial understanding of caring', and reshaping a society to honour the fullness of our humanity in yet a different voice.[22]

A feminist deconstruction of the family

If *this* feminist approach is unable to answer our question in the affirmative because of its doubts about the nature of justice, others are unable to do so because of their doubts about the family as a disciplining social institution which creates gender conformity, and as an inadequate social expression of our com-

[21] Ibid., 180.
[22] Ibid., 157, 169.

munal and interdependent nature. An essay by Marilyn Friedman can serve as the focus of discussion here, for in her analysis of 'Feminism and Modern Friendship', she considers how important it has been in feminism to speak, not of fundamentally isolated individuals as the atoms that make up a society, but of persons who are constituted by social relationships and human community.[23] On the face of it, there would seem to be some overlap between this feminist interest and the new communitarians who also are critics of liberalism with its dependence upon individual subjectivities. What communitarians emphasise is, she suggests, both the 'metaphysical view that *all* human selves are constituted by their social and communal relationships', and secondly the claim that the communities which 'become the points of reference for self-definition' are involuntary ones that are discovered and not created.[24] The family is one of these, for it is a human community which one is born into, or finds oneself within, and furthermore it provides a paradigm for the kind of human relationships that are most fulfilling of our metaphysical nature, namely ones shaped by 'spontaneous affection and generosity'.[25]

What troubles Friedman in her feminist critique of this privileged family, is two-fold:

1. The notion of being involuntarily bound within families has quite a different significance to women than to men. It has been a continuing theme of modern feminism that women have been made into the beings they are through the demands of the family, and more specifically through the appropriation of their sexuality and reproductive capacities by men in all the varied forms of patriarchy throughout history.[26] If the constitution of women's identity has been shaped for them, and has been justified through prevailing metaphors of their inferior nature and proper subor-

---

[23] Marilyn Friedman, 'Feminism and Modern Friendship: Dislocating the Community', in Eve Browning Cole and Susan Coultrap-McQuin, eds., *Explorations in Feminist Ethics: Theory and Practice* (Bloomington: Indiana University Press, 1992), 89.

[24] Friedman: 'Friendship', 90.

[25] Okin, *Justice*, 28. See her full critique of Michael Sandel's communitarianism, 26–33.

[26] Gerda Lerner, *The Creation of Patriarchy* (Oxford: Oxford University Press, 1986), 8–9.

dination, then to privilege the family as paradigmatic of our communal nature is to seal women up once again within a space immune to moral challenge. What is needed is a recognition of communities of choice, which are also significant in mature self-identification, and an acceptance of these as 'supplementing, if not displacing, the communities and attachments that are merely found'.[27]

2. Language about the family can overlook the diversity of patterns which exists, and within that diversity, the potential for resistance and critique which even involuntary associations may hold. Thus, Friedman suggests, 'the commitments and loyalties of our found communities, our communities of origin, may harbor ambiguities, ambivalences, contradictions, and oppressions that *complicate* as well as *constitute* identity, and that have to be sorted out, critically scrutinized'.[28]

Friedman's criticisms here are instances of broader feminist concerns about the family. Postmodern feminism has questioned the ways that social institutions shape gender identity, in particular by the cultural imposition of compulsory heterosexuality. The shaping of identity into two gendered forms which are set in opposition to one another is considered a manifestation of the ubiquitous dualism in our thinking and language, from which it is difficult to free ourselves. This kind of feminism tends to reverse the slogan mentioned earlier into 'The political is personal', for it finds in all forms of social order the insecurities of personal freedom and the tendency to domination of what we cannot understand.[29] Underlying this critique is a conviction that the self exceeds these bounds, that its nature cannot be confined by linguistic or social conventions, and that its nature, if that is the right word, is a very ephemeral web of constantly changing interactions and entanglements.

Thus Friedman's positive suggestions, to encourage both the varied forms of chosen friendship, and to place these in the context of modern urban communities, are ones that seem particularly appropriate in a postmodern context. Friendship, as

[27] Friedman, 'Friendship', 92.
[28] Ibid., 93.
[29] See Lynne Segal, *Is the Future Female? Troubled Thoughts on Contemporary Feminism* (London: Virago Press, 1987), 96.

a form of voluntary association, she believes 'is more likely to be grounded and sustained by shared interests and values, mutual affection, and reciprocal esteem', and in addition, it has 'socially disruptive possibilities, for out of the unconventional living that it helps to sustain, influential forces for social change may arise'.[30] Likewise, urban life is the setting for the formation of numerous social networks, providing women especially 'with jobs, education, and the cultural tools with which to escape imposed familial demands'.[31] Through such networks, a woman is able continuously to constitute and reconstitute her identity, not believing it to be fixed but fluid, and finding in communities of choice a source both of resistance to 'oppressive and abusive relational structures', and of new creativity in relationships.

Theological issues

This very brief sketch of some feminist responses to an ethical question regarding the appropriateness of justice to the family has, I hope, served to illustrate the diversity of feminism itself, as well as to indicate some of the implicit theological issues with which feminisms are struggling. Here it would be helpful to bring a few of these into the foreground as they relate to our central question, and as they point the way forward for a feminism that seeks to make distinctive and crucial contributions to the Christian theological task and method.

It is clear from this sketch that the existence of norms in ethical and political judgement has become a matter of considerable ambivalence in the contemporary world, as within feminism, and that discussions of the family highlight this very particularly. On the one hand, there seems to be a general loss of confidence in normative language, and there is no doubt that feminists have made significant contributions to this. They have questioned the false gender neutrality around which moral norms are formulated, expressing without acknowledging the perspective and lifestyle of men, and rendering invisible that of women. In this way, moral norms have hidden the exploitation and alienation of

---

[30] Friedman, 'Friendship', 94.
[31] Ibid., 94.

women, upon which they may be shown to depend. These attacks are particularly directed against the language of justice within the liberal tradition, and have served to unsettle the politically significant role that liberal feminism has played in considerations of justice. Added to this are more postmodern challenges, that normative language of all kinds is responsible for creating the very persons whose lives it means to discipline and to punish, and that it is therefore inherently oppressive. Like definitions of things, norms impose upon complex and chaotic reality, structures that limit possibilities and ensure conformity. Norms therefore give a voice to the winners, to those powerful enough to have a hand in their formulation, and render speechless the others who become non-persons. Feminism is thus encouraged in its postmodern form to move beyond morality altogether, to doubt its contributions to the improvement of life, to lose hope in its vision of better human relationships, and to question its right to challenge anyone else's communal practices.

On the other hand, each of the writers sketched here has recognised the need for some kind of normative language in order to evaluate both the requirements of justice and the shape of the family. Okin appeals to the original position as the place for the formulation of the principles of justice, beneath a veil of ignorance which allows one to speak from the standpoint of all. While suggesting that the person involved in this kind of debate is no longer real, Tronto nevertheless acknowledges also the need for a theory of justice to provide norms more appropriate to our interdependent nature as human beings.[32] Friedman too recognises that feminists need 'a *normative* account of what might be wrong or excessive about competitive self-seeking behaviours or other individualistic traits or dispositions', in order to provide a critique of the metaphysical naturalism of communitarian thinking.[33]

What these pleas may be understood to express is both the need for a critical distance which ethical thinking may be believed to provide, and a sense of sadness, perhaps even bewilderment, and certainly not a little anxiety about the loss of this

---

[32] Tronto, *Boundaries*, 166–7.
[33] Friedman, 'Friendship', 90.

distance as understood within the terms of liberalism. Christian ethics is in much the same place, and because of its own questions about the influence of liberalism upon biblical hermeneutics and theological anthropology, and because of its own challenges to the kind of naturalistic thinking that renders moral reasoning redundant, it is not in a position to provide ready-made answers to the feminist quest. It is in a position to go forward in partnership with those feminists who believe that there is something of a false dichotomy here, and who recognise that the recovery of norms of justice which count women in is crucial to our world.

One way forward in this recovery is to speak again about human nature, and to begin to reconstruct something of the natural law tradition of moral thinking. Feminists enter this terrain with even greater trepidation, for it is especially here that what Gerda Lerner terms the 'founding metaphors of Western civilization' are bred and nurtured. This is the framework within which both the 'symbolic devaluing of women in relation to the divine' and the natural subordination of women have been described, and justified, and concluded.[34] It is thus not an easy place for women to re-enter with dignity. Most especially, it is here that feminists will meet a common Christian response to considerations of the family, namely that it has been ordained by God, that its purposes are incorporated in our very bodiliness as women and men, and that the fulfilment of its obligations constitutes the proper end for which we have been created. For many feminists, this argument has the same subtle effect as running headlong into a solid wall, yet it is not my understanding that such an impact is either necessary or intrinsic to the natural law tradition. To invoke this response and, what is worse, to offer the rationale that it has been ordained because of sin for which women are held originally responsible, is to present not only feminists, but moral thinkers generally with an intolerable impasse. It of course gives a clear answer to our central question, that justice means obedience to the orders of creation.

What sustains natural law thinking is continuous reference to human reasoning about experience, and what provides its justification is its appeal to our deepest discernments and intuitions

[34] Lerner, *Patriarchy*, 10.

about life, and what nourishes its insights and judgements is the presence of divine wisdom which is to be found in our midst. For feminists to use this way of moral reasoning is to begin to discover and to describe our humanness, not as autonomous subjectivity, nor as decentred selves, but as persons intended for love, love of self, and love of others, and love of the earth, and love of God. Such reference to the ultimate purpose of human existence holds out the hope of happiness, as Helen Oppenheimer has so aptly put it, and requires of us the very difficult task of discerning what love is in the circumstances and dilemmas of our everyday lives.[35] What is so challenging to Christian feminists is to provide a thick description of this good life in which human beings may flourish, ranging through all of the dimensions of our humanness, and to find there the context in which to reassess the new needs, new features, new crises and new possibilities of families in our world.[36] Thus we are asked to consider whether nuclear families are good for us, whether permanence is an essential feature of good human relationships, whether children in single parent families may flourish, whether serial monogamy is a good thing for human beings, whether reproductive technologies are good, whether a free market economic system is good for human beings. It is this account of the good life which is needed both to sustain a conception of justice and to provide the common ground upon which the demands of justice and of love may grow together in mutual nourishment, critique and support.

This brings us to one final theological consideration regarding our relationships as women and men. To take our human nature seriously as a renewable source of norms for human living is to present us with the need to understand human sexuality, and especially its meaning as a manifestation of the image of the divine in which we are made. The philosopher, Kate Soper, has noted recently the changing mood of feminism as it moves from what she calls its 'heterosexual utopianism' into a new phase of 'uncoupling discourses', in which hopes for better relations

---

[35] Helen Oppenheimer, *The Hope of Happiness: A Sketch for a Christian Humanism* (London: SCM, 1983).

[36] See Martha Nussbaum, 'Human Functioning and Social Justice: In Defense of Aristotelian Essentialism, *Political Theory* 20.2 (May 1992), 202–46; 'Justice for Women! Susan Moller Okin's *Justice, Gender and the Family*', *Women: a cultural review* 4.3 (Oxford University Press, 1993), 328–40.

between women and men have been abandoned, and heterosexuality becomes 'the reviled norm'.[37] This strikes a chord with
reflections amongst Christian feminists, who initially understood
the liberation of women to be a necessary sign of the new
relationships made possible by the kingdom, in which women
were accepted as equal in dignity, value, and responsibility, but
who in more recent times have questioned the limitations of this
relationship and the loss of power which it entails for women. Its
vision of the kingdom is now considered too confining to the
plural possibilities of identity and relationship which are possible
in the Spirit, and in addition, its terms have been set by the
powerful with whom women sought to become identified. Such
thoughts have made problematic the rooting of marriage and the
family in the divine creation of two persons, whose sexual
attraction for each other is understood to be a manifestation of
the divine life, and whose conjugal love, a sacrament.

The theological tradition is full of assumptions about the
nature of this original creation, assumptions which distinguish
women from men on the basis of man's own self-understanding,
and which use language that has been deconstructed as a form of
coercion. Criticism of these assumptions leads some feminists to
describe a spectrum of possible identities along which different
persons may find themselves, and a spectrum of types of relationship which are of equal but differing value. However, many
feminists are unwilling to abandon the possibility of recovering
the *imago dei* as women, in a way that requires women's own
spiritual reflections upon the meaning of female sexual desire,
upon the nature of their difference, and upon their own relation
with the divine.[38] For them to give voice to these things may begin
to open up the possibility that women and men could speak to
each other as two different beings, and could realise in new ways
the giving and receiving of their otherness in love. And what a

[37] Kate Soper, 'Heterosexual Utopianism', *Radical Philosophy* 69 (Jan/Feb
1995), 5–15.
[38] See Luce Irigaray, '*La Mysterique*', in *Speculum of the Other Woman* (New York:
Cornell University Press, 1974) translated by Gillian C. Gill; *An Ethics of Sexual
Difference* (London: The Athlone Press, 1984) translated by Carolyn Burke and
Gillian C. Gill.

transfiguration of relationships that might bring is the disturbing and promising outcome of our greater openness to God.[39]

---

[39] It is interesting to see some of these same theological issues addressed in a different way by Linda Woodhead in 'Faith, Feminism and the Family', *Concilium* 1995/4, 43–52.

16

Ecology and the Family

Edward P. Echlin

Introduction

The interdependence of the family with the wider earth community is hardly a central theme in conferences on the family. Yet without more reflection on relationships with other creatures under God, reflection which flows into reconciling practice, neither human families nor the biosphere of this planet have a pleasant future. In this era of the Stockholm Conference, the Brundtland Report, the Rio Earth Summit, and the Copenhagen, Cairo and Beijing meetings, it seems appropriate, to say the least, for Christians to reflect, as Christians, on the family presence within the wider earth community.

In reality the primary community on this earth is neither the family, the church, nor secular society, but the whole soil or earth community, whatever flies in the sky, moves in the waters and dwells on the land with their varied habitats. *This* is the primary living community which precedes and includes the human family. The primary community with which we have to reintegrate, which we must begin to reinhabit sustainably, is the whole earth community. The primary *fact* of our late twentieth century context is the disintegration, under the impact of our species, of the whole earth community of which we are members – and the perplexing delay of many religious people adequately to respond. Devastation of the earth and the widely recognised disintegration of family life are not unrelated. For human work, technology, procreation and ecological education are inherent to human family life.

For our unprecedented context of gathering biocide, we need to rethink and recontextualise the social sciences, sociology, child development and primary education, Christian ethics and moral theology.[1] The primary 'spiritual and social needs' are of the whole earth community within which are human needs; the primary 'justice' is owed to the earth within which is human justice; the primary mission and ministry today is to respond, in families and as committed single people, to the deterioration, under human impact, of the planet. Ecocide is injustice, especially to human persons and to the future.

Contemplation

In radically new historical contexts Christians turn to the Bible seeking discoveries in the inexhaustible depths of God's word. When we contemplate the Bible heuristically, seeking new insights for new contexts, our discoveries, if we read the Bible imaginatively, will not be stranded like a boat on the shingles when the tide goes out. Imagination connects. One discovery leads to another. Manlio Simonetti observes:

> The history of doctrine is the history of exegesis, in that the whole development of catholic doctrine is based on the interpretation of a certain number of passages in Scripture in the light of particular needs; but the same could be said of any other aspect of the Church's life: organisation, discipline, worship.[2]

In our 'particular needs' of earth and family disintegration we had best go beyond the historical-critical exegesis of most recent biblical scholarship. In Richard Bauckham's words:

> It is becoming painfully obvious that much modern interpretation of the NT has been consciously and unconsciously influenced by the prevalent ideology of the modern West which for two centuries or so has understood human history as emancipation from nature.[3]

---

[1] Feminist discourse ethics can uncritically accept the exclusive anthropocentric assumptions of conventional 'ethical rationalism'. Cf. Seyla Benhabib, *Situating The Self: Gender, Community and Postmodernism in Contemporary Ethics* (Cambridge: Polity Press, 1992), 32–3, 50–1, 58–9.

[2] Manlio Simonetti, *Biblical Interpretation in the Early Church* (Edinburgh: T. & T. Clark, 1994), 1.

[3] Richard Bauckham, 'Jesus and the Wild Animals (Mk 1:13): A Christological Image for an Ecological Age', in J. B. Green and M. Turner, eds., *Jesus of Nazareth Lord and Christ* (Grand Rapids: Eerdmans, 1994), 3.

We need to contemplate, with imagination, the Bible and the whole Christian reality within the living memory of the church, including privileged early interpretations of the Bible which for medievals and ascetics comprised *sacra doctrina.*

There is within God's word inexhaustibly more than scientific exegesis alone can fathom. We are wise to proceed always with deference to good exegesis. Especially do we depend on the learning of exegetes for the literal sense of important texts: what the authors and compilers intended and conveyed to their contemporaries in their contexts.[4] But there is wisdom in the mordant words of the late Cardinal Yves Congar: 'I respect and refer increasingly to the knowledge of the exegetes. But I refuse their magisterium.'[5] It has not been the exegetes, still less systematic or moral theologians, who have preserved, within the church's living memory, the holistic depths and inclusive connotations in God's word. But artists, poets and Christian environmentalists have. Exegetes and theologians should have listened, they may still have time to listen, to the wisdom of Christian environmentalists, artists and poets.

I am not suggesting an ecological eisegesis for our context, that we read a family ecology into the Bible, but that we listen and discover what *is there*, often in the silence, with our hearts. 'It is only with the heart that one can see rightly,' said the Little Prince, 'what is essential is invisible to the eye'.[6] The heart which has its own reasons will discover in God's word more than salvation history, or covenant history, or even family histories. Contemplating the Bible within the living tradition we listen to and discover wisdom in the tacit, the silent, we winkle out what is implicit and between the lines, we discover the inclusiveness of good kings and good families, we connect. Imaginative contemplation of God's word is creative, but it is also perceptive. Imagination puts flesh and visage onto the bones of thought. The

---

[4] For a good discussion of the importance of 'the historical context of meaning', cf. 'Foreword to Second Edition', in James D. G. Dunn, *Christology in the Making: An Inquiry into the Origins of the Doctrine of the Incarnation* (London: SCM, 1989), xiv–xvi.

[5] Yves Congar, *Vrai et fausse reforme dans l'Église* (Paris, 1950), 498–9; cf. Stephen C. Barton, *Discipleship and Family Ties in Mark and Matthew* (Cambridge: Cambridge University Press, 1994), 19.

[6] Antoine de Saint-Exupéry, *The Little Prince* (New York: Harcourt, Brace and World, 1943), 87.

imagination is a faculty, says Noel Dermot O'Donoghue, 'that perceives what is really there, though it comes, like all perceptions, not only as a pure datum, something given, but in a fruitful marriage of what is in the mind and what is outside it'.[7]

The creation stories

The whole canonical Bible, with its wisdom, its poetry and chronicles, its many pictures and stories, is God's word wherein we discover the mutuality of people and the natural world, the harmony of creation, incarnation and redemption. We observe in the Bible that salvation does not free people from the earth community but heals relationships within it. There is an *order* in the earth community ordained by the Creator which our fellow creatures instinctively and 'naturally' respect. Waves do not defy but defer to the sands' restraints. Human creatures, God's image, who are free and responsible, transgress that order to their peril and that of their fellow creatures.

> I placed the sand as the bound for the sea,
>   a perpetual barrier which it cannot pass;
> though the waves toss, they cannot prevail,
>   though they roar, they cannot pass over it.
> But this people has a stubborn and rebellious heart;
>   they have turned aside and gone away.
> They do not say in their hearts,
>   'Let us fear the Lord our God,
> who gives the rain in its season,
>   the autumn rain and the spring rain,
> and keeps for us
>   the weeks appointed for the harvest.'
> Your iniquities have turned these away,
>   and your sins have kept good from you.
> (Jer 5.22–25)

When we contemplate the primeval Genesis stories, whether we ponder the creation accounts separately or as a composite, we notice that 'the Adam', our species, is inherently and forever

[7] Noel Dermot O'Donoghue, *The Mountain Behind The Mountain* (Edinburgh: T. & T. Clark, 1994), 23.

co-existent within the primary earth community. Adam needs, depends on and is responsible for trees and fields, soil and animals and plants and warm sweet rain. We also notice that only another sensate thinking being, of his marrow and flesh, is a fully 'fit' companion for a man, that women and men are complementary co-existents and that together (even before or without descendants) they are interdependent with the rest of the earth (Gen 1.26; 2.8, 15).

Humanity, God's image, is God's responsible representative, a kingly presence under God, within the earth community. Adam names the animals, which is a royal prerogative. Kingship under God connotes wise and just rule, compassion for fellow creatures, fertility and continuance for the whole earth community culminating in a shalom which transcends an anthroposolic (for people alone) rightness and peace (Ps 72.3, 6, 16; Isa 11.1–9; 65.25).

It should be said, and in the mythical stories of the Fall, Genesis memorably says it, that people from our origins, from the moment our species becomes conscious, need redemption. In the words of the Second Vatican Council (1962–65), 'Man has disrupted also his proper relationship to his own ultimate goal as well as his whole relationship toward himself and others and all created things.'[8] In our frailty, moreover, we remain, says Genesis, responsible co-existents within the primary earth community, dependent on each other and all creatures, destined to work with thorns and thistles, with animals and fields and plants, until we die. Man, said Blaise Pascal in a pre-critical age, is the glory and the scandal of the universe and a mystery to himself. Women and men, co-existents sharing love and the sweetness of life and struggling with congenital internal divisions, are responsible for the future of creation (Gen 3.15–17; 1 Cor 7.15, 23–25).

In the familiar antediluvian succession of sins, Eve and Adam's blunder in the garden, Cain's fratricide, Lamech's casual homicide, 'angel marriages', and the general ambience of human crime – 'the wickedness of man was great in the earth, and ... every imagination of the thought of his heart was only evil continually' (Gen 6.5) – we notice that human sins have cosmic

---

[8] 'The Church in the Modern World, I, 13', *The Sixteen Documents of Vatican II* (Boston: Daughters of St Paul, n.d.), 525.

consequences (Gen 6.7). Moral disorder damages not only human malefactors but all other dependent creatures for which humans, God's sovereign delegates, are responsible. Not only is sin, even sexual sin, never a private affair, it is a profoundly cosmic affair. The sin of the client sovereign disrupts relationships with the whole earth community. 'Therefore the Lord God sent him forth from the garden of Eden, to till the ground from which he was taken' (Gen 3.25).

The blessing to procreate, which our species has accepted with some enthusiasm, first granted to Eve and Adam in the garden, is repeated after the Flood to Noah's patriarchal family and to those other pairs of sensate creatures who shared the ark (Gen 8.17). The biblical blessings connote open land and abundant forests, wilderness, air and water. When relatively few people become a community numerous enough to possess and till a land, when, from Dan to Beer-sheba, every man sits at peace under his own fig tree and his vine, the blessing to *expand* is accomplished (1 Kgs 4.20, 25). On the other hand, when humans procreate more than the carrying capacity of their bioregion can sustain, disorder proliferates (Ex 1.7f). There is no mandate for unsustainable procreation in the Bible (Josh 18.1).

Noah and the flood

If, as Manlio Simonetti says, we turn to 'certain passages' of scripture for 'particular needs', then the Noah story is a passage for our season. According to the Flood myth a few people temporarily occupied the ark with pairs of their fellow creatures. When Noah disembarked with his wife, his sons and their wives, they did not reinhabit the earth alone, for 'every beast, every creeping thing, and every bird, everything that moves upon the earth, went forth by families out of the ark' (Gen 8.19). People in the Jewish tradition live in mutuality with other creatures. We notice the imagery of the rainbow covenant in which people, with animals as covenant partners, are bound in 'an everlasting covenant' with God. There are important implications here: to be covenant partners with animals means we share creaturehood, we have a relationship with them, moreover we share a common destiny with the flora upon which we and other animals depend. 'Our common future' includes the whole earth community which shares the global commons. The Flood sequence recedes when Noah, the first post-diluvian 'tiller of the soil', plants a vineyard where he lives with his patriarchal family. Human relationships with other creatures perdure as the land gradually is re-inhabited.

Into the New Testament

The Jewish people, Jesus' ancestors, would have been familiar with hopes of ecological peace enjoyed by the righteous individual who lives at peace with the vines, fields and flocks, and with the wild animals. In the ancient Near East a man's fields and harvests were shared in part with the wider earth community including widows and orphans and transient visitors and the wild animals (Ex 23.9–12). Eliphaz the Temanite reminded Job of the hope that the righteous person will live at peace with the domestic and wild animals. The reference to stones perhaps refers to successful husbandry in burning and rocky lands:

> At destruction and famine you shall laugh,
>   and shall not fear the beasts of the earth.
> For you shall be in league with the
>   stones of the field,
> and the beasts of the field shall be
>   at peace with you.
> (Job 5.22–23)

There was, moreover, after the trauma of Babylonian exile, in the centuries immediately before Christ, a Jewish hope in a future Davidic king who would bring eschatological peace to all creation.[9] The Jews were aware that wild animals competed with people and with their plants and domestic animals for habitats, space and food. They were less conscious that people are also a threat to the very existence of wild animals – as our generation reluctantly is beginning to learn. The anointed eschatological king, a descendant of Jesse and David, hopefully would bring cosmic harmony between humans, their domestic animals and the wild animals. The vulnerable young of different species

---

[9] Anthony Phillips, 'Animals and the Torah', *Expository Times* (June 1995), 260–5.

would play peacefully with predators. Even serpents, the traditional adversary of people, would live at peace with children. The
Isaian poem, probably composed during or after Babylonian
exile, is our most familiar portrayal of the peaceful kingdom.
'Isaiah 11 goes a stage further than the kingdom of justice and
righteousness prophesied in Isa. 9. It now carries a remote
eschatological hope which extends the just rule of the king to
include the re-establishing of that very order of nature as originally intended by God', writes Anthony Phillips.[10] There may be
a hint of dominion, human responsibility for other creatures, in
the leadership by the child, a dominion which is *with* the wild
animals and not domination. The vegetarianism – lions eat straw,
serpents dust – recalling the first Creation account in Genesis,
may imply peace *among and between* the wild animals themselves.
Certainly 'piecemeal peace is poor peace': the poem evokes in us
a yearning for a future in which all predation ceases. Neither in
the Isaian poem nor its summary in Isa 65.25 is there *explicit*
mention of the human *family*. Yet the central image of the serene
child implies parenting and nurture:

> The wolf shall dwell with the lamb,
>   and the leopard shall lie down with the kid,
> and the calf and the lion and the fatling together,
> The cow and the bear shall feed;
>   their young shall lie down together;
>   and the lion shall eat straw like the ox.
> The sucking child shall play over the
>   hole of the asp,
>   and the weaned child shall put his
>   hand on the adder's den.
> They shall not hurt or destroy
>   in all my holy mountain;
> for the earth shall be full of the
>   knowledge of the Lord
> as the waters cover the sea.
> (Isa 11.6–9)

Against the background of these hopes Jesus appeared at the
Jordan. Mark, our earliest canonical gospel, introduces Jesus as

---

[10] *Ibid.*, 264.

Messiah and Son of God. God's Spirit anoints him in his baptism by John in the river. From the heavens God testifies to Jesus' kingship (Mk 1.11; Ps 2.7). According to Mark Jesus immediately goes into the wilderness where he meets Satan, angels and 'was with the wild beasts' (Mk 1.13). In this brief Marcan imagery (not repeated by the other gospels) Jesus is *with*, not over against nor above, the wild animals, an apparent indication of faith in Jesus as the eschatological Davidic king whose peaceful reign would include peace with the wild animals.[11]

There are in the New Testament and early Christian writings clues for our imaginative contemplation connecting Jesus the eschatological king with Nazareth and family life, not least early in his life and at its close in John's passion account. Mark notices that Jesus 'came from Nazareth' to the Jordan (Mk 1.9). Jesus, says Matthew, is the descendant of Jesse and David, and his parents return with him to *Nazareth* after an exile in Egypt. Matthew connects that family move to Nazareth with the *nazir* from Jesse in Isaiah's poem: 'He went and dwelt in a city called Nazareth, that what was spoken by the prophets might be fulfilled, "He shall be called a Nazarene"' (Mt 2.23; Isa 11.1).

In Matthew's infancy account gentile magi, following Balaam's star which 'shall come forth from Jacob', found at Nazareth with his parents Jesus the awaited king to whom they brought gifts (Mt 2.10–11; Num 24.17; Ps 72.10). Luke portrays the infant Jesus at Bethlehem in a manger, a word associated in the familiar Septuagint scriptures with an ox and ass at peace with their owner (Lk 2.7; Isa 1.3). Also unique to Luke is the messianic story of the boy Jesus lost in the temple who returns with his parents to Nazareth, 'their own city', and is subject to them (Lk 2.39; 41–51). Jesus, as a young adult, after he leaves home returns to Nazareth 'where he had been raised' and in the synagogue chooses for his reading a messianic text, again from the Isaian literature (Lk 4.16–20). John who, like Mark, has no infancy stories ironically connects Jesus with *both* Bethlehem *and* Nazareth. 'But some said, "Is the Christ to come from Galilee? Has not the scripture said that the Christ is descended from David, and comes from Bethlehem, the village where David was?"' (Jn 7.41–42).

[11] Robert Murray, *The Cosmic Covenant* (London: Sheed & Ward, 1992), 105–8; Bauckham, 'Jesus and the Wild Animals', 19–21.

A final gospel reference to Nazareth and kingship during Jesus's brief earthly life is in the only words we know were written about him during his lifetime, the royal trilingual words on the cross: 'Jesus of Nazareth King of the Jews' (Jn 19.19). This written insult, which for us has both family and eschatological kingly connotations, was by an adamant gentile named Pilate – what he had written he had written. According to John, Jesus' mother and his beloved disciple were with him at his death. Jesus entrusted Mary to the disciple. Jesus, said John, called his mother – and later the Magdala – 'woman'. John adds, 'in the place where he was crucified there was a garden', possibly a hint of the primal garden where the first Adam and the woman originally lived peacefully with other creatures (Jn 19.26–27, 41).[12]

Salvation, reconciliation, redemption in Jesus of Nazareth, risen and glorified, to use but three of the ten Pauline metaphors for our healing, includes all families and all creatures, past, present and future, the whole earth community. God's raising of Jesus is the initial transformation of our cosmos, our families and ourselves. All earth creatures, as Paul wrote to the Romans, groan expectantly awaiting the completion in ourselves of the peaceful kingdom symbolised by Mark when Jesus, God's Son anointed at baptism in the Jordan, 'was with the wild beasts' in the Judean wilderness, inaugurating eschatological salvation which includes peace with the wild animals (Rom 8.19–23; Mk 1.13).

The Sabbath, worship and sacraments

Sabbath observance recognises Christ as eschatological sovereign. The Sabbath is *the Lord's* day (Ex 20.10). Recognition of the Sabbath *as God's* in market-driven societies is a peaceful countercultural sign: the Sabbath is not for the market, but the market for the Sabbath; men and women are not for work, but work for men and women. Sabbath people, with our domestic animals, owe allegiance neither to the Egyptians nor to the market (Ex 23.12). Work, especially with the awesome power of modern technology, can breach the restraints under which this

---

[12] R. E. Brown, *The Gospel According to John XIII–XXI; A New Translation with Introduction and Commentary*, The Anchor Bible (New York: Doubleday, 1970), 943.

planet grants us life. Work which is not sustainable damages the life support systems of this planet, destructive work, sometimes justified as 'economic growth', damages human families, the whole earth community, the future. Pope John Paul II said perceptively to a Youth Conference in Rimini, 'The ecological catastrophe confronting humanity is profoundly ethical in the forgetfulness of the true nature of human work, especially of its subjective dimension, its value for the family and society.'[13]

By respecting and, where necessary, purifying our local seas and aquifers with their teeming life we participate in Christ's sanctification of the waters. Jesus's baptism by John sanctified the cosmos including all the waters of the world. Jacob of Serugh wrote, 'seas, deeps, rivers, springs and pools all thronged together to receive the blessing from your footsteps'.[14] Families, including sponsors of newly baptised Christians, may draw sacramental water from local aquifers and return water to the soil perhaps in a churchyard, a garden or at a baptismal tree. The planting and 'watering in' of baptismal trees, especially indigenous or fruit trees, is a perduring reminder of the cosmic significance of Christian initiation: a baptised Christian shares in Christ's eschatological kingship.

Confirmation, a sacrament of strengthening, prepares people for adult Christian life which may include sacrifices. There are Christian people who risk their lives for other creatures, in the rainforests, in wildlife reservations, at wild bird shoots, in bull runs, in peaceful demonstrations about animal exports, to mention a few examples. As sharers in Christ's kingship Christians may have to make sacrifices for other creatures, possibly by consuming less, by bicycling or sharing transport instead of driving a car, by sustainable holiday in one's own bioregion, or by restoring habitats in a neighbourhood. The planting of confirmation trees either in one's local bioregion or in more degraded parts of the world is a living symbol of strength, courage and healing.[15]

[13] Pope John Paul II, 'Address to Youth, Rimini, 1982', *The Pope Teaches* (London: Catholic Truth Society, 1989), 748.

[14] Quoted in Kilian McDonnell OSB, 'Jesus' Baptism in the Jordan', *Theological Studies* (June 1995), 217.

[15] The Woodland Trust plants commemorative trees and sends a certificate (Autumn Park, Grantham, Lincs. NG31 6LL). Third World Link plants com-

At the Eucharist, families, especially on the Sabbath, with all creation offer the transformed cosmos in Jesus to God. In the third Catholic Eucharistic Prayer we say, 'all creation rightly gives you praise'. We petition the power of God's Spirit upon all which goes into local bread and wine including human work. We offer 'bread which earth has given and human hands have made' and wine 'fruit of the vine and work of human hands'. The Lutheran liturgical theologian Gordon Lathrop notes the inclusiveness of the local eucharist:

> Bread unites the fruitful goodness of the earth with the ancient history of human cultivation. Bread represents the earth and the rain, growing grains, sowing and reaping, milling and baking, together with the mystery of yeast ... The translucent liquid also holds together the fruitful earth, the sun and the rain, the ancient history of human cultivation, and the mystery of yeast and fermentation. It also is a food that has been made in endless local varieties, bearing the mark of local cultures. It too is meant for a group – the cup for sharing, the bottle too much for one – and seems to be misused when drunk alone. Here, poured out for a human circle, there flows the goodness of the earth pressed out, the sun made liquid.[16]

The use of locally grown organic bread and wine has more than mere symbolic value, it supports family growers, preserves soil fertility, wildlife and habitats, and reduces environmentally ruinous 'food miles', the long-distance transport of food. Locally produced organic bread and wine were used at meals by Christ and the first Christians.

The sacrament of Penance and the various penitential rites in our liturgies should recognise structural ecological sin. 'Sin', says John McCarthy, 'is anthropological, but has far-reaching cosmic consequences'.[17] When 'we call to mind our sins' let us include ecological sin. The words of Alan Gear, Chief Executive of HDRA

memorative trees in Rajasthan, India and sends a certificate (40 All Saints Close, Wokingham RG11 1WE). The offering to both charities is £10 for tree and certificate.

[16] Gordon W. Lathrop, *Holy Things: A Liturgical Theology* (Minneapolis: Fortress, 1993), 91–2.

[17] John McCarthy, SJ, 'The Expectant Groaning of Creation: Cosmic Redemption in Romans 8.19–22', *Theology in Green* (January–March 1994), 29.

(the UK national centre for organic gardening) deserve prayerful, perhaps repentant consideration:

> It is a scandal that organo-phosphate insecticides should ever have had any place whatsoever in food production. How anyone could have imagined that a group of compounds originally manufactured as chemical weapons that attacked the nervous system, could be sprayed on to crops and animals and not have an adverse effect on human health, is beyond my comprehension. Yet, despite an alarming body of evidence, there are still no official moves to ban them.[18]

This challenges all of us even in cities, because the soil of this island is our responsibility, indeed we are within the soil community, we are baptised and confirmed to be, in Christ, 'with the wild beasts'. Harmful things are done to the soil so that we may select cheaper food, in the short term, on the shelves for ourselves and our families. Are we not structurally implicated when damaging things are done to our soil, our countryside, its wildlife and habitats, and to our food? Can we with impunity enjoy the cheap food, in wasteful packaging, with its residues, often bought at pollution-generating, edge-of-town retailers? Is it true that 'the government knows best' and 'is taking care of that for us'? Environmental sins can be family sins which damage the elderly, the children, the future of human families.

Some 'infrastructure' projects such as the TERN (Trans European Road Network) which maims part of the earth community for which 'the EC' is responsible, may involve us in structural sin. Long distance and jetting holidays should be included in our examinations of conscience. What would happen, what will happen to what remains of this earth, when Chinese and Indian people travel like Americans and Japanese? Family ecological sin demands family repentance; ecological sin, as an injustice, requires restitution. Personal and monetary support of local conservationists, including Christian groups, is an obvious way to make restitution. Commemorative trees and glades, fruit trees and orchards, contributions to green charities, sustainable transport and holidays, use of local produce, insulation of homes, schools and churches, effectively symbolise – 'contain what they

[18] Alan Gear, 'Comment', *HDRA News* (Summer 1995), 2.

signify' – our repentant transformation of God's earth. Green burials, and contributions to green charities in lieu of flowers at funerals, assist earth healing. A prayer of Sister Ancilla Dent of Minster Abbey, Kent, may be useful at penitential services, funerals, private penance – and in all rites of passage:

> O God enlarge within us
>   a sense of fellowship with all living things
>   to whom you gave the earth in common with us.
> May we live gently with our fellow creatures
>   and through the work of our hands
>   may the voice of the earth go up to you
>   not in sorrow but in a song of praise.
> (Adapted from St Basil)

The church's 'holy orders', its ordained ministry, is the visible profile of the church to people outside and to many within. The *ecological* profile of the ordained ministry, in lifestyle and transport, in ordination rites, in liturgies and homilies, in daily ministrations large and small represents the whole Church. The importance of ecologically inclusive liturgies, intercessions, homilies and leadership by visibly commissioned 'priests and people' cannot be exaggerated. Through an ecologically sensitive ministry that which is holistic in the living tradition flows visibly into 'the preaching and life of the believing and praying church' (Constitution on Divine Revelation, 8). The permanent diaconate – with other similarly commissioned ministries – is a leading *ecological* ministry. The deacon's ministry includes support of local conservationists, living churchyard projects, sustainable use of church land, the integration of worship with efforts to preserve threatened seed and fruit varieties, and leadership in ecologically inclusive theological study, spiritualities, worship and family prayer.[19]

Responsibility for the earth community comes to women and men together. Evolutionary biologists observe that the whole cosmic history of life is contained in the human body. Therefore when we Christians love our own bodies and when we love our spouses we love the cosmos. When husband and wife pray

---

[19] Edward P. Echlin, *The Deacon and Creation*, (London: Church Union, 1992), esp. 12–18; cf. also Echlin, *The Deacon in the Church* (New York: Alba House, 1971), 135–6.

together they are the cosmos at prayer, they pray in creation's name. Hippolytus, in the third century, noted that some husbands and wives prayed together, with all creatures, at night when one day ended and another began:

> The elders who transmitted the tradition taught that at this hour the whole creation rests for a moment to praise the Lord: stars, trees, waters stop for a moment, and the whole host of ministering angels, to praise God together with the souls of the just.

(*Apostolic Tradition*, 41)

With diminished need to multiply our human numbers and with expanding need for women and men *together to nurture* the elderly and children and other creatures already living on this earth, there is a need for dedicated single people and for childless marriages. When married people, together with those who are single, love and nurture elderly people and children, including handicapped, fostered and adopted children, and all creatures, present and future, without reproducing many biological children of 'their own', they are within an alternative marriage community which, because it cares for the whole creation, we may call cosmic marriage.

Conclusion

The primary created community is the earth community within which human communities, including the family, are dependent, interconnected and derivative. We may discover, and in our urban wasteland, retrieve, the ecological inclusiveness of the Christian family through imaginative contemplation of the Bible within the living tradition of the church. Contemplation of the Bible, alone and in small groups, always with a good commentary, and with imagination which makes connections and embodies thought can, indeed should, flow into ecologically inclusive worship and transformative practice. Families, as creation at prayer, lead the whole creation in praise of God.

17

The Want of Family in Postmodernity[1]

The sword without, and terror within.
(Deuteronomy 32.25)

Gerard Loughlin

It would seem that family and postmodernity have little in common. On the one hand, family would seem to be about affective relationships and bonds that are generational and irreversible, establishing a person in past and future as well as in the present. Postmodernity, on the other hand, would seem to be about the continual realignment of relationships, asserting an atomistic individuality which is free to rove an infinite web of connections, without need of past or future because situated within simultaneity: everything is always-already to hand. There is truth in this contrast. However, if with Fredric Jameson we understand postmodernity as the cultural logic of consumerist or late capitalism, we must allow that postmodernity has claimed the family for its own, as it claims everything else.[2]

[1] This essay is a revised and shortened version of a paper given to the Durham Seminar on the Family in Theological Perspective, February 1995. I am grateful for the comments of those who participated in the seminar, in particular Stephen Barton, Colin Crowder, Ann Loades and Peter Packer. I am also indebted to Gavin D'Costa and Stanley Hauerwas for subsequent comments that have also informed and modified my own remarks. Needless to say, remaining infelicities are mine own. After giving the paper, Stephen Barton introduced me to Rodney Clapp's marvellous book, *Families at the Crossroads: Beyond Traditional and Modern Options* (Downers Grove, IL: InterVarsity Press, 1993). Because it better says many of the things I try to say here, I have provided references to it throughout. This is not to say that Clapp endorses all the views advocated in this essay.

[2] See Fredric Jameson, *Postmodernism or the Cultural Logic of Late Capitalism* (London: Verso, 1991), and Gerard Loughlin, 'At the End of the World: Postmodernism and Theology' in Andrew Walker, ed., *Different Gospels*, second revised edition (London: SPCK, 1993), 204–21.

Long before contemporary political parties sought to sell themselves on the back of 'family values', commercial advertising had understood that it could sell its products through want of the family, through people's desire for the family they feared they lacked. Contemporary society has want of family, and both commerce and politics have an interest in sustaining that want, for in a consumer society no want can be met unless replaced with another, more voracious one. Families are big business.

In this essay I argue that there is no one proper sort of family: or rather that there is, but that it includes all others. In the light of this proper family all actual families – as we know them in history – are 'pretend' families. I come to the one proper family at the end of the essay. Here it is sufficient to note that 'family' is used, and has been used, of many different groupings. There is, as Wittgenstein might have said, and the *Oxford English Dictionary* will confirm, a family of family meanings.

Nuclear territory

Hollywood projects various images of family,[3] among them the nuclear family of father, mother and child as a subordinated trinity offering safe haven from social chaos: a world at war.[4] These trios survive amidst urban decay, deprivation and death, constituting a territory of relative calm, support and mutuality. They alone are bonded. Such families are given to group hugs.

The image of the familial three against the world appears in many different genres and to differing degrees of imaginative depth. In Warren Beatty's *Dick Tracy* (USA 1990), an expensively staged comic strip performed by real actors, Dick Tracy (Warren Beatty) is not only the fearless cop confronting the unlawful rule of the mobster, but a hero who gathers to himself an admiring and loving family.[5] Already able to resist the temptations of wealth and power offered to him by the mobsters, the love of a

[3] See Andrew Ross, 'Cowboys, Cadillacs, and Cosmonauts: Families, Film Genres, and Technocultures' in James A. Boone and Michael Cadden, eds., *Engendering Men* (New York: Routledge, 1990), 87–101.

[4] On why the family as 'haven' is deeply unchristian see Clapp, *Families at the Crossroad*, 149–69.

[5] For a comparison of *Dick Tracy* with Arthur Penn's *Bonnie and Clyde* see John Pym, 'Black Hat, Yellow Hat', *Sight and Sound* 59/4 (1990), 264–5.

good woman also enables him to resist the seductive charms of the mobsters' moll, Breathless Mahoney – even though she comes in the form of Madonna.

Like everything else in the film, Tracy's family is the instant production of an artist's sketch. At one moment Tracy is alone in the world, a single action hero; the next moment he has a family. His 'son' comes to him on a stormy evening as an orphan rescued from an abusing thug. There is something about the kid that leads Tracy to take him into his own home, and something about Tracy that leads the streetwise scamp to trust his new 'father'. Almost as suddenly Tracy has a 'wife' and his 'son' a 'mother', Tess Trueheart (Glenne Headly), and the three are pictured in the local diner, discussing their problems and those of the city, their affection for one another inarticulate but palpable. It is a dream family conjured from nowhere, instantly produced without labour.

Tracy gathers his family to him because he is an action hero, able to fight violence with violence. The bond between father and son is established as the latter excitedly watches Tracy shooting numerous hooligans, riddling their cars with bullets. The bond between husband and wife is ensured because she knows that while her man is gentle at home he is tough on the streets, able to secure desired domesticity. Mayhem reigns outside the home, and while Tracy will always be drawn out there – as he is at the end of the film – he will also always return, his venturing the condition of the home for which he fights.

Similar themes are present in more adult action yarns – more adult because the terror that is society outside the home is portrayed more extensively, imaginatively and expensively, and because the terror now reaches into the home itself. The family visibly struggles to survive. A good example of this fearful fantasy is James Cameron's *Terminator 2: Judgement Day* (USA 1991). As the title suggests this is a sequel to Cameron's earlier film, *The Terminator* (1985), in fact a remake of that film, with Arnold Schwarzenegger reprising his role as the cyborg T800 (now reprogrammed for 'good' rather than 'evil').[6] The new termina-

---

[6] On Schwarzenegger's roles in the two films see J. Hoberman, 'Nietzsche's Boy', *Sight and Sound* 1/5 (1991), 22–5. See also Tony Rayns' review of *Terminator 2* in the same issue (p. 51).

tor of the second film, the cyborg T1000, is a virtually indestruct-
ible killing machine, brought into the present from the future,
from beyond Armageddon. But this future – in which the world
is laid waste, and the last remnants of humanity are hunted down
by the machines of its own making – is already our present. The
film not only projects the possibility of nuclear holocaust – scenes
of which are some of the most spectacular in the film – but
projects images of present social disorder as the condition of that
holocaust. The killing machine from the future comes to a world
already violent; the world we think already too real beyond the
comforting warmth of the cinema's auditorium.

Against the terror, *Terminator 2*, like *Dick Tracy*, conjures an
almost instantaneous family. This family is materially grounded
in a way that Tracy's family is not. The child is the fruit of its
mother's womb, and we are left in no doubt that she has laboured
to rear her offspring. But once joined by Schwarzenegger as their
adoptive father/husband, they constitute a similar family territory, except that while Tracy remains the sole protector of his
family, Schwarzenegger has a 'wife', Sarah Connor (Linda Ham-
ilton), nearly as violent as himself. In the world of the terminator
all members of the family must fight if they are to maintain a
territory in which habits of the heart may be nurtured.

Cameron's film has mythic pretensions. His family is not set
simply against a world of gangsterism, but against a world on its
way to nuclear holocaust; nor does it stand simply for the territory
of the familial, for home comforts, but for the whole world,
perhaps even for the world as home and humanity as family. This
is because Cameron's family has the possibility of changing the
future that otherwise leads to the destruction of humanity.
Cameron's family is the holy family that brings salvation. The
conceit of time travel, of heroes and villains coming from the
future, allows Cameron to place the holy family of Nazareth in a
sci-fi world of the late twentieth century. Cameron's holy child,
John Connor (Edward Furlong), is literally fathered from the
future. The child will grow up to defeat the future killing
machines, just so long as they do not kill him first. Thus they send
a machine from the future to destroy him, as do the last survivors
of humanity to protect him. It is the story of a child saviour, beset
by demons and protected by angels.

The families of both films are without substance, not simply
because they must finally serve the constraints of their genres, of

the comic-strip and the action-yarn, but because they have no basis outside of themselves. Set against a violent world, there is nothing in that world that can account for their appearance. As a consequence they offer no real alternative to it. They are unable to imagine any other way of being than as the world is: they cannot imagine an alternative to violence. This is most evident in Cameron's film, whose saviour and holy family contrast markedly with the saviour and family of the gospel story, who not only flee but finally refuse violence as a possibility.

While Cameron's film is not alone in failing to imagine any alternative to violence – it is perhaps impossible for Hollywood to do so – it nevertheless articulates the want of such a possibility in Western society, and constructs this want, this lack and desire, as the possibility of the nuclear family. An altogether more thoughtful and disturbing projection of such a want can be found in Neil Jordan's *Interview with the Vampire: The Vampire Chronicles* (USA 1994) based on the novel of the same name by Anne Rice.

This is the story of Louis (Brad Pitt), who shortly after the death of his young wife and sunk in depression, meets the vampire Lestat (Tom Cruise) who offers him the choice of death or immortality, though it is no more a choice than any of us have on being born.[7] Louis accepts vampiric immortality, little comprehending that it is the stasis of life: a living death. Louis will remain for ever as he was at the moment of his human death and vampiric rebirth. While he is now immortal he has no future, no possibility of change and thus no possibility of redemption. He is condemned to the endless repetition of death in the death of others, surviving as he does on the blood of the living.

In the course of the story Lestat saves the life of Claudia (Kirsten Dunst), a 12-year-old girl who is dying from the plague, by making her like himself: an immortal vampire. The anguish of a life without a future, without hope, is most poignant in her. As the years pass her body remains that of a 12-year-old child. In one scene she tries to deny her child's body by cutting off the golden locks of her hair, only to find them immediately regrown. She is terrifyingly trapped within her immature body.

The three vampires, Lestat, Louis and Claudia constitute the family of the film. At one point Claudia asks her adoptive

---

[7] See further Kim Newman's review of the film in *Sight and Sound* 5/2 (1995), 46–7.

vampiric parents if they are not now a family, three against the world. This question, which is delivered almost straight to camera, as if addressing the audience, is intentionally provocative. For they are the bogey family of the moral majority: a homosexual couple with an adopted child; though they are of course blood relatives. That they are literally bloodsuckers, feeding upon honest God-fearing folk, serves to confirm their degeneracy.[8]

In Jordan's film, as in Beatty's and Cameron's, we have a family that constitutes a territory of affection and mutuality, set against a hostile world. And like the other families, the vampiric family is violent, destroying to survive. Yet unlike the other families, violence does not seem forced upon them through a necessary engagement with the world, but emerges from within the family as of its nature. Lestat seeks to ease Claudia's unhappy conscience by arguing that it is simply in the nature of the vampire to feed upon the living; it can do no other.

Jordan's film represents a distrust of the nuclear family that the other films do not. Here the family is the unholy family. Nevertheless it is the only territory of mutuality displayed in the film. That at the same time it can offer only nostalgia in place of hope, suggests that even this last vestige of humanity will soon disappear. But what of the wider society, against which the story of Lestat, Louis and Claudia is set? The film opens and closes in contemporary San Francisco and in between takes us from eighteenth-century slave owning New Orleans to nineteenth-century decadent Paris. At best the wider society is briefly sketched, but what we see is telling.

At one point in the film, there is the suggestion that Louis is the spirit of the century. Which century is a little unclear, the nineteenth century in which the line is spoken or the twentieth in which Louis recalls the line for us? If it does speak of our time, then we are all finally like Louis, endlessly feeding upon one another as of necessity rather than choice, without hope of a different future, seeking solace in melancholia, a weakening regret for what has been: and the family does not escape this condition.

[8] Here there must be a question of how much Rice and Jordan are confirming conservative homophobia, but that the film boasts some of Hollywood's hottest properties – Tom Cruise, Brad Pitt, Christian Slater and Antonio Banderas – complicates the sexual politics.

With Hollywood as our guide, the nuclear family in post-modernity appears as a nostalgic enclave, a haven against a violent and terrifying world, a territory in which mutual bonds of affection are still possible, but only just. In *Dick Tracy* the family is a confident possibility, in *Terminator 2* it has to struggle for survival; but in *Interview with the Vampire* it is already invaded by the forces it would resist. It is this recognition that makes the latter film more insightful than the others, since they display but do not recognise families predicated upon destruction.

On this reading, postmodernity does not perceive the family as a real alternative to a feared and fearful society; at best it is a barricade against the wider terror. Where then might we look for an alternative family?

The Holy Family

In 1893 Pope Leo XIII instituted the Feast of the Holy Family on the third Sunday after Epiphany. It was reassigned to the first Sunday after Epiphany in 1920, and in 1969 it was moved again to the first Sunday after Christmas. The family feasted is that of Jesus, Mary and Joseph, the family of Nazareth, but it is also the family as such, as an ideal of Christian life. Devotion to the Holy Family of Nazareth is accompanied by promotion and protection of the family in society. This is evident, for example, in the work of the Sons of the Holy Family, a congregation of priests and brothers founded in 1864 to 'promote devotion to the Holy Family and to foster true Christian family life'. As the *New Catholic Encyclopaedia* notes, this apostolate is 'accomplished through the education of youth and the organisation of a family movement consisting of instruction in the faith and in the management of the ideal Catholic home'.[9]

The nineteenth century saw the founding of many such congregations,[10] ecclesiastical sororities and fraternities that sought to foster family life through education and through care

---

[9] L. Hoffman, 'Holy Family, Sons of the', in *New Catholic Encyclopaedia* (New York: McGraw-Hill, 1967), 7.67.

[10] The Sisters of the Holy Family of Villefranche in 1816, the Congregation of the Sisters of the Holy Family in 1842, the Sisters of the Holy Family in 1872, the Sisters of the Holy Family of Nazareth in 1875, and the Congregation of Missionaries of the Holy Family in 1895. See *New Catholic Encyclopaedia*, 7.66–9.

of those not otherwise supported by families. For them the Holy Family is the family of piety, both as pictured in devotion to Jesus, Mary and Joseph, and as practised in the care of others. They promote the life of the Holy Family through their own in the life of others. Yet at the same time they refuse to constitute the sort of family they promote; they refuse marriage and the production of children. They themselves are family insofar as they are brothers or sisters of Jesus, and thus members of the Holy Family; but they are not family insofar as they have denied themselves the possibility of producing children. They are devoted to the reproduction of a family that at the same time they refuse for themselves. Nor is this the only anomaly between the three families they seek to relate, for the Holy Family itself is unlike their own congregational family. While it denies sexual relation between father and mother – Joseph and Mary – as do the congregations, it remains heterosexual in a way that the homosocial congregations do not, as well as maintaining a relation of material production between mother and son that can be only figural in the mediating brother and sisterhoods.

As the dates for the founding of these brotherly and sisterly congregations suggest, the families they refuse for themselves are very much nineteenth-century constructions, both the Holy Family of Nazareth and the ideal of Christian family. As such these families[11] were not only in the province of the Catholic Church, but were more widespread in Christian society, as shown in the discussion of both families – the Nazarene and the ideal – in the work of the philosopher G. W. F. Hegel at the beginning of the nineteenth century.

For Hegel, in his lectures on aesthetics (1823–29), the Holy Family is the 'absolutely ideal subject' for the concrete representation in art of 'love *reconciled* and at peace with itself.'[12] The Holy Family is the site of a spiritual love without taint of sensuous desire or self-interest. This is seen especially in the relation of the Virgin Mother to her child:

> The natural depth of feeling in the mother's love is altogether spiritualized; it has the Divine as its proper content, but this

[11] On the ubiquity of the 19th-century bourgeois family – and its perpetuation in Christian evangelicalism – see Clapp, *Families at the Crossroads*, 30–4, 54–7.

[12] G. W. F. Hegel, *Aesthetics: Lectures on Fine Art*, translated by T. M. Knox, 2 vols. (Oxford: Clarendon Press, 1975), vol. 2, 819.

spirituality remains lowly and unaware, marvellously pen-
etrated by natural oneness and human feeling . . . a pure
forgetfulness and complete self-surrender which still in this
forgetfulness is from the beginning one with that into which it
is merged and now with blissful satisfaction has a sense of this
oneness.[13]

In the *Philosophy of Right* (1821) loving union is central to
Hegel's idea of the family as such. The family is 'characterized by
love', such that in the family a person experiences individuality
'not as an independent person but as a member'.[14] Marriage, in
its ethical and objective aspect, is that act of self-restriction in
which a person is paradoxically liberated through union with
another. It is the transformation of contingency – dynastic
alliance or sexual desire – into substantive self-consciousness. As
such it is a love like that of the Madonna for her child, a spiritual
union that transcends self-interest:

> The ethical aspect of marriage consists in the parties' con-
> sciousness of . . . unity as their substantive aim, and so in their
> love, trust, and common sharing of their entire existence as
> individuals. When the parties are in this frame of mind and
> their union is actual, their physical passion sinks to the level of
> a physical moment, destined to vanish in its very satisfaction.
> On the other hand, the spiritual bond of union secures its
> rights as the substance of marriage and thus rises, inherently
> indissoluble, to a plane above the contingency of passion and
> the transience of particular caprice.[15]

In its essence, marriage is not a contract, since contract is a
relation between individuals as 'self-subsistent units'. Marriage
transcends such a relationship, forming one 'ethical mind': the
family as 'one person', one substance, whose members are its
accidents. It is in this unity that the 'religious character of
marriage and the family, or *pietas*, is grounded'.[16] This idea of
marriage and family as an ethical unity does not deny or deni-
grate the physical or sensuous, but puts it 'into its ethical place as

[13] Hegel, *Aesthetics*, vol. 1, 542.
[14] G. W. F. Hegel, *Philosophy of Right*, translated by T. M. Knox (Oxford:
Clarendon Press, 1952), 110.
[15] Hegel, *Philosophy of Right*, 112.
[16] Ibid.

something only consequential and accidental, belonging to the external embodiment of the ethical bond, which indeed can subsist exclusively in reciprocal love and support'.[17]

For Hegel marriage is not simply one possibility among others, but an 'objectively appointed end', such that it is 'our ethical duty to enter the married state'.[18] This is because the difference and union of the sexes has a 'rational' basis in the ethical 'concept' as it 'internally sunders itself in order that its vitality may become a concrete unity consequent upon this difference'.[19] Thus the ethical concept, in its Hegelian history, dirempts itself between the two sexes. It is perhaps unremarkable that in this diremption between universality and particularity, there is found a philosophical basis for patriarchal gendering, so that 'man has his actual substantive life in the state, in learning, and so forth', while woman finds 'her substantive destiny in the family'.[20] In marriage these differences or personalities are surrendered to one another, such that each comes to know itself in knowing the other.[21] Hegel founds both monogamy and exogamy in the 'mutual, whole-hearted' surrender of one to another in the marriage union. It is an absolute and exclusive surrender of oneself to another, thus ruling out other partners and a partner like oneself: 'for individuals in the same circle of relationship have no special personality of their own in contrast with that of others in the same circle'.[22]

While the Hegelian idea of marriage as difference-in-unity seems to indicate a certain mutuality between the surrendering parties, it nevertheless remains skewed. As Hegel notes, the unity of marriage is 'only a unity of inwardness or disposition; in outward existence . . . the unity is sundered in the two parties'.[23] Man, labouring and struggling in the external world, may have to

[17] Ibid., 113. Hegel notes that denial of the body in relation to divinity or spirituality is 'in keeping with the monastic doctrine which characterizes the moment of physical life as purely negative and which, precisely by thus separating the physical from the mental, endows the former by itself with infinite importance' (112–13).
[18] Ibid., 111.
[19] Ibid., 114.
[20] Ibid.
[21] Ibid., 115.
[22] Ibid.
[23] Ibid., 117.

fight to gain a 'self-subsistent unity with himself', but he can always find a 'tranquil intuition of this unity' in the family, where 'he lives a subjective ethical life on the plane of feeling'. But there is no suggestion that woman, in her turn, might engage in the external world: her destiny is the family.[24] Thus the lines are drawn between world and family, public and private; and while man might labour in one and find haven in the other, woman knows only her domesticity.

The Hegelian philosophy both establishes the liberal division of public and private, and shows why the latter could never have the influence on the former that the former has on the latter. As Laura Gellott notes, in nineteenth-century liberal polity the family 'served not only as a counterweight to the vicissitudes and the amorality of public society, it was the source of moral formation, emotional satisfaction and renewal for individuals. Separate from the public sphere and sheltered within the walls of the home, the family would shape individuals equipped to venture forth daily to do battle in the marketplace and the political assembly'.[25] Here we are not so very far from the territory of the Hollywood family in *Dick Tracy*; and just as the cartoon family cannot finally resist the violence it holds at bay, so the bourgeois family succumbs to the marketplace outside its door. It becomes one more institution that serves, rather than counters, 'the interests of atomistic individuals'.[26] This outcome is presaged in Hegel's idea of the family 'as person', as the unity of an unequal diremption.

Hegel's discussion of the family is of course set within a larger dialectic of family, civil society and state, which I cannot pursue here. Rather I now turn to a twentieth-century rendering of the family as difference-in-unity. Pope John Paul II, in his exhortation *Familiaris Consortio* (1981), presents a picture of the family in some conformity with the Hegelian unity, and thus the family of nineteenth-century liberalism.

<hr />

[24] Ibid., 114.

[25] Laura Gellott, 'The Family, Liberalism, and Catholic Social Teaching', in *Catholicism and Liberalism: Contributions to American Public Philosophy*, edited by R. Bruce Douglass and David Hollenbach (Cambridge: Cambridge University Press, 1994), 269–95 (272).

[26] Gellott, 'The Family', 273.

Like Hegel, the Pope is concerned to go beyond mere appearance and discern the innermost truths of marriage and family, but now rooted in the will of God rather than the motor of the Hegelian 'mind'. However, like Hegel, these truths consist in the possibility of a man and woman so totally surrendered to one another that they constitute a harmonious unity and secure a real freedom in fidelity.[27] Marriage 'aims at a deeply personal unity, the unity that, beyond union in one flesh, leads to forming one heart and soul; it demands indissolubility and faithfulness in definitive mutual giving; and it is open to fertility'.[28] As with Hegel, the totality and exclusivity of this unity rules out polygamy;[29] and as with Hegel this unity is constituted between different but complementary personalities. This unity is rooted in the will of God, expressed in the Genesis creation story and in the analogy between the relation of Christ and church to that of husband and wife. Marriage is the type of Christ's 'spousal covenant' with his church.[30] This analogy means that the Pope is in danger of reproducing that imbalance of man to woman that we found in Hegel's conceptuality.[31]

If both the Hegelian and papal families are finally patriarchal in structure, the family of the latter achieves a degree of openness lacking in the former. While both conceive the family as unified territory, the Pope insists on the family as community in a way that opens it to a wider conception of the family than the merely

[27] Pope John Paul II, *Familiaris Consortio* (London: Catholic Truth Society, 1981), sec. 11, pp. 20–1.

[28] Ibid., sec. 13, pp. 25–6.

[29] Ibid., sec. 19, p. 36.

[30] Ibid., sec. 13, p. 24.

[31] This is to broach a large question concerning Pope John Paul II's attempt to understand 'woman' (which abstraction is part of the difficulty). It is addressed in Mary C. Segers, 'Feminism, Liberalism, and Catholicism', in R. Bruce Douglass and David Hollenbach, eds., *Catholicism and Liberalism: Contributions to American Public Philosophy* (Cambridge: Cambridge University Press, 1994), 242–68. See more recently the *Letter of Pope John Paul II to Women* (London: Catholic Truth Society, 1995), and 'Women Respond to the Pope', *The Tablet* (15 July 1995), 920–1. The difficulties attendant on the Pauline analogy of ecclesial and spousal covenants is considerably eased by understanding the relation of 'Christ/husband' to 'Church/wife' in (Johannine) terms of 'service', and in freeing-up the mapping of this gendered relation on to male and female bodies, so that *both* men and women may be 'Christ/husband' *and* 'Church/wife' – in the same way that all Christians are called to be both 'sheep' and 'shepherd', followers of Christ and Christ for others.

nuclear. 'In matrimony and in the family a complex of interpersonal relationships is set up – married life, fatherhood and motherhood, filiation and fraternity – through which each human person is introduced into the "human family" and into the "family of God", which is the Church.'[32] The idea of community allows the family to exceed the triangular structure of the nuclear family, and returns it to an earlier conception of family as household. While the 'communion of the family, of parents and children, of brothers and sisters with each other, of relatives and other members of the household' is still rooted in 'conjugal communion',[33] the family is understood to be animated by a wider communality. 'The Christian family constitutes a specific revelation and realisation of ecclesial communion, and for this reason too it can and should be called "the domestic Church".'[34] There is much wisdom in the Pope's teaching on the family as that place in which people learn to be church: the brothers and sisters of Christ – though this is not a model of which he much avails himself. However there is a darker side to papal thinking about the family, which, when taken with its potential patriarchalism, renders it seriously flawed.

Laura Gellott identifies the flaw as a lack of inclusivity.[35] Just as Hegel sought to render marriage and family a metaphysical necessity, so papal teaching posits marriage and family as the divinely willed *telos* of human life. Of course it allows for certain exceptions, such as the Pope himself. 'Christian revelation recognises two specific ways of realising the vocation of the human person, in its entirety, to love: marriage and virginity or celibacy.'[36] Outside of these possibilities, love is not really love. Yet

---

[32] Pope John Paul II, *Familiaris Consortio*, sec. 27, p. 27. The Church is the primary family of Christian existence, into which all members are 'born' at baptism. The Holy Family (Jesus, Mary and Joseph) of the gospel narratives – as opposed to that of a later piety – is, in the course of the gospel story, dissolved and reconstructed as the family of the church. See further Clapp, *Families at the Crossroads*, 67–88.

[33] Pope John Paul II, *Familiaris Consortio*, sec. 21, p. 39.

[34] Ibid., sec. 21, p. 40. But here it is important to remember that the nuclear family of modernity is not the only form of *domus* or household within the larger domesticity of the church.

[35] Gellott, 'The Family', 285–6.

[36] Pope John Paul II, *Familiaris Consortio*, sec. 11, p. 20.

there are those who insist on a vocation to love who are neither celibate nor (yet) marriageable: gay men and lesbian women.[37]

In relation to the family it is obvious that while all homosexuals are children, few will be parents. Consequently, where a nuclear model of the family predominates, they are effectively excluded from occupying any familial place other than that of child or sibling. A wider model of the family – such as that advocated in *Familiaris Consortio*: the household as extended conjugal community – allows them to take up positions such as uncle or aunt, or akin to such when there is no blood connection. Laura Gellott suggests that 'for those individuals – married or single – who do not have children the full meaning of family is to be experienced in the ties of "filiation and fraternity", as aunts and uncles, as partners in the work of transmitting identity and shared values across the generations'.[38] No doubt there are many homosexuals who, along with other single people and childless couples, engage in generational family life in just such a way. Nevertheless, within the familial imagination of the church, they are unable to constitute a legitimate household in their own right. Here it is not so much a matter of wanting heterosexual familiality, as a different but still legitimate familiality: that is, a different but legitimate way of realising the vocation of the human person to love.

The idea of the Christian family turns sour when it ceases to promote fidelity, mutuality and the dispossession necessary for the reception of children as gift, and instead becomes a means of attacking those whom it itself excludes and constructs as 'threat'. This is when the practice of familial virtues becomes the ideological promotion of 'family values'. Thus the papally approved *Letter to the Bishops of the Catholic Church on the Pastoral Care of Homosexual Persons* (1986) constructs the homosexual as the enemy of the family, arguing that the equal valuing of homo- and heterosexual relations 'has a direct impact on society's understanding of the nature and rights of the family and puts them in jeopardy'.[39] In a

---

[37] This is not the question of 'singleness'. Finally there are no singles in the church, unlike postmodern society where there are only singles finally. See further Clapp, *Families at the Crossroad*, 89–113.

[38] Gellott, 'The Family', 286.

[39] Sacred Congregation for the Doctrine of the Faith, *Letter to the Bishops of the Catholic Church on the Pastoral Care of Homosexual Persons* (London: Catholic Truth Society, 1986), sec. 9, p. 10.

similar – though more viciously paranoiac – way, the Ramsey Colloquium, an American group of Jewish and Christian writers, including priests and rabbis, constructs homosexuals as libertines who, allied with proponents of abortion, adultery, divorce and feminism, threaten 'innumerable individuals' and 'our common life'.[40]

Faced with such attitudes, it is important to learn that the church has no long-term interest in the heterosexual family, either nuclear or extended. The family of which the church is in want is altogether different.

Heavenly families?

Are there families in heaven? In the 22nd chapter of Matthew, Jesus tells the Sadducees that in heaven there is no marriage, for people are then like angels.[41] This has proved a protean text for speculation on post-mortem existence. The medieval mind was much concerned with the nature of the resurrection body, and in this followed Augustine, who worried about what would and would not be raised. Caroline Walker Bynum provides a useful conspectus of his questions:

> Will aborted foetuses rise? Will Siamese twins be two people or one in the resurrection? Will we all be the same sex in heaven? the same height and weight? the same age? Will we have to eat? Will we be able to eat? Will deformities and mutilations appear in heaven? Will nail and hair clippings all return to the body to which they originally belonged? Will men have beards in their resurrected bodies? Will we 'see' in heaven only when

---

[40] 'The Homosexual Movement: A Response by the Ramsey Colloquium, *The Month* (July 1994), 260–5. As so often, many of those who bewail the demise of the family celebrate the consumer capitalism that is its true enemy, because the enemy of all authentic human relationships. In so far as they succeed in promoting the one they fail in protecting the other, since capitalism has already made the family a commodified simulacrum, of which we are in want. It should be understood that sexual libertinism, gay or straight, is but one aspect of that more generalised promiscuity which is the 'market'. See further Clapp, *Families at the Crossroads*, 48–66.

[41] Matthew 22.30.

our eyes are open? Will we rise with all our internal organs as well as our external organs?[42]

It would seem that Augustine thought we might all be raised aged thirty, and that we will be raised with our internal and external organs, including our sexual organs, they being part of our perfection.[43] But while we will have our genitals, we will not enjoy the use to which we put them at present, for while the body in all its particulars is important for our salvific identity, its processes must be arrested, for process is change and change is decay. Tertullian was certain that we will have mouths but not eat, genitals but not copulate, for 'eating and procreation are aspects of the biological change that is part of corruption. . . . Such organs will have no function in the resurrection, but they will survive for the sake of beauty. We will not chew in heaven, but we will have teeth, because we would look funny without them.'[44] Origen, on the other hand, said that we will not have age or sex, for in heaven there is no growth, excretion or copulation. We may not even remember the relationships we have enjoyed or endured in this life.[45]

Speculation on our future state is not an idle exercise, for thinking about how we will be is thinking about how we are, from the perspective of our eternal destiny. Christian thought on the present is not complete until it is thought from the future: it must always finally be retrospective or eschatological. Therefore we must think body and sexuality, marriage and family, from the future. Are there families in heaven?

Karl Barth's theology of marriage and family is an attempt to think these realities from the future, that is from the eschatological event of Jesus Christ. In doing so, he has, in some though not all respects, a very different view of these matters from those of John Paul II. For the Pope, marriage is given for procreation, for family:

> The biblical account [in Genesis] speaks of God's *instituting marriage* as an indispensable condition for the transmission

[42] Caroline Walker Bynum, *The Resurrection of the Body in Western Christianity, 200–1336* (New York: Columbia University Press, 1995), 97–8.

[43] Bynum, *The Resurrection*, 99–100; Augustine, *The City of God*, Bk. 22, Chs 17–18.

[44] Bynum, *The Resurrection*, 37.

[45] Ibid., 67.

of life to new generations, the transmission of life to which marriage and conjugal love are by their nature ordered: 'Be fruitful and multiply, and fill the earth and subdue it' (Gen 1.28).[46]

For Barth, however, marriage is commanded for some as their vocation to love. 'There is no necessity of nature nor general divine law in virtue of which every man is permitted or commanded to take a wife, or every woman a husband. If this is permitted and commanded, it is a special distinction, a special divine calling, a gift and grace.'[47] And procreation, though natural, is an inessential part of marriage. The latter is not given for the former:

> In the sphere of the New Testament message there is no necessity, no general command, to continue the human race as such and therefore to procreate children. . . . *Post Christum natum* there can be no question of a divine law in virtue of which all these things must necessarily take place. On the contrary, it is one of the consolations of the coming kingdom and expiring time that this anxiety about posterity, . . . is removed from us all by the fact that the Son on whose birth alone everything seriously and ultimately depended has now been born and has now become our Brother. No one now has to be conceived and born. . . . Parenthood is now only to be understood as a free and in some sense optional gift of the goodness of God.[48]

---

[46] Pope John Paul II, *Mulieris Dignitatem: On the Dignity and Vocation of Women* (London: Catholic Truth Society, 1988), sec. 6, p. 21.

[47] Karl Barth, *Church Dogmatics* (Edinburgh: T. & T. Clark, 1961), vol. III/4, 183.

[48] Barth, *Church Dogmatics*, III/4, 266. That this is little understood in the churches, let alone outside them, is illustrated by the remark of the Church of England bishop, the Rt Revd Mark Santer, that married couples need a good reason for not having children. See *The Tablet* (1 July 1995), 851. On the contrary, Christian couples need a good reason *for* having children, since faith in the resurrected Christ frees them from the necessity to reproduce; or rather, there are no Christian reasons for having children outside the *ratio* of God, which comes to us as grace and gift. Here, as elsewhere, I am indebted to the teaching of Stanley Hauerwas and Samuel Wells in his unpublished paper on 'Why Christians Have Children'. See further Clapp, *Families at the Crossroads*, 100–1, 133–48. For Clapp, God gives children to Christians so that they 'can become the kind of people who welcome strangers' (138).

For Barth there is finally only one proper family: the eschatological family of Christ, who is our brother and whose father is our father, and whose mother – at least in Catholic thought – is our mother also. Thus while Barth devotes over 45 pages to the subject of parents and children, he refuses to discuss the 'family' as such:

> In the more limited sense particularly the idea of the family is of no interest at all for Christian theology. . . . When the New Testament speaks of a 'house', it means the *familia* in the comprehensive sense of a household fellowship which can become the centre of the message heard and reproduced in the wider life of the community. . . . Parents and children are still emphasised, like men and women, masters and servants, but as persons and for the sake of their personal connections and duties. The family collective as such plays no further part at all.[49]

Barth's teaching on parenting, which emphasises the fifth commandment to honour father and mother, reminds us that in Christian thought the territory of the family, especially the nuclear family, is already passing away with the coming of Christ and the one family of heaven.

There are two points to stress about the coming heavenly family. The first is that it is precisely that, a family that is *arriving but is not yet here,* just as the old world, with its various earthly families, is *passing but has not yet gone.* It is only in the proleptic presence of the Kingdom of Jesus Christ that we begin to live ahead of the future that is not yet fully arrived. The church, as has often been said, lives in the interim, in the Saturday between the Friday and the Sunday, between the ascension and the parousia. It lives in hope.

Christians are always seeking new ways to live the coming Kingdom now, new ways of being the heavenly family on earth, one of the most striking of which has been the monastic movement, which has sought to recognise all as brother or sister in Christ, and to imitate that asexuality which the medievals, following the teaching of Jesus, believed part of heavenly joy. Thus what the Pope calls 'consecrated virginity or celibacy' is not so much

---

[49] Barth, *Church Dogmatics*, III/4, 241–2.

a renunciation for the sake of the Kingdom as the enactment of the Kingdom in the sphere of sexuality. As the Pope writes, the celibate 'anticipates in his or her flesh the new world of the future resurrection'.[50] Such celibacy is denial only because heavenly life is not now natural to us, who still live in the old world.

The Catholic church has always deemed celibacy more perfect than conjugality, being a more perfect living of heavenly life. As the Pope writes, the Church 'has always defended the superiority of this charism [celibacy] to that of marriage, by reason of the wholly singular link which it has with the Kingdom of God'.[51] And yet we might still wonder about this 'wholly singular link'. Why is asexuality deemed such an important aspect of heavenly life that the denial of sexuality in this life must be thought 'superior' to its practice? Is the denial of sexuality any closer to the asexuality of heaven, than the embrace of sexuality in this life?

Even if the celibate does not escape his or her sexuality – as seems likely – and may even be dominated by it, nevertheless he or she, especially when living in community, becomes a sign of other possibilities than those imagined by the world. And this brings me to the second and last point I want to stress about the heavenly family as it even now presses upon us.

Postmodernity as the culture of consumer capitalism has claimed the family as its own; but it has done more than this. It has claimed the heavenly family also. Indeed postmodernity is the family of heaven now, a realised eschatology. The family of heaven is radically egalitarian, for everyone has the same father and mother, and each is the brother or sister of all. In the same way postmodernity imagines a radical equality of relationship, an ideology which is perhaps nowhere more evident than in the discourse of the computer internet. And just as the heavenly family dissolves all earthly hierarchies and familial bonds, so postmodernity renders everything and everyone an equal consumer and consumable, such that sexual and family ties are infinitely variable: if you can think of a new way to connect then connect. Promiscuity, which is the logic of postmodernity, is one realisation of the heavenly family. If everyone is a family member, then all sexual relations are incestuous, and either no one or

---

[50] Pope John Paul II, *Familiaris Consortio*, sec. 16, p. 29.
[51] Ibid., sec. 16, p. 30.

everyone may have sex with anyone else.[52] Both options have been tried in Christian history. The fraternal and sororal congregations represent the first option, and sexual congress between such spiritual brothers and sisters was once clearly understood as incestuous, as when Thomas More denounced Martin Luther's marriage to Catherine von Bora as 'shameful inceste and abominable lychrye'. On the other hand there were those Christians who took to heart St Paul's teaching that 'all things are lawful',[53] and practised sibling incest, free in the Spirit from guilt. As Marc Shell notes, the difference between the celibate brothers and sisters and those Brethren of the Free Spirit that are said to have flourished between the thirteenth and seventeenth centuries, is but polar opposition or inversion of the same logic:

> A celibate in the normative orders gracefully overcomes sexual desire and loves everyone (the same) as universal siblings; a libertine in the Brethren of the Free Spirit gracefully overcomes sexual desire or conscience and loves everyone (as the same). For both groups, sexual intercourse with a sibling is no worse or better than sexual intercourse with any other person. The religious celibate seeks liberty from physical desire; the libertine seeks liberty from rules that restrict physical intercourse. But for both, in the words of Saint Paul, 'Where the Spirit of the Lord is, there is liberty' (2 Corinthians 3.17).[54]

Postmodernity simply follows through on the libertine's interpretation of familial love. Post-modern promiscuity is in its root Christian eschatology, an understanding of present society as now already the heavenly family in which all siblings may love all other siblings, freed from the taboo of incest through the spirit of infinite consumption. Postmodernity does not wait for the coming of the heavenly household but instantiates it now already, perversely as we may think.

---

[52] See Marc Shell, 'The Want of Incest in the Human Family or, Kin and Kind in Christian Thought', *Journal of the American Academy of Religion*, 62/3 (1994), 625–50.

[53] 1 Cor. 10.23.

[54] Shell, 'The Want of Incest', 636. See further Robert E. Lerner, *The Heresy of the Free Spirit in the Later Middle Ages* (Berkeley: University of California Press, 1972).

But where does the perversity lie? Is it in opting for promiscuity rather than celibacy, or rather is it in thinking sexuality the 'wholly singular thing' about the heavenly household? Might it not be that what matters about the heavenly family are forms of relationship other than the sexual? Might it not be that the heavenly family arrives through those relationships of mutuality, fidelity and dispossession that render sexuality a means rather than an end in itself? But this is where postmodernity most differs from churchly practice, for when heaven has arrived there is no longer an end in view, a point beyond: the end is the means.

The church, on the other hand, still prays for the end which has not yet arrived, knowing that neither asceticism nor libertinism can be ends in themselves. It knows that it cannot finally imagine the heavenly family, but must await its arrival, discerning the signs of God that are its anticipation. The church seeks to promote the family insofar as the family seeks to repeat in its own circumstance the family of heaven. There is thus no one sort of earthly family that repeats the heavenly; but all families that listen for the command of God in faithful trust, already, in some measure, participate in the family of heaven.

18

The Family Reunion: Reflections on the Eschatological Imagination

Colin Crowder

And Sadducees came to him, who say that there is no resurrection; and they asked him a question, saying, 'Teacher, Moses
wrote for us that if a man's brother dies and leaves a wife, but
leaves no child, the man must take the wife, and raise up
children for his brother. There were seven brothers; the first
took a wife, and when he died left no children; and the second
took her, and died, leaving no children; and the third likewise;
and the seven left no children. Last of all the woman also died.
In the resurrection whose wife will she be? For the seven had
her as wife.' Jesus said to them, 'Is not this why you are wrong,
that you know neither the scriptures nor the power of God?
For when they rise from the dead, they neither marry nor are
given in marriage, but are like angels in heaven. And as for the
dead being raised, have you not read in the book of Moses, in
the passage about the bush, how God said to him, "I am the
God of Abraham, and the God of Isaac, and the God of Jacob"?
He is not God of the dead, but of the living; you are quite
wrong.'[1]

What kind of answer is that? Not once, but twice, Jesus accuses his
questioners of having gone astray – not so much being *wrong*, as
the RSV has it, and still less being *mistaken*, with the NEB, as if
their only problem was a touch of amnesia, but rather *deviating*
in some way. The accusation, *planasthe*, is about erring, or
straying, or wandering, and the metaphorical extension of this
idea is scarcely puzzling in this or any other context. Yet I cannot

---

[1] Mk 12.18–27. (Cf. Matt 22.23–33 and Lk 20.27–40.)

help being intrigued by the idea of deviation, and I sometimes wonder whether the questioners might not have found the accusation a bit rich, given the circumstances. Their question, after all, concerned what would happen to the seven successive marriages 'in the resurrection', and it is hard to see how the teaching of Jesus constitutes a proper answer.

Jesus argues that those who rise from the dead 'neither marry nor are given in marriage', but there remains the question of what happens to those who married in *this* life. In short, the problem is not the future of marriage as such, but the future of particular marriages. This is not a quibble over tenses, but a recognition that what Jesus says is logically compatible with more or less any response to the hypothetical example; in other words, it is consistent with many possible resurrection worlds, in which the woman would be married – in whatever sense – to her first husband, or her last, or all her husbands, or none of them. There might be a presumption in favour of this last option, which has the virtue of simplicity, but the logical gap remains. This gap has been a window of opportunity for many generations of interpreters, who have tried to reconcile the teaching of this passage with a profound longing for the perpetuation of relationships: the hope that we will not only *know* one another as wives and husbands, sisters and brothers, children and parents, but still *be* these things to one another. This hope, for the ultimate family reunion, is something that is neither confirmed nor denied in the teaching on the resurrection. Jesus accuses his questioners of straying, of erring, but there is a certain deviation, it seems, in his refusal to give a straight answer to a straight question.

But was it a straight question? In a sense, it was not, as the fact that the Sadducees didn't believe in the resurrection was one of their defining characteristics.[2] They challenged the Pharisees to derive resurrection from the Torah, but we also know that they were fond of a good resurrection riddle of the kind posed in the gospels. On one occasion, for example, they asked if the resurrected would require ritual cleansing, since by definition they had been in contact with a corpse.[3] The question in the gospels is, therefore, a trick question; but commentators sometimes

---

[2] Mk 12.18, Matt 22.23, Lk 20.27, and Acts 23.8; Josephus, *Antiquities* 18:1:4, and *War* 2:8:14.
[3] *Niddah* 70b.

appear anxious that we might give the Sadducees the benefit of the doubt in this case, and so they go out of their way to tell us what they were really like:

> The Sadducees were the aristocratic party, made up of the high priestly and leading lay families of Jerusalem. They were wealthy and worldly. Their arrogance and their harshness in the administration of justice were notorious. Conservative in doctrine, they rejected what they regarded as Pharisaic innovations; but their main concern was for the maintenance of their privileges, not for doctrinal purity.[4]

Given this kind of press, it is not surprising that commentators think that Jesus *did* give a straight answer: his answer concentrated on the fact of the resurrection, rather than its precise character, for the simple reason that it was the fact which the Sadducees denied. Yet the historical-critical perspective runs the risk of blinding us to the fact that the question is only a riddle because it is put by the Sadducees; *their* motive for asking it is plain, and Jesus responds accordingly. To those who look for the resurrection of the dead, however, questions like this can matter very much. The history of eschatology is full of attempts to imagine some kind of restoration for relationships disrupted by death, a family reunion beyond the grave – and these attempts are obliged to exploit the strangely tangential quality of the answer Jesus gives to the Sadducees. It is not hard to conceive of versions of their question which would be motivated by concerns other than sectarian polemic; nor is it hard to come up with an example which would be anything but artificial.

Most of the commentaries I have consulted serve to disguise the problem. The way in which Jesus argues with the Sadducees is impeccably rabbinic, and quite different from the way in which Paul and the early church typically defended faith in the general resurrection. As a result, the critics can get on with comparing and contrasting the teaching of Jesus with the teaching of his fellow Jews at the time, mapping out a position for Jesus in relation to the theological co-ordinates of Sadducees, Pharisees, and a variety of specialists in apocalyptic. But the routine

---

[4] C. E. B. Cranfield, *The Gospel According to Saint Mark* (Cambridge: Cambridge University Press, 1977⁵), 373.

contextualisation of Jesus in the eschatological disputes of the first century can make us think that we understand him better now, as if the proximity of his perspective to that of the Pharisees or the Essenes somehow lessened its distance from our own. The first-century horizon of this text does matter, of course; but unless we face up to the radically different horizons of later ages, including our own, we will fail to recognise that the teaching of Jesus does not solve the eschatological puzzle, but intensifies it. The small theological distances measured by biblical critics scarcely register alongside the distances between the world of Jesus and the world in which we now live. A gulf between the eschatology of Jesus and the eschatology of the later church has been axiomatic for a good deal of twentieth century theology, of course; something similar, I think, is presupposed by our anxiety about the relation between the gospels and 'Christian family values'. Since the question about the resurrection is a passage in which the themes of the future and the family come together, it is no wonder, perhaps, that we do not really know what to *do* with it.

The rise and fall of the 'modern heaven'

Eschatology, of course, has always been a good deal more than 'futurology', as almost every theological study of the last things is quick to point out. These days, in fact, even the original apocalyptic tradition – which has often been suspected of having corrupted Christian belief with its futuristic fixations – is seen to have been much more interested in revealing the truth about what *is* than in revealing the truth about what is to come.[5] The point which I want to make, however, is that the eschatological is inevitably and unintentionally a revelation of its own time. As Gerard Loughlin remarks in his essay, 'thinking about how we will be is thinking about how we are', but I would put the emphasis upon the diagnosis rather than the prescription – by which I mean that this is not something which has to be achieved so much as recognised, since the eschatological imagination is

---

[5] Christopher Rowland, *The Open Heaven: A Study of Apocalyptic in Judaism and Early Christianity* (New York: Crossroad, 1982).

always a mirror to its age. Much as I agree with the spirit of Loughlin's conclusion, moreover, I cannot help wondering whether thinking about the family *sub specie aeternitatis* may ultimately do more to hinder us than to help us in trying to think about the family today, but I shall let this pass for now.

Loughlin cites Caroline Walker Bynum's most recent contribution to the history of the body, an investigation of medieval thought about the resurrection which combines philosophical, theological, and social history in a quite outstanding way.[6] Few scholars, I think, would challenge the opinion that such 'eschatological histories', whether interdisciplinary studies or traditional exercises in the history of ideas, have shed fascinating new light on some specific periods of the past, not least on the nineteenth century.

The concept of heavenly existence as an everlasting sabbath of praise and worship goes back to the origins of the Christian faith, and countless hymns bear witness to the enduring power of this vision. At times, however, it has had to compete with the attractions of a less austere image of the life to come, in which the relations between the resurrected are at least as much a matter of interest as the relations between resurrected individuals and God. In some forms of this vision, the continuity between this life and the life to come is particularly pronounced, and the restoration to one another of families and friends is a crucial concern. While the two strands have been woven together throughout Christian history, the second of them came very close to eclipsing the first in the modern era, and especially so in the nineteenth century. The tension between these two visions of heaven has often been noted, and sometimes explicitly related to the teaching of Jesus on the resurrection which I discussed at the beginning of this paper.[7] Recently, however, it has been systematised by Colleen McDannell and Bernhard Lang in an eclectic but influential 'history' of heaven, in which the distinction between the 'theocentric' and the 'anthropocentric' image of eternal life is

---

[6] Caroline Walker Bynum, *The Resurrection of the Body in Western Christianity, 200–1336* (New York: Columbia University Press, 1995).

[7] Ulrich Simon, *Heaven in the Christian Tradition* (London: Rockliff, 1958), 217; John Hick, *Death and Eternal Life* (London: Collins, 1976), 204.

presented as the interpretative key to the Christian eschatological imagination.[8]

The 'theocentric' vision stresses the *discontinuity* between this life and the life to come, defining the life of heaven in contrast to the life of earth. It owes much to the teaching of Jesus, McDannell and Lang suggest, and governed the eschatological thinking of the patristic and medieval eras to a large extent. Its last great revival, inspired by the Reformation, can be seen as a reaction to the process of accommodating classical images of heavenly reunion which accelerated greatly during the Renaissance.

The 'anthropocentric' vision, on the other hand, stresses the *continuity* between earth and heaven. Minimally, this approach values interpersonal relationships in such a way that it can conceive of no life without them. But rather than be satisfied that the form of the social will be the Church Triumphant, it looks to heaven for the restoration of relationships in the order of nature. As a result, it posits a heavenly existence which is not only social, but may even be sexual, depending on the degree of continuity between this life and the life to come which a particular account affirms. Correspondingly, it is dynamic, whereas the theocentric vision is typically static: it imagines a heaven in which there will be spiritual and even material progress. In its most extreme forms, the anthropocentric vision yields descriptions of life after death which seem to be no more than idealised accounts of the life before: a heaven complete with family and friends, work and play, the arts and the sciences, and opportunities for personal growth, is scarcely another country.

Such radically anthropocentric images of life after death make up what McDannell and Lang rightly describe as 'the modern heaven', the presence of which is felt in the eighteenth and especially nineteenth centuries throughout high and low religious culture. To McDannell and Lang it was a necessary reaction to the theocentric eschatologies of Protestant and Catholic orthodoxy alike, the return of elements which had been suppressed for too long – but the origins of the phenomenon need not concern us here. What matters is that the ultra-anthropocen-

[8] Colleen McDannell and Bernhard Lang, *Heaven: A History* (New Haven: Yale University Press, 1988, 1990).

tric heaven seems to have answered so many needs, and that those needs can and should be taken seriously even though 'the modern heaven' itself strikes the contemporary reader as ridiculous.

There is no point in playing down the fact that the exhaustive accounts of heavenly society which poured from English and American presses in the nineteenth century do strike us in this way. This has something to do with the *character* of the details, of course, but I think that our reaction has as much to do with the sheer *existence* of so many details – and, correspondingly, the complete absence of any sense of the eschatological reserve which is so typical of our own time. For comprehensiveness, in fact, nineteenth-century descriptions of life after death never really surpassed the writings of Emanuel Swedenborg – the Swedish mathematician, engineer and visionary who founded the genre in the third quarter of the eighteenth century. Swedenborg's descriptions of an emphatically material and social heaven were published in order that 'the simple in heart and the simple in faith' might be protected against the 'negative attitude' of the eschatological sceptics.[9] Swedenborg's work remains fascinating, but our sympathies are likely to be with the sceptics of the era, like Kant, for whom Swedenborg's *Arcana Caelestia* was 'eight volumes quarto full of nonsense'.[10] Before dismissing Swedenborg as a marginal figure in the history of religious thought, however, we ought to consider the scope of his influence: his successors have included not only the Swedenborgians, the spiritualists, the Mormons, and so on, but also those 'mainstream' Christians who contributed to the triumph of the modern heaven in the nineteenth century. In a sense, therefore, the eschatological *chutzpah* of a Swedenborg is not quite as 'eccentric' (properly speaking) as it seems.

As this genre developed, in the nineteenth century, the latent sentimentality of the anthropocentric approach began to blunt the speculative edge which, in Swedenborg, had helped to preserve some measure of difference between the life of this world and the life of the world to come. In the new celestial

---

[9] Emanuel Swedenborg, *Heaven and Its Wonders and Hell* [1758], ed. D. H. Harley (Cambridge: Cambridge University Press, 1958), 3.

[10] Immanuel Kant, *Dreams of a Spirit-Seer Illustrated by Dreams of Metaphysics* [1766], quoted by McDannell and Lang, *Heaven*, 379.

literature, the concept of a radical transformation of human life died the death of a thousand qualifications, as the traditional 'discontinuities' were written off one by one as a series of theological errors. What earlier generations had failed to understand was not so much the New Testament, or the teaching of the church, it appeared, but the logic of love: we are what we are by virtue of our relationships to one another, and if heaven involves the perpetuation of our life it must involve the perpetuation of our relationships. In Swedenborg's wake, and under the influence of Romanticism, it was inevitable that the future of couples would be a question of central concern. But as the literature expanded, so its horizons widened, and increasing attention was given to the future of networks of relationships incorporating the couple yet transcending it and extending across the generations – in short, the future of families. The modern heaven offered the ultimate family reunion, and in doing so revealed the sentimentality which had long determined its development: there was a time when the souls of the departed travelled light, but the modern heaven raised the emotional baggage limit so far that it seemed nothing need be left behind – and, by stimulating ever greater demand, it was compelled to project ever more complex idealisations of the life of this world into eternity.

The results, as the literary critic Michael Wheeler notes, were rarely inspiring:

> Perhaps the most characteristic Victorian ideas of heaven are of a place in which family reunions and 'the recognition of friends' are to be achieved after death, and (more radically Romantic) of a site in which lovers are reunited as couples. Worked upon by imaginations less powerful than Blake's, such heavens are often more like a middle-class suburb in the sky than the city of God; less like the mystical marriage of Christ with his church than the consummation of erotic desire in an idealized form of safe sex.[11]

There is a case, however, for saying that the shift in emphasis from the couple to the family which gradually transformed the genre in the later years of the nineteenth century created new

---

[11] Michael Wheeler, *Death and the Future Life in Victorian Literature and Theology* (Cambridge: Cambridge University Press, 1990), 120–1.

opportunities for sentimentality, and the makers of the modern heaven were quick to seize them. No-one did so more enthusiastically than Elizabeth Stuart Phelps, the 24-year-old author of *The Gates Ajar* (1868), a novel which enjoyed considerable success in the United States and in England for the rest of the century. In it, a woman whose brother has been killed in the Civil War is consoled not by the eschatological commonplaces of the orthodox, but by her Aunt Winifred, a young widow who champions an ultra-anthropocentric eschatology. Those who oppose her, like the splendidly-named Deacon Quirk and Dr Bland, prove no match for her formidable debating skills.

To be fair, their creator makes them defend an improbably crude theocentric afterlife – mocked by Aunt Winifred, in a less than subtle parody of the seventeenth century hymn 'Jerusalem on high', as something to do with 'the harpers harping with their harps'.[12] The heaven of *The Gates Ajar* is a world in which reunited families enjoy various kinds of wholesome recreation in a picturesque natural setting, and in which the instrument of choice is not the harp but that cornerstone of family entertainment in the Victorian era, the piano. The novel's description of heaven is, in fact, so absurdly sentimental that to treat it as 'merely an extension of the Victorian home and its values' may be if anything a little generous.[13] First impressions count, and it would be difficult to beat Mark Twain's summary of Aunt Winifred's vision of eternal bliss as 'a mean little ten-cent heaven about the size of Rhode Island'.[14]

In retrospect, *The Gates Ajar* appears to signal the beginning of the end for the modern heaven. Now, towards the end of the twentieth century, we are acutely aware of the charge that Christian eschatology promises 'a sort of Disneyland, with fun for all the family',[15] and will go to great lengths to distance ourselves from the speculations of our ancestors. Theologians routinely

---

[12] Elizabeth Stuart Phelps, *The Gates Ajar* (Boston: Fields, Osgood & Co., 1868), 70.

[13] David Brown, 'The Christian Heaven', in Dan Cohn-Sherbok and Christopher Lewis, eds., *Beyond Death: Theological and Philosophical Reflections on Life after Death* (London: Macmillan, 1995), 46.

[14] *Mark Twain in Eruption*, ed. Bernard DeVoto (New York: Harper, 1940), 247, quoted by McDannell and Lang, *Heaven*, 273.

[15] A. N. Wilson, 'Life After Death: A Fate Worse Than Death', in Dan Cohn-Sherbok and Christopher Lewis, eds., *Beyond Death*, 188.

warn against the desire for a 'travelog eschatology',[16] and tend to stress the discontinuity between this life and the life to come. The so-called 'rediscovery of eschatology' in the present century has had a considerable impact on modern theology; but because the subordination of 'individual' (as opposed to 'general') eschatology to broader theological concerns was a necessary part of the process, life after death, as such, is no longer the focus of eschatological attention. When contemporary theologians do discuss heaven, however, their approach is invariably minimalist, by the standards of almost any other period, but recognisably theocentric. According to McDannell and Lang, the theocentric reaction was inevitable. Even though the history of heaven cannot be presented as 'a simple alternation between theocentric and anthropocentric models',[17] nonetheless they argue that these two approaches are mutually compensating over time: that which the eschatological imagination suppresses must re-emerge in some new form. And when I first came across this thesis I thought of Feuerbach and his brilliant, if deeply flawed, analysis of Christian belief in heaven, and of the irresistible forces which shape it.[18]

The future of the family

Feuerbach's interpretation of Christian eschatology deserves to be investigated, but in the space available I cannot begin to do justice to his contribution. Instead, let us make the most of the fact that to invoke Feuerbach as a critic of religion is, rightly or wrongly, to summon up the shades of Marx, Nietzsche and Freud – the 'masters of suspicion' – at the same time. Much twentieth century theology has been preoccupied with responding in some way to their criticisms of religion, as the student of modern theology very quickly learns; and although there are many who argue that Christian theology has no business letting something as hopelessly 'modernist' as nineteenth century athe-

---

[16] Hans Schwarz, 'Eschatology', in Carl E. Braaten and Robert W. Jenson, eds., *Christian Dogmatics* (Philadelphia: Fortress Press, 1984), volume 2, 567.

[17] McDannell and Lang, *Heaven*, 358.

[18] Ludwig Feuerbach, *The Essence of Christianity* [1841], tr. George Eliot (New York: Harper, 1957), ch. XVIII (170–84), and especially 183–4.

ism set its agenda, others would still say that it is important to acknowledge the extent to which Christianity *is* often sustained by various forms of alienation, and to show how these are transcended and subverted by Christian faith itself.[19] It would be irresponsible, therefore, to suppress the suspicions about *eschatological* belief which Marx, Nietzsche and Freud have sowed in the minds of many in the twentieth century.

The possibility that belief in life after death is the product of some kind of illusion, or projection, or whatever, is a theme which is routinely addressed in works such as John Bowker's *The Meanings of Death*, a comparative study of religious eschatologies,[20] and even if theologians do not always address the problem so directly, few have succeeded in exorcising it entirely from their treatments of the doctrine of the last things. Some, of course, have gone further, subjecting their hope to the critical fires of Feuerbach and the others so that it might be purified. Whether the 'masters of suspicion' are invoked or not, however, there can be no denying that some twentieth century reinterpretations of the discourse of eternity are radical enough to deflect the old charges at the outset. By disowning any interest in the survival of the individual subject, these theological explorations have attempted to outline an eschatology without fantasy.

It would be a mistake, however, to think that these reinterpretations are supposed to be completely original, since some of them conceive of themselves as the means by which forgotten spiritual insights might be recovered. I think this is true of the existentialist reinterpretation of eschatology, for example, in which the ultimacy of the last things is translated as the ultimacy of the present, the 'moment of decision'. At the very least, this vision is descended from the kind of Romantic reading of eternal life which one finds in Schleiermacher:

> The goal and character of the religious life is not the immortality desired and believed in by many ... It is not the immortality that is outside of time, behind it, or rather after it, and which still is in time. It is the immortality which we can now

---

[19] See, for example, Merold Westphal, *Suspicion and Faith: The Religious Uses of Modern Atheism* (Grand Rapids: Eerdmans, 1993).

[20] John Bowker, *The Meanings of Death* (Cambridge: Cambridge University Press, 1991), especially 10–18.

have in this temporal life; it is the problem in the solution of which we are for ever to be engaged. In the midst of finitude to be one with the Infinite and in every moment to be eternal is the immortality of religion.[21]

But for Bultmann, among others, it was nothing less than the recovery of an eschatology which in spite of the ecclesiastical redactors can still be seen within the New Testament itself.[22]

For a more self-consciously revolutionary approach, we have to turn to the reinterpretation of eschatology by Process theologians. According to Process thought, there are no substances, but only events, of which we are (like everything else) an aggregate or summary. At each moment the complex configuration of events which constitutes us passes into the past, and another one replaces it, until, at our death, the series of events as a whole comes to an end. It follows that we cannot survive death, as psychic or psychosomatic substances of some kind, since there are no such things. However, the events themselves cannot be erased, and they are recorded by the God in whom we live, and move, and have our being: incorporated in the life of God, as all past events are, we shall live forever in the divine memory. Therefore we are ephemeral, as Hartshorne puts it, but immortally so, and although nothing is added to our biographies after death, nothing can ever be lost: 'We write our book of life', as it were, '... for the one adequate Reader.'[23] Yet the 'book' is an interactive one:

> We can interpret 'heaven' as the conception which God forms of our actual being, a conception which we partly determine by our free decisions, but which is more than all our decisions and experiences, since it is the synthesis of God's participating responses to these experiences.[24]

---

[21] Friedrich Schleiermacher, *On Religion: Speeches to its Cultured Despisers* [1821³], tr. John Oman (New York: Harper, 1958), 101.

[22] Rudolf Bultmann, 'The Eschatology of the Gospel of John', *Faith and Understanding*, ed. Robert W. Funk, tr. Louise P. Smith (London: SCM, 1969), 165–83.

[23] Charles Hartshorne, *A Natural Theology for Our Time* (La Salle: Open Court, 1967), 112.

[24] Charles Hartshorne, *The Logic of Perfection* (La Salle: Open Court, 1962), 258.

Process eschatology does not pretend to be anything other than revisionist. Some in this tradition have left open the possibility that our consciousness might survive death,[25] and have even tried to bridge the gap between the old and the new concepts of eternal life.[26] Nevertheless, I suspect that Hartshorne's comment on our desire to meet one another after death is the authentic voice of Process eschatology, in its unmistakeably post-Freudian severity: 'if we know anything at all about the human condition it is that things do not always go as we might wish'.[27]

So what's wrong with this kind of eschatology? The problem is not just the speculative (and spectacular) metaphysics, which I wouldn't dream of defending, because the idea that immortality is no more (and no less) than a place in the eternal memory of God is to be found without the philosophical complexities elsewhere.[28] Nor, I think, is the problem exhausted by the kind of philosophical and theological objections which might well apply to the idea in almost any form.[29] Instead, it is as if something very big is missing from the picture, something so significant that radical reinterpretations of eschatology, like this, are often assumed at the outset to be illegitimate. What is it? What factor is missing from the equation?

According to some theologians, specific theological themes in the Christian tradition make the affirmation of life beyond death in an individual, conscious form simply non-negotiable. Stephen Sykes, for example, sets himself against the eschatology of Moltmann's *The Crucified God* – which, in its own way, is an attempt to reappropriate the eschatological without falling under the suspicion of the masters – by insisting that the themes of 'true life' and of 'judgement' are not only central to the Christian life but 'demand the notion of life after death'.[30] The usual

[25] Schubert Ogden, *The Reality of God* (London: SCM, 1967), 206–30.

[26] John B. Cobb, 'The Resurrection of the Soul', *Harvard Theological Review* 80 (1987), 213–27.

[27] Charles Hartshorne, *Omnipotence and Other Theological Mistakes* (Albany: State University of New York Press, 1984), 37.

[28] For example, David Edwards, *The Last Things Now* (London: SCM, 1969), and Jacques Pohier, *God in Fragments*, tr. John Bowden (London: SCM, 1985).

[29] John Hick, *Death and Eternal Life*, 219–21; Paul and Linda Badham, *Immortality or Extinction?* (London: SPCK, 1984²), 31–6.

[30] Stephen Sykes, 'Life After Death: The Christian Doctrine of Heaven', in Richard W. A. McKinney, ed., *Creation, Christ and Culture* (Edinburgh: T. & T. Clark, 1976), 260.

candidate, however, is *love* – the love of God for us, for the creatures made in God's own image, which death cannot change. In fact, whether the love of God entails that we must live forever is open to question, according to Grace Jantzen:

> 'Are not three sparrows sold for a farthing?' Jesus asked. 'Yet not one of them falls to the ground without your heavenly Father's knowledge.' These words of Jesus have often (and rightly) been taken as his teaching of the tender concern of the Father for all his creatures; what has not been noticed so often is that Jesus never denies that sparrows do fall.[31]

We might be 'of more value than many sparrows'; but does the difference between us really make the difference between not dying unnoticed and not really dying at all? Jantzen does not suggest for a moment that the 'logic' of divine love entails that we do *not* survive death, and the arguments she uses are open to criticism in more than one way.[32] At the very least, however, her reflections should remind us that theology is not a deductive science.

But if the history of speculation about the 'family reunion' teaches us anything, it is perhaps that the love from which we draw whatever eschatological conclusions we can draw is as much human as divine. By this I mean that the character of our convictions may have much more to do with the strength of human affections than with the force of any reasoning from theological first principles: it is the love we have for one another, for husbands and wives, for parents and children, for families and friends, which so often fires the eschatological imagination – and it is hard to see how it could be any other way without denying something essential to us. That is why, I think, we must take the anthropocentric tradition seriously, in spite of its comic excesses.

The 'eschatological realists' might argue, however, that their critics *cannot* take it seriously, because they refuse to recognise the reality of the dead. I am not so sure about this. Consider the following remarks from the notebooks of Simone Weil:

---

[31] Grace Jantzen, 'Do We Need Immortality?', *Modern Theology* 1/1 (1984), 42.
[32] For example, Charles Taliaferro, 'Why We Need Immortality', *Modern Theology* 6/4 (1990), 367–77.

To lose somebody: we suffer at the thought that the dead one, the absent one should have become something imaginary, something false. But the longing we have for him is not imaginary. We must go down into ourselves, where the desire which is not imaginary resides. Hunger: we imagine different foods; but the hunger itself is real; we must seize hold of the hunger. The loss of contact with reality – there lies evil, there lies sorrow. There are certain situations which bring about such a loss: deprivation, suffering. The remedy is to use the loss itself as an intermediary for attaining reality. The presence of the dead one is imaginary, but his absence is very real; it is henceforth his manner of appearing.[33]

Must we call this 'anti-realism'? To do so would, I think, betray an impoverished understanding of the idea of the 'real'. But that does not mean that Simone Weil's words are any less austere than they look: this is a hard saying, no matter how one categorises it. The discipline it suggests would be too much for most of us to bear, and I suspect in any case that the desire to be reunited with one another beyond death should not be suppressed. We *do* want to meet again, and there is something wrong with any approach – ultra-theocentric eschatology included – which explicitly or implicitly denies this.

The problem with 'eschatological realism' and with 'eschatological anti-realism' is that these constructions force us to distort the desire, making it an anticipation of an actual future state of affairs, or an expression of affection. Notes of Wittgenstein's lectures in the 1930s show very clearly that he rejected the former, but he was certainly no expressivist:

Suppose someone, before going to China, when he might never see me again, said to me: 'We might see one another after death' – would I necessarily say that I don't understand him? I might say [want to say] simply, 'Yes. I *understand* him entirely.'

Lewy 'In this case, you might only mean that he expressed a certain attitude.'

[33] Simone Weil, *The Notebooks of Simone Weil*, tr. Arthur Wills (London: Routledge & Kegan Paul, 1956), volume I, 28.

I would say 'No, it isn't the same as saying "I'm very fond of you"' – and it may not be the same as saying anything else. It says what it says. Why should you be able to substitute anything else?[34]

Is there an alternative? Some have suggested other possibilities,[35] and these deserve further exploration. A glance at the history of eschatological speculation shows that desire has often fuelled fantasy, but the desire, as such, is not the problem. It is true that hope has often been little more than nostalgia in disguise, and that the image of the family reunion can corrupt our thought about the family by representing complex human relationships in an impossibly idealised form. But critical, constructive thinking about the family today should still confront the tradition of anthropocentric eschatology since it reveals something which we ought never to neglect. The hunger is real, but it is what it is because we live within limits, and must make our relationships good – or 'good enough' – while we can.

Perhaps we can learn about these limits by exploring the modern heaven, a world in which they are suspended – making it familiar and foreign at one and the same time. Then we might be in a position to think about families without being tempted into theological excesses, and to understand that we do not need to give *reasons* for believing that families matter – because if we cannot see *this*, no amount of theological or philosophical debate is ever going to help us.[36] Correspondingly, we might be in a better position to resist the political manipulation of 'the family', that household god of the New Right, which, in its essential instrumentalism, constitutes a devaluing of actual families rather than the reverse. The critique of the eschatological imagination, therefore, is not just an academic exercise: as always, 'the criticism of heaven turns into the criticism of the earth'.[37]

---

[34] Ludwig Wittgenstein, *Lectures and Conversations on Aesthetics, Psychology and Religious Belief*, ed. Cyril Barrett (Oxford: Blackwell, 1966), 70–1.

[35] For example, D. Z. Phillips, *Death and Immortality* (London: Macmillan, 1970), especially 61–78.

[36] On 'mattering' as a fundamental ethical concept, see Helen Oppenheimer, *The Hope of Happiness* (London: SCM, 1983); and 'Mattering', *Studies in Christian Ethics* 8/1 (1995), 60–76.

[37] Karl Marx, 'Contribution to the Critique of Hegel's Philosophy of Law. Introduction', in Karl Marx & Frederick Engels, *Collected Works*, volume 3 (London: Lawrence and Wishart, 1975), 176.

Suggestions for Further Reading

Anderson, H., *The Family and Pastoral Care* (Philadelphia: Fortress Press, 1984).

Anderson, R. S. and Guernsey, D. B.: *On Being Family: A Social Theology of the Family* (Grand Rapids: Eerdmans, 1985).

Balch, D. L., *Let Wives Be Submissive: The Domestic Code in 1 Peter* (Chico, CA: Scholars Press, 1981).

Barton, S. C., *Discipleship and Family Ties in Mark and Matthew* (Cambridge: Cambridge University Press, 1994).

Berger, B. & P., *The War Over the Family. Capturing the Middle Ground* (Harmondsworth: Penguin, 1983).

Bogle, J., ed., *Families for Tomorrow* (Leominster: Fowler Wright, 1991).

Borrowdale, A., *Reconstructing Family Values* (London: SPCK, 1994).

Brown, P., *The Body and Society. Men, Women and Sexual Renunciation in Early Christianity* (London: Faber & Faber, 1989).

Cahill, L. H. and Mieth, D., eds., *The Family* (*Concilium*, 1995/4; London: SCM, 1995).

Catechism of the Catholic Church (London: Geoffrey Chapman, 1994).

Clapp, R., *Families at the Crossroads. Beyond Traditional and Modern Options* (Downers Grove, IL: InterVarsity Press, 1993).

Countryman, L. W., *Dirt, Greed and Sex: Sexual Ethics in the New Testament and Their Implications for Today* (London: SCM, 1989).

D'Antonio, W. V. and Aldous, J., eds., *Families and Religions. Conflict and Change in Modern Society* (London: Sage Publications, 1983).

Davies, J., ed., *The Family: Is It Just Another Lifestyle Choice?* (London: Institute of Economic Affairs, 1993).

Dennis, N. and Erdos, G., *Families without Fatherhood* (London: Institute of Economic Affairs, 1992).

Evangelium Vitae (Encyclical Letter of Pope John Paul II, 1995).

Familiaris Consortio (Apostolic Exhortation of Pope John Paul II, 1981).

Fiorenza, E. S., *In Memory of Her. A Feminist Theological Reconstruction of Christian Origins* (London: SCM, 1983).

Goody, J., *The Development of the Family and Marriage in Europe* (Cambridge: Cambridge University Press, 1983).

Greer, R. A., *Broken Lights and Mended Lives. Theology and Common Life in the Early Church* (Pennsylvania State University Press, 1986).

Harvey, A. E., *Promise or Pretence? A Christian's Guide to Sexual Morals* (London: SCM, 1994).

Hauerwas, S., *A Community of Character* (Notre Dame, IN: University of Notre Dame Press, 1981).

345

Humanae Vitae (Encyclical Letter of Pope Paul VI, 1968).

La Fontaine, J., *Child Sexual Abuse* (Oxford: Polity Press, 1990).

Letter to Families From Pope John Paul II (Boston, MA: St Paul Books & Media, 1994).

Morgan, P., *Farewell to the Family* (London: Institute of Economic Affairs, 1995).

Mount, F., *The Subversive Family* (London: Jonathan Cape, 1982).

O'Donovan, O., *Begotten or Made?* (Oxford: Oxford University Press, 1984).

Okin, S. M., *Justice, Gender and the Family* (New York: Basic Books, 1989).

Roper, L., *The Holy Household. Women and Morals in Reformation Augsburg* (Oxford: Oxford University Press, 1989).

Sacks, J., *Faith in the Future* (London: Darton, Longman & Todd, 1995).

Schluter, M. and Clements, R., *Reactivating the Extended Family: From Biblical Norms to Public Policy in Britain* (Cambridge: Jubilee Centre Publications, 1986).

Something to Celebrate. Valuing Families in Church and Society (Report of the Church of England Board for Social Responsibility Working Party on the Family, London: Church House Publishing, 1995).

Stevenson, K., *Nuptial Blessing. A Study of Christian Marriage Rites* (Oxford: Oxford University Press, 1983).

Stone, L., *The Family, Sex and Marriage in England 1500–1800* (London: Weidenfeld & Nicolson, 1977).

Studies in Christian Ethics 9/1, on 'Christianity and the Family' (Edinburgh: T&T Clark, 1996).

Thatcher, A., *Liberating Sex. A Christian Sexual Theology* (London: SPCK, 1993).

The Future of the Family (Report of the Board of Social Responsibility of the Church of Scotland, Edinburgh: Saint Andrew Press, 1992).

Utting, D., *Family and Parenthood: Supporting Families, Preventing Breakdown* (Joseph Rowntree Foundation, 1995).

Vasey, M., *Strangers and Friends* (London: Hodder & Stoughton, 1995).

Verner, D. C., *The Household of God. The Social World of the Pastoral Epistles* (Chico, CA: Scholars Press, 1983).

Walrond-Skinner, S., *The Fulcrum and the Fire. Wrestling with Family Life* (London: Darton, Longman & Todd, 1993).

Weber, H. R., *Jesus and the Children* (Geneva: World Council of Churches, 1979).

Wood, D., ed., *The Church and Childhood* (Oxford: Blackwell, 1994).

Wright, C. J. H., *God's People in God's Land. Family, Land, and Property in the Old Testament* (Grand Rapids: Eerdmans, 1990).

Index of Modern Authors